Kitty Ray graduated from St Martin's School of Art in 1968 and has worked as a designer, window-dresser, illustrator and even a stewardess aboard World War II DC3s for a regional airline. She lives in Suffolk, with her husband and two sons, and divides her time between writing and working with disruptive children in a local primary school. *Stoats and Weasels* is her first novel.

Stoats and Weasels

...

KITTY RAY

WARNER BOOKS

A *Warner* Book

First published in Great Britain in 1996
by Warner Books

Copyright © Kitty Ray 1996

The moral right of the author has been asserted.

'Keep on Running' written by Jackie Edwards
© 1966 Island Music Ltd
Lyrics reproduced by kind permission of the publisher.
'Do You Want To Know A Secret' words and music by
John Lennon & Paul McCartney
© 1963 Northern Songs
Used by permission of Music Sales Limited.

A CIP catalogue record for this book
is available from the British Library.

ISBN 0 7515 1590 6

Typeset by Solidus (Bristol) Limited
Printed and bound in Great Britain by Clays Ltd, St. Ives plc

Warner Books
A Division of
Little, Brown and Company (UK)
Brettenham House
Lancaster Place
London WC2E 7EN

ACKNOWLEDGEMENTS

• • •

My thanks go to Hilary Johnson at the RNA for her support and advice, to my agent Sarah Molloy for having faith in me when I had none in myself, and to all at Little, Brown, especially to Imogen Taylor for not cutting my baby to pieces.

To Giles, with love

CHAPTER ONE

• • •

'I might make a start on the attic today.' Emma rattled the breakfast plates in the big stone sink. 'George is coming next Sunday and I promised him I'd have it sorted out.'

He looked up from his sketching. 'What's the rush, George'll wait, won't he? It's not as if he couldn't have done it himself. I don't know why you agreed to the arrangement in the first place.'

'Yes, you do.' She slopped washing-up liquid over the dishes, turned on the taps and swished the water with her hand. 'If you hadn't been in such an inordinate hurry to move in he would have had time to clear it himself. Besides, George was very fond of his parents. It was bad enough having to sort out the rest of the house, he said, without tackling the attic as well. And I don't mind doing it. In fact I quite like sifting through the detritus of other people's lives.'

He put his pencil down, pushed his chair back, scraping it along the flagstoned floor and crossed the room to stand behind her. 'Only when they're dead: you wouldn't intrude upon the living.' He ran the backs of his fingers down her neck beneath her thick plait, causing a familiar ripple of pleasure. 'The dead can't complain, they can't sue for invasion of privacy.'

She laughed, leaning back into his warmth. 'And who will sift through the detritus of our lives when we go? Should we leave it to the dogs?'

They glanced across the room to where a tangled heap of hair and paws lay stretched out along the warmth of the Aga, then Emma picked the soapy plates out of the steaming water and set them to drain, changing the subject slightly. 'Perhaps we should convert the attic. It's so huge, and it's all wasted space, it would make a good selling point when we move on ...' She waited, turning to look at him as he gazed over her shoulder at the morning sun slanting across the lawn between the greengages, and smiled at his expression. 'Although I did think, listening to you snore last night, that perhaps this time we might stay.' She eyed him surreptitiously, gauging his reaction. 'You know, put down roots now we're middle-aged. I could join the Women's Institute, you could join the Rotary Club ...' She watched with amusement the look of utter horror creeping across his face. 'There's a postcard in the window of the village shop. They want a helper for the pre-school playgroup, three mornings a week. I thought I might volunteer ...'

'Feeling broody?' He frowned at her, the joke backfiring, and she rattled the last teaspoon round the sink then pulled the plug and dried her hands.

'No.' She turned to face him, sliding her arms around his waist in a gesture of reassurance. 'It was just one of those things, a biological hiccup.'

'But there's still time. Look at Silly Jilly.'

'If it was going to happen it would've by now. I'm forty-five next birthday.' She tightened her grip, making light. 'Think of all your seed, falling on stony ground over the years.'

'No—' he returned the pressure, clasping his hands behind her back '—think of all you have absorbed into your body. What a lot of me I've given you.' He smiled, bending his head to kiss her. 'And I don't snore.' He released her and moved across to the Aga to pour himself another cup of coffee. Two feathery tails wagged desultorily and an inelegant leg was raised, rewarded by a gentle stir of his foot on a pink stomach. 'More?' he asked, waving the pot.

'Mmm.' Emma leaned against the sink, watching him pour, letting the familiar rush of tender affection wash over her. 'So, are we staying or going?'

He shrugged. 'Staying if that's what you want. Norfolk's as good a place as any to be, I suppose.'

How transparent you are, she thought. Or is it just that we have been together so long?

'Thanks.' She took the proffered cup, transferred it to her right hand and sipped. 'Then if you think we're civilised enough to leave the decorating for a couple of days I'll start on the attic. Will you take the dogs out?'

She watched him moving easily about the kitchen, sipping his coffee, long legs in corduroy trousers, stoop-shouldered in a faded Viyella shirt. Your hair may be white, she thought, but it's still thick. You won't go bald. Your face is kinder than it used to be, too. Am I responsible for that?

'Why the sudden desire for permanence,' he asked, 'if it's not maternal instinct? It's never bothered you before.'

'Josie going, I suppose. She was my buffer against the end, my last hope of immortality.' Then, inconsequentially, 'I'm afraid of being left alone.'

'If parents are a buffer, I was derailed years ago. I shall do my best to live to a hundred.' He patted his thigh, said, 'Walk?' and waited for the two dun-coloured lurchers to erupt into life, stretching and shaking themselves, pawing at his trousers, barking and leaping.

Emma followed his progress, heard him call as he let himself out of the garden into the spinney beyond, 'Newton, Flotman, heel!' and smiled at the ludicrous succession of names, from Tooting onwards, that their dogs had suffered over the years. Then she turned away from the window and searched in a cupboard for black sacks.

The phone rang when she was halfway up the stairs. She paused, head on one side, listening, then continued up, turning right on to the landing, and made for the window along the passageway. She was laughing when she picked up the receiver.

'Share the joke, sweetie?'

'Oh, Bill!' She perched on the wide sill, still chuckling. 'How nice. You are responsible for me finding a telephone I didn't know I had.'

She heard his familiar throaty giggle. 'Of such stuff is pleasure made. Are you civilised yet, darling girl? Can we visit?'

'Oh yes, *lovely*. When?'

'Next weekend, Friday night to Sunday afternoon. It's the leaving party on Thursday and the Dear Old Thing's gone into a black depression. You know, nothing left to live for, no use to anyone, fit for the scrapheap, over the top as usual. I keep telling—'

'Tell the silly fool we're longing for a visit. Our lives won't be complete until you've been.'

'Shouldn't you check first? The Hermit might not be pleased.'

'The Hermit,' Emma's correction was firm, 'will be delighted. You are the only two people he doesn't count as outsiders.'

'Apart from you,' said Bill drily. 'Don't forget to include yourself in this select band.'

She laughed. 'Apart from me. George is bringing his brood too, by the way, for Sunday lunch, so you'll overlap. You can deflect the Hermit's barbs.'

'Good,' said Bill. 'It'll be like old times.'

There was an infinitesimal pause.

'Not quite,' they said in unison and were both silent, remembering.

'Right,' said Emma briskly. 'Friday night in time for supper. The Hermit cooks.'

'Thank God.' Another fruity giggle. 'We shall look forward to it. Bless you, dear girl.'

Bill and I, she thought as she climbed the steep stairs to the attic, slid into promiscuity at around the same time, and it didn't do either of us any good. We have been so lucky since. On the other hand, if Alison hadn't given up her flighty ways when she did, who knows what might have been ... ? She shook herself as she pushed open the attic door, which creaked forlornly on its hinges. Needs attention, she noted. Might have been, might have been. How many times over the years have I played that game?

We were so young, so absurdly young. 'I was just a child,' she said out loud to the dusty shadows, and she sighed, remembering.

CHAPTER TWO

• • •

She managed the train all right, but the Tube frightened her. She'd done it with Josie and with Auntie Mabel, on day trips to the V & A or the British Museum, but on her own it was unnerving. Her portfolio was embarrassingly unwieldy too; she wasn't used to gauging distances with such a large encumbrance under her arm and she kept poking people with it by accident.

The Tube made her jump as it thundered out of its tunnel and she was swept along by a great mass of bodies on to the train, then couldn't find a seat and had to strap-hang all the way from Liverpool Street. A man tried to fondle her bottom between Bank and St Paul's and in turning away to avoid him she poked another man in the balls. He made a loud *ooph*ing noise and clutched at himself, and everyone looked at her. By the time she emerged into the daylight at Tottenham Court Road she was hot, red-faced and almost in tears.

The office was on the third floor and she had to ask twice. The place was seething with students, all going somewhere, loud-voiced, confident, oddly dressed. When she delivered her work to the secretary, she didn't seem to be nearly interested enough in what it was.

'You know where it's got to go, don't you?'

'Yes, dear, don't panic, I'll see it gets there.'

'I swear this year's applicants are the youngest ever,' the secretary remarked to her colleague as they watched her walk away. 'That one looks about twelve.'

'It's the freckles that do it. And those eyes. Reminds me of those puppies you see advertised, Abandoned on the North Circular, needs a good home.' They laughed.

She'd had to get the folio together by herself. The Art mistress, new to the school and eager to assert her authority, refused to release any of her work. 'Certainly not. You should finish your education before you go gallivanting off to enjoy yourself.' She had failed to get into Art School herself and settled for teaching as a poor second.

So Emma did it on her own, got an entire portfolio together in less than six weeks: plant drawings, landscapes, pages and pages of fashion drawings – thin elongated women with spiky elbows and long legs, wearing narrow skirts, tight, skimpy tops. Skinnyrib jumpers were in, and hemlines were creeping up, but there was no chance she'd be allowed to flash her legs. Josie would *die*.

'For God's *sake*, Ma,' she said. 'It's nineteen sixty-four!' But her mother just sniffed and pursed her lips. She was tired, as usual.

Josie insisted on coming with her when she went for the interview, but Emma made her stay in the street and averted her eyes when she waved, disowning her. She was the last to be called.

There were three of them: the Principal, the head of the Pre-Diploma course and someone else whose name Emma didn't catch. She sat on a chair in the middle of the room while they picked over her work and fired questions at her. They were concerned about her age, kept coming back to it.

'Where would you live?' asked the Principal unexpectedly.

'At home.' Where else?

More conferring. Then the head of Pre-Diploma, tall, avuncular, bald-headed. 'How do your parents feel about you leaving school so early?'

'I haven't got a father, it's just Ma and she knows what I want to do. There's no point in staying on at school when I don't want to, is there?' The belligerence was involuntary, unconscious.

They conferred for hours before offering her a place.

'Ohhh!' Emma whooped, then bounced out of her chair and crossed the room, leaning over the table to shake their hands. 'Thank you, thank you, oh, *thank* you!' she said, red with embarrassed delight. They laughed. The third man, the one whose name she hadn't caught, rose to usher her out.

'Remember,' he said, 'this is strictly between us. There are a lot of hopeful kids out there who won't know one way or the other for a week yet.'

Emma walked with what dignity she could manage to the door. 'Thank you,' she repeated unnecessarily, her plait swinging heavily against her back as she turned to go, and she heard them laughing again as she shut the door.

There was a girl standing by the lift, a spectacularly beautiful girl, talking animatedly to a couple of boys. She was blonde, a rare dark honey colour, not from a bottle, cut in a fringe at the front and running smoothly down her shoulders at the back. It rippled heavily as she moved. Her skin was brown, almost foreign and her eyes nearly black, the surrounds startlingly white against the irises. She used them as she talked and laughed, flirting with them. As Emma passed she flashed her a blinding smile.

'Hi, how'd you get on?'

'Okay.' Emma smiled back, entranced.

'See you next term then. I'm Alison.'

Emma didn't notice the tall, dark-haired man leaning against the wall by the stairs, but he noticed her.

The letter came a week later, confirming the offer of a place and giving details of the enrolment procedures. There was a handwritten addendum to Josie from the Principal, asking for confirmation that in view of Emma's age, not sixteen until August, her living arrangements would be suitable. Her mother was still dubious.

'Think of all the things you can get up to during the day,' she pointed out darkly.

*

When she went up to enrol, Emma took more notice of the clothes, the make-up some of the girls wore. They all seemed dauntingly independent. No one said, 'I'll have to ask my mother', or 'No I can't, I have to be home by ten.'

She was on her way out, going to catch the train home, when she was hailed by the exotic-looking girl she'd seen at her interview.

'You made it then. Fabulous! We're all going for a coffee. You coming?' She swept past Emma, trailing an assortment of boys in her wake and leaped down the stairs two at a time. 'Come on!' Her voice floated up the lift shaft beside the stairwell and they all increased their speed, including Emma, frightened of being left behind, or worse, left out.

They turned off the Charing Cross Road into Soho, like children meekly following the Pied Piper. They passed strip clubs, bouncers in full evening dress accosting passers-by, 'Live-shows, lovely girls . . .' They passed prostitutes – painted tarts such as Emma had never seen before, with beehive hairdos and fish-net tights, short skirts, wide plastic-patent belts and bored expressions – and peered at the menus in the ethnic restaurants, Chinese, Greek, Indian, Italian. Alison led them effortlessly, skipping backwards and talking non-stop, waving her hands in the air, her golden hair swinging about her face. Her legs were long, her skirt daringly short, three, four inches above her knees.

When she dived into a coffee-bar they all trooped obediently after her, downstairs into the basement to order espresso coffees, hot, sweet and frothy. Alison clapped her hands.

'Now,' she said, 'we can all get to know each other. You first.' She pointed at the boy on her right.

'George, George Campbell, nineteen, um . . . I'm a Norfolk dumpling. Scottish originally, Dad's a solicitor . . . er, I've two younger sisters . . .' George hesitated, casting about for something else to say about himself, and Alison, bored already, switched her attention.

'You?'

'Jay Hammond.'

Alison waited. 'Is that it? Just name, rank and serial-number? How old are you?'

'Twenty-six.' He shut his thin mouth like a trap, forcing her to move on or to sit in silence.

'Emma Versey. Ma's a secretary and my father was a salesman, died two months before I was born. He was knocked down by a car outside our house, Ma says, on his way to buy me a cot.' And how long-suffering she has always been about it, she thought, playing the sacrificial martyr, struggling bravely to bring me up alone. 'I'm sixteen.'

'Why, you're just a baby,' said Alison kindly, leaning across the table to flash her brilliant smile. Her teeth were small, very white and even; she had the sort of smile that made you want to keep her happy so she would do it again.

Impatient to hear the sound of her own voice, she declared it her turn. 'Alison Brown. Dreadfully boring name, isn't it? But awfully apt. My mother was Malayan, very beautiful, so I'm told, and I get my looks from her.' There was no false modesty about her: she was well aware of the effect she was having on them all.

'Was?'

'Was. She died when my little brother Ricky was born. Dear Daddy, the bastard, brought us up on his own, and a rotten job he's made of it too.' She laughed again. 'Okay, your turn.'

William, fair-haired, round-faced and snub-nosed, a country boy down to the Metropolis for the day, was finding it all completely intoxicating. 'Appleyard. Bill. Nothing much to tell really. Dad's a doctor and Mum's a housewife, very boring.' He smiled tentatively at Emma and Alison's black eyes flicked from one to the other.

'You two go together,' she said. 'Both dutiful children of sensible parents judging by your clothes.' Emma was mortified. 'Bet your kids'll have red hair and freckles.' They were both mortified, blushed in unison.

'Leave them alone. Can't you see you're embarrassing them?' said Jay coldly.

Alison was instantly full of contrition. 'Sorry, my pets. I'm over-excited. It's nerves.'

'You don't look the type.' George, curly haired, brown eyed, pinkly handsome and full of his own importance, was already besotted, paying attention to the others only on the rare occasions when Alison was silent. Jay talked hardly at all. He sat back watching; loose, gangly limbs, hooked nose, dark straight hair falling heavily over a high forehead, long-lashed blue eyes. When he stared at Emma he made her feel uncomfortable.

Alison fancied him, turning to him frequently to ask questions, most of which he didn't answer; teasing him, resting her chin on her hand and using her eyes. George melted visibly when she did it to him but Jay seemed immune. It was he who ended the party.

'See you all next week,' he said, rising suddenly without warning.

Alison was crestfallen. 'Must you go?'

'Got a train to catch.' He was laconic, unmoved by her entreaties to stay, and they broke up, shouting goodbyes down the length of Old Compton Street, then dispersed to catch their buses and trains. Alison walked with Emma to Tottenham Court Road.

'Got far to go?'

'Cheshunt.'

'Ah, Suburbia. I'm at home too, Richmond. Could be worse, I suppose, and the Bastard says I can get a flat next year if I get on to the Diploma course.'

'Is he that awful?'

Alison laughed brightly. 'Yes, awful. He's so . . .' she paused, searching for the right word '. . .*pushy.*'

'How do you mean, pushy?'

Alison darted a sideways look at her with her black eyes. 'It's all right for you,' she said. 'I bet your father wasn't a genius.'

'I don't know. I never met him.'

'Oh Lord, there I go again, putting my foot in it. I'm sorry, I don't mean to, you know. Any brothers or sisters?' Emma shook her head. 'I've two. Brothers. Pete's twenty-three and he's a genius as well, so Daddy never had a problem with him. And there's me. I'm quite bright too. It was only because I threatened to run away that I'm here at all.' She laughed again. 'It's Ricky that's the problem. But you don't want to hear about that.' They walked down into the Underground together and Alison went off to catch her train. 'We're going to have a *fabulous* time,' she said. 'See you next week.'

Emma, watching the heads turn at Alison's passing, wondered why on earth a girl like that had decided to pick her out of all the others to be one of her satellites, then made her way down to her train, to Liverpool Street and the journey home to Suburbia.

CHAPTER THREE
• • •

Just when Emma was ready to leave for college on the first day, her mother noticed the hem of her skirt, turned up secretly the night before, and put her foot down.

'You are *not* starting your first day looking like a cheap tart and that's final. You either change or you don't go.'

Emma flounced upstairs to change into jeans and a sloppy-joe. 'Cow,' she muttered under her breath as she slammed the front door behind her. *Cow*, she repeated silently all the way in to London on the train.

A list was posted to tell her which room she was in. The boys were in the other group, as was Alison – their names were in the first half of the alphabet – and Emma panicked, milling about the noticeboard until she was late. When she finally found the room they'd already started and a dozen pairs of eyes turned in her direction at the interruption. Oh, to be invisible.

The fat, elderly man sitting in the middle of the room was wearing nothing but a black jock-strap and a bored expression. Emma had never seen so much flesh before. His breasts rolled over his stomach, skin meeting skin in white doughlike hillocks and his buttocks sagged, overflowing the sides of the chair on which he sat. Emma wondered what his penis looked like beneath his jock-strap. It was the nearest she had ever got to seeing one. Did penises get fat too, apart from when they were erect? Or were they penii? Why hadn't she paid more attention to the dirty talk at school?

The tutor found her a donkey – a wooden bench with a bar at the front to rest her drawing-board on – and the class continued in almost complete silence until mid-morning.

'Go and get a coffee,' he said then. 'Have a look around, get your bearings.'

They filed out meekly, down two floors to the canteen, and as the noise assaulted Emma's ears she was overcome by a sudden complete loss of confidence. She stood in the queue with her head down, pretending to search for something in her bag because she didn't know where to look, then when she had collected her coffee and a Wagon Wheel, she didn't know where to go. She felt enormous, conspicuous, a face to sink a thousand ships, gigantic hands and feet, a complete freak. She should have stayed on at school where they were used to her gargantuan proportions, her Quasimodo-like features.

When Alison arrived in the doorway a couple of dozen heads swivelled towards her. She looked around and posed, playing to the gallery, then saw Emma and tossed her blonde head, baring her teeth in that glorious smile; Emma heard the massed intake of male breath as twenty pairs of eyes followed Alison's progress across the room.

'Hi. Be an angel and save me a seat, will you? Shan't be a tick.' Alison set off for the back of the queue, then spotted George and pantomimed elaborately at him to get her a coffee. He looked ridiculously pleased, basking in the vicarious attention. 'Come on,' she said, 'let's find some space,' and a table was miraculously vacated, offered to her with a deep obeisance.

George was followed by Bill and Jay. Somehow, Emma didn't quite see how, Alison arranged it so that Jay sat next to her, upsetting George. The boys were calling her Ali already, vying for her attention, except Jay, who aimed his conversation at Emma, leaning close to fix her with intent blue eyes. Emma felt threatened again.

'So, where shall we go for lunch?' asked Alison. 'There's an Italian just up the road, shall we try there? Jay?'

Jay shrugged his acquiescence. 'As long as the others want to. Emma?'

'Yes, I'll come.' Emma would have agreed to almost anything to avoid having to face the canteen alone. Her Wagon Wheel lay untouched in her bag; she was too embarrassed to eat it.

'I'm in.' George was annoyed. Ali hadn't asked if *he* wanted to come. It was favouritism in his opinion; he was as good as Jay, wasn't he? Better looking too if it came to that.

Bill switched his gaze from face to face, round-eyed with excitement. He would do whatever the others wanted to do, he was easy.

'Good. Twelve-thirty then.'

The coffee break loosened tongues, eased the first-day nerves. Back in the art-room the other students began to hand round cigarettes, to swap jokes and innuendoes, girls and boys sizing each other up, pairing off already. I don't know how to do it, thought Emma, can't do it, won't do it. So she put up her 'do not approach' sign, the aloof, distant face that had always been her defence at school when anyone got too close. It worked here too, very efficiently; her peers found her cold, haughty, and left her alone.

They ate Italian, as much risotto as the plates would hold for five shillings, and drank lots of coffee. Emma, starving, wolfed hers down and could have done with more. Alison had a half portion for two-and-sixpence and struggled to finish it.

'Tomorrow,' she said, 'we'll go to the pub. There must be lots round here.'

George was thoroughly over-excited. 'We had this *fabulous* model to draw. Black, *beautiful* body.' They all laughed, Emma too, trying to look worldly and knowing.

'D'you know—' Alison continued '—she took everything off, every single stitch except...' she giggled at the incongruity of it '...except her belt. You know the ones they sell in Woolies, the three-inch wide elastic ones? She's got a black one with a big silver buckle and she kept it on all the time.'

'*Sensational.*' George sighed theatrically and they all laughed again, trying to ease the slight embarrassment the subject engendered.

'What was yours like?' Jay leaned across the table to Emma.

'Old. A fat old man. Like . . .' She searched around for some way of describing him. 'Like Magwitch in that black-and-white film, you know, *Great Expectations.*'

Jay nodded. 'I know the one, bullet-headed and a big nose.'

'Poor old you,' said George sympathetically.

Jay grinned contemptuously. 'I don't suppose Emma's quite so riveted at the thought of a naked bird as you are.'

Emma smiled too, grateful to Jay for sticking up for her and George felt humiliated and foolish.

It was a relief to be on the train going home. Emma managed to get a seat and sat idly watching the commuters doing their crosswords, catching up on their morning papers, surreptitiously picking their noses, avoiding each others' eyes. I have aged, she thought, twenty years in less than twelve hours, yet I know no more about the male sexual organ than I did when I set out this morning. How come the female models take everything off and the male ones don't?

It confirmed what she'd already suspected. Compared to all the intimidating, sophisticated experienced grown-ups she had spent the day with, she was just a child, practically an infant.

All your fault, Ma, she thought, almost twenty-eight years later, as she stood in the attic doorway peering into the gloom. So overprotective, so stiflingly careful of my virtue, you'd deprived me of the chance to mix like all those self-confident young people, talking and laughing together as if they'd known each other all their lives. You'd kept me carefully cooped up at home for fear I might escape and leave you behind. Perhaps with hindsight you were more percipient than I gave you credit for.

She smiled, remembering the conversation that first night, her mother so eager, so suffocating in her desire for information, so desperate to retain her hold.

'So?'

Emma cringed inside as Josie settled down beside Auntie Mabel with a large dry sherry and leaned across the empty plates, determined not to miss a single word.

'So, how was it? What are they all like? What did you do today? Tell us everything.'

'Nothing much to tell.' Emma twiddled her pudding spoon around her fingers.

'Don't be ridiculous, darling. You must have done *something*. Auntie Mabel and I have been dying to hear all day.'

Silly old bat. Interfering Nosy Parker. 'I drew a bit.' That won't hold her for ten seconds, you fool . . . I drew a man with no clothes on, and he had a big, fat willy, three feet long. That'll hold her all right. 'Is there any more pudding?'

'Yes dear. Custard?'

'Mmm. Please.' It's rude to talk with your mouth full; spin it out, make it last.

'So what did you draw dear?'

'A nak— a man.' With a three foot . . . No. It would spoil in the telling. 'Sorry Ma, I'm shattered. I'll tell you all about it tomorrow.'

Up in the attic, Emma searched for the round, old-fashioned light switch and snapped it on, then gazed at the sea of junk George's parents had left behind them and sighed. She might have told dear Auntie Mabel, her mother's sister, who had looked after her sometimes when she was small and who ran a boarding house in Earl's Court, mysteriously acquired many years ago from an unknown benefactor. Mabel had seen it all, understood about being young, and she had the added attraction that Josie disapproved of her. There was a skeleton in her cupboard, which made her more interesting than Ma.

Ah, Mabel, thought Emma as she threaded her way amongst the broken chairs, the tea chests, the chaotic remains of forty, fifty years of George's parents' lives; you tried so hard on my behalf, advocating youth clubs, coffee-bars, evening classes, standing up for my freedom, but Ma stuck out her chin as far as it would go and did what she considered best for her little girl, despite you.

She squinted in the gloom at the daunting mess, wondering where to start, then smiled again, recalling the tail end of a conversation she had overheard between the two women that first evening.

'My darling daughter,' Josie said decidedly, 'is going to live happily ever after.'

'Contradiction in terms,' riposted Mabel drily. 'Happy, and ever after.'

They walked round to the Coach and Horses on the corner of Greek Street and sat on stools at the bar. When Bill said, 'What d'you want, Em?' Emma didn't know. She didn't dare mention that she'd never been in a pub, or drunk alcohol before, so Bill shrugged his shoulders and ordered her a pint of bitter.

It tasted horrible to begin with, but Emma enjoyed the euphoria it induced, and by the time she was halfway down the glass she was getting used to the taste, losing her inhibitions. She had sneaked her short skirt past her mother, dressing after Josie'd left for work, in black corduroy and a black skinny jumper. They suited her. She grew flushed; very pretty, Bill said, encouraged by her departure from the previous day's reserve. They didn't notice the effect the beer was having on her until George made a suggestive remark to Alison and she smacked his hand, sticking out a pink tongue.

'Dirty boy,' she teased him, and Jay jerked his head at Emma, reminding them both that there were children present. Instead of blushing Emma began to giggle. They all stared at her in surprise.

'What's the matter?' She leaned against Bill and ran a playful finger down his cheek, enjoying the attention. 'Aren't I old enough to listen?'

Jay frowned at her. 'Emma, how much have you had to drink?'

'Only a pint. Is that too much?' Emma looked from one to the other in puzzlement. 'What's all the bother about?'

'I don't think she's used to booze.' Jay regarded her doubtfully. 'Are you?'

'Emma!' Alison shook her arm.

Emma focused on her with difficulty. She had been drinking not only her own pint but Bill's as well; more than a third of it, and she was fed up with being treated like a child.

'Why're you all making such a fuss?' she asked petulantly, reminding them that she was only sixteen, and under age. When she leaned heavily against Jay, enjoying the warmth of his arm against hers, it was Alison's turn to get annoyed.

Jay got down from his stool and guided Emma away from the bar to a table in the furthest corner where it was darker and less conspicuous, then Bill brought crisps and packets of salted peanuts. Emma demolished the food and demanded more, then when she had sobered up a little Alison took her to the loo, where they stood side by side staring at their reflections in the pock-marked mirror, two tall, striking girls, one fair-haired and dark skinned, the other redheaded and pale.

'Have you ever thought about letting your hair down?'

Emma giggled, then frowned. 'My bloody mother wouldn't like it,' she said, and waited for the rush of guilt. When it didn't come she felt a surge of euphoria, and smiled at her distorted image. She'd never said 'bloody' in public before and, oh, it felt good. 'My bloody mother,' she repeated, savouring the words.

Alison laughed, and moved round to take hold of the thick red plait. 'Well as your bloody mother isn't here let's take a risk, shall we?'

She unravelled the braid carefully, then fumbled in her bag for a brush. Emma's hair was thick and wavy; it spread out to frame her face, covered her shoulders and romped halfway down her back.

'You remind me of that girl, you know, the one in Millais' paintings,' Alison encouraged. 'It looks *fabulous*.'

Emma gazed with tipsy fascination, until the Pre-Raphaelite beauty in the mirror, with her generous mouth, her unfocused golden eyes and her great mass of vivid hair, began to make her feel uncomfortable. Then she turned hurriedly away, avoiding the peculiar conviction that she was looking at a stranger.

Whey they returned to the table Jay kept staring at her and the more she sobered up the more he intimidated her. It was time to go.

Bill took her arm as they walked back to college. 'You look sensational. Why don't you wear your hair like that all the time?'

'Her mummy won't let her,' came Alison's voice from behind, mimicking.

'Leave her alone.' Jay took Emma's other arm, sliding his hand down to encircle her wrist, and they took the stairs three abreast, George following with Alison. Why, Emma wondered, did it make her feel so peculiar, touching the boys? Especially the gentle pressure of Jay's fingers on her wrist.

They were all together for the afternoon life class. The tutor, Harry Passmore, was young, very good-looking in a smooth sort of way. He appraised the girls as they came through the door, leering suggestively at Emma as she passed.

'You seem to have made a conquest,' Jay laughed and sat down next to her, moving his donkey so his leg was almost touching hers. Alison sat the other side of him and glared, annoyed.

The rest of the day was blurred; Emma drew in a desultory fashion and listened to the tutor lingering over the girls, discussing the size of the female model's anatomical parts as if she wasn't there.

'Come on, give the poor bird some tits, for God's sake. She's quite well endowed if you look ... You've made her as flat as a pancake ... Good grief, her arse isn't nearly as big as that – you could put your effort in for a circus Fat Lady competition.'

He spent longer with Alison than with anyone else, leaning

over her as he explained his points, winking when he left her, coming back for a second, a third time. Emma was hazily shocked but Alison didn't seem to mind, flirted outrageously, glancing frequently at Jay as she did it. To her chagrin he took no notice at all.

Emma didn't tell Josie about the pub. By the time she got home she had begged her hairband from Alison and she was respectable again. To her surprise, she wasn't struck down by the wrath of God for daring to utter the words 'my bloody mother' out loud.

It was that day, as the beer worked on her system, that it dawned on her for the first time: her mother had only as much, or as little, power over her as she chose to let her have. That day marked the beginning of her independence.

CHAPTER FOUR

• • •

Jay wasn't the only one who intimidated Emma, merely the most daunting. Her reputation for haughty disdain spread over the first weeks of term, until someone nicknamed her the Ice Maiden. Someone else, more perceptively, dubbed her the Virgin Queen.

She was aware that she was cutting herself off from her peers, but still she guarded her right not to join in. She was learning about herself, discovering that she didn't care if they thought her strange, provided they let her alone.

Only a small part of her longed to be like Alison, who by halfway through the term had taken up and dropped five boys and been out for a lunchtime drinking session with the tutor Passmore. She was dumped back in the Common Room in a state of complete inebriation and Emma, standing over her wondering what to do, was disgusted. 'It's common knowledge,' she told her new friend indignantly, 'that Harry Passmore can't resist a pretty face. But he's married with three children, for heaven's sake. I suppose it was your fault for going with him, but even so, getting you drunk just so he can touch you up in the pub is a bit beyond the pale.' Alison groaned, and rushed for the loo.

Passmore thought it was very funny when the tall freckled kid accosted him in the corridor to give him a piece of her mind, but by the time she'd finished shredding his character a dozen others had congregated to stare and snigger and he was no longer amused.

'You were fabulous,' said George later. 'I wish I'd had the guts.'

'Well you didn't.' Jay smiled at Emma. 'And neither did I, Em did.'

Emma was retrospectively horrified at herself. It was like going to the headmistress at school and telling her where to get off.

'Tell you what,' Jay, watching Emma's pale face as usual, took his opportunity, 'we'll skip the last lesson and I'll take you for a coffee.'

Emma agreed without thinking. She was beginning to feel such a fool that she was grateful for the opportunity to escape, even with Jay. As they left, the secretary was escorting Alison along to the office to pour black coffee down her throat.

'Some of our beloved tutors should have warning signs on them,' she remarked to her colleague. 'Just look at the state of this one.'

When Alison was sober enough she was sent on her way home, but she saw them: Emma sitting with Jay in a coffee-bar. He was leaning across the table smiling at her and something he had just said was making her laugh. Bitch, thought Alison as she passed, you sneaky bloody *bitch*.

It was then, thought Emma, picking up a piece of disintegrating curtain fabric and clambering over a three-legged coffee table to get to the window at the far end of the attic, that her friendship with Alison really began – with reluctant confidences borne of guilt. How Ali laughed at her. What a fool she must have sounded.

She rubbed at the grimy glass, then huffed on the panes and rubbed again. The sun was sloping across the grass, green turning to grey where the dew still lay. She could see the Hermit's footprints, and the dogs', meandering dark across the wet ground. How beautiful this place is, she thought, and how apt that we should end up here when you had coveted it for so long. How odd that you and he should both have felt the same about it, and about me.

*

It was three days before Alison spoke to her, and even then she had to pursue her on her way to the Tube, and force her.

'Look,' she begged, 'will you please talk to me? I haven't the faintest idea what you're so angry about.'

Alison glared at her, then switched moods and shrugged. 'Come on,' she said resignedly. 'I'll buy you a coffee. You haven't a clue, have you?'

They found a café just off Oxford Street. 'It's Jay,' said Alison.

Emma was puzzled. 'What about Jay?'

Ali fumbled in her bag for a cigarette. 'I haven't got the hang of it yet.' She laughed at herself. 'I only took it up to look sophisticated. I fancy him like anything, and I saw you the other day, sitting in a coffee-bar gazing at him over the espresso.'

Emma laughed at her. 'You are silly,' she said. 'I don't fancy him at all.'

It was true. He had made no advances that afternoon, just talked about college, about illustration, and she had left him to go home feeling less in awe of him than before, had even decided she quite liked him. 'He only took me for a coffee,' she insisted. 'There wasn't anything in it, honestly.'

Alison was sceptical. 'Well if you don't fancy Jay, who *do* you fancy? You must fancy *someone*.'

What a clumsy farce she'd made of explaining … Emma started on a second pane, spitting on the cloth then rubbing again. She had told Alison, dear, cynical, self-confident Alison, that she was waiting for someone special, waxed lyrical about Love with a capital L, when really she simply didn't know how to start.

She chuckled, dropped her makeshift duster and made her way back towards the door to begin her task. What a ludicrous conversation she and Alison had conducted that day.

'There are masses of boys in Pre-Dip that fancy you, you know.'

'Are there? I hadn't noticed.' It was true, Emma hadn't. She had switched off that sort of thing.

'How could you not notice?' It was a thought completely alien to Alison that anyone could go through life unaware of the effect they were having on other people. 'So why don't you become a nun or something, if that's the way you feel? After all, Art School's hardly the place for a professional virgin. I just don't understand why you don't want to – I mean, I'm dying for someone to try it on with me. I can't wait to lose my virginity and here you are . . .'

'It's got nothing to do with sex.'

Twenty-eight years later, Emma laughed out loud, remembering that barefaced lie, and went warm with retrospective embarrassment. At the time she had been offended, bridled huffily at Alison's whoops of condescending laughter.

'We're poles apart,' Ali had said, when she could speak. 'Here's me, determined to try out every available male as soon as possible and you're doing your best to avoid surrendering to anyone. Still,' she added contemptuously, 'look on the bright side; at least I can stop worrying about you being competition.'

There had been a man in the Tube station exposing himself to an unmoved public, and Emma had stopped to stare, fascinated by the first male member she had ever seen. It was larger than she'd thought it would be (she'd seen a picture of Michaelangelo's David), a wriggling, flaccid sausage made of white tripe and Alison had had to move her on, sniggering at her naïve interest. They had parted at the bottom of the escalator to go their separate ways, closer friends than before and each the possessor of a couple of intimate secrets about the other; Emma's unacknowledged fears had been further increased by the sight of that fat, white sausage.

During that first term, Emma recalled as she sifted fading family photographs, they had settled in. She sat her Art A-level, essential to get on to the Diploma course, and the students got to know each other, their surroundings and their tutors, which ones they could get round and which would give them a rocket for being two seconds late, which were lechers (Passmore wasn't the only one), and which they could safely turn their backs on.

She put aside a moth-eaten album – George as a baby, fat and smiling; George as Andy Pandy at a Coronation Party in 1953; George as a sulky, adolescent Mod in a plastic mac, posing with his sisters – and sat back on her haunches, reminiscing . . .

They began to socialise with the Diploma students. They were the élite, already on a 'proper' course. They knew where all the parties were, parties like nothing the Pre-Dips, straight out of school, had ever experienced. Emma couldn't get to the first ones and neither could Alison, but they heard about them second-hand from the boys. They didn't have to ask permission; being boys they could always kip down on someone's floor. Their parents didn't worry about them being seduced, and getting drunk was part of growing up.

Alison was frustrated, her plan to try out life stalled for lack of opportunity. Wise by now to her friend's appetite, she took Emma to the Italian, stood her a mushroom risotto and two helpings of Neapolitan ice-cream, and enlisted her aid.

'If I pretend I'm staying with you, I can get away from the Bastard. I'll do it for you in return, I promise.'

'Okay,' said Emma. 'But you don't need to do it for me, I'm not interested.' Alison shrugged her shoulders and set out to enjoy herself.

She lost her virginity with a complete stranger at a party in Notting Hill Gate, didn't even ask his name. 'We did it on the floor in the bathroom,' she told Emma afterwards, giggling. 'There was a drunk in the bath, passed out cold, and I had terrible trouble with my knickers. They wouldn't come off with all the fumbling and stuff.'

'Was it good?'

'Not really. I liked the bit beforehand, the kissing and the messing about. He had a big tool. But it was a bit of a let-down in the end; it was so quick. I expect I just picked the wrong bloke.'

'So are you ready for Jay now?'

Ali shook her head. 'No, I'm leaving him for later. I want to get it right first, otherwise he'll run a mile. I've a feeling he's been around a bit and I want to be ready for him. Aren't I dreadful?' She laughed and lit another cigarette.

A week later Jay asked Emma out. 'Why not?' he asked when she refused.

Because, she might have explained, I'm terrified of you, of the air of world-weary experience you exude. She didn't though, she just mumbled, 'I'd rather we stayed friends,' and offended him.

'I'm not going to rape you,' he said angrily, and she felt a complete fool.

Ali was after a second-year Graphics student, a boy called Barry. He was tall, sleek and handsome, with a broad-shouldered, narrow-hipped body and she reckoned he'd do nicely to learn on.

There was a Hop in the Common Room after half-term: beer; crisps; loud music, Tamla Motown, the Beatles, the Stones, and a couple of slow ones thrown in every now and then to encourage the shy ones, Sandie Shaw, Dusty Springfield. Emma went, just to assert her independence, and danced during the early part of the proceedings exclusively with Bill and George because they were the only boys she felt comfortable with. Jay didn't go.

George was over Alison now, in love with a first-year Graphics student called Jilly Fox. 'But I can't get near her for all these other blokes,' he told Emma, shouting over the noise. 'What do you think I should do, Em?'

'How would I know?' she shouted back, preoccupied with her own problems, and he left her to pickle his frustration in alcohol.

Later, when she had a couple of drinks under her belt, she grew brave and danced with a boy called Ian, from the Fine Art department. She didn't catch his surname because they were playing the Animals' 'House of the Rising Sun' and the music was too loud, but he seemed nice, ordinary, unthreatening.

'Come to the flicks tomorrow?' he asked casually over the thumping music.

'Okay,' Emma mouthed, emboldened by booze, and he

wandered off; it was surprisingly easy.

Alison pounced on her. 'Well? What were you talking about? Is he a good kisser? Is he The One?'

Em laughed at her. 'No he isn't The One. He's just a nice boy. I don't know whether he's a good kisser – he didn't kiss me.'

Alison was disappointed, but she brightened up when Emma told her about the pictures. There was hope for her yet, she said.

He took her to the Wednesday Night Film Club at college to see Sternberg's *The Blue Angel*: Marlene Dietrich, oozing heartless decadence from every pore. The final denouement, when Dietrich's lover was humiliated and destroyed, brought a lump to Emma's throat at the cruelty involved. She didn't think anyone would be that cruel in real life.

Ian laughed at her. 'Course they would. Look at your friend.' Emma was puzzled. 'Alison, that friend of yours. She manipulates everyone, including you. She's got Barry dangling on a string already. He's dumped his girlfriend on the off-chance that he'll make it with her and you can see she's just messing him about. Can't you?'

Emma shifted uncomfortably. 'It's not her fault,' she defended Alison. 'She's got this terrible father.'

'Nah,' said Ian dismissively. 'She's just a bitch, that's all.' He didn't understand.

They caught the Tube to Liverpool Street and he waited on the platform until Emma's train pulled in. Then he kissed her on the cheek, squeezed her hand and said goodbye.

'Thanks,' she said. 'It was lovely.'

'I'm very honoured.' He grinned at her. 'You've got a reputation, you know.'

'What do you mean, what reputation?'

'For being unapproachable. There're two boys in my year wanted to ask you out apart from me, but neither of them dared.'

Emma felt humiliated, embarrassed.

'Look.' Ian smiled at her. 'It's quite all right. I admire you; you don't let anyone pressure you into anything. How old are you?'

'Sixteen.'

'I thought so.' He nodded pompously. 'There's plenty of time.'

Ali pounced the next afternoon. 'Good grief, what's the matter with the stupid boy?' she exclaimed when Emma told her he hadn't even tried to kiss her properly. 'Is he queer?'

'Queer?'

'You know, bent, a fairy, a hom-o-sex-ual. Do I have to explain that as well?'

'No. No, of course he's not.' Emma was sure he wasn't one of those. 'He knows I don't want to, that's all.'

Over the rest of the term Ian took Emma out half a dozen times, for a drink or a meal. They talked and laughed safely together like brother and sister and at the end of each evening she caught the last train home to Cheshunt and her mother. She told Josie she was out with Alison.

Josie was finding it harder and harder to assert her authority these days – Emma was becoming so distant, she was afraid of losing her altogether if she complained.

Jay wasn't speaking to Emma at all.

'It's common knowledge; he fancies you rotten. Didn't you know?' said Ian.

'No . . . yes, I suppose so.' Emma was reluctant to acknowledge Jay's obvious interest; it made her feel guilty about Alison. 'But I've already told him I don't want to go out with him. I don't see why that should preclude us being friends.'

'You insulted him; you turned him down and went out with me.'

'But that's different, you wouldn't—'

'Wouldn't what, try and get you into bed? He doesn't know that, does he?' Ian looked briefly annoyed before he changed the subject.

CHAPTER FIVE

• • •

The January term, 1965, was a step forward. The Pre-Dips were getting to know each other. Some of the older ones had found digs in town, bedsits in Earl's Court or in the streets off the King's Road, and Emma could walk into the canteen now without feeling like Quasimodo.

There was a rock concert at Chelsea Art School, featuring Long John Baldry and Julie Driscoll, and they went in a big gang together, all except for Jay. Emma stayed away from home for the first time; having begged and pleaded with her mother to let her go.

Josie insisted on ringing Ali's father to make sure it was all right and he nearly scuppered Alison's alibi when he said pompously, 'After all the times you've had my daughter, it's the least I can do.' Fortunately, Josie was tired that night and Emma managed to shrug the remark off as a mistake. It was a close shave though, and it gave the girls a shock.

They travelled back to Richmond on the top of the last bus, high on noise and Watney's Red Barrel, beating out the rhythms on the seatback, sweating from heat, physical exertion and too much booze.

The Bastard was still up when they got in. He was huge, six foot five at least, florid and fair-haired. Emma took an instant dislike to him. He had a cruel twist to his mouth and his conversation was like a third-degree interrogation. Why had Emma left school so early? 'How many O levels've you got? D'you know how many Alison has?'

'Shut up, Daddy. Em doesn't want to know about my boring exam results.'

'Ten O levels, all As or Bs, and three As, all top grades.'

Ali scowled at him. 'Come on Em, let's go to bed.'

'So what was your problem, Missy?' he demanded. 'Not bright enough for A levels?'

Emma, intimidated by his aggressive manner, mumbled, 'I just didn't want to stay on, that's all,' and hastily followed her friend.

The house was enormous, Georgian and elegant on the outside, opulent and flashy on the inside. 'Too much money and too little taste,' said Alison, whose room was quite different from the rest of the place, furnished with steel and glass, white bedspreads, white sofa, white carpet, big splashy prints on the white painted walls. 'When I'm as rich as Daddy I'll have real paintings,' she said.

She was over-excited, talked manically about the concert, about men, sex. It took her an hour to get round to the Bastard. 'Isn't he just horrible?'

'Why is he so keen on exams?'

Alison sprawled on her white bed on her stomach, bare legs crossed in the air and her chin in her hands. 'He's an intellectual snob, a genius with an IQ of God-knows-what, a self-made man who dragged himself up from nothing to all this.' She waved a dismissive hand at their surroundings. 'My grandparents were working class I think, but I've never met them, he never even mentions them. He made all his money doing deals just after the war, you know, buying surplus stuff cheap and selling it at an enormous profit, but he plays the stockmarket now, wheels and deals. He loves anything to do with power, and he thinks exams, degrees give you power, like money and titles. He'd love a title, but he doesn't know any of the right people.' She laughed, delighting in her contempt. 'He's got lots of money and no class.' She reached across to the bedside table, fumbling for cigarettes. 'He's a Grade A bastard. Pete, that's my older brother, he's at Oxford doing a doctorate in Maths and he's a genius too. Daddy's never had any trouble with him; he wanted to do it, all Daddy had to do was point him in the right direction. I'm bright enough as well . . .'

'How bright?'

'Very bright actually. I should be at university: I got a place at Somerville to read History and Economics.'

'So why didn't you go?'

'Two reasons.' Alison rolled on to her back and lit her cigarette, then contemplated the ceiling through the smoke. 'One was just to spite him – I was sick of being told what to do. And two, I didn't fancy it. He chose the college because it was all-girl; he thought there'd be fewer distractions.' She rolled on to her stomach again, showing her perfect white teeth in a grin. 'You can imagine how well that went down. I told him if he made me go I'd run away and he'd never see me again. But I've got to live at home this year so he can keep an eye on me. And then there's what he's done to Ricky.'

Emma was intrigued. 'What has he done to Ricky?'

Alison sat up, cross-legged. 'Ah . . . Ricky's my little brother. He's away.'

'And is he clever too?'

'Yes and no. They did some tests when he was eight, then again when he was thirteen, and they decided in the end that he had an IQ of between 125 and 130. That's not quite as good as me and nowhere near as bright as Pete, but it's pretty clever. Trouble was, he couldn't get it together. When he was six, his teacher called Daddy in and told him Rick was an idiot.' She paused to blow blue smoke. 'Daddy's always been hard on him. Perhaps it was being the youngest and having to follow me and Pete. Anyway, it turned out he has some sort of . . .' she shook her shoulders, fiddled with the ash she'd flicked into the ashtray '. . . um, perceptual problem. You know, he can't sort out words properly. If he looks at a book or a newspaper he doesn't see it like you or I would – it's just a jumble.' She leaped off the bed to rummage in a drawer. 'He wrote this when he was about ten.' She handed Emma a dog-eared piece of paper. There were gaps between some of the letters and occasionally Emma thought she could pick out a word. 'Nad' could have been 'and' and there was what might have been 'the', except that the 'h' was the wrong way round. The rest of it was virtually indecipherable. She handed it back.

'See what I mean? You can't *imagine* how badly Daddy took it. Here he was, self-made man, two clever children and then along comes this complete duffer. He wouldn't believe it for ages, kept blaming the schools; it couldn't possibly be his problem. Then at Rick's last junior school his headmistress took Daddy on one side and gave him a piece of her mind, said Rick was a very bright little boy with a learning difficulty. She did all sorts of funny tests on him, to confirm how clever he was, but that made Daddy worse. He thought if Rick was bright he must be failing because he wasn't trying, so he started coaching him at home, and when Ricky couldn't do it he'd scream and shout at him. Rick was petrified of him. He'd end up in tears and Daddy would throw the books across the room and slam out in rage.' Alison was smoking aromatic black Sobranie cigarettes with coloured filters, taking deep drags at each one, then lighting another from the glowing tip and stubbing out the remains, until she had a pile of multi-coloured cylinders in the ashtray.

'So what happened?'

'I went away. I was thirteen and Daddy packed me off to boarding school, but nobody would take Ricky so he decided to educate him at home. He was twelve by then, and Daddy could've done it, I mean he had the knowledge, but what he didn't have was the patience. He hadn't the faintest idea how terrified of him Ricky was. When I came home for Christmas that first year, Rick had developed a stutter, and by the time he was fourteen not only could he not read or write, he couldn't talk either.' Angry tears began to course down her cheeks. 'I *hate* him!' she shouted. 'I hate the bastard's guts!' Emma found her a tissue, nearly clean, and she wiped her eyes. 'Sorry.' She blew her nose loudly. 'It's the booze, makes me morbid.'

'So where is he now?'

'Who, Ricky? I told you, he's away, at a special school. But he finishes at the end of the summer term and then he'll have to come home so dear Daddy can torment him again.'

They undressed in silence, then Alison tumbled straight into bed and sleep. Emma lay awake, thinking about what she had been told and seeing her faded, overworked mother in a new light. They slept late and Alison woke with a hangover.

They didn't see much of each other for the rest of term. There had been too many raw edges exposed and they both stepped back from further intimacy. Ali didn't want sympathy. She wanted to be liked, loved, admired, but she didn't want to be pitied.

The vacation was a relief.

CHAPTER SIX

• • •

During the summer term it hit them all that if they wanted to get on to the Diploma courses they had to do some work.

Ali was going for Graphics. She fancied the advertising business, she said. 'Lots of money, lots of kudos, lots of men.'

'Poor saps don't know what's going to hit them,' said Jay acidly, deliberately goading her.

He and Alison were hardly talking these days. She'd made advances to him at a party in St John's Wood whilst under the influence of a joint and had been rebuffed. He wasn't speaking to Emma because she was still seeing Ian. No matter that he had fallen for her the first minute he set eyes on her – he didn't need her, he told himself, when the urge to strangle both of them was at its worst, didn't love her. She would only complicate his life. He began, after his run-in with Alison, to take his transitory pleasures well away from college, hidden from the prying eyes of his fellow students.

George was still pursuing the glamorous Jilly, who encouraged him one day, ignored him the next. He lived in a state of permanent sexual excitement, leavened by constant perplexity at the mysterious ways of women.

The lunchtime boozing had stopped, except for Bill, a fixture now in both the Coach and Horses and the Six Bells. Grigsmore, the senior tutor, took him to one side halfway through the term, catching him as he returned from a liquid lunch, and when he emerged his face was white as paper. Emma, who sat next to him for the afternoon session, asked him if he was ill.

'Not ill,' he said. 'More shell-shocked. Griggsy's just torn me metaphorically limb from limb and slowly roasted my gizzard over a hot fire. If I don't stop boozing I'm out on my ear at the end of term. No second chances, he says, starting now.' He grinned ruefully. 'So that's it. From now on I'm a teetotal celibate. No beer, no parties, no girls.'

Bill, with his open, honest face and engaging personality, had been cutting a swathe through the Pre-Dip girls that many a would-be college Lothario might have envied, but he took Griggsy at his word. For the rest of the summer term he worked like a Trojan, kept off the beer and the birds. He was surprised to find that it was a relief. His restless bed-hopping, searching for something but never getting close to finding it, had been tiring him out.

Barry was now Alison's devoted slave and therefore in danger of becoming a bore. She was getting restive, looking around for new excitement, and even Emma and Ian had progressed to hand-holding, and French kissing at the end of the evening.

The last few weeks were frantic, everyone trying to get a portfolio together and realising they hadn't done enough work. Except Jay, quiet, sardonic Jay, who knew he'd done enough. He was very good; very, very good, and arrogantly confident. He was opting for Graphics and had no doubts at all that he would be accepted.

George was going for Graphics too – he knew he could get a well-paid job at the end of the course, but to everyone's surprise Bill opted for Fashion.

'Dunno,' he said when they asked why. 'Just feels right that's all.'

Emma opted for Fashion too but, typically, Alison changed her mind three times before finally deciding to go with Bill and Emma, mostly because she fancied the Textiles tutor.

'And I can always swap if I don't like it,' she said flippantly.

All accepted, they decamped to the pub on the last day of term to celebrate and say their final farewells before the long vacation.

Ian found Emma in a corner, conducting a heated conversation with Bill. 'Of course you can,' she was saying. 'Why don't you ask her? George and Ali are going to.'

'Going to what?'

Emma turned and smiled at Ian. 'You never smile at me like that,' Bill complained, flirting out of habit, and she laughed at him.

'What are you talking about?' asked Ian again.

'My Auntie Mabel.' Emma made room for him to sit. 'Ali and I are going to try and persuade the parents to let us off the leash next year. I've been working on Ma. If she can't keep an eye on me herself then Mabel's the next best person to do it. She's in Earl's Court, you see. A lot of her students are moving out this summer, and we're all so respectable, she'll be delighted if I can persuade all my dear sweet friends to rent her rooms. Little does she know what a disgraceful lot of reprobates you are.'

Bill bridled. 'How dare you! Here am I, pure as driven snow and dear Alison, the Virgin Queen herself . . .'

They all laughed at the thought of Alison as the Virgin Queen, that title still belonged to Emma. Some wag had dubbed Alison 'the Bicycle' – anyone could ride her – but it didn't stop any of the boys from coveting her.

'If you're interested,' said Emma, 'you'll have to be quick. She's nearly full up already.'

'So's Alison,' said Bill drily.

Up in the attic, Emma moved a couple of broken lampshades, beginning a tentative pile of throwaways, then went back to sifting the faded photographs. George was getting older now, nearer to the age at which she had first met him; as his hair grew longer his expression lightened, sartorial rebellion easing his passage through adolescence. She sighed, remembering his parents, Doug and Morag, with a smile of affection, then began to clear a wider passage towards the window beyond which the sunlight beckoned.

She had never told the others the trouble she'd had, persuading Josie to let her go. 'How can you leave me on my own like this? All these years I've scrimped and saved, sacrificed myself for you, and for what? So you can run off the minute you get the opportunity?'

Emma was patient, practical. 'The fares will be less. Auntie Mabel is hardly asking me for any rent, so only the electric and the gas will be extra ... I'll come home every weekend.' Oh, the worthless promises of youth. 'It'll be less tiring for you, not having to rush back from work to cook for two, no more washing, bed changing for us both. And for me—' blatant emotional blackmail '—no more travelling across London late at night, or missing lectures so I can catch the early evening train.' Her mother gave in.

Too late now, thought Emma, as she gazed out at the sunlit garden far below, to be sorry for my callous disregard of Ma's needs. It didn't occur to me that she *had* needs, that she had dreams and aspirations, just as I had. She was old to me then, and I was young. It's too late now to say sorry.

CHAPTER SEVEN

Emma bagged the big back room on the ground floor. It had French windows opening on to the communal gardens, a stone sink with a wooden draining-board and a Baby Belling. Ali had her eye on the bedroom above Emma's, next to the shared bathroom, and the other ground and first-floor rooms were already let, to a law student and a girl reading English at London University. That left Auntie Mabel, who had the second floor, and the basement, which was reserved for the boys, although, for another few weeks it was still occupied by two students and a tutor from the London School of Economics.

Emma organised a meeting for the first week of the holidays, gave them all instructions, how to get there, what to wear, how to handle Mabel. Only Jay wasn't interested. He didn't want to share with anyone, except Emma.

It was a warm sunny day and Josie came up to London for the occasion. They had all made an effort: Ali in a fresh white blouse and a knee-length pleated skirt (where on earth had she got *that* from? wondered Emma); George, hair down to his shoulders but so clean you could almost hear it squeaking and a tie ('A *tie*?' she whispered as she let him in and he winked exaggeratedly at her).

Bill was pony-tailed, but his jeans were clean and his T-shirt was immaculately white. He brought with him two of the biggest bunches of roses Emma had ever seen and both Mabel and Josie were almost speechless with delight. It was a long time since anyone had given either of them roses. Ian was late, but his hair was newly cut and he, like George, was wearing a tie.

They sat round Mabel's dining-table on the second floor eating squashed-fly biscuits, drinking coffee and discussing rent and rules. 'No loud music after ten p.m., no members of the opposite sex in rooms after midnight, no alcohol on the premises, no rubbish left on the steps except on Tuesdays and Fridays . . .'

'No hawkers, no circulars, no pimps, no tarts,' whispered Bill to Ian, who choked on his coffee and had to be patted on the back.

Mabel was pleased with them on the whole. A bit outlandish, especially the pony-tail, but they were all clean, and scrupulously polite. None of them smoked.

'Filthy habit,' agreed Alison, flashing her most irresistible smile.

It was a long, hot summer. Ian gave Emma his telephone number before they parted, but she didn't get round to giving him hers. She got a job in a local supermarket, stacking shelves with dog food from eight until one-thirty, then rushing home for lunch before catching the bus to the local wholesale Cash-and-Carry where she worked on the checkout from three-thirty until half-past ten. She went to bed each night with swollen feet and an aching back, dreamed of cash registers and till rolls, and earned £8 10s a week.

By the end of September, when she handed in her notice, she had amassed nearly £100, but she didn't touch any of the money; it was for her new place. Having refused to accompany Mabel and Josie on their late summer holiday in Southwold, she went up to London ten days before term started. She hadn't seen Ian since the meeting at Mabel's, and she wondered in passing if she should have phoned him, but she didn't worry about it – it wasn't important. Or was it Ian that wasn't important?

Without Mabel there, she could do as she pleased and the freedom was intoxicating, like being drunk for the first time. She thought briefly of phoning Ali, but she didn't, she was enjoying herself too much, discovering the delights of being completely alone for the first time in her life.

She took down the dirty Regency-striped curtains, and painted the grimy walls of her room deep terracotta. The furniture was tolerable: a cumbersome Victorian wardrobe; a three-quarter size bed, halfway between a single and a double; a table and two chairs for eating, and two easy chairs with wooden arms and loose cushions covered in sprigged stretch Crimplene, the material discoloured by age and grease. She stripped them off and re-covered them in black corduroy, puncturing her finger over and over with the curved needle, and bought a couple of Indian bedspreads and a small sagging sofa with feather cushions, delivered for a quid in a scruffy van. The only bits of the room she left white were the ceiling and the beautiful wooden fire surround with its wide mantelshelf. There was nothing she could do with the ugly gas fire. She found a flaky, rickety screen in the same junk shop as the sofa, sanded and repainted it with shiny black lacquer, to hide the wash-basin and the cooker, then bought paper blinds, white ones, and a big white paper lampshade for the naked lightbulb. She picked up a threadbare but genuine Persian rug for a fiver, just what she wanted – rich, exotic, oriental looking. Ma, she thought gleefully, would *hate* it.

Josie and Mabel returned from Southwold a few days before the new term began, bringing with them her wireless and record-player, her books and the rest of her clothes. Josie had a headache and went to bed early; Mabel spent the evening sipping dry sherry and complaining about the landlady of their boarding house. Southwold was getting very common, she said, too many tourists and they'd actually opened a *supermarket* in the High Street. Emma began to wonder whether she'd done the right thing swapping her mother for her aunt and longed, for the first time, for the others to move in.

They turned up on the Saturday in an assortment of family cars piled high with boxes, tea chests, suitcases and long-suffering parents. Bill's were quiet and unassuming like Bill; George's instantly likeable, calm, self-assured and softly Scottish. Ian's parents made no impression upon Emma at all. The Bastard was as boorish as he had been the last time. Mabel, having suffered years of invisibility in a better cause than the bad-mannered Mr Brown, took instant umbrage.

'He may well be a perfectly nice person,' she confided to Josie, 'but frankly, I can see no evidence of it. The man is irretrievably common.'

'Oh!' Josie was alarmed. 'Do you think so?' She had already entrusted her precious daughter to the wretched man once. 'And yet dear Alison's so charming.'

They retreated upstairs, leaving the young people to it, and settled down with a dry sherry apiece. 'It merely goes to prove,' said Mabel decidedly as she eased her shoes off, 'that money can't buy breeding.'

The boys had all managed to get summer jobs. Ian had been working on a building site and looked brown and fit. Bill had been driving a fork-lift truck in a warehouse for six weeks and had hardly seen the sun at all; he was terribly pale. But it was George who had really fallen on his feet, working as a life-guard at the municipal swimming baths in Cromer, watching scantily clad girls sunbathing on the grass or frolicking in the warm water. He was smug and pleased with himself; he had plucked up the courage to be unfaithful to Jilly and he felt he had their relationship under control at last.

Alison had been on holiday to the South of France with Ricky and her father, and it had been horrible. 'The Bastard harangued Rick from start to finish and Rick finally lost his temper and told him to "B-b-b-b bugger off".' She mimicked her brother's stutter. 'Now he's really in the doghouse. I don't know what Daddy has in mind but it'll be something evil, you'll see. In the meantime Rick's at home. Can he come and visit sometimes, d'you think?'

Emma thought it would be all right. 'But I don't know whether Mabel'll let him stay in your room.'

'Maybe he could doss down with the boys in the basement then?'

When the others dispersed to their own rooms Ian hung around.

'You didn't phone me . . .'

'I'm sorry, it was just that I was working so hard—'

'And you didn't give me your number so I could phone you.' He stared at her belligerently. 'I've been very patient, Em, but sometimes I think you just use me as a convenient means of fending off more insistent suitors. It's not fair.'

He was plaintive, aggrieved, and Emma quickly became defensive. They'd had an arrangement; he'd accepted the rules. She felt invaded by his persistence, trespassed upon.

'I pay my share,' she offered sulkily, by way of expiation.

'That's not the point and you know it.' It was one of Ian's complaints; it was hard to put pressure on Emma when he couldn't even claim to have spent money on her. He'd not once managed to pay for a whole evening out and it wasn't fair of her to say so. He went to kiss her but she turned her head and offered her cheek.

'Perhaps I should have made alternative arrangements instead of sitting by the phone,' he said angrily and stumped downstairs.

She closed the door after him and went to sit by the open window. The summer had lasted long into autumn and the evening breeze smelled good, of petrol, warm tarmac and cut grass. She tried to imagine life without Ian and found it very easy. If he chucked her she would just go back to being on her own, except that now she really would be on her own. She could hear them settling in downstairs: muffled thuds, voices, laughter, then the thump, thump, thump of rock music. It didn't bother her, any more than the hum of traffic or the Australian next door singing a bawdy Antipodean ditty in his bath. She was alone.

Josie had left on the Sunday, tearful and depressed. 'The house'll seem so empty,' she snuffled into her handkerchief, her nose running, her eyes pink and watery with emotion. 'You won't eat properly without me to look after you.'

'Thank you for your confidence.' Mabel was dry and sarcastic, irritated by her sister's misery. 'Now do stop it, Josie. I'll see Emma stays on the straight and narrow, I promise.' Josie sniffed.

They walked her down to Earl's Court Tube station and waved her off at the top of the escalator, then grinned conspiratorially at each other.

'And you'd better behave, young lady,' Mabel threatened emptily, 'or I'll send you home to Mother.'

CHAPTER EIGHT
• • •

They travelled in to college together on the Tube, all except Ian who went in early, avoiding Emma. They made a lot of noise, deliberately, to annoy the other commuters.

'Look at them, poor saps.' Bill flicked his pony-tail contemptuously from his collar. 'Drabness personified.'

He was wearing a black Teddy Boy jacket with a velvet collar, deep pockets and squared-off shoulders, a bright turquoise shirt with a bootlace tie and black drainpipe jeans. Emma had painted her eyes at home for the first time, instead of surreptitiously on the train, and she was wearing her hair loose. She had on an ankle-length Indian skirt and a cheesecloth top beneath a second-hand airforce greatcoat. Ali was all in red – red blouse with a long, pointed collar, red A-line skirt, a wide black belt and a short jacket embroidered with flamboyant red and black flowers. Her legs were very brown and the toes of her high-heeled shoes were very pointed; she looked sensationally beautiful and she gathered dozens of admiring stares during the journey. George was wearing a very expensive plum-coloured leather jacket, bought with his life-guard earnings, but he still looked scruffy. He had risen late and forgotten to shave; his hair was greasy and his jeans were none too clean.

They swaggered up the wide stone steps, greeted familiar faces, stopped to talk. 'How was your vac?' 'Have you been working?' 'Where's so-and-so?'

The routines were different now and took some getting used to. It was hard to remember where they were supposed to be, and they spent their first week learning new names, new tutors, new places. They were over-excited, full of their own importance and difficult to control.

They saw less of George now they were in different departments and hardly anything of Jay. He wouldn't come for lunch at the Italian, and in his absence they talked about him.

'He's the best of us by miles,' said George, 'single-minded, meticulous. He's got an instinct for what looks right, "commercial instinct", our tutor calls it.' Jay was already getting freelance illustration work, just by word of mouth. 'Astronomical money,' George said wistfully. He had been back less than a week, and already his holiday earnings were dwindling. Jilly was bored with the Chinese, so they'd tried Dinty Moore's, the Italian round the corner from Mabel's where most of the student population of Earl's Court hung out, but that didn't suit either. She wanted more sophisticated venues.

'She's got me by the short and curlies,' George admitted ruefully to Emma, regretting his brief fling now that he was back under the influence.

It took Alison less than a week to realise she had chosen the wrong room. She tried to cajole Emma to swap with her, but Emma wouldn't budge so she turned her charm on the quiet, self-effacing law student currently occupying the ground floor front. The bathroom didn't make nearly as much noise as the traffic, she assured him and her room overlooked the gardens. '*So* much more peaceful,' she said, widening her eyes at him.

'What are you up to?' asked Emma suspiciously.

Ali winked at her. She was lounging on Emma's sofa, long legs dangling over the arm and a cup of coffee balanced precariously on her stomach. 'Thing is,' she explained, 'on the first floor I'm right underneath Mabel's bedroom.'

'So?'

'Well, I can't see your Auntie Mabel lying in her chaste little bed upstairs saying to herself "That's nice, young Alison's entertaining a friend for a bit of slap-and-tickle tonight", can you? She'd be downstairs in ten seconds flat, escorting me and aforementioned young man into the street if she thought I was having it off on her hallowed premises. Whereas, if I have the ground-floor front...' She threw back her golden head and howled with laughter.

The law student acceded to her wishes for nothing more than a devastating smile and a quick peck on the cheek, and Alison decided to throw a party to celebrate the move.

Auntie Mabel was invited, though not before Alison had carefully ascertained that she was going to stay with Josie for the weekend, which made it easy when Mabel declined the invitation to say how sorry she was. 'But you'll have to come to the next one, won't you? It's not as if it's a proper party, Mabel (she was on first-name terms already), it's only a few friends, and you've met most of them.'

Mabel was flattered to be invited but went off for her weekend relieved to escape the noise she knew would be inevitable. Over the years she had learned not to interfere in her tenants' lives; at her age all she wanted was peace and quiet, and besides, she thought, Alison was good for dear Emma, bringing her out of her shell and stopping her spending too much time on her own. She suspected that nice, respectable Ian of being sweet on her niece as well, and he seemed just the right sort of young man to stimulate her interest in the opposite sex, not the type to take advantage of her innocence. Mabel had wondered more than once whether she shouldn't take Emma to one side and explain the facts of life to her, put her in the picture about the propensity of the average male for ignoring any practical considerations once his mind had settled upon his groin. But it was a little early for that; no sense in putting ideas into the girl's head. Watching her, she would have sworn on a stack of Bibles that her niece was still a virgin, and set to stay that way for a while yet.

As usual Alison organised the move, and everyone else rushed around carrying out her instructions. At the last minute the reason for the party, the room warming, became irrelevant when she decided that her room was too small and Emma's would be much better. Emma didn't want her room used, it was private, but by that time so many people were involved that she was shouted down.

Ian waited for Emma in the canteen on the Friday.

'Coffee,' he said. 'I want to talk to you.'

Emma knew what he wanted to talk about; he'd been trying for days to get her on her own and she'd been avoiding him.

He came straight to the point. 'I need to know where I stand.'

She frowned at him across the table, resenting the pressure. 'You already know where you stand. Exactly where you did last term.' She stirred her coffee irritably. 'I like you.'

'Big deal.' Ian stared morosely into the sugar bowl, resenting her ability to shut him out, then tried another tack. 'What about the party, are we going together?'

'If you like.' *Stop pressuring me.*

'If you like's not good enough. I want a positive answer. And while we're at it, are you ever going to go to bed with me?'

Emma lowered her eyes hurriedly and fiddled with her spoon. 'I'm sorry,' she said at last, shaking her head, 'but you did ask.'

'But I *love* you.' He looked as if he was about to burst into tears.

'I'm sorry, I can't help it.' Emma was swamped by guilt; this must be her fault for leading him on. She leaned across the table to touch his hand but he shook her off. 'You don't really love me,' she began tentatively, 'you just think you do because I won't—'

'If that was all I was interested in I'd have found someone more accommodating months ago.' Ian was very angry. 'I asked you out because ... well, if you don't know why then you're more stupid than I thought you were. Anyway, you've answered my question. I'll make alternative arrangements.' He paused, waiting for her to change her mind, but she didn't look at him. She heard his chair scrape as he pushed it back and when she looked up he was shouldering his way through the crowd to get to the door.

Confusingly, she felt only relief. Why couldn't she be more like Ali? Ali would have gone to bed with him just to cheer him up and thought nothing of it. Was it possible that she was a freak?

They spent Saturday getting ready for the party, parading in front of the full-length mirror in Alison's room. By lunchtime there was a pile of rejected clothing lying on the floor and Alison had decided she had to have something new, so they took the Tube to Kensington and walked down Abingdon Road to Biba, where Alison stole a dress. It was short, black and superbly cut. It showed off her legs and her beautifully tanned arms; she tried it on, liked it, and walked out with it stuffed down the sleeve of her jacket.

'Don't look so shocked.' She laughed at Emma's expression. 'Everybody does it, and anyway, I couldn't afford three pounds ten.'

They got back just after five to find the others gone. They'd left a note, *Dinty Moore's 8 p.m.*, so Emma ate a tin of ravioli with grated cheese, and then they held a final dress rehearsal. She was wearing a jersey dress she had bought in the King's Road the previous week: an ankle-length T-shirt with a scoop neck and wide blue and yellow stripes, fitted very tight over her body. The material, stretched across her prominent hip bones, emphasised the lack of flesh beneath: she looked like a skinny wasp.

Alison examined her critically. 'You're too thin,' she said. She was looking sensationally, spectacularly beautiful, and she knew it.

Bill and George came up from the basement, but there was no sign of Ian. 'He said he'd see us later,' said Bill.

'Where was he going?'

'Dunno, didn't ask.'

'He's been in a foul mood all day.' George wasn't renowned for his tact. 'You been upsetting him, Em?'

Emma didn't answer. It was none of their business.

They walked down to Dinty Moore's to bag one of the big tables in the back of the restaurant, and the others arrived in ones and twos over the next hour. The party wasn't due to start until ten but by nine there were fourteen of them and they had got through eleven bottles of cheap red wine. Barry arrived at half-past, insinuating himself into the chair beside Alison's. The stolen Biba dress looked wonderful and the more she drank, the more Ali turned up the voltage of her personality, until she eclipsed everyone else in the restaurant.

'Now!' she announced, choosing her moment, and they all jumped, pushing back their chairs, rising in unison, draining their glasses and following where she led.

Emma resented her. She resented the stolen dress, the way her friend manipulated everyone, the fact that it was Alison who wanted this party but she had to have it in her room.

'What's up with you and Ian?' Bill took her arm as they emerged into the street.

'Nothing. We're just not seeing each other any more.'

She caught him by surprise. 'Poor old Ian. No wonder he was so bad-tempered.' He slid his arm further round her. 'Any chance for a nice country boy then? Very clean, highly recommended.'

Emma forced a laugh. 'Mmm, but by rather a lot of women, so I've heard.'

'Not lately, dear girl, not for at least a week.'

It was getting chilly and they walked fast, all except for Emma. She dawdled, prevaricating, wishing desperately that she hadn't agreed to let them use her room.

It was too late, there were already a dozen people waiting on the doorstep, and as she fumbled in her pocket for her keys a chorus of 'Why are we waiting?' began, accompanied by whistling and foot stamping. Emma's resentment increased.

The place looked different with so many people in it. It's just a party, she kept telling herself, swallowing the spleen, not the Rape of the Sabine Women, but over the next two hours more and more people appeared, friends, friends of friends, people she'd never seen before, the word passed from one to another.

George read her mind. 'Come on,' he said as he passed her on his way to get Jilly a drink, 'it's only a party.'

She gritted her teeth. 'Does it show?'

Ian had turned up with a tiny, wonderfully pretty Japanese girl and he was all over her.

'Yuk!' Bill stared in revolted fascination as they lolled in one of the armchairs. 'Why doesn't he just swallow her and be done with it?'

The party spread. There were people littered all over the house, on the stairs, in the hall; someone spilled red wine on the carpet then flung Emma's bath towel down on the spot to mop it up and the sofa filled up with an assortment of arms, legs and bodies, all mixed together in various stages of abandonment.

Emma negotiated the crowds into the hall, sipping from her glass of wine. The law student was sitting down on the stairs necking with a second-year Graphics girl, but of Alison, whose party it was supposed to be, there was no sign. She must be in her room with Barry. How convenient, thought Emma sourly as she wandered back to the party. It was coming up to midnight and they were smooching to the Walker Brothers' 'The Sun Ain't Gonna Shine Any More'. As she passed George and Jilly the sweet smell of marijuana hit her.

Alison returned just after one, towing Barry and looking smug. She put on the Stones' 'Route 66' and the loud, insistent beat galvanised them into their second wind, setting them dancing again. Someone organised a whipround and a couple of unattached boys were sent round to the corner shop for more booze while Ali stretched herself on the newly vacated sofa.

'Sit here, at my feet,' she commanded Barry, and Emma's choler rose again. The Empress and her Slave, how bloody apt. She was sitting alone on one of the floor cushions when they came in, with her knees drawn up to her chin and a glass of red wine in her hand. She could hear The Supremes' 'Baby love'.

She moved a rickety chair from beneath the sloping attic roof, burrowed behind it and found a pile of old wooden tennis racquets, one still in its press. Their strings were a tangle of gut, their frames bent and twisted by age, warped beyond repair. Remembering that first time, Emma paused and smiled. How beautiful he was, she recalled with a glow of remembered pleasure; how instantly she was smitten.

She made her way back to the pile of throwaways, growing higher as she worked ('Be ruthless,' George had instructed her. 'I'm not sentimental.') then gravitated towards the window again, searching the meadow until she found him at last, sitting on the bank of the stream that meandered along its edge, with a panting dog at either side, like bookends. As she watched he lay back, hands behind his head, long legs bent at the knee, and turned his face up to the sun. Oh, how I love you, she thought. But my God, when it came to it, the decision almost broke my heart.

'Ricky!' shouted Alison above the din and clambered over Barry's legs to get to the new arrivals, standing in the doorway clutching crash helmets in their hands. Emma recognised one of them vaguely, a Fine Art student who lived near Alison in Richmond. The other was unmistakably Ali's brother, Ricky.

He was tall, around six foot, with his sister's colouring, dark skin and eyes, rich golden hair, but thinner than Alison, painfully thin. He was round-shouldered too, stooped as if he expected a cuff or a blow at any moment. Despite that, despite the grim set of his mouth and the heavy frown mark between his brows, Emma thought he was the most beautiful boy she had ever seen. It was love, love at first sight, and she knew without any doubt at all from the moment she set eyes on him that she would love him for ever.

He didn't have his sister's ability to light up a room. After waving an airy hand at the drinks Alison went back to the sofa, then the other boy picked up a beer and wandered off too. It was Bill, on his own just then and at a loose end, who smiled a greeting and poured Ricky a glass of wine.

He wandered across to the window and stood staring out at the shadowy garden with his back to the thumping music, making no attempt to join in with what was going on, and no one took any notice of him. Alison was chatting up the boy he had arrived with and Barry was getting annoyed. Ian was still spread-eagled in one of the chairs, all over his Japanese girl, his hand up her skirt and his tongue in her mouth. George and Jilly were smooching to the Beatles' 'Ask Me Why'. Ricky Brown didn't see Emma, still sitting alone on her cushion drinking her wine, and she made no move. She just stared, wallowing in emotion.

By two o'clock fewer than a dozen people remained, but Alison wasn't ready to quit. She was enjoying herself, making Barry jealous. When someone shouted, 'Ali, coffee!' she looked around for her brother, unwilling to interrupt her game.

'Ricky? Be an angel and make some coffee . . .'

He moved reluctantly away from the window, in the direction of Alison's pointing finger and Emma watched him go. If he couldn't read, he wouldn't be able to find anything. She took her glass and followed him behind the black lacquered screen.

He was standing in front of the open shelf above the sink, his hand hovering uncertainly. He had very brown fingers; the bones stood out white beneath the dark skin and she wanted to stroke him.

There were three jars, all the same, labelled in flowing italic script: *Tea*, *Coffee*, *Sugar*. Ricky Brown didn't hear her coming and when she reached across in front of him she saw him jump, heard the sharp intake of breath as she took the coffee down, put the sugar next to it and smiled at him.

'This one's coffee and this one's . . .'

He stared at her, not eyeing her up like most of the boys she knew but staring as if he'd never seen anything like her before. She reached up and touched his face. She'd had an awful lot to drink.

'I think you're beautiful,' she said.

He smiled in return, a sudden blinding reminder of whose brother he was, and as her fingers left his cheek he caught her wrist and held on to it.

'S-s-s-s s . . .' He gazed in rapt concentration at her freckled face, cursing his handicap. Oh, he thought, oh, so are you, and he pressed her fingers hard against his mouth to still his wayward tongue. Emma wondered how she could have forgotten that he stammered. When he released her she smiled again, then picked up her glass and left him, returning to her cushion in the corner to shut her eyes and lean her head against the wall so she could listen to her pulse thudding in her ears without interruption. Something stupendous, something amazing seemed to be happening to her.

She heard him clatter cups, fill the kettle, then pour, stir. Someone had put on another record, the Beatles' 'Please Please Me' and she heard cups being distributed, Alison demanding more sugar. When someone sat down beside her she knew it was him.

He moved very close, touching her deliberately all the way down her side, but she didn't react until the internal quaking got too much to bear. Then she opened her eyes and fixed them on her glass, watching the wine slop over the rim in time with the shaking of her hand. She regarded it solemnly as if it belonged to someone else, then turned her head to see if he had noticed.

He was still staring at her, a deadly serious, intense examination, thinking how beautiful she was. As their eyes met he reached across and took her glass, putting it carefully on the carpet beside her, then he took both her hands in his. She watched, fascinated, as he wrapped his brown fingers around hers.

'Ricky!'

He jumped convulsively and so did Emma, so engrossed in what was happening to them they had forgotten the rest of the room existed. Alison had had enough and it was time for everyone to go.

Ian had already vanished downstairs to bed with his Japanese girl; as the others trailed out one by one, Ricky relinquished Emma's hands and knelt in front of her, running his knuckles slowly down her face.

'Will you come back?' She wanted to touch but she didn't, in case Alison was looking. He nodded.

'N-n-n-n ...'

'Next week?'

He flashed another of Alison's smiles, turning her to jelly, then rose and walked across to his sister, waiting by the door. Emma watched him go. Oh God, he was so beautiful. Oh God, leaning back on her cushion and closing her eyes the better to savour the sensation, she was in love.

The Beatles were still playing, crooning in flat, Liverpudlian accents, 'I'm in love with you, ooh-ooh-ooh...' Barry had disappeared, tired of being made a fool of, and Alison was draped all over the boy who'd come with her brother. Emma gravitated across the room in time to hear her explaining to Ricky that there was no room downstairs.

'The lads are busy.' She winked at Emma as she joined them. 'And so am I. You'll have to go home. Will you remember how to get there?' She turned to Emma. 'John had to direct him here – the poor darling can't read a map.'

The frown mark between Rick's eyes deepened and he flushed with anger and embarrassment.

'Strictly illegal of course.' Alison was oblivious. 'John's got no licence and Ricky's riding his motorbike on L-plates, but it's a crafty way of getting him mobile. I forged his signature on the application and he can ride on a provisional licence for ever as long as the bike's under 250ccs, so they don't know about his little problem.'

Emma hated her, a great surge of vitriolic loathing at the easy way she humiliated him, but Alison didn't notice.

'Go on kid, beat it,' she said, then patted him affectionately and strolled past him into the hall, towing her new conquest towards her room and her bed. Ricky hesitated, then picked up his helmet and followed.

There was one couple left, stretched out on the floor entwined in a passionate embrace and he had to climb over them to reach the front door. He looked back briefly before he disappeared into the night, then Emma heard the roar of his bike as he kicked it into life, the sound rising and falling, then fading into the distance.

She stood listening, alone but for the half-naked couple on the floor, as cold air swirled down the corridor from the open front door and unmistakable noises began to emanate from Alison's room, then looked down. It was Barry. His jeans were undone and the girl's skirt was rucked up round her waist, exposing a pair of brief knickers and laddered black stockings. Emma was suddenly, savagely, disgusted.

'Get *up*,' she said angrily through clenched teeth and watched, astonished, as her foot connected with Barry's half-naked buttocks. He yelped with pain and sat up indignantly. 'Go home, Barry.' She turned on her heel and walked back into her room, slamming the door hard behind her. She heard the front door shut, then the *thud*, *thud*, *thud* of Alison's bedhead hitting the wall.

It took Emma nearly four hours to tidy up; by the time she had emptied the last ashtray and tipped the last dregs of beer down the sink it was getting light. When she'd finished she picked up the wine glass Alison's brother had taken from her shaking hand and took it across the room to the sofa. Then she sat, running her fingertips up and down the stem, staring at nothing in particular, and tried to remember his beautiful face, his smile.

She couldn't conjure him up, the only thing she could recall was the sensation when she had first seen him, the emotion she had felt when he touched her. She closed her eyes and let it sweep over her again in a heavy, delicious wave. Love, love, oh ... *love*.

She kept the catch on the door the next day, sitting silently on the floor with her knees drawn up to her chin when Alison knocked. She could hear her outside with John, complaining, 'She must be there, where else would she have gone?' She took a long time to give up and go away.

Emma worked hard that week, even harder than usual and she easily avoided Alison, who was preoccupied with her new man. When Mabel asked how the party had gone, she said casually, belying the violent trembling inside, 'Oh, it was fine thanks, Auntie Mabel,' leaving her aunt with the impression that she hadn't had much of a time. Early days yet, thought Mabel comfortably, plenty of time for that sort of thing.

When Emma ran into Ian in the middle of the week, he was smug, guilty.

'Good party,' he said, watching her face for some sign of jealousy or resentment.

'Mmm. She's very pretty, your Japanese girl. Where'd you meet her?'

'What do you care?' He was insulted by her lack of reaction to his defection. He'd enjoyed Saturday night but by Sunday morning, suffering from a hangover and a nagging conscience, he'd begun to feel sordid and uneasy about using the girl just to get at Emma. And now Emma didn't care anyway.

'You're a bitch,' he said bitterly. 'You do know that, don't you?' and he walked away, leaving her standing in the corridor staring in bewilderment at his departing back.

By the end of the week the whole thing had begun to seem like a half-remembered dream, taking on something of the quality of those black-and-white films at the Wednesday Night Film Club.

Alison barged in on Friday night as Emma sat by the window working on a design. She was clutching a bottle of red wine and two glasses.

'I've come to say sorry.' She turned on her most disarming smile. 'I've been shitty all week. I meant to come and thank you for the party—' as if, thought Emma, it had been my idea '—and I didn't get round to it.'

They sat by the window until midnight. Alison drank most of the wine and Emma made toast and Bovril while they discussed Ian and his new bird.

'He's only doing it to make you jealous,' said Ali.

'I know.' Emma sipped at her wine. 'Trouble is it doesn't bother me at all. Talking of which—' she refilled Ali's glass '—where was Jay?'

'Sent his apologies, via George. Otherwise engaged apparently.' Alison stared morosely into her glass. 'Why is it I can pull anyone I like except him? Is it me or is he just contrary?'

Emma shrugged her shoulders. 'I don't know what makes people fancy other people. And you're luckier than most. Perhaps you should be content with the ninety-nine per cent of the male population that does fancy you and stop hankering after the one per cent that doesn't.'

'But I think that's why I fancy him,' Alison sighed, 'because I can't have him. They're all so *easy*.'

Emma laughed suddenly. 'I should be so lucky,' she said. Then, because the boy had been on her mind ever since the party, added, 'Is your elder brother as beautiful as you and Ricky?'

The minute the words left her mouth she wanted to take them back but Alison didn't notice, she was too wrapped up in her own thoughts.

'D'you think Rick's beautiful?' She giggled at the thought. 'It never occurred to me. I don't think he's ever had a girlfriend. It must be pretty difficult to get turned on by someone who can't even string two words together, mustn't it?' She didn't register Emma's silence. 'Pete's gorgeous. He and I got all the looks. I s'pose that's part of Ricky's problem, having to live up to us. Pete can dominate a room just by walking into it; I learned it from him.' She poured more wine and changed tack, losing interest in Ricky and his problems. 'I know I manipulate people. I don't mean to be a cow, I just seem to open my mouth and out it comes.' Tears of self-pity welled unexpectedly in her eyes. 'I wish I was like you, Em. You don't seem to need other people. You don't mind being on your own; I hate it.'

She leaned forward in her chair, suddenly intensely, un-characteristically serious. 'It frightens me to death, being alone. I'm scared as hell I might find out who I am.' Then, dropping the subject abruptly, 'I'm talking too much. It's the booze.' She shivered, then rose to carry her glass to the sink. 'Night Em,' she said, 'thanks for putting up with me,' and she made her way unsteadily across the room to disappear down the hall to bed.

*

She came back the following night with half a dozen friends, each carrying a bottle of wine, 'just to say thank you for the party', and she smiled brightly, showing Emma all her white teeth, silently pleading to be welcomed. Emma smiled reluctantly in return and opened the door wide, then resigned herself, found glasses and a bottle opener while they dispersed around the room and went to sit in the same place she had occupied before, on a big cushion against the wall. Watching them all she felt like a stranger, looking in through a lighted window at a tableau that had nothing to do with her.

Someone put on The Rolling Stones' 'I Just Want to Make Love to You' and she didn't hear the door. It was the sound of his name that brought her head up.

'Em, get Ricky a drink, would you?'

She left her place and slipped behind the lacquered screen without looking around the room at all. Her hand was shaking again and she had difficulty with the bottle, stared stupidly at the spreading pool of wine on the draining board. She knew he would come and find her, but still she wasn't prepared when he did.

She saw his brown fingers out of the corner of her eye and watched fascinated as they moved to stroke the inside of her wrist.

'Hello,' she said lamely.

She felt a tremendous surge of emotion when she turned to look at him, overwhelming. He held out his hand, the one he had just touched her with, palm down, fingers spread and she laughed because it was shaking nicely. Then she took hold of it and wrapped it round the bottle.

Between them they poured a glassful of wine, giggling at their inability to aim straight, then Rick picked it up and took a long swig at it. Emma topped it up carefully and without speaking they left the privacy of the screen for the cushions.

They sat as they had before, touching from hip to ankle, from shoulder to elbow, heads resting against the wall. The Searchers were on now, 'Needles and Pins', and the others were laughing at some joke Alison had just made. When Emma turned her head Rick was already staring at her. She wanted to stroke his face, but not in front of so many people. It doesn't matter, she thought, I can wait, you can wait, and she kept quite still, returning his stare, stroking without touching.

They sat without exchanging a word for two hours, until Alison looked at her watch and shouted at her brother, 'God, Ricky, have you seen the time? Get a move on or the Bastard'll have your guts.' She didn't register how close he was sitting to her accommodating friend. She was looking, not seeing.

Rick stretched his long legs, then rose, walked to the door, picked up his helmet and left. Come with me, he begged Emma silently, please.

'Cheers,' called Alison. 'Take care.' She returned to her conversation, didn't notice Emma leave her place against the wall.

Ricky knew she would follow him; he was waiting for her in the hall, his helmet on the floor beside him. She went to kiss his cheek but he turned his face until he was so close she was breathing his exhaled air and she could taste the wine, then he put his brown fingers on her cheeks and kissed her clumsily on the mouth.

When he let her go she lost her balance, disoriented by emotion. He steadied her and she buried her face against his shoulder while he stroked her hair. His jacket smelled of leather and engine oil and she could feel his heart beating, or her own, she wasn't sure which. Whichever it was, it felt wonderful.

They stood quite still until the door behind them opened, then Rick released her abruptly, retrieved his helmet and disappeared down the steps into the street.

Alison assumed she'd been to the bathroom. 'Night Em,' she said, patting her shoulder affectionately. 'Coming down the pub for lunch tomorrow?'

Emma slept well, deliciously well, and she was outgoing and boisterous on Sunday.

'What's got into you?' asked Bill, gazing with interest at her animated face.

'Nothing,' she lied. Her cheeks were flushed with anticipatory excitement.

She was as high as a kite all week, even flirted with Jay when she ran into him at college, accusing him of neglecting them all. 'No time for old friends now you're a star.'

He was becoming increasingly successful, so successful he was in trouble with his tutor for falling behind with his college work, and he'd bought himself a second-hand car out of his earnings. He laughed at the jibe, then said, suddenly serious, 'Do me a favour?'

'What?'

'I need some advice and you're the only one I know who won't spread it all over college.'

They went for a Chinese, down a little lane off Gerrard Street. Jay was preoccupied, didn't talk much until near the end of the meal and Emma didn't ask what was bothering him. She liked him better minus his usual overpowering arrogance.

'I'm making a lot of money,' he said at last.

'So what's the problem? I wish I was.' She smiled at him but he didn't smile back.

'I don't know what to do.'

He put his chopsticks down, then picked them up again and began tracing a pattern on the tablecloth. You have nice hands, Emma thought irrelevantly, like Ricky, lovely long fingers.

'You see, the thing is, I've been offered this commission. It's a lot of money and it could make my name, hundreds of pounds, but I've only got three days to make up my mind. It's six weeks' solid work, black-and-white illustrations.'

'So what's the problem? Just take it; it sounds too good to be true.'

'It is. If I take it I'll have to drop out of college. I'll never get my Diploma.'

'Oh.'

'And I don't know what to do. I want the Diploma; I've worked for it this year, but I'm not sure I can afford to turn down such an enormous opportunity. They might not give me another chance if I blow this one.'

'Can you do it?' asked Emma. 'I mean, if you take it can you do it well enough . . . ?'

'Of course I can.' She had made him angry. 'I'm good, Em. I'm damn good, better than anyone else in our year in college. If I stay I'll get a First.' His face clouded. 'I'll get a place at the Royal College. I'm brilliant.' He said it as if he was merely stating a fact. 'What I can't decide is whether I'm prepared to wait another three to four years to prove it.'

He saw her back to the Tube station and kissed her cheek.

'Thanks, Em,' he said. 'It's helped talking it through.' It was only as she turned to go that he caught her arm. 'Em, would you . . . ?'

She shook her head, knowing what the question was, and he shrugged. 'Let me know if you change your mind.' He watched her walk away. Christ, he thought, if you knew how I feel about you, you wouldn't do this to me.

Sitting on the Tube, watching the multicoloured tide of humanity sweeping on and off the train, Emma wondered why he had picked her to confide in.

As the week progressed, she had trouble keeping the lid on her excitement. She mooned about on Saturday afternoon, tidying her room, picking things up and putting them down again, rearranging the furniture, fiddling about. She wandered upstairs to soak in a hot bath and wash her hair, then afterwards, still pink and damp, sat in front of the mirror by her bed and examined her reflection. Her hair clung to her neck in red snakes, curling across her skin. She was too thin, the bones at her neck and beneath her breasts showed, her hips stuck out. She wondered what she would do if Ricky didn't want her, and watched with detached interest the blush that climbed up her neck to suffuse her face at the assumption she was making, that she was going to go to bed with him.

By eight o'clock she was dressed, in jeans and a T-shirt, no make-up, deliberately unprovocative and her hair in its usual plait. When he knocked at nine she was ready for him, and she was in his arms before the door closed. She startled him so much he dropped his helmet with a loud thud.

Neither of them spoke. Emma didn't feel the need and Ricky couldn't; the silence made them even.

She traced the contours of his face instead, running her fingers over his cheeks and down along his jaw. She touched his eyes and his mouth, buried her fingers in the hair at the nape of his neck where it curved against his skin, then closed her eyes and stood quite still while he explored her in return. This was how it should be, she told herself – special.

They sat down on the big cushions, holding hands, and Rick stared at the wall opposite while he struggled with his tongue.

'You're in m-m-my h . . .' He closed his eyes and leaned back against the wall, cursing his recalcitrant tongue. 'My h–*head*.' He expelled the word as if it might bite him on the way out.

'You're in my head too.'

There didn't seem to be anything else that needed saying and when they began to kiss things just progressed naturally.

They were inept, fumbling and incompetent. It hurt Emma, Ricky came almost immediately and it wasn't how either of them had imagined sex would be at all. It gave Emma no physical pleasure, but it didn't matter. Alison had said the first time was a let-down and anyway, the emotion, the love, made up for the lack of excitement. Emma was relieved that Ricky's penis wasn't like the white tripe sausage she had seen in the Tube station. She decided she rather liked it, could even, she thought, grow quite attached to it.

The closeness they felt with each other, the overwhelming strength of the bond between them, was undiminished by the failure of their lovemaking and it made Emma cry. He wiped the tears from her cheeks with long brown fingers, then held her until she slept. When she surfaced he was on the other side of the room, pulling on his jeans.

'Ricky?' It was the first time she had spoken his name aloud. She liked the sound of it, said it again. He looked up from buckling his belt, smiled dazzlingly, and came back to kneel beside her. 'I have to g-g . . . g-g-g—'

Her eyes filled with tears again. She found his difficulties almost unbearable.

'It's all right,' she said. 'You can go. You're in my head.'

He nodded vehemently. 'You're in my h-h-h—' He gave up, shrugged, then tapped his forehead, leaned across and kissed her mouth again. You're in my head, he told her silently.

'I love you,' said Emma, wanting him to know. He didn't reciprocate, just went back to his clothes, pulled on his T-shirt and his jacket, laced his boots. He hesitated at the door though, turning back to squat in front of her. She was propped up on one elbow, her plait hanging heavily down her bare arm; he bent down and rearranged it, then kissed her one last time, picked up his crash helmet and left.

She heard his bike starting up in the street, listened to the sound dying away, then picked herself up, went slowly to bed and slept.

On Sunday conscience reared its tiresome head; she found it difficult to look Auntie Mabel in the eye.

Mabel reassured Josie when she phoned. 'She doesn't come on strong like some of the girls,' she told her. 'You mustn't worry, Josie, you can trust her to be sensible.'

'But she's so young,' said Josie. 'She's bound to be more impressionable than most.' She sighed. 'I wish you'd persuade her to come home at the weekend. I haven't seen her all term, and she *promised*.' Her voice was heavy with unshed tears and Mabel frowned irritably at the telephone. Silly woman, she thought, you haven't the foggiest idea what it's like, being young.

Emma was sure they'd know. She thought everyone would be able to tell but the only one who guessed, when she ran into him the following Wednesday, was Jay.

'You look different.' He stared at her suspiciously. 'What have you been doing?'

'Nothing,' she protested too vehemently.

'Good. If I can't have you I don't fancy the idea of anyone else poking you.' He laughed at her offended expression. He'd just handed his letter in to the Bursar. 'I'm dropping out,' he told her. 'But you don't get rid of me that easily: I'll call you.' He didn't say any more, but she knew he knew.

She overheard Alison on Thursday, talking to Ricky on the phone. 'Where the hell were you last Saturday? I got back early from a party 'specially. I'd arranged for you to stay with the boys for the night, and you couldn't even be bothered to let me know . . .'

A long pause, then Alison again. 'For God's sake try and be a bit more coherent. I can't understand a bloody . . . What? What pub? What do you mean you went to the pub instead? For crying out loud, Ricky, can't you remember *anything*?' Another long silence, then Alison, angrily, 'Oh, bloody hell, just leave it. Look, I'll be here Saturday night. Eleven o'clock. Don't be late. And don't forget. If I'm not home just bang on Emma's door.' Then she slammed the receiver down.

He came at six. Emma was drying her hair, sitting on the floor in front of the gas fire in her dressing-gown and she'd left the lock on the catch for him; he dropped his things by the door and went to kneel beside her.

'I missed you,' she said.

He nodded. He was excited but it took him twenty minutes to tell her in fits and starts, and the frustration made him angry. He touched her all the time: face, neck, shoulders, and her hands, holding them up to his mouth to stop his tongue from misbehaving, pressing them against his cheek when he wasn't using them. He grew more and more distressed, gripping her until it hurt as he tried to communicate his news and she had to bite her lip because the pain brought tears to her eyes. He'd got a job.

Nothing brilliant, working on a building site.

'C-c-c-cash,' he managed finally, after a long struggle with the 'c' sound. 'Da ... D-D-D-Dad d-doesn't have t-t-t—' he took a run at it '—doesn't have to know how m-much.' But his triumph didn't last long. When he started again, the word he wanted to use was glued to the roof of his mouth. In his agony he stood up, pulling Emma with him, then forgot what he was going to say and instead took her face in his hands and said fiercely and quite clearly, 'I love you.'

Emma laughed at him. 'I know.'

He searched around the room, then dragged her across to sit on the bed, grabbed the pad and pencil that lay on the table beside it and, holding the pencil awkwardly in his left hand, began to draw an intricate filigree pattern, very beautiful. When he'd finished he drew another, with what looked like a pin across it, and Emma saw that it was a brooch. Then he drew a man, working at a bench, hunched up with concentration, peering at something small.

He stared at her intently, willing her to understand. 'M-Money,' he said. 'I w-w-w-want t-to t-t-t-tr ...' He started again. 'I want t-to t-t-t—'

Emma got it, suddenly. 'You want to train. To make ...' she pointed at the drawing, 'jewellery?'

He pushed her backwards on to the bed, grinning, and kissed her hard. Then he forgot the sketch-pad, dropping it on the floor so he could concentrate.

She was bruised from the first time, on her hips and the inside of her thighs. Had he done that? He was careful, trying not to hurt her, and slower. It was better this time, nice, gentle, even, for a moment, exciting, and afterwards they lay for ages still joined, their arms around each other.

'I w-want to be a ... s-*silversmith*.' He forced the word out before it had a chance to get stuck to his tongue. 'But I have to t-train. I've found a man who'll t-take me on, but I have to p-p-pay him.'

'I could help. I could get an evening job. That would raise some money.'

He stopped her mouth with his hand. 'I h-have to d-d-do it mys-s-s-s-self.' The 's' was an effort and he lapsed into silence. She didn't try and dissuade him.

They got up and dressed, then Emma made coffee and they sat on the sofa, close together. She talked a bit, about college, vague plans for the future, but mostly they were silent, and Ricky drew. His talent as an artist was in inverse proportion to his ability to understand the written word. He drew Emma over and over again, interspersed with hearts and arrows, like lovers carve on trees. His drawings were better than anything she'd ever done, better than anyone else she knew, except perhaps for Jay, but he'd never get to Art School unless he could learn to read.

She caught at his arm, enthused by the wild idea that she could teach him, love succeeding where all else had failed but he already knew what she was going to say and he shook his head at her.

'They've t-t-t-tried.' His stammer was increasing again. He rose to go, kissed her, and she pulled his head down so she could comfort him.

'It doesn't matter,' she told him. 'It doesn't matter at all.'

She heard them next door when they got back, clattering into Alison's room, loudly drunk and all talking at the same time. Ali sent a runner for her but she pleaded a headache and went to bed; she didn't want to see Rick with everyone else. She could hear the talk, occasional bursts of laughter as she lay staring at the ceiling, arms behind her head, wondering what had happened to Auntie Mabel's rules. Had they been just for Ma's benefit? Oh, how she had underestimated her aunt . . .

Ricky knocked on her door just after midnight. When she let him in he shut it carefully, then took her back to bed. He was distraught, angry, and afterwards he cried in her arms.

'Why do you do it?' she asked. 'Why do you let them humiliate you?'

'It g-gives me an excuse to s-see you,' he said, adding inconsequentially, 'That G-George is an idiot,' which was what

George, drunk and irritable with Jilly, had called Rick, when he couldn't tell him where the booze was.

When he left around three, Emma slept at last, surrounded by a warm glow of love. Just before she dropped off it occurred to her: she was no longer the last virgin left in the world. She was like everyone else now . . . she was normal.

He didn't come the next weekend. Emma, wound up with anticipation, couldn't cope with the disappointment his absence induced. It was a dull physical pain which nothing would shift and which got steadily worse. She couldn't concentrate at college and she was snappy and aggressive at home.

'What on earth's the matter with you?' complained Alison after Emma'd bitten her head off for the third time. 'You been disappointed in love or something?'

'Don't be stupid.' Emma stared at her with unconcealed dislike.

'All right, all right, I'm going.' Alison backed away towards the door. 'I can take a hint.'

It was halfway through the second week before she plucked up the courage to ask casually, 'What are you doing this weekend?'

'Dunno, why?'

'Just wondered.' Emma fiddled nervously with her plait. 'Are you staying in for your brother?'

'Ricky? No, Daddy's taken him away for a month. They've gone on some residential thing; you know, they counsel the parents as well as the kids.' She laughed. 'The Bastard'll love that. He's the one that needs the counselling. Shan't see Rick before the end of term.' She didn't notice Emma's face. 'Bit of a relief to be honest. It's all very well, but the poor lamb does tend to be a bit of a blot on the landscape. He just sits there and *watches* all the time. Some of the girls think he's sweet, but the boys all think he's a drip. What are you doing this weekend?'

'Nothing much,' said Emma and went back to her room, feeling sick.

*

The ache in her belly refused to go away. As the last few weeks of term dragged to a close she got worse rather than better. This is stupid she told herself. If you can manage for a week, you can manage for a month.

Jay rang and asked if he could see her. 'Nothing heavy, I just need to talk.'

'Okay,' she said. Anything was better than sitting in her room.

He came to pick her up in a second-hand Sunbeam Rapier, with a soft top and fins at the back. He looked very affluent, even more arrogant than usual, and took her to a restaurant somewhere in the suburbs where the clientele oozed money and she felt under-dressed in her patchwork skirt and muslin top. He was in perfect tune with their surroundings: expensive leather jacket, well-cut dark trousers. He looked like a well-heeled, if slightly uncoordinated, advertising executive.

'I'm doing well,' he told her. 'Over the past six weeks I've earned over five hundred quid and been commissioned for another seven hundred and fifty pounds worth, to be finished by Christmas.'

'D'you think you did the right thing?' asked Emma.

He nodded. 'I'm good. I'm never going to be out of work. What about you? How's college?'

'Okay, I s'pose.'

'Still keeping yourself to yourself, little Em?' He examined her closely. 'What's the matter? Last time I saw you, you looked like the cat that'd got the cream. Now you look like it's gone sour. Boyfriend chuck you?'

He caught her by surprise and she couldn't think of an answer. 'Come on,' he persisted. 'Tell me. You know I won't talk.'

She picked at the food on her plate. 'It's nothing really, just this . . .' she hesitated '. . . chap.'

'Chap, what chap?'

'Just someone I know, someone I've been . . .' another hesitation '. . . seeing.'

'You mean sleeping with.' He stared at her belligerently. 'Don't look at me like that, Emma, it's written all over your face. So you finally gave your all and the rotten swine walked out on you. Is that it?'

'No!' she said fiercely. 'He's just had to go away, that's all. For ages. And I miss him.' To her intense annoyance her eyes filled with tears.

'So who is the lucky bastard, anyone I know?'

'Ali's brother.'

'What, her elder brother?'

'No, her younger brother.'

'But I thought he was . . .' Jay hesitated, at a loss for once '. . . handicapped, you know, not all there.'

'Well, he's *not*.' Emma was suddenly furiously angry, not just with Jay, with everyone, and she shouted, 'He's not stupid at all!' She was aware that people were looking at them, but she didn't care. 'He's cleverer than me, or you. But nobody ever bothers to find out. None of you look beyond your stupid, narrow-minded noses.' She shoved her plate violently across the table and stood up. 'Now you can take me home, please.'

He followed her out to his car without a word, slid in beside her and started the engine. I don't think I can bear this, he thought, and switched it off.

'Look Em, I didn't know it was so serious. I didn't mean to hurt you.'

Emma stared resolutely ahead. 'It's okay,' she said, 'it doesn't matter.' A tear slithered down her cheek.

'Emma . . .'

'What?'

'If you ever need me, you know I'm always here, don't you?' How pathetic, he mocked himself, what a bloody stupid thing to say.

'Yes, I do.' She turned to face him. 'Do me a favour?'

'Anything.'

'Don't tell anyone about Ricky. Please.'

'I've already said I won't. You do me a favour in return. If you're ever in trouble, let me know.' Please, I *love* you.

He started the engine again, then caught her by surprise. 'Have you thought about the possibility of getting pregnant?' She stared at him blankly. 'I thought not. Be sensible, Emma. Whatever this boy's like he's hardly in a position to support himself from what I've heard, let alone you and a baby. You've got to get yourself on the Pill soon, before it's too late. It's important. You could ruin your life.' And mine. A baby would tie you irrevocably to him, leave me no hope at all. Oh *God*, how I hate this.

They didn't speak at all during the journey. As he drew into the kerb he asked to come in, but she said no, and when he leaned across to kiss her she offered her cheek, not her mouth.

'I'm sorry,' she said. He shrugged easily, betraying no hint of pain.

'I can wait,' he said. ''Night, little Em.'

She went to the Brook Advisory Centre the following Tuesday, and submitted to an embarrassing examination by a brusque lady doctor. She got her pills, along with a lecture about the addictive nature of promiscuity and, oddly, felt better. If she was going on the Pill, Ricky must be coming back.

College broke up on the 17th of December and Mabel closed down for the holidays as she did every year. She and Emma left last in the Morris, driving out to Cheshunt with all the presents and enough possessions to last the festive season.

Alison had been invited to phone, Emma hoping that if she saw Ali over Christmas, she might just see Ricky too. The ache in her stomach refused to go quite away, it kept her awake at night, but it was bearable now she knew where he was.

She was very good, kind and patient with her mother: told her frequently, and insincerely, how glad she was to be home; explained what she was getting up to at college, pattern cutting classes, making up *toiles*, fashion illustration; regaled her with tales of visits to the V & A to study historical costume, and to the

Central School for weaving classes. About her private life, her sex life as it was now, she told her absolutely nothing.

Josie was pleased and flattered that her only child should be so forthcoming. 'You're looking much too thin,' she accused Emma, and set about feeding her up with pies and puddings, and nourishing stews. Emma ate voraciously whatever was put in front of her, assuaging a hunger that had nothing to do with food, and ignored her guilty conscience, rumbling below the surface like a volcano, reminding her that it was not enough to make pious noises, and that she should feel more grateful for Josie's efforts. She longed to be in London, living out of tins, with a boy who could hardly string two words together, who couldn't, she thought wistfully, even write her a letter.

Christmas was as it had always been, just the three of them; New Year was dreary, and the first week of January was cold and miserable, matching Emma's mood. She spent much of her time in her poky bedroom, making up for all the work she had neglected towards the end of last term.

She had a phone call just after New Year.

'Can you meet me at Mabel's tomorrow?' Alison sounded frantic. 'I'll only be up for the day; the Bastard wants us all at home for the last week of the vac.'

'Are you bringing R—?' Emma bit the word off.

'Bringing what?'

'Er . . . records, are you bringing any new records?'

'No, why should I be?' Ali sounded puzzled. 'I must go. See you tomorrow . . . Oh and Rick says hello, or rather h-h-h-hello.' She laughed, high pitched, slightly hysterical, then the line went dead. Emma stood in the chilly hall listening to the dialling tone and hated her, missed Ricky painfully.

She travelled up on the train the next day, telling Josie she had equipment to buy before the beginning of term. It was seven weeks since she had seen Ricky and she should have got over it by now. Alison wouldn't pine for a boy for seven minutes, never mind seven weeks.

*

Ali was already there when Emma walked through the front door and she dragged her straight into her room. She had stamped her personality on it, white like her other room in Richmond: white bedspread, white walls, white curtains. The chairs were covered in unbleached calico stolen from college and there were big splashy prints on the walls, like the ones she had at home.

It was cold. Their breath steamed and they kept their coats on. Alison made coffee then went to sit cross-legged on the bed.

'I'm pregnant,' she announced without preamble. 'Well say *something*, even if it's only serves you right.'

'I thought you were on the Pill.'

'I am. I was.'

'So how—?'

'How d'you think? Because I'm a bad girl. I forgot to take it. I missed four last month.'

'Who is it?' Emma stared at her frivolous friend in despair. 'The father I mean.'

Alison shrugged. 'Dunno. There're three candidates – Barry, John or . . .' she took a long gulp at her coffee, avoiding Emma's eye 'Harry Passmore.'

'Passmore?' Emma shouted. 'Oh Ali! Oh, you bloody fool!' She rose from her chair and went to sit next to her on the bed. 'How could you?'

'Easy, you just open your legs and away you go . . .'

'Don't be facetious. You drag me all the way up here to tell me you're pregnant, possibly by a tutor with a wife and three children, and all you can do is make stupid jokes about it.'

Alison's face crumpled. 'I'm scared, Em,' she whispered. 'What am I going to do?'

They sat without speaking while Alison made a pretence of contemplating the options.

'Do you want to keep it?' asked Emma at last, frightened of the silence.

A vehement shake of the golden head. 'God, no. It'd spoil everything.'

Emma's education had come on apace by now. 'So there are two alternatives. You either have it and give it away, or you have an abortion.'

Ali took around ten seconds; she had already made the decision, even made the appointment; Emma was merely there to listen. 'An abortion.'

'Do you know how to go about it?'

'Yeah. You know Lizzie Dawson in Graphics? Remember she was away for a couple of weeks last term?'

'Mmm. Stomach trouble, she said.'

'It was a one-night stand, some pop star she met at a party. Her mum paid for the abortion. It cost around a hundred and fifty quid.'

Emma gasped. 'Where on earth will you lay your hands on that sort of money?'

Alison laughed, recovering now she'd got the worst bit out of the way. 'I've already got it.'

'Where from? Surely the Bastard hasn't . . .'

'Don't be stupid.' Ali pulled a derisive face. 'Ricky's lent it to me. He earned it over the holidays, working on a building site.'

Oh God, thought Emma, all that money, all that hard-earned money, and you've just handed it over to your bloody, bloody sister to pay for an abortion.

Ali had no idea what she'd done. 'I'll pay him back of course,' she continued blithely. 'I might try and persuade Harry Passmore it's his. He's the only one with any money.' She giggled nervously. 'I could always blackmail him.'

'You would too, wouldn't you?' Emma was aghast.

'Mmm,' said Alison, suddenly subdued. 'I might.' Her mind leaped on. 'Did I tell you I reckon Rick's got a bird somewhere? He went all pale and wan over the holidays and when I accused him of pining he turned bright red and walked out. He was really embarrassed.' She was so busy talking she didn't notice Emma's face. 'I need you to come with me. It's in Stanmore, the clinic. *Please* Em, I don't want to go on my own.'

'All right,' said Emma reluctantly. 'When?'

'Thursday.'

'That soon?' So it was all settled long before she arrived. She was merely there to give moral support, to act as a crutch for Alison to lean on.

'I'm already eight weeks gone. If I leave it much longer, it'll be too late.'

'All right,' said Emma again, 'but for God's sake don't let on to Auntie Mabel what's happening. If she ever gets wind of this she'll throw you out, and she'll send me home.'

'I'm not completely daft.'

'That's debatable.' Emma didn't even try to disguise her disapproval.

They arranged to meet at ten o'clock on the Thursday. When Alison said, 'Ricky's coming too,' Emma had to turn away to hide the wild elation that hit her. 'The appointment at the clinic is for twelve and if you're late you miss your slot so he's bringing me up on the back of his bike. We've told the Bastard we're going shopping.'

Going home on the Tube, Emma wondered how Alison could have been so stupid, until it occurred to her that there but for the grace of God and some timely advice from Jay, went she. She was briefly grateful, then rattled that she and Ricky had been too naïve to think of the obvious by themselves, that it had taken an outsider to point them in the right direction. And how much of his hard-earned savings, she wondered resentfully, would Ricky have left after paying for his sister's little accident?

She was at the flat by nine-thirty. She fed the meter with shillings and lit the fire, then sat down in the cold to wait, but she couldn't keep still; after a couple of minutes she got up and began to wander about, picking things up, putting them down, rearranging the bits and pieces on the mantelpiece, almost frantic with impatience.

She'd put some music on, loud throbbing stuff to drown the sound of the blood thumping in her ears, so she didn't hear the bike, or the door. The first she knew he was standing there when she turned round.

Her insides tumbled into a heap in the pit of her stomach, just like a roller-coaster ride she'd been on once, and she found herself momentarily unable to breathe. When he held out his arms she ran into his embrace, sliding her arms around him, inside his jacket as far as they would go.

By the time Alison walked in they were kissing, absorbed, oblivious to everything but each other. Standing in the doorway watching them she was assailed by a wave of vicious jealousy. It caught her unawares, roaring up unexpectedly from the depths of her diaphragm, straight out of her mouth.

'How sweet,' she said succinctly, just as the thumping music stopped, 'the Virgin and the Halfwit.'

They leaped apart, turning startled faces towards her. The words sounded loud in the sudden silence and Rick abruptly turned his back on his sister.

'Oh, Christ,' Alison backtracked. 'Ricky, I didn't mean it. I'm sorry.'

Emma put her hand up to Rick's face, reassuring him, then kissed him again. The bitch.

'Emma? Em, what on earth's going on?'

'Can't you tell? I thought you were so terribly clever.' The bitch. The nasty, cruel, vindictive *bitch*.

'Ricky?' As Alison moved into the room Emma turned away, wanting to scratch her face, pull her hair out.

'Are you and Em . . . ? I don't understand.' The contrition was already fading from her voice. 'How long have you been . . . I mean, how long's it been going on? How did you think you'd get away with it?'

Emma took Ricky's hand and moved very close, putting herself between him and his sister to protect him. 'We got away with it because no one noticed, because no one was looking, least of all you. You were too wrapped up in yourself to see what was right under your nose.'

'But why the secrecy?' asked Alison.

Rick opened his mouth and months of pent-up spleen spilled out uncontrollably. 'B-b-b-because of b-bloody sh-shits like y-you.'

Alison felt a prickle of fear; if she antagonised him beyond redemption he might demand his money back, or worse, tell the Bastard.

'But I think it's lovely, you two being together,' she wheedled. 'Really ... really *sweet*. I'm just hurt you didn't trust me.' She bathed them both in the glory of her smile.

Emma snorted bitterly but her resentment was blunted, as Ricky's was, as Alison meant it to be, by the full force of that irresistible smile, by the effortless power of her charm. Anyway, it was too late to go back now: the damage was done.

They travelled across London together, first on the District line, then changing at Embankment for the Bakerloo line and the long journey out to the suburbs. Alison sat opposite Rick and Emma, watching them. They didn't speak, and they didn't take their eyes from each other unless she spoke to them, but they touched all the time and she felt as if she was choking, suffocating with furious, unreasoning envy.

That journey was a turning point, Emma recalled as she crouched in the attic sifting through a knitting bag full of carefully preserved lengths of string. For the few brief times she and Rick had been together they had been confined to her room. They had never been anywhere, to a restaurant, or even to the pub for a drink; out in the open surrounded by other people they felt exposed and vulnerable, their fragile relationship threatened by the outside world, by people like Alison.

She heaved a pile of ancient tennis shoes from beneath a broken umbrella, caught the faint smell of sweaty feet and added them to the pile. And yet I enjoyed that journey, she thought, treasured it as a new beginning, despite its dreary purpose. If I had known what our foray into the big wide world would lead to, would I have done differently?

Alison was puzzled by their silence. She needed to talk, to hear the sound of her own voice and they seemed to communicate without words. She didn't recognise her little brother in the intense, silent young man sitting opposite her, or her friend in the distant young woman beside him.

They blinked in the daylight as they emerged from the last tunnel and passed through Neasden and Wembley. After Wembley Park the suburbs began in earnest, mile upon mile of red-brick villas with neat gardens and net curtains. Rick produced a tiny sketch-pad from his pocket and began to draw, while Emma stared out of the window at the drizzle which had just begun, linking her arm tightly with his.

'Ricky?' began Alison, desperate to hear someone speak even if it was only herself. He looked up. 'I'll pay you back.' She leaned forward in her seat, needing attention. 'I promise.' She widened her eyes at him, smiled, and he nodded, smiled back reluctantly. She felt overwhelming relief.

The train terminated at Stanmore and they left the station for the cold drizzle outside. As they turned off the main road Ricky and Emma separated, moving without a word to flank Alison, linking arms with her to give her moral support.

The street was full of large detached Victorian houses, with sash windows and fanlights over the front doors. Number 29 was no different from any of the others except that the front garden was given over entirely to shingle for parking and there was a discreet brass plate by the front door.

When Emma rang the bell a brisk middle-aged woman let them in and conducted them along a corridor to a big waiting room where five girls already sat. The girl nearest the door was with her boyfriend, crying quietly into a handkerchief while he patted her hand and looked uncomfortable. The other four were alone. They differed, thought Emma, staring at their pasty faces, only in the degree of their misery.

One by one they disappeared. The boyfriend wasn't allowed to go with his partner so he sat on, staring blankly out of the window at the dead winter garden and chewing his fingernails. When they called Alison's name she bounced up eagerly.

'Okay,' she said brightly, 'let's get it over and done with, shall we?' Her voice sounded very loud in that quiet room.

Rick and Emma sat and waited, until another girl was shown in. 'Llarsson,' she told the receptionist, 'I am Llarsson. Pliss, I am com-ink to the right place?'

The nurse who had let her in explained that she was late.

'Not late. Today iss Wednesday, pliss?' She was Scandinavian – Danish, Swedish? 'I am com-ink over exact-lee for the terminu-tion.'

The receptionist kept telling her they wouldn't do it. 'Don't you understand?' she repeated in that loud slow-motion voice the British reserve for stupid foreigners. 'It was yesterday. It's too late now.'

For fifteen minutes the girl pleaded, begged, cried, but the woman remained obdurate. 'No, you cannot be fitted in ... No, you cannot make another appointment; we're fully booked for the week ahead.'

She shuffled the papers on her desk. 'It's not my problem,' she said, spreading her hands wide at the tear-stained young woman. 'Why don't you go home and talk to your boyfriend again?'

'Pliss.' The girl blew her nose loudly, pleading through her sodden handkerchief. 'I haff not money for go-ink home ant com-ink back again. Iss not possible.'

It was too much for Ricky. He pulled Emma from her seat, dragged her outside into the cold street and walked her back to the main road, to a dingy café, where they sat drinking black sludgy coffee that left an after-taste of greasy chips in their mouths, and

Emma ate three stale doughnuts and a Penguin biscuit, because the waiting had made her hungry.

'Can you stay late tonight?' she asked.

'Yes,' he said vehemently and coherently and she leaned across to kiss him, tasting the oleaginous coffee on his lips. Then they dawdled reluctantly back to wait for Alison.

She was pale, groggy and unsteady on her legs. Her stomach hurt, she complained.

They took her back in a taxi to Earl's Court and saw her safely in, then left her with a cup of tea and walked the short distance down the hall to Emma's room. There they went to bed for the rest of the afternoon, falling asleep in each other's arms as dusk fell and the street lamps began to come on. Their lovemaking grew more accomplished each time.

Alison lay on her white bed with the curtains drawn, listening to the traffic outside and the sounds filtering through the wall, trying to imagine Emma and her little brother having sex together. She could feel the blood seeping between her legs, warm and sticky against her thighs. She clasped her arms over her aching stomach, curled herself into a tight ball and cried herself to sleep.

CHAPTER NINE

• • •

By the beginning of term Alison seemed to be recovered in both mind and body. She found a job as an usherette in a local cinema and began to pay Ricky back a little every week, but she didn't ask Harry Passmore for anything.

Emma saw Rick every Saturday now, Alison acting as his alibi. It was her turn, said Ali in a rare moment of guilt-induced generosity, to return previous favours. But he never stayed beyond the early hours and Emma longed to sleep with him properly, lie with him through the night and wake to find him beside her in the morning.

Jay rang early in February. 'I'm snowed under,' he said. 'Can you get a portfolio together to show someone? It'll take the load off my shoulders.'

The someone turned out to be *Honey* magazine. They liked Emma's work and the pay was good too, but she was conscious of Jay's barely concealed hostility towards her new-found happiness, and resolved not to see him again.

Rick began to spend two or three evenings a week in Earl's Court. It was a novelty to begin with: they went out, to the pub, to the cinema, to eat. After a while though, Emma noticed how reluctant Ricky was and their forays into the outside world petered out, until they were back to their original routine, staying in her room. Rick was more comfortable with that, and she told herself it didn't matter.

They worked or read or sat side by side on the big cushions

listening to music or went to bed. Some nights they didn't even make love. Their couplings were good now, more intense, more satisfying, but the physical side of their relationship was less important than the tender closeness they felt for each other, the mental rapport between them. Emma glowed with quiet happiness.

Most of her college friends knew by now that she had a boyfriend, although she kidded herself that Jay and Alison were the only ones who knew who he was. It was inevitable too that Mabel would begin to take an interest in the motorbike parked so frequently outside. But when she asked about it, Emma said casually, 'Oh, that's just Ali' brother's,' and, reassured, Mabel left it at that.

Emma and Alison started at the annexe, silk screen printing, and both of them turned out to have a talent for it. Between them (a small contribution from Alison and a larger one from Emma), they bought a bolt of cotton lawn and printed it with wild, vividly coloured abstracts. They sold it for a vast profit, to a shop in Pimlico which dealt in Casa Pupo rugs and expensive rattan furniture, and bought another bolt. They sold that to a shop off the King's Road where it was made into cheap circular skirts and long-tailed shirts, enabling Alison to pay off the last of her debt and leaving them with enough for a party. 'Please, Em?'

Emma's room was the biggest after all.

It was only a small party (Mabel was in residence that weekend), just the boys downstairs, of whom they saw so little these days, and a few others. Between them, Emma chopping and Alison cooking, they made a curry and a huge plate of popadums, stinking the room out with smoking oil while the boys trooped up from the basement bringing bottles and extra plates.

Jilly had brought a camera and insisted on taking a photograph of Ali, George, Bill and Emma, standing two by two on the stairs before the others arrived, and then George opened the first bottle of wine, starting the party early. They were going on to the

Marquee later; that way Mabel would have no cause for complaint.

She inspected them at around nine o'clock, on the spurious pretext that they might all be cold. Emma could see her from where she sat on her cushion, straining her neck to peer past Alison in an attempt to see what was going on.

Mabel felt a complete fool. Normally she would have left them to their own devices, but Emma was involved and she felt an obligation, to Josie if not to her niece. She didn't recognise the smell of marijuana mingling with the curry, and returned, reassured, to her sherry.

'If only she knew,' Alison giggled at Emma as she passed, towing the reinstated Barry.

Emma was on her own, because Ricky had refused to come. 'I w-won't b-be hu-hu-hu-miliated,' he had announced stubbornly and nothing Emma could say had budged him.

'Face it, Em,' said Alison irritatingly when Emma asked her advice. 'If you want to stay with Rick you'll have to come to terms with the fact that he's a hermit. And he's not going to change just because you want him to.' So she sat alone as she had at the first party, and watched.

Ian had split up with his current girlfriend, and came on his own. Towards the end of the evening he took his glass and went to sit down beside her.

'How are you?' he asked.

'Okay, you?'

'Fine. Someone said you'd got a boyfriend, is that true?'

'Yes.'

'So where is he?'

'Couldn't come.' Emma sipped at her wine without looking at him.

'Who is it, anyone I know?'

'No, you've never met him.' When she turned her head to look at him he was staring across the room at Alison.

'It's that half-witted brother of hers, isn't it?'

'Yes,' said Emma evenly. 'It's that half-witted brother of hers. Cheers.'

She raised her glass in salutation, poured the contents over his head, then rose and walked stiffly across the room. She picked up her keys on the way out, and her coat, and she slammed the door hard behind her.

She returned just before eleven to stand at the end of the gardens, leaning against the basement railings of the last house in the row to watch them all tumble down the steps and disappear round the corner. Then she walked slowly along the street to the front door, standing wide open to the night.

She was swept by a new sensation, a longing to be just like the others, to be a joiner, a participant instead of always standing on the sidelines observing. She wanted to go with them, to show her boyfriend off instead of hiding him as if she was ashamed of him.

Her room smelled of curry and stale cigarettes, and she tidied up in a rage, then poured herself a glass of wine. It was cheap stuff and it hit the back of her throat, making her cough, but she took it to bed anyway, with a book and a plate of broken popadums. She missed Ricky, wanted his company. She felt – another new sensation – lonely.

She had left the catch off and he came just after midnight, letting himself in without noise. She had gone to sleep with the book still in her hand and he kneeled by the bed, watching her sleeping face until she woke, suddenly aware of his presence, and stared at him with blurry hazel eyes.

'You should have been here,' she accused him indignantly. 'I missed you.'

'I m-missed you t-too.'

'Then why didn't you come?'

'B ... b-b-b-because ...' He thumped the side of the bed, aching with helpless frustration. 'You kn-n-n—'

'No, I *don't* know why.' Emma was only half awake, still irritable. 'I'm tired of hiding away pretending I'm nothing to do with you. I want to be like everyone else. I want to be . . .' She sat up in bed and took his face in her hands, trying to explain how she felt. 'I want to be with you at parties, instead of always on my own. Why is that so awful?'

He stared at her angrily, loving her and hating her at the same time. 'You d-d-d-don't underst— unders-s-*stand*.'

'Yes I *do*.' She was still upset about Ian, incapable of being tactful. 'I just want to be *normal*, that's all.' As soon as the words left her mouth she wanted to rescind them. He wasn't normal.

How can you understand? he thought. How can you know what it feels like to be trapped in here, to want to shout, to scream with frustration and not be able to explain? To love someone as much as I love you, and not be able to say? He began to kiss her fiercely, not as he usually did at all, and when they made love he was rough, wanting to hurt her. Afterwards he got up almost immediately and began to dress.

'Aren't you going to stay?' asked Emma, feeling used and unloved. Rick shook his head, still angry. 'Please . . .'

He paused by the door, his jacket and helmet in his hand, then hesitated and dropped them on the floor, neither staying nor going, until she padded naked across the room and put her arms round him.

'I love you,' she pleaded. He held her until she stopped crying, kissed the top of her head and put her back to bed. Then he left, unable to handle any more emotion. She didn't ask when she would see him again.

The following week started badly and got worse. Emma spent most of Wednesday feeling vaguely queasy and retired to bed at seven with a splitting headache. She struggled into college on Thursday, but she didn't even make it to lunchtime, staggering home on the Tube with her stomach heaving, her head banging and coloured spots distorting her vision.

Ricky arrived at five o'clock, in time to hold her head while she threw up her breakfast, and stayed until she fell into an exhausted sleep in the early hours of Friday morning. That was when Mabel caught them.

She had heard Emma being sick on her way back from the corner shop, but when she knocked Emma shouted, 'Go away. I'm fine.'

Worried about her niece and suspecting the demon drink, Mabel found it difficult to sleep, so she donned her dressing-gown and tiptoed down the stairs. I'll just peep in, she thought when she saw the line of light under the door, be on the safe side.

Emma was in bed, a bare arm half obscuring her face and her eyes shut. Kneeling on the floor by her pillow was a boy in a T-shirt and a pair of grubby jeans. Mabel almost fell over the crash helmet he'd left by the door.

When he heard her he turned. Mabel found herself staring into a pair of startled black eyes beneath a thick curtain of golden hair and thought, I know you. Just Alison's brother indeed.

'And what do you think you are doing, young man?' The boy flushed (shifty, thought Mabel) and gestured towards the invalid.

Rick was off-guard, worried about Emma who had been only spasmodically aware of his presence for the past three hours. He didn't need this large, grey-haired, disgruntled matron, wearing her disapproval like a voluminous coat. She's ill, he yelled silently, can't you see? 'Sh-sh-sh-sh—'

'Don't you shush me in my own house!' Mabel was incensed. 'How dare you! And come away from my niece. You shouldn't be in here at all.'

Rick stood abruptly, dropping the bowl he was holding and disturbing Emma, who groaned and heaved beneath the blankets.

'Where's your sister?' Mabel demanded, further infuriated, then added when no reply was forthcoming, 'What's the matter with you, why don't you answer?' She took a couple of steps towards him. 'Are you stupid or something?'

Ricky tried again. 'Shh—' he went. 'Sh-sh – Oh C-Christ! I – Sh-sh – Oh *shit*!' He moved towards Mabel, waving his arms and stuttering as tears of frustration collected in his eyes then, despairing of making himself understood, picked up his jacket and his helmet and walked past her out of the room. He slammed the front door behind him.

'Well!' Mabel stood listening to the motorbike's starting roar, then rounded on her niece. 'Perhaps you'd like to explain what's been going on, young lady. Did I get here in time, or am I too late?'

'Too late? Too late for what?' The noise banged inside Emma's head.

'To stop whatever has apparently been going on right under my gullible nose!'

'What are you talking about, Auntie Mabel?' Emma reached over the side of the bed for the bowl, feeling sick again.

'Drinking too much for a start, and then goodness knows what else besides. I suppose you thought you'd worry about the consequences later, did you? Well, it won't do, you know. That's how girls like you end up in trouble.'

'Auntie Mabel.' Emma retched, heaved, spat, wiped her mouth on a strip of loo roll and fell back exhausted. 'Whatever you're talking about, can you tell me tomorrow? My stomach hurts.' She peered vaguely round the room. 'Where'd Rick go?'

'I sent him packing.' Mabel's voice was rigid with disapproval. 'Which is what you should have done hours ago.' The door thudded shut behind her.

Alison woke Emma on Friday morning, barging in without knocking.

'What on earth's the matter with dear old Mabel?' She perched on the edge of Emma's bed and frowned at her in the gloom. 'And what's the matter with you? You look terrible.'

'I feel terrible. I've been sick. Ricky was here, at least I think he was. And Mabel came in and shouted a lot. Or perhaps I dreamed that bit, I can't remember.' She rubbed her hand over her eyes. 'Can you tell them at college I'm not well?'

Ali nodded. 'What is it?'

'Dunno.' Emma dragged herself up on the pillows, her head swimming unpleasantly. 'Some sort of bug. You ought to stay away from me.'

'Right.' Alison rose swiftly and made for the door. 'Let me know if there's anything you want.'

They left her alone for the rest of the day. Mabel didn't quite know how to handle the situation. If I do nothing, she decided in the end, the problem will go away by itself. I'm probably overreacting.

It was dark when Alison put her head round the door. 'Ricky's just phoned; he's coming over.' She peered into the gloom, reluctant to venture nearer in case she caught something nasty. 'Mind you, it took him ten minutes to tell me.'

'What time?'

'What time what?'

'What time's he coming?'

'Good grief, if I'd waited for that I'd have been there all night. Want anything?'

Emma shook her head and turned over to sleep.

She didn't hear his bike, but Mabel did and it made up her mind. She was waiting by the front door when Rick arrived, arms folded, lips pursed, ready to nip things in the bud before they got out of hand. This retarded, grubby biker who couldn't string two words together simply would not do.

'Where do you think you are going, young man?' she asked as he appeared on the top step. 'I thought I'd made it quite plain that you weren't welcome here. Have you come to apologise?'

Ricky froze.

'Well?'

Ricky scowled at her. Miserable old cow.

'Well?' Mabel's voice rose with her temper. I am *in loco parentis*, she berated herself. I've let poor Josie down and it's all the fault of this dim-witted boy.

'I w-w-w-want—'

'You want!' Mabel, fuelled by guilt, swelled with righteous indignation. 'And by what right do you want anything, you – you scruff-budget!' *Scruff-budget*? What on earth was the matter with her?

Ricky subsided into sulky silence as Alison emerged from her room to see what was going on, and Mabel proceeded to make things worse. 'I suppose you knew all about this?'

'Me? Knew all about what?'

Mabel waved angrily at Ricky, hovering white-faced and scowling on the doorstep, remembering what she had seen the previous night, justifying herself. 'Took her out, got her drunk, then . . .'

'I d-d-d-didn't!'

'You did!'

'I d-*didn't*!'

Good God, thought Mabel, we sound like a pair of five-year-olds. Did! Didn't! Did! Didn't! What is the matter with me?

'He wouldn't. What do you mean? Ricky hardly drinks at all.'

'Don't you soft-soap me, Miss. I know what I saw. She was stark naked in bed, being sick into a bowl when I saw her. It was disgusting. And I won't put up with it, do you hear?' Even as she was complaining she was thinking, I am overreacting; I am handling this all wrong; I should stop it.

Ricky glared from one to the other. I don't care, he raged silently, what either of you think, I have to see Emma, and he pushed unceremoniously past them and strode down the corridor.

He kneeled by the bed and stroked her hair. Her skin felt better, cooler, but although she tossed and murmured in her sleep, she didn't wake. *I love you*, he bellowed at her inside his head, then groaned and clenched his fists, lowering his head briefly to touch her hot shoulder before he left her. He ignored both Mabel and his sister as he passed them on the way out and Mabel was outraged.

'Who does your brother think he is? Barging in here as if he owns the place, then off again without so much as an excuse me?

Well, you can tell him from me, Miss, if I catch him near Emma again he'll be in serious trouble. I'll tell your father what's been going on and then you'll both be sorry.' She gave Alison an old-fashioned look, then added, 'I'm beginning to think you're a bad influence on young Emma,' and stumped upstairs to pour herself a large dry sherry and calm down.

So what to do now? Why couldn't Emma have picked someone more suitable, a boy with brains and a little basic breeding? Her condescension shamed her. Hark at you, Mabel lashed herself, a humble boarding-house landlady, full of the airs and graces you despise so much in Josie. And even after all those years of playing the invisible housekeeper you still haven't got out of the habit of assuming most of your fellow human beings to be your inferiors. But oh Henry, she sighed, missing her long-dead partner more than usual, that half-witted Brown boy really won't do at all.

She didn't tell Josie. Alison seemed to think nothing had happened between the two children (all weekend she had worked on Mabel, flashing the smile and the eyes until Mabel succumbed to her charm and relented through sheer exhaustion) in which case there was no harm done. And she'd sent the wretched boy packing now. He wouldn't dare show his face again.

When she tried to talk to Emma on the Sunday, her niece slammed the door in her face.

The virus affected Emma's mood. She began to brood on Rick and their relationship. Perhaps they were too intense? Perhaps they should be more casual? Except that she wasn't sure what she meant by more casual. Did it mean seeing more of other people or less of each other? She saw little enough of him already. Perhaps, she thought, as she sat by her window at night, watching the lighted windows behind which other people lived their lives, she ought to make it official, tell Mabel they were going out together and take Ricky home to meet Josie. But when she tried to imagine him stammering his way through an evening in Suburbia with Ma, she knew it wouldn't work.

*

He came after dark, leaving his motorbike round the corner and bringing a bunch of flowers. Emma ached with the pleasure of seeing him, touching him, and he sat in her armchair, his thin legs sprawling and his cheek resting on his hand, as she told him about her week. But he didn't stay long, unwilling to risk another confrontation with Mabel, and she was left unsatisfied, wanting more. Just before he went she broached the subject of the end of term. There was a dance at college on the last Saturday, with music and a bar.

'Everyone's going.'

He didn't answer, but she saw that stubborn look come into his face, watched his mouth tighten into that hard line and the frown deepen between his eyes, and she knew she'd spoiled the evening.

By Saturday afternoon she had made up her mind he wasn't coming, but she dressed carefully just in case, in a silky cream-coloured top and an ankle-length black skirt that fitted over her hips, then flared out to the hem. She left her hair loose and painted her eyes carefully with black liner.

'Go without me,' she yelled when they banged on her door, 'I'll catch you up.'

She could hear them along the street, laughing and jostling, fooling around, as she sat down on the stairs to wait for him.

'You look b-b-beautiful,' he said when he finally arrived. He was wearing black jeans, a T-shirt and his leather jacket.

'Don't be nervous,' she reassured him. 'It'll be all right, I promise.'

From the moment they got there she held on to him very tight. She calculated that their best chance of survival lay on the dance-floor – it was too noisy to hear oneself think, let alone hold a coherent conversation – and she even caught a couple of girls casting covetous looks in Rick's direction. But when the DJ decided to take a break it went quiet suddenly; people began to wander away, dispersing to the corners of the building. There were couples everywhere, twined round each other, sitting on floors, leaning against walls, up on the roof.

'Let's get a drink,' Emma suggested, limp with heat and nerves.

'Well hul-*lo* there!' Red-faced and sweating, Ian barred their way. He was drunk, clutching a paper cup from which beer slopped to trickle down his arm, and swaying unsteadily on his feet.

'I say, I say, if it isn't little Emma and the mystery boyfriend,' he sniggered, focusing with difficulty upon Ricky's face. 'Good lay, is she? You're a lucky sod, you know. She wouldn't let me in her knickers.' He waited for a reaction, then when none was forth-coming, quipped merrily, 'What's the matter, old son, not been in there either? I should give up if I were you. Know what Em's nickname is? The Virgin Queen.'

He laughed again, a high-pitched snort cut off abruptly as Ricky grabbed the front of his shirt and slammed him back against the wall.

'*Ooff*!' he grunted, and his beer went everywhere, down his shirt and trousers, all over the floor. But once he'd got him there Ricky didn't know what to do with him. He was too drunk to hit and Rick wasn't in a position to abuse him verbally. So he silently cursed him, then let him go and walked away.

'See you haven't managed to tame your pet gorilla yet then,' Ian jeered, flicking beer at Emma's face, and she flinched. All around them people stared.

Rick walked on, but he heard the jibe. When Emma caught him up, running, his face was red with anger and humiliation.

'We'll go home,' she said, trying belatedly to put things right, but he kept on as if he hadn't heard, towards the stairs and escape. He was already on his way, with or without her.

They travelled back to Earl's Court in silence, then sat on Emma's sofa and went round and round in circles for over an hour, neither really understanding the other's point of view, but both trying hard to be placatory. It was Ricky who abruptly terminated the conversation, exhausted and frustrated by the effort of making himself understood.

Their lovemaking when it began was more emotional than anything Emma had experienced before; we are part of each other, she told herself, overwrought by the events of the evening, locked together for all time.

They didn't hear Mabel's key in the door. It was only when she said, 'Emma? Emma, where are you?' and switched on the overhead light that they knew she was there.

'I'll deal with the little tykes! Leave it to me.'

'Oh G-God!' murmured Ricky and rolled off the sofa on to the floor.

If Josie hadn't phoned that night, worried as usual about her daughter's moral well-being, Mabel would have left well alone. As it was, when she saw Emma from her window, strolling home as bold as brass, hand in hand with that idiot boy, she rang his father without thinking about the consequences.

Brown was rich dark red with rage, the veins in his forehead and his neck standing out like knotted rope beneath the skin, huge fists bunched by his sides.

'Get up, you little tart!' he roared. 'Get your bloody clothes on!'

He flung Emma's dressing-gown at her head while Rick scrabbled frantically for his jeans. As he struggled to pull them on, his father began to hit him with the flat of his hand, leaving first white, then red marks on his back and head and shoulders, wherever he connected.

'Stupid little shit!' he roared. 'Frigging moron!'

Rick hopped about on one leg like a long brown stork, his penis still standing incongruously to attention, and yelped as each blow landed. He couldn't find his underwear and when he finally managed to get one leg into his jeans, Brown hit him again and he lost his balance. He found his pants halfway down the other leg and Emma was assailed by a wild, hysterical desire to laugh as he pulled them out, like a conjurer producing rabbits, then stuffed them in his pocket while he untangled himself, trapped half in, half out of his jeans.

Once she'd struggled into her robe, she joined in, flailing wildly at Brown's enormous bulk and screaming 'Leave him alone!' as she pummelled at him with her fists. He swatted her off easily with one hand.

It wasn't what Mabel had had in mind at all. 'Oh Lord!' she exclaimed, horrified at the frightening success of her telephone call in breaking up the two children. The boy might be a simpleton but he didn't deserve this. 'Oh Lord! That's enough! Stop it! Do you hear?'

Rick managed to get his T-shirt over his head and stand but he had to keep one arm up to fend off the blows while he struggled with his zip. Brown raged at him as he fumbled. 'Half-wit! Bloody imbecile! Moron! Is that the best you can do, you little runt, spending your time screwing some teenage tart when you should be learning to read?' He rounded on Emma. 'As for you, amuses you, does it, silly little cow, going to bed with a worthless, gutless, illiterate idiot who can't even answer his father back? I knew you were stupid, but I didn't think you were that dumb!' When he stopped the room went so silent that Emma could hear her own breathing, and Ricky's. Then Rick hit him.

He put all his strength behind the blow and he broke the Bastard's jaw, Emma heard it crack. Brown fell backwards against the wall and Rick followed him, fist clenched for a second blow. He raised his arm, slowly, deliberately taking aim, but he couldn't do it, not in cold blood. Instead he squatted down in front of his prostrate father and pulled him up by his collar, almost over-balancing with the effort, until he was staring him straight in the eye.

'That,' he said, quite distinctly without any trace of a stutter, 'is the very last time.' Then he picked up his jacket and his helmet and walked out, past Mabel, struck dumb with horror in the doorway, past his sister, just back and standing in the front hall with her mouth open, down the steps and into the street.

Mabel was horrified. This is my fault, she acknowledged guiltily; this appalling violence is being perpetrated in my house because I couldn't leave well alone. But how could I have known the man would behave like that?

Emma pulled her dressing-gown tight, then went back to the sofa, and slumped. Alison stepped gingerly over her father's outstretched legs and sat down beside her.

'What's happening?' she hissed.

Emma barely glanced at her. 'They caught us,' she said flatly.

'What, you mean ... *doing* it? Christ. So why is Daddy lying over there looking like a felled ox?'

'Rick hit him.'

'Christ,' said Alison again, and lapsed into silence.

They heard him getting up behind them and Alison made the mistake of turning to look.

The left side of Brown's face was swelling rapidly and his mouth was distorted. At the sight of his daughter his colour rose again, and she made hurriedly for the door, trying to get away from him. As she passed he grabbed her hair and hung on, twisting until she squealed with pain. Mabel had disappeared.

'Get your things. We're leaving.' His speech was muffled by the bruise that was already closing his eye.

'No!' Alison writhed under his grip. 'That's not fair, it's not my fault.'

'Course it's your bloody fault. You were supposed to be looking after him, weren't you? Where were you while he was screwing that stupid bitch?'

'God, Daddy, this is 1966, not the Dark Ages. Everybody does it. It's *normal* for Crissakes.'

'Not in my book it's not. Now get your stuff. We're going home.'

'*Bugger off!*' screamed Alison.

Mabel had called the police. When they arrived father and

daughter were still hurling abuse at each other and they had to be separated by force. They woke half the street as they spilled down the steps, and heads appeared at lighted windows to see what was going on. Bill and George, home from the dance, wandered up from the basement to watch the dubious entertainment while Alison enlisted the two young constables in her defence.

'He can't do this, can he? He can't make me. I'm nearly twenty-one, you know.'

The constables agreed, seduced by the smile. Between them they prised the protagonists apart and Brown was manhandled into his car. 'Or we can make it the station, sir, if you prefer?' One of them suggested pleasantly. Brown was practically unrecognisable, almost apoplectic with rage.

Emma was still sitting hunched on the sofa in front of the fire when Ali and Mabel got back. She had found a bottle of wine and she was drinking steadily, gazing sightlessly into the fire and trying to block out the words reverberating in her head, *tart*, *screw*, *half-wit*, *bitch*, as if she and Ricky were a couple of mindless animals on heat. She was getting more drunk than she had ever been in her life.

Lord, thought Emma, stumbling over a pile of bottles in the uncertain light of the attic, all that wine – I should have passed out by rights. Maybe it would have been preferable. I wished I had the next day; I wished, I seem to recall, that I was dead. She added the empty bottles – gin, whisky, vodka – to the discard pile. What a little fool I was, she mused, so melodramatic, so self-pitying. And what a revelation was Auntie Mabel. Why, oh why didn't I appreciate her at the time? She was so calm, made no fuss, just quietly shut the door and left us to it. Dear Mabel. And yet it was months before I forgave her.

'What's so awful,' Emma demanded when Alison returned, rubbing her sore head, to flop down beside her, 'about going to bed with someone you love?'

'Don't ask me.' Alison made a face at her. 'How the hell would I know?'

Emma was staring into the fire, wondering through the alcohol how grown-ups could turn loving someone into such sordid filth, and why the tiled fire surround should be undulating so alarmingly. 'I can't live without him,' she moaned, maudlin with wine and misery, 'it'll kill me.'

'I'm seeing Harry Passmore again.'

'Tut, tut. Who's a naughty girl then?' Emma, drunkenly sarcastic, wagged a disapproving finger at her friend and overbalanced, spilling her wine on the carpet. Alison propped her up again.

'Right now,' she accused, irritated, 'you're not exactly in a position to criticise, are you? Come on, sunshine, time for bed.'

She tucked Emma between the sheets, found her a bowl just in case, and left her to it.

She came back the following morning; she'd rung home on the kitchen line, she said, so she wouldn't get her father, and she'd spoken to the housekeeper.

'She was in a dreadful state. Ricky woke her in the dead of night, falling down the stairs, and when she went to investigate she found him sitting on the bottom step with his face all bruised and a big bag open on his knee, picking up piles of clothes and pound notes and stuffing them in the bag. When she asked him what he was doing he just said "leaving". Mind you . . .' Ali was dubious. 'You know how incoherent he is. He could have meant anything.'

Emma was quite sure that leaving was exactly what he'd done. He would come and get her; they would run away together. And she was never going to drink again.

''S all very well, this true-love lark,' Ali sniffed, 'but it hasn't done either of you much good, has it?'

Afterwards Emma remembered little of the words Alison used, upstairs in Mabel's sitting-room. All she retained was an abiding memory of overpowering charm, of the sweetness that was Alison's unique talent for persuasion. And Auntie Mabel was no more immune to her wiles than anyone else.

They went back to college on the Monday secure in the knowledge that the status quo would be maintained. From Ricky there had been no word, no sign at all.

The last week of term. Every night Emma sat in her room waiting for Ricky, and every night she was disappointed. The dull, aching sensation in the pit of her stomach began as her hangover receded, and worsened as the vacation approached, until on the day they broke up she had a telephone call. She knew it was Ricky when she went to pick up the receiver, even before the operator said, 'I have a call for you.'

He was in a phone box. He sounded quite clear to begin with, but his stammer got worse.

'I h-have to s-see you.'

'Where?'

'Your p-place.'

'When?'

'S-s-s-s-s . . .'

'Saturday?'

Silence.

'Sunday?'

'Yeah.'

'Sunday . . . But I'm supposed to be going home with Auntie Mabel on Saturday.'

'G-good. T-tell her you've g-g-g-got t-to . . .'

'All right, I'll think of something.'

What a romantic conversation.

She told Mabel she had some work to finish for a commission. She even showed her what had still to be done, because as it happened it was perfectly true. She was working on a set of sketches for a shop in Carnaby Street. They weren't paying much but they were displaying the drawings, blown up to life size, in the window and she was hoping more work would come from it. Mabel was sceptical.

'How do I know I can trust you?' she asked, still playing the heavy-handed guardian.

Emma opened her eyes wide, as she'd seen Alison do so often, and said demurely, 'Because I've learned my lesson, Auntie Mabel, I promise.'

He didn't risk leaving the bike outside but Emma was waiting for him, sitting on the top step in the sunshine with her chin in her hands. She didn't move when she saw him come striding round the corner, although she wanted to run down the street and throw herself into his arms; she just sat there watching his approach and thinking how beautiful he was, how much she loved him.

He paused on the pavement, then climbed the stairs almost reluctantly, hesitating at the top before he sat down, beside her but just far enough away that if she wanted any physical contact she would have to make a positive move towards him.

His eyes never left her face. He had big, black rings under them, because he hadn't slept, and he looked even thinner than usual. There was a barrier between them, invisible, untouchable, but both of them felt it. Emma needed him to talk, to tell her that everything was going to be all right, but too many words had already been said. *Screw*, *bitch*, *moron*; they played like a refrain in the background, never quite clearly audible but insidious, so they both hummed the tune subconsciously without knowing they were doing it.

'Tell me it will be all right,' she said without looking at him.

'I c-can't.'

'Please, Ricky. I *love* you.'

'I c-c-can't.' I would, if I only could. And I love you too, more than I can ever tell you. He put his hand in his pocket and fished out a small parcel. It was wrapped in tissue paper, twisted at one end; he handed it to her without a word.

'Do I open it?' She tore the paper off eagerly, her spirits soaring. It was going to be all right.

It was the brooch he'd drawn for her all those months ago. It was gorgeous, ill-finished, but lovely nevertheless, and he had added a heart, pierced by a tiny silver arrow, with an initial at each end, R and E. The R was back to front.

She began to cry and he moved closer at last, holding her, crying with her. Afterwards Emma had no idea how long they sat, but in the end he pushed her away from him and, cupping her tear-stained face in his hands, he kissed her.

It was not a beginning kiss, a prelude to lovemaking, it was a parting kiss, a goodbye, and they both knew it. It went on, Emma thought, for ever, and was over in an instant.

When it ended Rick stood up and left her. She didn't try to stop him, just watched as he walked down the street and round the corner, the tears running down her cheeks unchecked. Then she sat on for ages in the sun, leaning against the railings, pretending he was coming back, even though she had heard the bike roar and fade into the general traffic hum. As she rose to go inside, she heard the sound of Spencer Davis drifting from an open window, 'Keep on runnin' . . . Keep on hidin' . . .'.

Ha, she thought bitterly, ha bloody ha.

CHAPTER TEN

• • •

Ian moved out shortly after the beginning of the summer term; he'd found his own place, he said, and he was sick of living in a permanent shambles with a couple of slobs. George was perfectly happy to admit that he was a less than ideal flatmate, but Bill, who in his college work was almost obsessively tidy, took umbrage.

'Bloody nerve,' he complained. 'It wasn't me that left a half-empty can of baked beans in the bathroom for a fortnight, with the spoon in.'

Emma, outwardly fine, went down with Alison to help the boys clear out his room.

The place was a shambles. They set Bill, whose room was comparatively civilised, to cleaning the bathroom, arming him with a large container of Vim and copious instructions on how to use it, while George, protesting, hoovered carpets and the girls started on the kitchen.

They threw out all the blue bread, the half-finished can of pineapple chunks coated in thick green mould, the lamb chop that had been in the fridge since George's mum left it for him when he moved in. They unblocked the sink and swept up the remains of a packet of salted peanuts that had burst all over the floor one night and been left to decompose over the ensuing months.

It took them all of one day and half of the next to get the place civilised enough to show potential tenants and the boys took them out to dinner to show their appreciation. Bill couldn't get over the luxury of having a clean, tidy kitchen.

'Absolute bliss,' he kept saying. 'I don't know why I didn't do it myself.'

George told him to shut up. 'You're in danger of becoming a domestic bore.'

They went for a Chinese, just the four of them, and it was almost like old times, no boyfriends, no girlfriends, no worrying about flirting with the wrong person, or trying to impress. The only one missing was Jay. If Emma's pain wouldn't go away, it was her problem, not theirs and she kept it to herself.

'I, er ... I got ...' George paused, waiting for a gap in the conversation. 'I got engaged during the hols.'

'What?'

'Engaged. Jilly and I got engaged during the hols.'

'Blimey!' Alison was aghast. 'Are you sure you know what you're doing?'

'Not really,' George excused himself, feeling foolish. 'I was drunk at the time.' It wasn't strictly true. He and Jilly had been a serious item for months now and everyone knew it. They spent most of their free time in the Common Room sharing one of the sagging leatherette armchairs and canoodling. Now that he had tamed her, Jilly suited George. She would be an asset, he was sure, in his chosen career. Anyway, he was crazy about her. He looked around at his friends.

I am the only one of we five, he congratulated himself, who has managed to achieve a steady relationship. Look at them all: Ali, messing about with a married man; poor Emma's disaster; Jay, hankering after Emma and bedding any girl that'll have him to compensate. And as for Bill ...

Bill had gone completely quiet on the girlfriend front. 'Resting,' he had said evasively when asked, and George remembered something Alison had said.

'I think he's getting rather ambivalent about women, if you must know, or perhaps he always has been and we just didn't notice.' I mean, *really*, thought George, Bill, a queer?

Bill wasn't about to tell any of them about his seduction by a man he had met at a party two months previously; he was finding it hard enough already, coming to terms with the fact that he was a fag.

No one asked Emma about her love-life. Everyone was disappointed in love, it had happened to them all at one time or another, but you got over it and Em seemed to be healing up nicely. There was none of the tearfulness, the sudden mood swings that tended to send girls scurrying from the room with a handkerchief clutched to their eyes because someone had mentioned the wrong name, no outward signs of pining. Alison made a mental note, though, that she must organise another boy to take Em's mind off Ricky. First love was supposed to be the most difficult to get over, specially if you were as naïve as poor Em. She hadn't asked what had happened at their final meeting, didn't want to know, but she did know that Ricky was gone, presumably for good.

They wandered home replete with food, wine and companionship, to part at the steps. Emma closed her door carefully behind her and crossed the room to the armchair by the fire. She fumbled in her big bag for the filigree silver brooch then, holding it tightly in her clenched fist, she curled up in a ball and began to cry. When she felt better she put the brooch back in her bag and went to bed.

CHAPTER ELEVEN

• • •

The loneliness that had hit her for the first time so recently refused to go away. She began to avoid being home alone, stayed on at college working late, went out for coffee, or to the pub afterwards, even began to go to parties.

With a perception rare for her, Alison began to wonder whether all the frenetic socialising was doing Emma any good. She seemed so restless, so on edge all the time and it wasn't as if she went to any of the parties with anyone – apart from Bill, who didn't count – or left with anyone for that matter.

On impulse Ali prised Jay's number from George and rang him. He sounded surprised to hear from her, suspicious.

'Look,' she protested irritably, 'I'm not chasing you, I'm ringing about Em.'

'What about Em?'

'She's on her own.'

'So?'

Alison couldn't think of the best way to put it. 'Look, I know this'll sound silly, but she's taking it too well.'

'Taking what too well? You're talking in riddles.'

'Ricky. He's gone, done a runner.'

There was silence for a moment then Jay said, 'You mean he's chucked her?'

'No, well, yes I suppose so, in a way. It's more complicated than that.'

'You're certainly making it sound complicated.' Jay's tone was acid. 'What do you expect me to do about it?'

Alison hesitated again. 'I … um, I thought you might, er, perhaps you could take her out or something, you know – take her mind off things.'

There was another silence, longer this time. 'Ah,' Jay came back at last. 'I get the picture. I play the sucker's part.'

'I suppose so, if you like.'

'I don't.' He sounded surly, almost angry. 'I'll think about it,' he said, and put the phone down.

It was a week before he got in touch. 'I have a job for you,' he told Emma. 'If you're interested we could meet for lunch.'

'No.' She was struggling to catch up with all the work she had neglected over the past few months. 'I can't manage lunch, I'm working flat out and the lunch-hour's my only chance to get on a sewing machine.'

'Okay.' He kept his voice casual, friendly. 'Dinner then.'

Emma hesitated, then saw in her mind her empty room, her empty evening. 'All right,' she agreed reluctantly. 'I suppose so.'

'Good. I'll pick you up at seven then. Bye.'

He had a different car, a Jensen, sleek, dark rust-red, and he was wearing an expensive-looking woollen coat. Em had been expecting a Chinese, not proper dinner, and she made him wait while she changed out of her jeans behind her lacquered screen. She emerged wearing a short black dress she'd finished making that afternoon, with a gold link belt fastened round her hips in an attempt to look sophisticated, but she left her hair plaited, hanging heavily down her back as usual.

'Shame,' said Jay, tugging at it. 'I like it loose.' When she looked disconcerted he changed the subject.

He took her to a discreet restaurant in Knightsbridge, all soft lights and obsequious waiters, and talked business, deadlines, the sort of work she would need in her portfolio to impress.

'I'll take anything you can send my way.' Emma was grateful to him for taking so much trouble. 'I really appreciate it.'

'Why, are you short of money?'

'No.' Emma attacked her chicken ravenously. 'I just need something to do, that's all.'

'Why? I thought you said you were up to your neck at college?'

'I am, but that's only during the day.' She stared at him defensively, then when he stared back began to feel uncomfortable and lowered her head to her food again. 'I have plenty of free time in the evenings.'

'Oh?' He was all innocent curiosity. 'I thought you were seeing Alison's brother.'

'Not any more.' To Emma's profound embarrassment she began to cry. 'Oh blast,' she said.

Jay handed her a handkerchief, large, clean, white. 'I didn't know,' he lied, restraining himself from flinging his arms around her.

'No reason why you should.' She blew her nose loudly. 'Sorry. I don't know why I did that.'

''S okay. D'you want to tell me about it?'

'Nothing to tell.' She blew her nose again, then shrugged. 'He's gone away, that's all, and I miss him.' She'd had this conversation before with Jay, she realised. 'Only difference is, this time it's for good.' She hadn't said that before, even to herself. She found the words profoundly depressing and her eyes filled with tears again.

Jay didn't comment. He just topped up her wine, ordered coffee, and began to talk about work again. Emma felt a surge of gratitude.

He took her home early and kissed her on the cheek. He didn't ask to come in and he didn't ask to see her again. It was one of the hardest things he had ever done in his life. To her surprise Emma was slightly disappointed, but it wasn't important; after all, he wasn't going to turn into Ricky overnight.

Over the next few days she got some examples of her work together and took a couple of hours out of college to see the advertising agency in Soho Square. Jay had already put in a good word for her and she came away elated. They liked her work, gave her two commissions to complete by the end of June and promised her more if the client was pleased with the result. The money was terrific.

There was no word from Ricky, no calls. Mabel didn't tell Emma that he had been to the house. She had sent him away, forcing herself to be practical. Her niece was too young to know her own mind and the boy was unsuitable.

Rick hung around outside college one Thursday, but a few minutes before Emma came down the steps, Ian emerged.

'She's already gone,' he said dismissively, and smiled to himself as he watched the tall thin boy turn and disappear into the rush-hour crowds.

They broke up the next day for the summer vacation.

Josie was irritating. She wanted to participate; her little girl was slipping away from her, so she hung around, taking an interest, peering over Emma's shoulder while she worked, fiddling with her equipment.

'What's this, darling?'

'A Rapidograph.'

'What a funny name. And what does it do?'

'It's for drawing. It's got a needle running through the middle so the ink—'

'Dear me, how complicated . . . What lumpy paper.'

'It's for watercolours, it's extra absorbent—'

'How fascinating, dear.'

She brought cups of coffee and put them down in all sorts of inappropriate places.

'Not there, Ma, or there. No! Ma, I'm *working* on there.'

With the holiday stretching endlessly ahead, Emma decided she wouldn't be able to stand it; over the next few days she finished the last of her college work and her commissions, then found herself a job in a local pub. It wasn't much, but it was better than nothing and it got her out of the house.

Josie disapproved – apart from any other considerations it was illegal (Emma was still under-age until August), but Emma wasn't interested in her opinion. How like her father, that feckless, charming wastrel, Arthur Versey, Emma was turning out to be, thought Josie. The same rangy build, the same pale, freckled skin and thick wavy red hair, the same capacity for shutting her out, excluding her. She was in danger of losing her, and she didn't know what to do about it.

CHAPTER TWELVE

• • •

The pub suited Emma. A great deal of good-natured banter went on across the bar, but as long as she stayed on her own side of the invisible line she drew and the punters stayed on theirs, she was perfectly safe. She was learning how to wield the power she had always unknowingly possessed, to attract and manipulate the opposite sex.

It was that summer, pondered Emma, catching her breath at the stench of camphor as she opened a big metal trunk full of old clothes, it was that summer that Bill and I began our respective slides into degradation. She dragged the trunk to one side, found a picnic hamper with a broken handle containing three school caps, a straw panama and a beret, then straightened up and looked around for a chair. Time for a rest.

Sifting through a pile of mouldering beer mats, she recalled the cruel games she had played with her customers. She toughened herself up that summer, grew a protective shell. And she discovered that conscience is only a hard taskmaster if you allow it to be.

She stopped taking the Pill soon after she got home, flushing the two months' supply she still had down the sink, and she began to drink on a fairly regular basis.

Josie complained that she never saw her daughter: as she got home from work, Emma was going out for the evening shift; when the pub offered her a Sunday lunchtime session she took it with alacrity. If Emma had stopped to analyse it, she might have realised how unhappy she was, but she never stood still long enough to think about her state of mind.

Josie worried about her, blaming the college for her daughter's surly attitude. 'I shouldn't have let her live away from home so young,' she confided to Mabel as they sat drinking dry sherry in the back garden one Saturday. 'That place isn't doing her any good; she's getting hard. I want her to come home.'

Mabel busied herself pouring another sherry, and avoided her sister's eye.

'Yes?' said Emma sulkily through her throbbing head. 'What?'

'I want to talk to you. And you'd do well to listen, my girl.' Another hangover, guessed Mabel, noting Emma's red-rimmed eyes, her sullen expression; you're pushing your luck, young lady.

Emma heaved herself up in bed, frowning at the effect the brief movement had on her ability to focus. How thin you look, thought Mabel, and how unhappy.

'Your mother wants you to come home.'

'What do you mean? I am home, aren't I?'

'Don't be ridiculous. She wants you home permanently.'

Emma began to pay attention. 'No! I won't. She can't make me!'

Mabel sighed, exasperated. 'I know that. I'm not here to persuade you, I'm here to make sure that when you turn her down you don't hurt her feelings too much. Perhaps if you could manage to wake up occasionally without a hangover you might care to give it some thought.'

Emma rubbed her heavy eyes and tried to pull herself together. 'So I went over the top last night,' she said belligerently. 'So what?'

Mabel snorted. 'Every night, you mean. It's time you grew up, young lady. You're not the first to be disappointed in love, and you won't be the last.' Why does one always talk in clichés under such circumstances? she wondered. 'Now pull yourself together and start acting like an adult. I don't mind how you do it, but you let your mother down gently, understand?'

'Yes, Auntie Mabel.'

'Thank you.'

'Is that it, Auntie Mabel?'

'Yes, dear,' said Mabel briskly and left her to it.

Disappointed in love. What a ludicrously inadequate phrase. Emma lay back and thought about it. Was that all it amounted to? After all, Alison didn't get so overwrought about love. Ali never got hurt.

Emma rang her.

'Hi!' Alison sounded pleased. 'You okay?'

'Mmm. Have you heard from him?'

'Who?'

'Ricky. Who do you think?' Emma found it difficult to keep the irritation out of her voice.

'Oh. No, not a word. But he came to the house, didn't Mabel tell you?' She had been unable to leave her room when she heard her brother's stuttering voice. She was entertaining, and naked at the time.

'Which house, your house?'

'No, not my house, silly, I haven't been home this vac, not after . . . He was here, Earl's Court. Mabel sent him away, told him you didn't want to see him again. Didn't she mention it?' Crafty old witch, of course she didn't.

Emma tasted bile in the back of her throat. How *dare* Mabel interfere, how *dare* she try to run her life for her? She swallowed the lump.

'So what do I do now?'

'Christ, I don't know.' Alison sounded embarrassed. 'If it was me I'd sleep with any man who'd have me, just to show the stupid sod. You've had these Victorian morals drummed into you for so long it's stunted your emotional development.'

'That's rich coming from you. So what do you suggest I do, waltz up to the first bloke I see and ask if he'll please take me to bed so I can see if it'll cheer me up?'

Alison was offended. 'I'm only trying to help,' she protested. 'This has very little to do with you, you know. Oh, I know you think you're playing Juliet to Ricky's Romeo, star-crossed lovers and all that, but you don't have any idea how much Rick hates Daddy.' She changed the handset from one hand to the other. 'Far more than he loves you.'

The silence that followed was broken only by the faint crackling of the line. 'Thanks,' said Emma at last, and put the phone down.

She started the supper before Josie got back from work, called in sick to the pub then found some chicken pieces in the fridge and made a watery stew, peeled the potatoes and some carrots, laid the table and poured a large glass of sherry ready for when her mother got home.

Josie was touched, pathetically grateful for her daughter's thoughtfulness, if less impressed by her culinary skills, and Emma watched her surreptitiously as she ate, picking her moment.

'I haven't been here enough this year. I miss your cooking, Ma, and my own bed.' Then, without giving Josie a chance to agree with her, 'It's a shame. I'm getting so much freelance work now, I really need to be in London, otherwise I think I would've been tempted to come home to live.'

Watching her mother's expression change from hope to disappointment she felt nothing, except satisfaction that she'd won. We're growing apart, she thought, and there's nothing we can do to stop it.

Three weeks later she went back to London, her troublesome conscience relegated to a dusty cupboard at the back of her mind, and the carapace hardening nicely.

CHAPTER THIRTEEN

● ● ●

Second year of the degree course, new techniques to learn, new classes with new tutors, more self-confidence. One step further away from the bottom rung of the ladder, one year older. Emma began to build upon what she'd learned about the art of flirtation.

She went to a party in Swiss Cottage, tried marijuana for the first time and embarrassed herself by not inhaling the heavy aromatic smoke because she didn't know she was supposed to. She sat next to a pretty, dark-haired boy, an architectural student, drinking wine and discussing the inadequacies of the student grant. After a while his hands began to wander and she arrested their passage, but he was quite good-natured about it, settled for just kissing without complaint. It was a pleasant enough sensation, purely physical, and Emma enjoyed it. She had imbibed enough alcohol not to care that he was a stranger. This, she told herself, is a new start. From now on, I cut out the pain and stick to the pleasure.

The pretty boy saw her home, kissed her goodnight on the step and begged to come in. She said no, but she gave him her telephone number willingly enough and went to bed feeling better than she had for ages.

He called her later that week. 'Hi,' he said cheerfully, 'this is Ben.'

'Who?' she asked.

She arranged to meet him at Gloucester Road Tube station and they went to a nearby pub for a drink. Ben had trouble keeping his hands to himself again, and Emma had to smack his wrist a couple of times. He walked her home to her front door, then kissed her wetly, pushing up against her in the corner of the porch. 'Oh, Emma,' he whispered in breathless tones in her ear, 'can I come in? I won't stop long, I promise.'

What the hell, thought Emma, why not? 'But you can only stay for a little while.'

Almost before she had removed her coat he was wrestling her to the bed, pushing her backwards until they fell in a tangled sprawl of arms and legs and then he got stuck into the serious seduction routine.

Emma let it go on too long, trying to analyse whether there was any enjoyment to be had from the experience, and by the time she had decided she ought to cool the whole thing Ben was well into his stride and she had trouble stopping him. In the end she had to clout him across the side of the head and push.

'Get off, you great elephant!' she complained, and he rolled on to the floor with a loud thud, then lay on his back and groaned. She could see the outline of his penis, standing erect inside his trousers.

'I say, Emma, I'm terribly sorry. I thought you were enjoying yourself,' he protested ingenuously and she had trouble keeping a straight face.

'Do you always carry on like that?' she asked, adjusting her dishevelled clothing.

He sighed lustily. 'No, not usually, but you're so delicious I can't keep my hands off you. I fancy you like anything.'

Emma laughed at him. 'Well if you'd just give me a chance I might find out whether I fancy you or not.'

He reached across tentatively and touched her hair, escaping in wisps from its plait with all the strenuous wrestling. 'I really do think you're gorgeous,' he said. 'I'm sorry I rushed you.' Then he started again, slower this time.

It's going to be all right, thought Emma, I'm enjoying myself. She felt a surge of pleasure. He was a good kisser. But when his hand began to wander again she slapped it, hard.

'Time to go,' she said firmly and he went like a lamb, kissed her chastely on the cheek, asked her to a party the next Saturday night then waved cheerfully and decamped into the night like a docile puppy.

After he had gone Emma sat on the edge of her bed in her underwear and analysed the evening. On the whole, she decided, it had been all right; it had made her feel normal. Tonight, she determined, was the beginning of her rehabilitation. She was getting better at last.

She saw Ben again the following weekend. A week later she renewed her prescription for the Pill, and three days after that she went to bed with him.

He was energetic, moderately skilful and extremely, almost pathetically, grateful. He saw her home the following morning and kissed her tenderly on the doorstep, then whispered, 'I love you, Emma,' as he left. She couldn't have been more shocked if he had slapped her face.

She shut the door, snapping the catch carefully behind her, then crossed the room to light the fire. It was November now, and the nights were getting cold. Then she sat for two hours staring at the hissing blue flames, clutching Ricky's brooch and fighting the unwelcome waves of loneliness that threatened to overwhelm her newly formed defences.

Anything's all right as long as you want to do it, she told herself. That's Alison's *raison d'être*. Do what you like as long as it feels good, and it *did* feel good. So what the hell is the matter with you? Why can't you just take it for what it was and leave it at that?

She blew her nose hard, then stood up, straightened her shoulders and made her way upstairs to the bathroom to get ready for bed. 'I'll do it again,' she said out loud, defying nobody in particular. 'And I'll enjoy it too.'

She did. She went to bed with Ben twice more, and then she ditched him, going with him to a party in Notting Hill and leaving halfway through the evening to go home alone.

She didn't even try to analyse why she had treated him so badly. Too much close scrutiny might have breached her shaky defences. She just threw herself into her college work and tried not to think about anything at all. The following week she went to a party in Blackheath, picked up a boy who lived just round the corner and went home with him.

It was easier than the first time, and she was careful not to let slip her address, or her phone number. As she lay soaking him out of her system in the bath the next morning, she realised she hadn't even asked his name.

After that, it became easier each time.

She never spent a night in a strange bed, or allowed her partners to spend the night in hers. She bathed frequently, almost obsessively, and she began to dream, the same dream night after night. She was walking on a wide headland when the ground gave way beneath her feet and she tumbled down a deep, narrow shaft into a tiny black cavern filled with stifling sand, its roof so low she couldn't even stand. She screamed and shouted for help but she was hundreds of feet down, buried alive, and there was no one to hear, no one to rescue her. The only way out was inch by inch, her back wedged against one side of the crumbling shaft, her legs braced against the other, shuffling upwards an inch at a time. Again and again she made it almost to the top, to the sunlight and fresh air, only to slither inexorably down again to the bottom, to the black depths of despair; she woke each time sobbing hopelessly, drowning in loneliness and longing for the feel of Ricky's arms around her.

She developed a dislike of enclosed spaces, lifts especially, and the Tube. If she had been able to forgive Mabel for interfering she might have gone to her for help, but Mabel had sent Ricky away, and it was easier to blame than to understand. She hardly saw Alison or the boys; they were conducting their own affairs, with varying degrees of success.

*

At the beginning of December Jay phoned. 'I've got a commission for you; shop in the King's Road wants some drawings like the ones you did for Carnaby Street. Can you meet me for lunch?'

Emma left college early and they went to a Greek place on Frith Street, all checked tablecloths and tinkling ethnic music playing in the background. 'How are you?' asked Jay.

'Fine.' Emma was bright and brisk.

'You don't look fine.' As usual Jay's scrutiny made her feel uncomfortable. 'What've you been up to?'

'Nothing.' That didn't seem to be enough of an answer so she elaborated. 'Absolutely nothing. I've just done some growing up.'

'What is that supposed to mean?'

'Exactly what I say.' He frowned at her and it made her defensive. 'I've just stopped behaving like a precious little virgin, that's all.'

She shocked him, she could tell, and the power she felt in catching him off balance caused an unexpected surge of pleasure.

'If you mean you've decided to spread yourself around like dear Alison you're a damn fool, Emma Versey.' Jay stabbed an angry finger at her and she was taken aback by his vehemence.

'I thought we were here to discuss business,' she said frostily. 'I wasn't aware that my private life was any concern of yours.'

'Then why tell me about it?' It cost him a visible effort to get his temper under control and Emma was disconcerted when he finally sat back in his chair and smiled coolly at her. 'You're right,' he said. 'It's none of my business.' Then he changed the subject.

They discussed the commission briefly, and then Jay, rarely for him, began to talk about himself. 'I'm diversifying, buying in work from young, unknown artists then selling it on. Nothing modern, I'm specialising in traditional work. There's a steady market for it, and I'm building up a loyal clientele, not connoisseurs, just people who want something they understand to hang on their walls.'

'And what about your own work?'

'I've got more than I can handle, I'm turning offers away

nowadays.' He shrugged indifferently. 'I can make more this way. Are you busy tonight?' Emma shook her head. 'Good. I've something to show you; I'll pick you up outside college at five o'clock. And make sure you're on time, I don't want to have to cruise around.'

He took her back to college, then left her with a brisk 'Bye', not even a peck on the cheek. For the second time Emma was vaguely disappointed, wanted more; more of what she couldn't have said.

He was waiting when she reached the pavement at ten past five, engine running, ready to go.

'You're late,' he greeted her impatiently and Emma was reminded of the early days, when she had found him so intimidating; she quailed.

'Don't shout at me,' she pleaded. 'I was busy.'

'Huh!' He turned briefly to look at her and she caught a startling glimpse of vitriolic anger before he cloaked it. Just because I was ten minutes late, she thought defensively, stupid man.

As they drove down Oxford Street and round Hyde Park Corner she closed her eyes and leaned back wearily into the expensive leather upholstery. What was it about Jay? Why did she find keeping him at arm's length so exhausting? Why did it seem so terribly important that she shouldn't give him any hold over her?

She'd fallen asleep, Emma remembered, resting her aching back on the rickety chair in the attic, but then she was almost always tired at that time. She'd woken with a start just as they stopped by Brompton Cemetery, snarled up in the traffic.

She moved back to the attic window, her eyes quartering the meadow for the three familiar figures, but they were gone out of her range of vision. Odd, how things turned out in the end.

They crossed the river at Putney Bridge, then turned off the road that ran alongside the river, into a courtyard surrounded by tall tenements built of red brick.

'This is it,' said Jay.

'This is what?'

'This is what we're here to see. Come on, I'll show you.'

The flat was on the third floor. There were three bedrooms, a kitchen and a long, narrow sitting-room with big windows looking out north-east across the Thames, just opposite the starting point for the Oxford and Cambridge boat race. It was a wonderful outlook, but the place was dingy, brown and beige, with hideously patterned carpets everywhere, except for the kitchen, painted purple and jade green.

'What do you think?'

Emma was nonplussed, bereft of encouraging platitudes. 'The view's great,' she said at last and he roared with laughter.

'A model of tact and discretion. I'm proud of you. All right, so it's awful, but it won't be by the time I've finished with it.' He paused, then added, in a voice Emma hardly recognised, 'And it's mine, all *mine*!'

He picked her up suddenly, without any warning, and swung her high in the air, round and round until she was dizzy. Then he put her down and kissed her.

It was quite different from Ricky's kiss, from What's-his-name's, from anyone she'd tasted before. It triggered a physical reaction in Emma that she had never felt before and it frightened her. When he released her she was profoundly disconcerted, embarrassed at how eagerly she had responded.

Jay was exultant, not the slightest bit abashed. He grinned at her.

'I've been wanting to do that for a long time,' he said, 'and now that you're no longer a – what did you call it? – a precious little virgin . . . What's the matter?'

'I . . . er, um . . .' Emma waffled. 'Well, I wasn't expecting . . .' She stared at her feet, and he watched her, amused by her discomfort.

'You thought I'd be good old uncle Jay for ever did you, ready to listen to your sob stories and stroke your hand sympathetically without expecting anything in return?' He ran a long finger down her face. 'A little naïve, don't you think?'

She'd never seen him like this before, so *predatory*. She backed away from him and made for the window, even more intimidated than usual.

'Yes,' she acknowledged reluctantly, 'I suppose it was.'

'I'm not Ian. I'm not going to give up and go away.' He crossed the room to stand behind her, resting his hands on her shoulders. 'It's time you considered the possibility.'

'Don't rush me,' Emma blustered.

Dear God, he thought, *rush* you? 'You'll have that engraved on your tombstone,' he said. He turned her round to face him and she wriggled uncomfortably, resenting the easy way he manipulated her and thinking vaguely that she probably ought to slap his face, but wanting instead to be kissed again.

'You're very sure of yourself, aren't you?'

'Not very, but I bluff well.' Jay released her and moved away. You enjoyed kissing me, he crowed silently, you loved it, and that's the only thing that matters.

He made no further attempts to touch her, just talked about his plans for the place as if nothing had happened, until Emma found herself doing the same, forced against her will to behave normally.

'You need a painting party,' she suggested, talking too much in an effort to regain some sort of equilibrium. 'Get plenty of people along and ply them with copious amounts of booze while they're decorating. You know what our lot are like, they'll do it for nothing if you provide enough liquid refreshment.'

'All right.'

Emma, talking just for the sake of talking, was caught off balance by his easy acquiescence.

'If you'll find the decorators I'll get the booze and the painting materials. But not too many, I don't want the place overrun with strangers.'

They arranged it for the following Sunday, then Jay ran her home in a silence which made Emma acutely uncomfortable and appeared to bother him not one bit. He didn't kiss her again either, and she found herself wishing that he would. If only so she could push him away, slap him down to size.

She rounded up seven people: herself; Ali; Bill; George and his Jilly; Ian's successor in the basement, a third-year student from the LSE called Adrian; and Joe, a friend of Bill's on the fashion course a year ahead of them. It was the first time that term they had all been together. Bill was spending more and more of his time in Joe's company and Joe was as bent as a nine-bob note. He was quite open about it, called everyone 'ducky' including most of the tutors, and performed a convincing drag act at college dances. The frocks he designed were over the top, flamboyant, frilly, and determinedly feminine. Emma wondered in passing whether Alison's theory about Bill was right. At the last minute Adrian roped in Dave, another LSE student.

Dave was impossibly handsome: his blond hair was smooth and shiny and he had big, baby-blue eyes. 'Corr...' whispered Alison as they piled down the front steps into the street, and she made eyes at him all the way to Putney.

Adrian was nice. They had known him less than a fortnight but already they were comfortable with him. He was funny, friendly and rather good-looking in a slightly effete upper-class sort of way, with wavy mouse-coloured hair, pale, almost colourless eyes and elegantly defined eyebrows. His father was something big in the City.

Emma was wearing her airforce greatcoat. As they trooped over Putney Bridge Adrian edged close to her and linked arms.

'You look better in a man's coat than any girl I've ever seen,' he told her.

Emma grinned at him, said, 'Thank you, kind sir,' and flashed hazel eyes. She was getting good at the come-on.

They leaped up the stairs two at a time, laughing and shouting;

Jay heard them while they were still on the first floor. By the time they got to the third there was a row of beer bottles laid across the landing, tops off, fizzing, and they followed the trail through the hall into the kitchen, where Jay was waiting for them, leaning against the sink.

Emma wondered why no one else seemed to notice the wary, almost hunted look he gave his guests as they spread out around the room, and wondered why, since he clearly didn't like them being there, he had agreed to the idea in the first place. She felt a surge of loneliness, standing there surrounded by her friends; what was the matter with her?

Jay had laid out all the equipment, pots, brushes, rollers, trays, and he waved an expansive hand. 'Take your pick.'

All the paint was white. 'Ah,' said Alison, 'a man after my own heart.' She opened her eyes wide at him, flirting, but Jay didn't notice; he was watching Emma fighting Adrian over a paint roller. She was strangely wound up, and she was flirting too, showing Jay that he had no claim on her.

They split into pairs: George and Jilly in the big bedroom, Bill and Joe in the kitchen, Alison and the handsome Dave in the second bedroom. That left Jay, Emma and Adrian to paint the third bedroom and the sitting-room. Jay glanced at Adrian, then at Emma.

'I'll take the bedroom,' he said. 'You two can do the sitting-room.' Emma was stupidly, ridiculously disappointed, and felt another stab of loneliness.

Jay had rigged up a sound system: Stones, Tamla Motown, Everly Brothers, loud stuff with a beat, and they downed more beer as they worked. Jay kept his door firmly shut, and Emma, struggling with the black cloud of depression that was threatening to engulf her, wished he would come out of his self-imposed isolation and join in with everyone else.

By lunchtime they had just about finished the first coat and Bill and Adrian went out for a Chinese takeaway. By the time they got back, laden with leaky containers of chop suey, brown paper bags containing crispy noodles and chunks of battered chicken, and plastic cups full of glutinous orange sauce, they were ravenous. They sat cross-legged on the floor amongst the half-empty paint pots, devouring the food like wolves, attacking each others' dishes with plastic forks and throwing prawn crackers at each other, all except for Jay, who leaned against a dry wall and watched. Then Emma and Adrian went out for wine while the others started on the second coat.

'How come you get out of painting twice?' she asked as they took the stairs two at a time.

'Because,' Adrian grinned suggestively, 'I am a deeply reliable person. People look at this honest face and think, now there's a man I can trust to get a Chinese takeaway. There's a man who's responsible enough to come back bearing unopened bottles of wine. Lesser souls would drink it on the way home.'

He did, insisting that only a complete jerk would take it back without testing it. 'Anyway, these screw-top bottles are so cheap they need to breathe for hours before they're fit for human consumption. I'm performing a noble act of self-sacrifice, sampling the filthy stuff.' He swigged deep, then grimaced dramatically. 'God, I hope they're well pissed before they start on this. I would be doing a service to mankind if I was to pour it down the nearest drain.' He hovered over a convenient grille in the gutter and perused the murky depths beneath his feet. 'On the other hand, that would be unfair to the rats.'

By the time they got back to the flat and the thumping music, he was a third of the way down the bottle and fairly drunk. The others joined in with a will, except for Jay, who had consumed, so far as Emma could tell, no more than a pint of beer since they arrived. He drank no wine at all. Whenever she looked at him he was staring at her.

By mid-evening they were nearly finished, so they decamped to the nearest pub, all looking like refugees from a WI jumble sale except for Jay, who had managed to stay virtually paint-free and looked his usual elegant, if somewhat gangling self.

He paid for sandwiches, bought more beer, and it occurred to Emma that the exercise had probably cost him as much as hiring a professional decorator. He didn't seem to mind; once he was on neutral territory he cheered up, smiling indulgently at them like a kindly uncle as they got sillier and sillier. He was the only sober one amongst them.

He saw them on to the bus then turned and walked away by himself, back to the flats to pick up his car. Fuddled by drink, Emma watched his diminishing back, illogically annoyed that he hadn't offered to take her home, irritated that he was clearly so relieved by their departure, and curious about his private life. It occurred to her that she knew nothing about him at all, and never had. Oh, Rick, she thought, as she swung on to the bus, where are you? And why do I feel so lost tonight?

George and Jilly sat opposite her holding hands; Dave and Alison whispered and sniggered in the seat behind her. Joe and Bill were strap-hanging, trying to be discreet. When Adrian began to nuzzle her ear she let him. She was vaguely aware that she would regret all the booze tomorrow but just then it didn't seem to matter. The pain that had been gnawing at her all day was dulled by his warm breath against her neck, eased to manageable proportions, and she was grateful.

They meandered back to the house, shushing each other loudly then exploding into hysterical giggles for no reason at all. Dave and Alison disappeared but Emma staggered down to the basement with the rest of them, reluctant to be on her own, and Bill made coffee.

George and Jilly went to bed almost immediately, then Joe stood up, ostensibly to go home; there was a show of loud goodbyes on the step, a slammed door, then shuffling and whispering.

'Night,' called Bill from the hall, then closed his bedroom door firmly.

The necking was starting to get serious now. Emma put up a half-hearted show of resistance, but Adrian was insistent and she was in need of comfort. He was more than willing to supply it.

Afterwards, as she lay next to him in the dark, she realised she had made a mistake. Adrian fell asleep almost immediately and she felt more, not less lonely than she had before. She got up and dressed, tiptoed up from the basement to her own room, then put on her dressing-gown and made her way upstairs to have a bath.

She wallowed in the hot water for nearly an hour, until her fingers went crinkly, listening to the Ascot hissing and popping above her and a voice in her head saying over and over, 'I'm lonely, I'm lonely, I'm lonely.' Tonight, she couldn't even conjure up Ricky's face, but she missed him more than ever.

Adrian came upstairs the next afternoon. He looked as embarrassed as Emma felt, fiddled with his collar and stared at the ground.

'Look,' he began, 'I feel really bad about yesterday. Must've been pissed.'

Emma felt sorry for him. ''S okay,' she said. 'We were both pissed. Anyway, it was nice.'

He brightened. 'Oh, good. Does that mean we can do it again?'

Feeling better, she laughed at him. 'Maybe, but not now, I'm in the middle of a bowl of cornflakes.'

Adrian waggled his eyebrows. 'A bowl of cornflakes? Do you have any idea how turned on I can get watching a girl eat a bowl of cornflakes?' He leaned against the doorjamb and panted.

'Get out of here,' said Emma, laughing at him again, and he went, whistling as he skipped down the steps two at a time. He was so uncomplicated, he lifted her out of her despair.

He took her out for a drink, only orange juice, they were neither of them ever going to drink again, and spent the evening telling her funny stories. It seemed perfectly natural that he should end up seeing her to her door.

'Shhh,' she cautioned. 'Auntie Mabel has ears like an early warning radar station,' and they tiptoed along to her room, where one thing led to another.

It took them a long time to get going – Adrian fell out of bed twice and there was an awful lot of giggling and shushing – but Emma enjoyed it. It gave her a fair amount of pleasure without breaching her carefully constructed shell. After she had agreed to go to the Christmas dance with him and kicked him downstairs she had a bath, then went to bed and lay staring at the ceiling, thinking about what she'd just done. It had been better, she decided, than the anonymous couplings in which she had indulged so often recently, and it had made her feel only moderately dirty afterwards. She congratulated herself on having found a nice (that word she had always been told to avoid in school essays, so meaningless) boy who wouldn't make demands on her; an easy, uncomplicated relationship was just what she wanted if she couldn't have Rick.

She tucked the thought away in the back of her mind to be dealt with later, turned over and went to sleep.

They went to the Christmas dance with Alison and the handsome Dave. 'I'm not sleeping with him,' Alison told Emma. She was still seeing Harry Passmore, using Dave as a convenient cover for her less permissable activities. 'Harry's wife is beginning to suspect, so he has to be a bit careful for the moment. He could lose his job if the college finds out about us.' It made her feel very virtuous, going out platonically with a boy. 'Well, almost platonically.' She grinned wickedly.

They met Ian as they were going in. 'Found yourself a new gorilla, Em?' he greeted her.

'Who's the jerk with the mouth?' asked Adrian contemptuously.

'Only an ex-boyfriend.'

Alison found her halfway through the evening, sitting on Adrian's lap in the Common Room, sipping beer from a paper cup while he nibbled her ear. 'There's hope for the dear girl yet,' she told the uncomprehending Dave.

Emma and Adrian left early for Earl's Court and lay on the rug in front of the fire. Afterwards Adrian found a half-full bottle of brandy, pouring generous measures into chipped mugs, and while they drank he asked Emma for her home number: 'So we can spend New Year together.'

She gave it to him. 'But don't call until after Christmas.' That would give her time and space to breathe without him. It would make a pleasant change not to spend the year's end sitting with a dry sherry staring at Josie and Auntie Mabel.

'I'm making a resolution to bed a willing wench as early as possible on New Year's Day,' Adrian explained. 'Although it could be different if the fountains are crowded.'

Mabel took Emma home the next day. Emma spent the journey pretending to sleep and Mabel wisely kept her mouth shut. Don't interfere, she told herself, you've already got it wrong once, give the child some space to do her growing up.

CHAPTER FOURTEEN

• • •

Mabel had earned her boarding house. Of the two Bentley girls it was she who had been destined for great things. Not only was she handsome, she was clever too, a blue-stocking with a place at Cambridge University, well earned, and a future. Her elderly parents, refined, snobbish, ambitious, were thrilled that at least one of their girls was going to set the world on fire, until the war came and, like a great many others of her generation, Mabel was swept along on a tide of patriotic fervour, postponing her higher education and going instead to London to find work with the Ministry of Information. That had been bad enough, but Henry was the last straw.

Mabel Bentley met Henry O'Neal, crippled by childhood polio and unfit for active service, in October 1940 during the Blitz. They were on firewatch duty on the Ministry roof and it was a week before she saw him in daylight. During that week, against a backdrop of falling bombs, air-raid sirens and searchlights, despite Harry's twisted leg and an age difference of almost thirty years, they fell in love. They began a passionate affair, and by the time he plucked up the courage to tell her he was married, Mabel was in too deep to walk away.

Henry was Irish, Catholic. 'So there's no chance of a divorce,' he told her. 'But you could come and work for me. You could be my housekeeper.' They laughed together, planned it all, then decided, crazily, to carry out their ludicrous idea and make it work. It was only when Mabel took on the role that she discovered what a consummate actress she was. As the weeks turned into months she became what she was supposed to be, flattened her vowels, changed her appearance, mothered her employer/lover's wife, as if the woman was younger, not older than she, and deviated from her new persona only at night, when she shared her master's bed.

Henry's wife knew from the beginning. A sensible woman and a devout Catholic, her terror of childbirth was exceeded only by her disgust at the act of procreation; the new housekeeper solved her problems at a stroke. And besides, Miss Bentley was frightfully good at her job.

Mabel's role-playing suited her. She watched with amusement as Henry's friends, her intellectual inferiors, ignored her presence as they discussed their pompous bits of business, tolerated with ironic patience his wife's silly friends, and kept her own counsel. She cut herself off from her disapproving parents and became, to all intents and purposes, invisible. When Henry's wife died they merely carried on as before.

'Why rock the boat?' said Mabel, when he went down on one arthritic knee and proposed.

'I'll see you're all right when I'm gone,' he promised, and he had.

Oh, Henry, she sighed silently as she drove her sullen niece north on the A10, how I miss you still.

CHAPTER FIFTEEN
• • •

Josie wasn't back from work when Mabel parked the car, and they unloaded the bags in silence. The house was cold, gloomy, and Emma fought to keep her spirits up as her aunt bustled about.

'We must organise some supper for your mother. She'll be tired when she gets in.'

Emma waited until Mabel wandered off to the kitchen, then slipped out and walked down to the pub. By the time she got back she had taken on some evening shifts behind the bar.

'Where've you been? I could have done with some help, young lady, instead of you skiving off like that.' Mabel was not pleased. 'It's about time you started thinking about your poor mother.'

'I *have* been thinking about my poor mother. I've just been organising a job so I can pay my way over the holiday.'

Mabel stared at her stolidly. 'Don't pull that one, my girl. Paying your way's got nothing to do with it.'

'How would you like me to put it, then? I've got a job so I can avoid spending any more time than I have to at home? Is that what you'd like me to tell Ma?'

'At least it would be honest. Now do the carrots for me before you make me really angry.'

They chopped and peeled in unfriendly silence; it was a relief when they heard Josie's key in the lock and her tired voice calling, 'I'm home.'

She was desperate to hear about college. 'How are you doing, darling? Are you enjoying it? Do you (a sidelong glance, and an irritatingly coy giggle), do you have a boyfriend yet?'

'Yes.' Emma enjoyed the startled expression on her aunt's face, suspicious, she guessed, that she was still seeing Ricky.

'Oh! Oh, how *lovely*. Oh, *Emma*! What's his name? Tell me all about him.'

'Adrian. His name's Adrian.'

'Adrian? You mean Adrian Ward from downstairs?'

'Yes, Auntie Mabel, is there some problem?' Emma's look dared her to tell and Mabel, seeing Josie's eager, innocent face, subsided. 'I've been seeing him for a while now.' Her voice was too loud but she couldn't help it. 'You'd like him, Ma, he's a nice boy.'

'Well bring him home, darling, whenever you like.' Josie was thrilled; this was communication on a grand scale.

'Yes, do,' said Mabel heavily. 'Good idea.'

Emma shot her aunt a venomous look. 'I'd love to, Ma, but I can't, I haven't got his number.' It was true enough, she hadn't asked for it.

She could sense Mabel watching her, wondering what had been going on under her nose, and a bubble of malicious glee welled up. That'd teach the old cow to interfere in her life as if she was a child.

She went to bed early, pleading a headache, and half an hour later Mabel marched into her room to confront her.

'What are you playing at, my girl?'

'Nothing. Stop treating me like a ten-year-old.'

'Have you been—'

'Having it off with Adrian? What if I have?'

To hear the coarse phrase tripping so lightly off Emma's innocent tongue was a shock. So was the revelation that a mild case of calf-love had turned so quickly into casual promiscuity. I misjudged you, thought Mabel, considered you young and silly, too immature to know what you were doing. This is my fault.

'It's not what you're up to, you're a big girl now and I can't stop you.' Emma's mouth fell open in astonishment; she had been expecting another lecture. 'What concerns me is your mother. She's trusting me to look after you while you're in London, and if you're not careful you're going to find yourself in trouble. How would we explain that to Josie? Do we just pop home and mention in passing that her precious daughter has managed to get herself pregnant?'

'I won't get pregnant.'

'Oh? And why not? Do you have some magic formula I don't know about?'

'Because I'm on the Pill, that's why not.'

'Oh!' That stymied Mabel a little; she had thought her niece too naïve to have gone so far. Her relief was tempered by guilt, that she had so underestimated how much Emma had grown up, and suspicion, too, that the child was doing it just to show she could. It was too late now, though, to put the genie back in the bottle.

Mabel went back to London the next morning, her normally cheerful demeanour blunted by her niece's casual revelations. As soon as she'd left the house Emma walked down to the phone box.

Alison was still in bed.

'Mabel's on her way.'

'Damn,' came the sleepy voice the other end. 'Okay, thanks, Em,' and she put the phone down.

When Mabel returned for Christmas, Josie greeted her like a saviour, Emma like a stranger.

'I can't remember her ever being so difficult,' complained Josie. 'I don't know how to cope with her at all.' The atmosphere grew daily more icy.

On the 23rd of December, Emma received a rather large cheque for some freelance work she had done, forwarded by Alison, and the money hardened a resolve that had been growing since November. On the 27th she called in sick to the pub and went to London.

'Don't know,' she replied briskly when Josie asked how long she would be away.

*

She bought a paper at Liverpool Street station. Her aunt wasn't due back in Earl's Court until the 7th of January which, allowing for New Year, gave her about five days.

'Do you know what you're doing?' asked Alison as they leafed through the Accommodation section. 'Surely you can't afford anywhere else?'

'Yes, I can. I've saved everything I've earned over the past year, give or take a pound or two, and I reckon if I can find somewhere cheap enough I can manage for months, even if I don't earn another penny. I won't stay here any longer with that bloody woman breathing down my neck.'

'But Mabel's a dear. She never gives me a moment's bother. You can't blame her for what happened – that was down to Daddy.'

'Ha!' Emma bit savagely into her third chocolate Swiss roll. 'It was she who called him. And it wasn't the Bastard who sent Ricky away.' She glowered heavily at her friend. 'Anyway, she doesn't interfere with you; you're not her niece.'

'True enough.' Alison grinned and settled down cross-legged to concentrate on her task.

Most of the advertisements were for sharers, but there was a sprinkling of bedsits – plenty of students gave up their digs at Christmas because they couldn't afford to keep them on.

The spent two days traipsing round grotty rooms all the way from Swiss Cottage to New Cross and found nothing even remotely reasonable. 'You'll have to pay more,' said Alison, and they started all over again.

They found a room in Baron's Court on the 30th of December, two flights up, with a door to a tiny balcony serving a fire escape, and a window with a spectacular view over the skyline.

'It's got a proper kitchenette,' the landlord proclaimed, 'and its own bathroom. Won't get a bathroom anywhere else for the kind of money I'm asking.'

The room was poky, only nine foot by twelve, but the sun was shining and Emma was getting desperate. There was a single bed to act as a sofa during the day, an easy chair covered in hideous knobbly tweed and the much-vaunted bathroom was tinier even than the kitchen, with a shortened bath. But there was a deep built-in cupboard for clothes, the light was good and it was private. Pretty nearly perfect, Emma told herself, and put down three months' rent.

The phone was ringing when they got back. 'Why didn't you tell me you were going to be in London?' complained Adrian. 'I could have come up to see you. And what's the matter with Mabel? I just rang your place and when I asked to speak to you she practically snapped my head off. She's usually such a cheerful old girl.'

'She knows we're sleeping together.'

'What? How'd she find out?'

'I told her,' said Emma shortly. 'I was fed up with her ordering me around, so I told her.'

There was silence for a moment, then Adrian said, 'That was a bit silly, wasn't it? I mean, you know what they're like, that generation; it's all right as long as you don't rub their noses in it—'

Emma cut him short. 'What did you want, Adrian? I'm packing.'

'What for?'

'I'm moving.'

'Moving?' Adrian sounded stunned. 'But I . . . Can I help? I can come up early if you like. I was going to pick you up tomorrow night, but I can come in the morning if—'

'Tomorrow night? What for?'

'New Year.' Adrian was getting confused. 'Remember? "Auld Lang Syne", Scottish dancing, fountains, drunks? And sex of course.' He laughed uncertainly. 'Don't forget the sex.'

Oh God, how could she have forgotten? 'Yes!' she said hurriedly. 'Of course, come up early. That'd be great, we could use an extra pair of hands. I've got a place in Baron's Court.'

'Oh.' Adrian sounded flat now, hurt. 'Okay, I'll be there around ten. Bye.'

'Well?' said Alison.

'Well what?' It occurred to Emma that she had felt nothing hearing his voice, no pleasure, no excitement, no anticipation, *nothing*. Oh, Ricky, she thought, aching with misery, I miss you so much. When are you going to come and rescue me?

'Well, what are we going to do about this flat?'

'We're going to move my stuff tomorrow. Adrian's coming over to help.'

Alison stared at her. 'Christ, she really has made you mad, hasn't she?'

Alison was spending New Year with Harry. 'He's talking about leaving his wife,' she told Emma.

'Come on.' Emma was dismissive. 'He's got three children. He might consider leaving his wife, but there's no way he'd walk out on his kids.'

Ali regarded her with disfavour. That was not what she wanted to hear. 'You're so naïve.' She lit a cigarette and took a long, greedy drag at it. 'He loves me. It's the real thing this time; take my word for it, I know.'

Emma, remembering Jay, wondered whether part of Harry Passmore's attraction was his unavailability. If Alison was heading for trouble, there was nothing she could do about it, because Ali didn't want to listen. She didn't want to hear anything that didn't fit her picture of the future, and she wasn't used to losing.

They packed up most of Emma's stuff using as many suitcases as they could find and cardboard boxes begged from the shop round the corner. By the time Adrian arrived the next morning almost everything was done, just the bed to strip, the last cups and plates, a few tins and packets of food.

Adrian had got hold of a van, and he insisted they move Emma's stuff in it instead of getting a taxi. He made her feel terrible, guilty as hell, for being so cold on the phone.

'Doesn't matter,' he said when she apologised, and kissed her on the cheek. Then he began to shift boxes, whistling cheerfully as he worked. Emma was attacked by guilt again. Her hard shell was not yet quite impregnable.

Alison appeared in her dressing-gown around eleven, still bleary-eyed with sleep. 'Did we wake you?' she asked. 'Harry left about three. We had an almighty row. I asked him to stay tonight and he said he couldn't. In the end he stormed out and slammed the door behind him.' She giggled, seemingly unperturbed. 'I'll bet he gave his wife a hard time when he got in.'

While the girls talked, Adrian continued to doggedly hump boxes out to the van, studiously ignoring the conversation. Alison raised her eyebrows at his uncharacteristic silence.

'What's the matter?' she whispered while he was outside. 'You two had a row as well?'

Emma shook her head dismissively. 'Just busy,' she said shortly.

The traffic was heavy. It was Saturday and everybody in the world was trying to get home to prepare for the year's end. It took them nearly an hour to get to Baron's Court, but by half-past four they had nearly finished unloading and Adrian unexpectedly produced a bottle of wine.

'Quite decent stuff,' said Ali, examining the label. 'Here's to freedom from interference.'

'I'll drink to that.' Emma raised her glass and took a hefty gulp, then Alison, in a rare display of tact, made her excuses and left. Emma wished for once she could have been her usual undiplomatic self. She didn't want to be left alone with Adrian.

She sat as far from him as possible, on the end of the bed with her knees drawn protectively up to her chin. Adrian sat in the tweedy chair, his legs dangling over the arm, his glass in one hand and a rare cigarette in the other. The conversation petered out very quickly.

Emma didn't know what was the matter with her. She'd got what she'd been hankering after: a place of her own and the freedom to live as she pleased. Adrian, she thought, watching him surreptitiously over the rim of her glass, is a sweet boy. But he's not Ricky. I want Ricky.

'I wish you'd tell me why all this is going on.' Even his voice grated.

'It's like Ali said. It's about freedom from interference.' Emma glared at him, willing him to leave.

'But . . .'

'But what?'

But what about us, Adrian was going to say, what about *me*, where do *I* fit into all this? Instead he rose from his chair, placed his glass carefully on the table and picked up his jacket.

'I must take the van back. Are we still all right for tonight?'

'Yes, of course,' said Emma briskly, 'why not?' I have nothing better to do, no one better to see.

'Okay, I'll pick you up at nine.' Adrian hesitated. 'Bye then.'

'Bye. And thanks for your help.' She watched him stonily as he made his way to the door. When he'd gone she poured herself another glass of wine.

Emma paused in her dusty labours, staring at the cardboard box she had rescued from the darkest corner of the attic. Inside, carefully kept over the years, were a dozen or more champagne corks, each with a half-crown or, from later years, a tenpenny piece embedded in its top. Adrian had given her a similar one, she remembered: he had cut a slot with his knife, as Big Ben chimed in the New Year, then pushed the coin in and pressed it into her reluctant hand. 'Keep it,' he said, 'it'll bring you luck.' I threw it away, Emma recalled, the moment he left. God, what a bitch I was.

She shook herself, put the box down carefully in the 'saving' pile, then smiled at her own foolishness and moved it. She must be more ruthless, she scolded herself. George wouldn't want all this junk.

She was ruthless that New Year's Eve. She confused poor Adrian, bewildered him, finally insulted him and still expected him to understand, when she didn't understand herself why she was behaving so badly. I used him, she thought, allowed him to fill me up with expensive food, drown me in champagne, and when I was sufficiently drunk, I took him home to my new bed in Baron's Court. Then when I had taken my pleasure, such as it was, I told him to go.

And after all these years I can hardly remember what poor Adrian Ward looked like, let alone all the ins and outs of that drunken evening.

It was a good romp, funny, sexy, and ultimately almost seriously satisfying. Emma, drunk on champagne and exhausted by her move, hadn't the faintest idea why afterwards she was swept by such desolation, such revulsion.

When Adrian, relieved that they were on intimate terms again, tried to take her in his arms once more, she froze and turned her back.

'Em?' he begged. 'Emma, what's the matter?' He pleaded with her, stroked her, kissed her neck, but she lay resolutely turned away from him, and finally whispered in a voice heavy with distaste, 'Please go.'

He rose reluctantly and dressed. She heard him stumbling as he made his way to the door and she added belatedly, 'I'm sorry.'

There was a long pause, then his voice from the doorway. ''S okay, Em. Too much champagne, I expect.' She registered the hurt in his voice, wished he wouldn't be quite so bloody reasonable.

'Why do you have to be so bloody reasonable?'

'What?'

'I said why— Oh, never mind, just *go*.'

When he'd gone she rolled on to her back and stared miserably at the ceiling. It didn't make any sense; she went to bed with him quite willingly, because she enjoyed it, and tonight the sex had been good. So why did sex with Adrian make her miss Ricky so much?

She dreamed he was waiting for her, sitting astride his motorbike in a dark alleyway, and in the dream she ran to him, delirious with happiness that he had come for her at last, desperate for his embrace. He took her face in his hands and kissed her: a long, passionate kiss that, oddly, brought her nearer to a climax than she had been all evening. Then, just as the excitement became almost too painful to bear, she was caught from behind and dragged away from him, crying and protesting, until his face faded into the gloom and she knew she'd lost him again.

When she turned to beat at her captor with her fists it was Adrian, but as she lashed out at him he turned into Jay, and he began to laugh at her, louder and louder, until finally he threw his head back and roared like a lion.

She woke up shaking, and lay awake for an hour before she could sleep again, unsure what the dream had meant, but drunkenly positive that it proved she still loved Ricky and no one else.

When she finally closed her eyes again she slept like the proverbial dead.

Over the days that followed Emma fought fiercely to retain a tiny pocket of optimism in the face of everything that logic and practical common-sense told her, holding on to a small echo of hope that it wasn't over, that it never would be.

Adrian phoned one evening. 'Are you all right?'

'Yes. No.' *Leave me alone. I need to be on my own. If I can hang on to Ricky, he'll come back to me. If I don't keep hold of him now, I'll lose him for ever.*

'Do you want to stop seeing me?'

'I don't know.' *She was hedging her bets.*

'All right.' Adrian sounded awkward, hurt. 'Let me know when you've decided. You know where I am.'

She replaced the receiver, climbed the stairs to her room and went to sit by the window, watching the multi-layered patchwork of tiled roofs without moving until it grew too dark to see. Then she had a bath and went to bed.

When Alison came round the next morning she stayed where

she was, hunched up under the bedclothes, and shouted, 'Bugger off!' through the door until Alison gave up and went away.

She survived the next three days on a diet of water biscuits and Bovril, her normally voracious appetite completely absent.

It was midday when Jay turned up, but Emma was still in her dressing-gown. He caught her by surprise when he knocked, she thought it was Alison again and bellowed fiercely from the bed, 'I told you to bugger off!'

'Open the door, Emma,' he said calmly through the woodwork, 'or I'll break it down.'

Emma jumped at the unexpected sound of his voice. 'Sod off!'

'I mean it. It's no skin off my nose and you'll get the repair bill.'

'Leave me alone.' She climbed off the bed and moved warily towards the door.

'I'm waiting.'

Reluctantly she padded the last few feet and opened the door an inch to peer through the gap at the dimly lit landing.

'What do you want?' She was surly and suspicious.

'You.' Unexpectedly Jay pushed hard, and Emma stumbled backwards, overbalanced by the pressure. 'God, you look a mess. How long since you washed your hair?'

'None of your bloody business. How did you find me?'

'Alison rang me. Now go and have a bath and tidy yourself up; you're a shambles.'

'Why the hell should I?'

'Because,' Jay stared at her impassively, 'I have just told you to, and if you won't do it by yourself I shall remove your dressing-gown and put you in the bath personally. I might even join you if you don't get your act together quickly enough.'

A small, unexpected *frisson* of excitement ran down Emma's spine at the thought, followed by a spasm of murderous anger; he was *laughing* at her. It didn't occur to her to disobey though. She drew her dressing-gown protectively around her and flounced into the bathroom, slamming the door behind her.

She ran the bath and washed her hair in it, then pinned it up, climbed into the soapy water and lay back, seething with rage. She could hear music, the Third Programme, violins and flutes, and the sound of spoon, cup and kettle as Jay made himself at home. Her anger seeped away; the warm water felt wonderful, better than anything had for days, and she relaxed, closing her eyes and letting her mind go blank.

Jay grew restless and banged on the door. 'Are you clean yet?'

Emma panicked, alarmed that he might decide to see for himself, yelled, 'Yes! I'm out!' and leaped up, swaying as the combination of hot water and an empty stomach made her head spin.

'Good. Hurry up or I'll assume you need some help.'

Another flicker of excitement. Emma climbed gingerly out of the bath, towelled her hair as best she could and struggled into her dressing-gown again, then hesitated, suddenly conscious that the man standing just the other side of the bathroom door had always intimidated her, and that her clothes were in a cupboard out there with him.

When she emerged Jay was waiting for her, lounging against the wall with a cup of coffee in one hand. 'Well,' he said approvingly, 'you look a damn sight better than you did when I arrived.'

She slid along the wall as far from him as possible to rummage in the cupboard for her clothes.

'Not jeans.'

Her temper flared again; who did he think he was? But she flung the offending denims back in the cupboard anyway, too flustered to argue, and pulled out her Indian skirt.

'Will this suit, Your Lordship?'

'Admirably.' He never once took his eyes off her, never ceased to be amused by her furious discomfort. She grabbed a cotton jumper and flounced back to the bathroom, shielding herself with her clothes, then slammed the door in his face for the second time and leaned against it, waiting for her heart to stop hammering. She heard him laugh as she dressed, as slowly as possible, putting off facing him, and when she appeared at last he was pacing the room impatiently.

'What are you going to do with your hair?'

She shrugged dismissively. 'It'll dry. I'm not going anywhere.'

'Yes you are. Where do you keep the towels?' When she didn't answer, he disappeared into the bathroom, emerging with a couple in his hands. Then to Emma's impotent fury he propelled her across the room to the bed and pushed her down to sit on the floor.

'Ow!' she complained. 'Get off!'

'Shut up.'

He moved her big bag out of his way, then sat on the bed, long legs stretched out either side of her, and began to rub her hair. He was rough and she moaned and whimpered, but she got no sympathy; he just told her again to shut up and she capitulated, too tired to fight him, closing her eyes and submitting sulkily to his ministrations. When it was nearly dry he dragged her bag across and rifled through it until he found a comb.

'Ow!' squeaked Emma indignantly as he set about untangling her thick mane, but when he began to plait it she lapsed into silence, enjoying despite herself the feel of his fingers at the nape of her neck.

Jay felt the change in the almost imperceptible softening of her tense muscles, in the slight movement of her head against him, and his hands moved further afield.

'Stop it!' said Emma angrily and he chuckled, returning obediently to his task.

When he was finished he handed the thick braid across her shoulder. 'Find something to tie it with. And a warm coat.'

She rose swiftly, anxious to get away from him, and dived for the safety of the bathroom again, then stood staring at her white face in the mirror, shocked by her own appearance. She looked awful, black rings beneath her eyes and hollows under her cheekbones. When she went back to the sitting-room he had found her coat and was holding it out, ready to leave.

'But I don't want to go out,' Emma protested indignantly, making a last-ditch attempt to stop the steamroller that appeared to be moving her.

Jay shrugged his shoulders. 'Okay, we'll stay in.' He grinned. 'I'm rather good at indoor games.' He placed his hand on the back of her neck, pressing her damp hair against her skin and pulling her towards him. Emma panicked again. Jay wasn't controllable, not like Adrian or all those others. She stepped back sharply and knocked his hand away, snatching her coat as she went.

'All right!' she snapped. 'All right, for God's sake. Let's get it over and done with. Then perhaps you'll go away and leave me alone.'

He took her to a dark, old-fashioned hotel, all overstuffed plush seating, Axminster carpets and heavy oak furniture. He marched her across the dining-room to the remotest corner, despite protests from the *maître d'hôtel*, then pushed her unceremoniously down into a squishy velvet chair. Emma glared at him, hating him. Ricky would never have treated her like this.

He ordered roast beef, Yorkshire pudding, three vegetables and she scowled, insisting, 'I'm not hungry and I won't eat it.' But when the food came she demolished a huge plateful at such speed that she had finished before Jay was halfway through his helping.

'Better now?' he asked sarcastically.

'Must've been hungrier than I thought,' she mumbled, and Jay raised an eyebrow, put his knife and fork down, and leaned back in his chair.

'Now perhaps you'd like to tell me what's going on.'

'Nothing's going on.' Emma stared defensively at her empty plate. 'I'm just a bit fed up, that's all. What's Ali been telling you?'

'Not much, just that she thought you were depressed and that you'd barricaded yourself in and told her to bugger off, which sounds familiar. Also ...' Jay paused to pour himself some water; Emma watched the ice bouncing and tinkling in his glass, then looked away when his eyes returned to her face. 'She said you'd sent – what's his name?'

'Adrian.'

'Adrian, thank you.' I think I will probably kill him if I ever see him again. 'That you'd sent Adrian packing as well. She was worried about you.'

'She didn't need to be. I'm perfectly all right.' Emma's voice wobbled on the last word and she lowered her head hurriedly to hide the tears that had appeared from nowhere and were threatening to overwhelm her again.

Jay gave her no sympathy. 'Is this about Alison's brother still? Or something else?'

'Don't know. None of your business.'

He placed his hands in his lap, clenching his fists under the tablecloth. 'Either way, it's time it stopped. And what about this other boy, where does he fit in?'

'He doesn't.' It was nothing to do with Jay, except that she had just eaten vast amounts of food for which he was paying, which meant she owed him. 'He's just a nice boy, that's all; he makes me laugh.'

'Is he good in bed?'

'None of your business,' she said again. Then to get back at him, because she didn't think he'd want to hear the answer, 'Yes he is, since you ask.'

She got no rise out of him at all, and his next question was even more offensive. 'So if he's such a good screw why don't you just lie back and enjoy it, instead of still pining after Ali's brother?'

'You don't understand.' When she looked up he was regarding her with barely controlled hostility, waiting for an explanation.

'I can't explain,' she said. 'It's got nothing to do with being good in bed.'

'Is it because he was the first then? He was, wasn't he, the first, I mean?' And you will never know how much I hate him for that.

'You wouldn't understand.'

'Try me.'

She shifted uneasily in her chair and greeted the arrival of the waiter with a wide, insincere smile of relief. Jay waved him away peremptorily.

'Apple pie,' he said shortly. 'For one. Come on, Em. Explain.'

She stared at him until his intent, unblinking gaze made her feel uncomfortable.

'It was right, from the first minute I saw him.' Go on, laugh, she dared him silently. Ali did. Ridicule me, belittle what Rick and I have been to each other, all the others have. 'I just *knew*, that's all. It was like he'd been put there for my benefit.' She began to spoon little piles of salt from the blue glass dish in front of her, a neat row of small white hillocks on the tablecloth. 'And now he's gone, its as if . . .' She tailed off into silence, then started again, wanting him to know what it felt like, needing him to understand. 'It's as if someone's cut off one of my arms or something.'

She stopped again, momentarily unable to trust her voice, then added pathetically, 'I feel as if I'm slowly bleeding to death.' Her eyes filled again and as if to emphasise her misery a single tear ran slowly down her cheek to land in one of the piles of salt, and was absorbed as if it had never been. She wiped her face angrily with the back of her hand then carefully flattened all her white hills into neat round circles.

Christ, thought Jay, shaken by a sudden spasm of fierce, possessive love, I hope the bastard dies. 'Okay,' he said calmly. 'So how do we staunch the wound?'

He startled Emma. She had no idea why she had unburdened herself in the first place, and if she had expected any sort of reaction it would have been derision. Jay wasn't the sympathetic type. She glared at him as the waiter placed a large portion of apple pie on the table, trying to work out whether he was mocking her.

'Why should you care?' She stirred a hole in the first circle of salt, then progressed along the line until Jay took the spoon away, exasperated by her endless fiddling. 'Why are you wasting your valuable time stuffing roast beef down my throat just because I'm fed up? Haven't you anything better to do?'

'Not today, no. If you were to be depressed next week I'd be unavailable. I'm up to my neck then.' I *love* you, he shouted silently, you fool, you idiot, you cretin, just like you love him.

Despite herself Emma smiled, and he leaned forward, resting his elbows on the table and his chin on his hands.

'We're alike, you and I,' he said. 'We're both loners. And there's a girl I was in love with once, that I couldn't hook. So maybe I know how you feel.'

'I'm sorry.' Emma hadn't the faintest idea what mattered to Jay; she'd never been interested enough to ask. 'You didn't say. I didn't mean to . . .'

'It's not your problem.' He shrugged dismissively, then pushed the apple pie across the table through the white circles of salt. 'Eat.'

'Did she go off with someone else?' She looked straight at him for once, at his dark haunted face, the straight, heavy hair flopping over his forehead, the ironic twist of his mouth, and saw him as a person for almost the first time, not just as intimidating, sardonic Jay, the one who refused to fit in with everyone else. 'It wasn't Ali, was it?' She could see Jay wouldn't want to share, and Ali wasn't exactly the faithful sort.

He laughed derisively. 'No, it wasn't Ali. She's not my type and never was. Now eat your apple pie and shut up. You're becoming ridiculous.'

He deflected her as he had always done, avoiding any question that threatened to get too close by ignoring it, and Emma finished her meal in silence, rebuffed. Jay ordered coffee, then sat back as he always did, giving nothing away whilst managing at the same time to make her feel exposed and vulnerable. After he had paid the bill, Emma followed him meekly out of the hotel to his car and allowed him to settle her in her seat, exhausted by the effort of parrying his conversational barbs and by the vast meal she had just eaten.

Jay fitted the key in the ignition, but instead of starting the engine he rested his hands on the steering wheel and stared out through the windscreen at the sleet that was beginning to fall.

'What shall we do now?'

'You've done your bit for humanity. Just drop me off and you can go on your way glowing with the knowledge that you've saved me from certain starvation.' Emma stared down at her hands, neatly folded in her lap, and ached to be on her own. 'Jay?'

'Mmm?' He was still gazing out through the windscreen at the blurred car-park, miles away.

'Thanks for lunch.'

'Right,' he said absently, then started the car, and pulled out into the slushy road.

Emma leaned back and closed her eyes, grateful to be on her way home.

When Emma opened her eyes, they were travelling south down the Fulham Road in the gathering gloom in completely the wrong direction.

'You've been snoring.' Jay barely glanced at her as she pushed herself up in her seat, protesting. 'And it's no good complaining, it's your turn to perform an altruistic deed and I'm still in need of company.' Emma subsided resentfully as they crossed Putney Bridge and they swung into the car-park behind the flats in silence.

Jay cut the engine. 'Aren't you even slightly curious to see what it's like now it's finished?'

'Are you in then?' What a stupid question, why else would he drag her halfway across London on a freezing winter's afternoon in what was threatening to become a full-blown snowstorm?

They crossed the short distance from the car to the entrance hall with their heads down and their coat collars up, protecting themselves against the biting wind that was hurling icy rain into their faces. Emma couldn't face the lift. They had to climb three flights of stairs, and she was breathless before they reached the second landing, suffering from an immediate surfeit of food and her previous self-induced starvation.

'I'm glad I don't have to escort you up this way very often,' said Jay drily. 'It would probably kill me,' but he wasn't puffing. He unlocked the door, then stood back and bowed mockingly as Emma preceded him.

Apart from the kitchen, pale wood and French navy, it was as Emma remembered, painted white everywhere, but not white like Alison's rooms. The floorboards were polished and scattered with rugs, lustrous antique beauties that made her want to get down on her knees and stroke them. The colours glowed jewel-like in the uncertain light, unobstructed by clutter, by coffee-tables or knick-knacks or stools.

There were pictures too, hung on every vertical surface, not big, splashy modern prints like Alison's but watercolours, sub-dued, subtle. They weren't Jay's, though. He showed her every room in the house, including the big double bedroom at the end of the corridor and there wasn't one example of his work anywhere. They were all, he said, for sale, part of his business. Emma thought it typically odd.

He had turned the second bedroom into a study, with a big oak desk overlooking the car-park far below, and the third, smallest one into a studio, facing north over the river, with a stainless-steel workbench lit by an anglepoise lamp. He was working on a layout, a restaurant interior in full colour. Bottles of ink were ranged neatly in trays alongside. He came and stood beside Emma as she examined his drawing.

'You always were better than the rest of us put together,' she said, moving away from him.

'Yes I was, wasn't I?'

Arrogant bastard, she thought, and let go the breath she had subconsciously been holding. But when he left her, making for the door and the kitchen, she was oddly disappointed. Part of her wanted him to kiss her, needed the stirring of pleasure he kindled in her.

'Coffee?'

He took the mugs to the sparcely furnished sitting-room; more beautiful rugs, a big sofa, a plain, pale oak table set against the wall with two chairs, but no curtains, and lots of books – an eclectic mix of art, typography, biography, fiction: Steinbeck, Hemingway, John Hersey, P.G. Wodehouse, Proust, Bernard Malamud, Evelyn Waugh – and records, not so eclectic, all classical. How little I know about you, she thought again as she sipped nervously at her coffee.

Jay found a bottle of brandy in a corner cupboard and poured two generous measures. He handed one to Emma, then raised his glass and proposed a toast.

'To the staunching of old wounds.'

Emma pursed her lips and sniffed, offended by the irony implicit in the words, then took a hefty gulp, coughing as the fumes hit the back of her throat. Jay tossed his back in one, poured himself another, drained that too, then crossed to the window, still holding his empty glass. How odd, thought Emma again. It was the most she had ever seen him drink in one go.

The snow was coming down in earnest now, thick, heavy flakes falling steadily from a sombre sky. Already the far bank of the river was barely visible and the cars moving along the Embankment had their lights on.

'Come and look,' said Jay.

Emma took her glass and went reluctantly to stand beside him, staring out at the yellowish light filtering through the snow, street lamps and twilight mingling with car fumes and river mist. Looking up, one could imagine that the snow was standing still, that the warm room was rushing through the thick flakes into the leaden sky. She could hear car tyres swishing faintly on the wet road below.

'Do you think your hair's dry yet?'

The change of subject startled her, and she shifted uneasily, awkward and suspicious. Jay balanced his glass on the window-sill, then moved round behind her and began to unravel the thick braid that hung down her back. It was set now, kinked into impossible curls by its tight confinement. He spread it slowly across her shoulders, running his hands through it, stroking it, twisting it round his fingers.

It took Emma a while to realise she was being seduced and by the time she had worked it out, it was too late. Jay's fingers were too persuasive, the effect they had upon her too hypnotically pleasurable; by the time he picked her up and carried her, there was no fight left in her at all.

She noticed nothing of the shadowy room to which he took her. She only felt physical sensations she had never experienced before, delights she had not dreamed existed.

She climaxed helplessly, then collapsed, awed by the intensity of her arousal, by her latest lover's casual expertise. But when Jay came, whimpering out loud like an animal, antipathy flared. He didn't sound in control and she resented the noise, resented Jay, not only for giving her something no one else had, but for that small, unexpected sign of weakness when she was in need of strength. This is just sex, she reminded herself desperately; there is no emotion involved on either side. If she could confine herself to physical pleasure she could keep her defences intact.

When Jay moved up close and tried to take her in his arms again, she resisted, pushing hard against his hot skin, rejecting him as she had Adrian, as she had all the others, because he wasn't Ricky.

Jay wouldn't let her. He knew what she needed and he chose not to let her have it, wouldn't allow her the space to be alone.

Where Emma had allowed his physical violation of her carefully erected barriers, she didn't want this more cruel invasion, his refusal to let her be afterwards; she lay stiff and unyielding in his arms until he moved his mouth close to her ear and pleaded in a voice quite unlike his own, soft and shaking with emotion, 'Stop it, Emma, please.'

He caught her by surprise; she snatched at her breath as his warmth, the smell of his skin surrounded her and, exhausted, gave in.

'Oh, bloody hell!' she swore savagely, and Jay tightened his grip, drawing her in while she sobbed as if her heart would break.

*

When she woke she was covered to the waist, and for a moment she had no idea where she was. She rolled on to her back, frowning at the ceiling, fuddled with sleep. It was only when she turned her head and saw Jay, propped up on one elbow watching her, that she remembered.

'Good-evening.'

She blinked, startled by the prosaic greeting then, suddenly aware that she was stark naked, drew herself sharply into a hunched-up ball, curling round and pulling the sheet up protectively to her chin.

'I have seen everything you possess, little Em,' he ridiculed her. 'You've been asleep for over an hour and I'm not gentleman enough to pass up such an opportunity to explore.' He smiled and she opened her mouth in outrage, her cheeks burning. She felt as if she had been raped.

'Why? How could you do that to me?'

Wilfully, Jay misunderstood. 'Seduce you? Because I wanted to; because I've wanted to for two and a half years and I couldn't wait any longer.' He lowered his head to her shoulder, sighed. 'Would you like me to pretend my motives were altruistic? I will if you like; I could tell you I took you to bed in order to stop you bleeding for your amputated limb.' She turned her face away, grossly offended by the crude insult; he turned her back again. 'It wouldn't be true. I just wanted you, that's all. Have since the first time I set eyes on you. And you wanted me, just as much.'

It was what Emma had told herself she needed to hear, that Jay had no feelings for her, any more than she had for him, but said out loud so baldly it degraded her, made her furiously angry.

'I'm going home.' She struggled out of bed and fumbled on the floor for her clothes, gathering them up in her arms to cover herself up.

Jay made no attempt at first to stop her. Only when she had her skirt, jumper, shoes, knickers, all clutched to her bosom, and was about to leave the room, did he speak.

'Stay with me, Emma. Please . . .'

She stopped, disconcerted.

'Why should I?'

He rolled over and swung his legs on to the floor. It was almost dark now, she could see only a blurred outline, hunched shoulders, bent head. 'Because I love you,' he mumbled.

'What?' She caught his eyes glimmering in the light from the window as he turned his head.

'*Because I love you!*' he bellowed.

Emma stood quite still and strained her eyes to see him. She felt as if she was in some silly play, and Jay had departed from the script without warning, leaving her with no cue, no line to follow.

He rose and crossed the room, took her clothes and dropped them on the floor, then led her back to the bed and pushed her down into the warm patch she had left behind. Emma lay rigid as he climbed in beside her, watching his shadowy outline in resentful silence. I don't have to put up with this, she thought, I will go home. But she couldn't seem to make herself get out of bed.

When Jay wrapped his arms round her again, she sucked in her breath, resisting him, and he sighed, wafting warm, brandy-laden air against her cheek.

'It's all right,' he murmured. 'I'm not going to hurt you. I just want to *sleep* with you.'

He began to stroke her, patiently, gently, until despite herself Emma felt her tense muscles unknotting. Then just as the feel of his skin against hers began to arouse her and she turned involuntarily towards him he fell asleep. He had hold of her hand and he wouldn't relinquish it, sighing and muttering like a frightened child when she tried to pull it away.

For the second time that night he was vulnerable when she expected him to be strong, and the chaos in her head made her tired. It was warm beneath the blankets, his skin was smooth, and he smelled nice. I must get up, she told herself, and go home before it's too late. She was just wondering how she would find her clothes in the dark when she fell asleep.

CHAPTER SIXTEEN

• • •

He began the moment she woke, as if he'd been waiting for her: hands, mouth, tongue; seductive, compelling, irresistible. Emma lay still, holding her breath, feigning indifference until she ached excruciatingly all over, until he bent his head and she felt his lips against the hollow of her throat.

'Love me back,' he whispered hoarsely. 'Please, Emma,' and she yelped as if he was hurting her.

'Oh,' she complained. 'Don't!' Begging him to help her resist him. He wouldn't play. He teased her, tantalized her beyond endurance until she had no choice but to give in.

She caught him by surprise, relaxing unexpectedly beneath his hands, then reaching out, the suddenly obedient pupil, to touch in her turn. It took Jay a moment to recover his equilibrium, then she felt him shake with triumphant laughter and he leaned close again to whisper in her ear, 'Catching, isn't it?' as if sexual desire was an infectious disease.

'Frankly, I'm surprised you managed to keep your virginity for as long as you did.' Jay stretched languidly, his hunger assuaged. 'Once you get going, your appetite for sex is almost as voracious as your taste for food.'

He laughed, getting his own back for her unsuccessful attempts to repel him, then rose and began to move around the room. Emma watched him as he found a dressing-gown and picked up her discarded clothes, then threw them casually on the end of the bed in a tumbled pile. His body was more powerful than Rick's:

loose jointed, heavily built; watching him made her want him again.

And yet how alike Jay and Ricky were, she thought, standing in George's dusty attic twenty-six years later: the same straight, floppy hair, one dark, one fair. The same long limbs, beautiful hands, the same shuttered faces, the same aversion to (or was it terror of?) people – the great mass of humanity.

She gravitated towards the window, drawn by an invisible line, tripped over a pair of binoculars and picked them up. One eyepiece was missing and she focused with difficulty, then search-ed the meadow until she found what she was looking for, shutting one eye to improve the wavering image.

He was standing thigh-deep in buttercups and ox-eye daisies while the dogs cavorted around him, their presence betrayed only by the violent trembling of the long grass. He was laughing; Emma laughed too as Newton (or was it Flotman?) shot suddenly out of the green on stiff, straight legs, ears and tail flying, then plunged again into the waving sea and disappeared. Watching him, she thought, you have grown more tolerant of your fellow man over the years, as long as they don't come too close. Is that partly due to me?

'Breakfast in fifteen minutes,' said Jay, and disappeared in the direction of the bathroom. Emma lay back on the pillows for almost ten minutes before she plucked up the courage to reach for the dressing-gown, sliding gingerly out of bed as if he might be watching her.

It was far too long for her and she had to roll the sleeves up, but it got her to the bathroom where she showered and scrubbed her face until it was pink and shiny, then brushed her hair with Jay's brush and tied it back into a ponytail. She cleaned her teeth as best she could with her finger and rinsed her mouth, avoiding her reflection in the mirror, then crept out into the corridor to listen to Jay clattering about in the kitchen.

He was lying in wait for her. 'You look about twelve,' he taunted her. 'I should be prosecuted for having sex with a minor.' His laughter pursued her as she fled back to the bedroom.

There was toast, orange juice and black coffee, but Emma wasn't hungry. Jay was amused by her lack of composure.

'Please,' she begged at last, 'will you stop looking at me all the time? It makes me feel uncomfortable.'

'Why? You should be flattered that I want to look at you. It's a good test if you think your partner's still worth looking at the morning after. There's nothing to stop you doing the same.'

She rose to the bait, returning his straight stare, but she couldn't do it for long, and he ridiculed her again.

'Well? Will you kick me out of bed next time?'

Emma grimaced. 'I'm not sure you'd go if I did.'

'No, I'm not sure I would. But I don't think I'd be asked to.' His thinly veiled triumph embarrassed and infuriated her. She felt as if she was sitting at the table stark naked.

'I must go home,' she said abruptly but he caught her wrist and pulled her down again.

'Finish your toast. I don't do seduction scenes over breakfast.' He paused. 'Although I could make an exception for you.' He drained his cup and rose to fetch more coffee.

He was dressed casually, in jeans and a faded blue shirt, and he seemed to take it for granted that she would stay all day.

'I have the rest of the week off,' he said pointedly, as if she might stay even longer. 'What papers do you like to read?' He put on his jacket to go and get them, then stopped in the doorway. 'Did you take your pill last night?'

'No.' Panic. 'I haven't got—'

'They're in your bag. Shan't be long,' and he was gone.

Emma found her bag, flung carelessly on the hall table, but her pills were on the bathroom shelf, back at Earl's Court. Except that they weren't – they were in her bag where Jay had put them.

She took the pill for Thursday then flounced back to the

bedroom, dressed in a fury and grabbing her bag left the flat, slamming the door behind her. I hope you haven't taken a key, she cursed him savagely. I hope I've locked you out.

She leaped down the stairs two at a time and arrived in the entrance hall just in time to cannon into him, knocking the papers out of his hand and winding herself. Then she froze, trying to catch her breath while he picked them all up again.

'Why?'

Emma was paralysed by his unexpected return, rendered speechless by the awkwardness of getting caught, as if she was playing hooky from school and Jay was the headmaster. The self-righteous spleen seeped slowly out of her.

'Where are you going? Why are you running away?'

She swallowed. 'I'm going home. I don't know why I let you bring me here in the first place. I don't know why I went to bed with you.'

'That's easy.' Jay smiled indulgently, as if she was a child. 'You're lonely, and you fancied me. You enjoyed it too, although you don't think you ought to have done.' He put his hand under her chin and turned her face up to his. 'No, that's not true ... you loved it, didn't you?'

'I ...' Emma closed her eyes, feeling the same swift arousal as she had an hour earlier, then opened them again to ask plaintively, 'What do you *want*, Jay? I don't know what you expect of me.'

'Two questions.' He dropped his hand, stared down at her impassively. 'Since you seem to be so concerned, I will try and answer both. What do I want?' He took a deep breath, let it out very slowly. 'You. I'll marry you if that's what you'd like.'

Emma gulped, suddenly short of oxygen.

'Don't look so shocked. Why not? I love you. I'll have you on whatever terms you choose, just so long as I can have you. What do I expect of you? Nothing, yet. Except that if there's a choice I'd rather you stopped seeing other men. I'm not good at sharing.' No good at all, I want to kill them all, beat them into a bloody pulp.

'I don't love you,' said Emma flatly. 'I love Ricky.'

'So you've said.' Especially him. God, how I hate that bastard. 'That will come in time. I can wait.' He made it sound as if she had a mild case of measles, didn't want to understand. 'Would you like to go home now?' She nodded vehemently and Jay turned abruptly on his heel and led the way out into the icy wind that was swirling round the car-park. Emma waited patiently while he scraped the windscreen, her feet getting cold and her head aching with tension, then he drove her home without a word, once again as happy with silence as with conversation, and dropped her off in the street outside her flat. Before he let her out he scribbled, then handed her a folded piece of paper.

'My phone number,' he said. 'Sort yourself out and call me when you're ready.'

'Ready for what?'

'Ready to give me what I want.' The cool words matched his neutral expression.

'You're very sure of yourself,' Emma complained.

Jay nodded his head, his dark hair flopping on his brow. 'I'm banking on you coming back for more. You've acquired a taste for what I can give you, and sooner or later you'll want to do it again.'

'Thank you for lunch,' she said idiotically, then fumbled for the doorhandle, desperate to get out. He leaned across and caught her wrist.

'I mean it,' he said. 'And don't leave it too long, I'm hungry already.' Then he kissed her, deliberately not on the mouth, on the cheek.

She was intensely disappointed, and quite unable to hide it. I've got you, he thought, and felt a surge of triumphant satisfaction.

'Next time,' he promised. As she tumbled out of the car its engine roared instantly into life and he began to pull away almost before she had slammed the door. She was left standing on the pavement staring at his disappearing exhaust, longing already, as he had promised she would, for more.

There were three notes on the floor, and the flat was freezing. Emma picked up the bits of paper, glanced at them, threw them on the table and bent to light the fire. Then she removed her coat, flung herself full-length on the bed and went instantly to sleep. She was startled into wakefulness by a frantic banging on the door.

Alison was breathless from the stairs and bursting with curiosity. 'Where were you last night?' She lit a cigarette and peered at Emma through a cloud of smoke. 'I called and called. I gave up at midnight. They said you were out.'

'I was.'

'Who with? Adrian was downstairs all evening, Bill told me.'

Emma looked around vaguely, avoiding Alison's suspicious scrutiny. 'That reminds me, there was a note somewhere . . .'

It was on the table where she had left it, along with the two telephone messages saying Alison had called. She held it out hurriedly, as if it might contaminate her.

Darling Emma,

    I assume you don't want to see me any more I'm sorry if I've done something to upset you I didn't mean to honestly I'm writing this in the hope that I'm wrong and it isn't me at all and if that's the case please please, ring me as I miss you.

Lots and lots of love
Adrian
xxx

'Hasn't anybody told this boy about full-stops?' Ali giggled as she handed it back. 'When are you going to put the poor lamb out of his misery?'

'I don't know,' said Emma, reminded that it was Alison who had set Jay on her trail and resenting this further interference in her affairs. 'But what I am going to do, right now, is throw you out, lock the door and go back to bed.'

'All right, so don't tell me.' Alison sized her friend up shrewdly, then blew a meditative cloud of smoke at the ceiling. 'Seen Jay lately?'

Emma shifted uncomfortably.

'Ah ... Tell me all.'

'He came round and ... took me out to lunch.' She paused, reluctant to elaborate, perversely longing to tell. 'What's today?'

'The sixth.'

'No, what day of the week?'

'Friday.'

'Thursday then. It was Sunday lunch, you see.'

'What was?'

'That Jay took me out for.'

Alison sighed. 'Is any of this relevant? What I want to know is, where were you last night?'

'Um, well, he took me back to Putney, to show me the flat. It's fabulous Ali, you'd love it, all white walls and rugs and paintings and things.'

Alison was beginning to despair. 'And?'

'And what?' Emma was running short of breath, and out of prevarications.

'And you stayed the night. Didn't you?'

Emma stared fixedly out of the window.

'Ah. Good, was he? Now let me guess ... he's got you hooked, and you don't know what to do about it. Well, I know what I'd do if it was me, you silly fool.'

'He frightens me.' It tumbled out, the muddle, the confusion and resentment. 'He seems to know exactly what he wants and it doesn't occur to him for a second that he might not get it.'

'And what he wants is you.'

Emma lowered her head, avoiding those black eyes, and Alison tossed her golden hair and laughed. 'Oh, don't worry about me, I got over that one a long time ago. I'm after much bigger fish.' She blew another cloud of smoke. 'Just the same, if he crawled into my bed tonight I wouldn't kick him out. So what now? Where do you go from here?'

'Nothing. Nowhere. That was it, the first and last time.'

'I don't understand. He's got to be the most exciting man

you've ever had. Admit it, Em, he's—'

'He's not. Ricky's the most exciting—'

Her words were lost in the sound of Alison's ribald laughter and Emma took immediate and violent offence. Alison ignored her.

'I need a cup of coffee. This is giving me a headache. You got any food?'

'In the cupboard next to the sink.'

Alison rummaged around and found a packet of stale digestives. 'Is this it? God, no wonder you're looking so thin. Where's the nearest shop?'

'Dunno.' Emma sulked furiously. 'Never investigated.'

It was no good; Alison bullied and browbeat her until she wearily put her coat on again and they went out to find some food. Then they made soup and sandwiches.

Once she'd started eating Emma couldn't stop, polished off two bowls of soup and her own sandwiches, then finished Ali's, cut the remaining cheese and toasted it with the last of the bread. After that Alison started on her in earnest.

'Josie's phoned every day, and I've been lying my socks off on your behalf. Mabel's due back in London tomorrow too. You've got to *do* something, go home, preferably today, and tell them face to face before they find out the hard way...'

'You sound just like Mabel,' said Emma sourly.

'Good. Christ, is that the time? I must get back. What are you going to do?'

Emma sighed, resigned. 'I'll go home. Just wait a minute and I'll come with you.'

She stuffed her washbag and a change of clothes into her rucksack and they left together, parting at Earl's Court. Emma leaned her head against the train window to watch the blonde head bobbing along the platform towards the exit, and wished her life was as uncomplicated as Alison's seemed to be.

CHAPTER SEVENTEEN

• • •

She walked from Cheshunt station, her coat collar turned up against the cold, her body aching with fatigue, and let herself in just as the clock in the hall struck seven. They were eating, sitting in the kitchen over bowls of home-made oxtail soup.

'Hello, Ma,' said Emma, and stiffened with embarrassment as Josie leaped from her chair and embraced her. Mabel didn't move.

'I just needed to be on my own,' she repeated stubbornly in response to all her mother's questions, but she ate everything Josie put in front of her. She knew she was behaving badly but somehow she couldn't seem to stop herself. When Mabel began to hover meaningfully by her chair, she pleaded exhaustion and retreated hastily to her room, to lie on her narrow bed with her eyes shut and think about sex, about how simple life would be without it, about how much she would like some more of it, with Jay.

'I'm worried about Josie.'

Emma sat up abruptly, startled out of a heavy sleep.

'I said, I'm worried about Josie. She's taking it very badly, you not spending any time at home. I know it's difficult; I was young once, whatever you might think, but I don't want your mother hurt.'

Emma was still on a short fuse. 'You don't want my *mother* hurt? What about me? You didn't care about *me* getting hurt, did you, when you sent him away—?'

Oh Lord, thought Mabel, I got it wrong. It must be nine months, and she should have got over it by now. That's what comes of being an interfering old woman.

'You mean Alison's brother?' She sat down heavily on the end of the bed and Emma shrank, drawing her legs up and tucking them under her so there was no possibility of being touched. 'Is it still about him, all this unhappiness? I thought it was just—'

'What, just another teenage infatuation? Well it wasn't. It wasn't at all. It was the most important thing that ever happened to me, and you spoiled it.' Emma began to shout. 'You and Alison's bastard father spoiled it, and I'll never get over it, *never*!'

She hadn't thought about Ricky at all for more than twenty-four hours. She had been really, truly unfaithful to him for the first time; she had forgotten to pine for him, and she couldn't forgive herself.

'Emma dear, I'm sorry.'

'Oh!' Mabel's apology caught Emma by surprise, disarmed her. She sat up and crossed her legs, gripping her ankles with her hands. 'I've found a flat.'

'You've what?'

'I've moved. I've found a flat in Baron's Court. It's got its own kitchen and bathroom and everything so you don't need to worry about me any more.'

'Slow down!' said Mabel, taken aback.

'I'm nineteen this year; it's time I was independent; I need a place of my own—'

'All right! Just stop talking and give me a chance to get used to the idea. It's done, whatever I think of it, and we're going to have to explain to your mother. Young Alison's been pulling the wool and she's got Josie wrapped round her persuasive little finger. She thinks you're still in Earl's Court.'

'And where did you think I was?'

Mabel chuckled, surprising her niece for the second time. 'I thought you were off somewhere with Adrian, asserting your independence.'

'I was,' Emma lied, because it was easier than explaining.

'Nice boy.'

Emma laughed suddenly. 'Mmm, poor Adrian. Much too nice
for me.' She untangled her legs and climbed off the bed. For the
first time since it had happened, it occurred to her that perhaps
Mabel had only been doing what she thought best. Besides, she
was too tired to fight any more. 'Come on, Auntie Mabel,' she
said. 'Let's hit the sherry.'

They poured three large sherries, then broke the news, clumsily,
between them. Josie took it very badly.

'Why didn't you ask me? How will you afford it? You'll be
lonely all on your own. You won't eat properly.'

'Josie, you're being ridiculous,' protested Mabel, exasperated.
'It won't make a blind bit of difference to how much Emma eats.
I don't spend all my time peering at the contents of her larder to
see how many slices of toast she's eaten in the last two days, and
neither does—'

'Why not?' Josie was outraged. 'Why did I trust you with her
in the first place if you had no intention of looking after her?'

'Because she's a grown woman. Haven't you noticed? It's only
you that persists in the delusion that she's six years old.'

Josie began to cry. 'I can't help it,' she sobbed. 'She's all I've
got.'

Emma couldn't bring herself to put her arm round her
mother's heaving shoulders, so she talked instead. 'I'm only
moving five miles up the road. Just a couple of stops on the Tube,
that's all. I'm nearly nineteen now. I need peace and quiet to
work.' She gulped at her sherry, needing Dutch courage, then
added pompously, ludicrously, 'You have to understand, Ma, I'm
an *artist*.'

But Josie, not listening, continued to bewail her loss, her
daughter's disloyalty, incapable of either understanding or accepting Emma's need to break free.

The sherry made Emma sleepy. She packed her things for the
morning and got ready for bed, then went through her bag
throwing out all the old receipts, sticky sweet papers, grubby

hankies. She transferred her pills to her washbag, recalled the previous night with a quick glow of pleasure, then remembered Jay's parting words, the outrageous arrogance of the man. She frowned, then smiled. Outrageous or not, she thought, you screw like an angel, Hammond.

She found his folded note at the bottom of her bag and brought it out reluctantly, aware that it had been sharing space with Ricky's brooch. At the top was the Putney address and his telephone number. Below, in longhand, he had written, '*Come live with me and be my love.*' That was all, apart from his signature, the only untidy thing about him, a great looping aggressive scrawl across the page. She threw it in the bin with the rest of the rubbish, then undressed and climbed into bed.

Just before she turned the light out, she retrieved it, pushed it deep into the recesses of her bag, then dived beneath the bedclothes again and turned over to sleep.

College started the following week. Emma took Mabel over to Baron's Court at the weekend, mending fences, and made coffee while Mabel poked into cupboards and peered under the bed.

'Looking for my secret lover?' asked Emma from the kitchen, amused.

'Dust,' said Mabel shortly, puffed from bending, and Emma felt a twinge of sadness, thought how tired her aunt looked, how worn.

'Well, do you approve?'

'Bit small.' Mabel sniffed. 'But I suppose it'll do. How are you going to afford it?'

'Freelancing. I've enough put by to pay the rent for six months and I've already paid three in advance, so I'm covered until September.'

Mabel nodded briskly. 'Tell me if you need any help.'

'Thanks.' But I won't ask, and you know it. I'll go under rather than be beholden. Emma walked across the room to hug her aunt spontaneously, and wondered why everything was so much easier with Mabel. Was it because she didn't want to possess her, to smother her as Ma did? Poor Josie. Conscience niggled, told her she was cruel to her mother, that she ought to try harder, love her more. But oh, she did make it so difficult sometimes.

'Get off.' Mabel went pink with pleasure. 'I must go. Now don't forget to invite your mother over as soon as possible. And don't forget to eat properly or she'll make my life a misery.'

'Yes, Auntie Mabel. No, Auntie Mabel.'

'And don't be sarcastic either, young woman.'

They parted on better terms than they had managed for months, and they both knew that Josie wouldn't get to see the flat.

'Auntie Mabel,' Emma shouted down the stairs on impulse. 'Ask Adrian to call me, would you?'

She met Alison to pick up her grant cheque and they went for coffee. Ali was as high as a kite. She'd been to Foyles and bought a book of Expressionist landscapes.

'Wonderful prints!' she enthused. 'Fabulous colours!' They were glorious. Alison waved her hands about, gloating over red and turquoise sunsets, swirling blue and green seascapes, then they pored over them together, deciding which they would buy when they were rich. But Emma wondered, why all the excitement? After all, it was only a book. It took Alison twenty minutes to get to the point. 'I'm pregnant again. And this time only one candidate for father.'

'Have you told him?' Emma felt sick.

'Not yet. I was going to tell him yesterday but I didn't get the chance. I'm going to have this one, Em.'

'What will he say?'

'He'll look after me.' She was very sure of herself. 'I know he will. His wife knows all about me. He swore he'd tell her. He was going to leave her sometime anyway; he's just been waiting until his kids are older. We're going to get married.'

'So when are you going to break the news?'

'Dunno.' Alison lit her fourth cigarette. 'I've got to choose my moment. I shan't see him tonight, he's got to go to some dinner or other. Maybe tomorrow.'

'How far gone are you?'

'About six weeks. Oh, Em, I can't *wait* to see his face.'

She was delirious, glowing with vitality and happiness. Emma was aware of all the males in their vicinity watching her flushed, beautiful face, her golden hair, some surreptitiously, others in open admiration. She didn't doubt for one second that Alison had done it deliberately.

They had lunch in a sandwich bar on Oxford Street, then at Alison's insistence took the Tube to Notting Hill Gate and changed on to the District Line for home.

'I can't get used to not having you next door,' Ali complained.

'Neither can I,' said Emma, wiping her clammy hands on her jeans and wishing they had taken the bus.

Adrian was sitting on her stairs, chin resting on his knees, arms wrapped around his legs, in a dejected heap. He brightened visibly when he saw her. If he had been a cat he would have purred.

'Can I take you out?' He was eager for some sign that they were still a couple, that this wasn't the brush-off.

'Give me a break,' protested Emma, feeling nothing but irritation. 'I've only just had lunch.'

'Have another. Have three.'

She laughed. 'What is this? Is it because I was beastly to you? It's a plot, to make me die a horrible death from over-eating.'

Adrian nodded, taking his cue. 'I cannot tell a lie, I've lain awake night after night, plotting revenge for your callous ill-treatment of me, and this way is completely foolproof; they'll just think you were a piglet.'

'Shut up.' Emma forced herself to laugh again, wished he would go away. 'Come and have a cup of coffee.'

Her room was freezing. They sat huddled over the fire in their coats, as far apart as space would allow, eyeing each other warily over their mugs. They had lost whatever easy familiarity there had once been between them, and they both knew it.

'Well?' asked Adrian at last.

'Well what?'

'Well, are we on or are we off? I would rather like to know.'

'We're on.' So up yours, Jay Hammond, you arrogant bastard. 'I'm sorry about New Year. I didn't mean to spoil it, honestly, it was just—'

'It doesn't matter.' Adrian was ecstatic, granted a reprieve when he had thought she was going to send him packing. 'Really, it doesn't.' He moved along the floor to sit close beside her. 'Let's forget it, please?'

He went to kiss her, and she was willing enough, except that when their lips met she compared. And Adrian didn't make her feel anything, not after Jay. There was no plunging swoop of pleasure, no anticipation deep in her belly; there was no desire for more. It was pleasant, nothing else.

'Ohh,' he said, enjoying himself. 'That reminds me ...' he began to nuzzle her ear '... when do we get back on a more intimate footing?' Emma stiffened, leaning away from him, and he flinched. 'Not yet obviously. I don't suppose there's any chance of an explanation, is there? It's a bit hard on a chap all this.'

'You said it didn't matter.'

'I lied.' He moved reluctantly away from her and stared at his hands. 'Look, Em, if you'd rather not see me I wish you'd say. Then at least I'd know where I stand.'

Emma was hit by another wave of guilt; he was so *nice*. She leaned across and kissed him firmly on the mouth. 'Oh, Em,' he murmured, and she was in need of a little tender loving care ...

They spent the afternoon in bed. Emma, feeling Adrian's arousal, waited for him to kindle reciprocal desire in her and felt nothing, except increasing frustration. His hand was in slightly the wrong place, he moved slightly too early, or slightly too late. It just, she thought irritably, isn't *right*. She wondered as they rested afterwards why he didn't seem to notice whether she was satisfied too, since Jay had seemed to take it as part of his pleasure that she was.

She sent him home, pleading an early start in the morning, and blamed herself for the failure of their lovemaking. But she kissed him good-night on the landing and arranged to meet him at the weekend. Then she ran a very hot bath and soaked for an hour, washing him out of her system. She felt guiltily disencumbered by his absence, a weight lifted from her shoulders.

CHAPTER EIGHTEEN
• • •

Second term, second year of the degree course. Familiar faces, familiar places. Work is uncomplicated, and the hours pass swiftly when your head is full of stitching techniques, fabric repeats, deadlines.

Emma received a redirected letter offering her another commission. The money wouldn't make her rich but it would be steady, every week, and it took care of that nagging doubt about the rent. She splashed out on some coloured inks on her way in to college, and an easel so she could work on fabric designs at home in the evenings.

She didn't see Alison all morning, and she was tied up during the lunch-hour. By the time they left together, catching the bus at Emma's insistence, she was dying of curiosity. They stood near the exit, hanging on to the straps with their free hands, Alison with her folio tucked under her arm, Emma clutching her new easel, and they whispered.

'Well?'

'Well what?'

'Well, what did he say?'

'Nothing, absolutely nothing. I only saw him for five minutes, in the store cupboard, and I was just going to tell him when someone came in.'

Emma glanced at Alison's flat stomach, at the tightly cinched belt she was wearing, and wondered how long before she would start to bulge. She knew as much about pregnancy as she'd known about penises when she first started college. At least some of my knowledge has expanded since then, she thought, inappropriately amused. 'So when are you seeing him properly?'

'Tomorrow, he's coming round tomorrow night. He'll be thrilled, Em, you'll see. He loves kids.'

'I'm sure he does.' After all, he's sired three already.

'I wonder whether it'll be a boy or a girl? I'd like a girl I think; I don't know anything about boys.'

Emma pulled a face at her. 'Join the club.'

'I think I just have.' Ali began to giggle and she set Emma off. They spent the rest of the journey sniggering like a couple of schoolgirls. 'Come back with me,' pleaded Alison as they pulled into her stop. 'I could do with some company.'

'I can't.' Adrian might be around and Emma didn't want to run into him; he'd read too much into it. 'I've a commission to finish by tomorrow.'

She spent the evening hunched over her new easel, absorbed in her work. She slept well, peacefully, without dreams. She was on her own at last, free, utter bliss.

Alison wasn't in college on Friday, and Emma went out with Adrian that night, so she didn't get a chance to phone her. No news was good news anyway, she would have heard if anything was up. It was all right with Adrian: easy, uncomplicated, unexciting. He took her to bed, she stared at the ceiling analysing his performance and found it wanting. When she asked him to go he did, without complaint.

When she called Ali on Saturday morning the law student answered. No, she wasn't in, he said. No, he didn't know when she'd be back, she hadn't left a message.

Ali phoned early on Saturday afternoon, as Emma was on her way out. She and Adrian were going to feed the ducks in Hyde Park, with two bags full of stale bread and gloves to keep out the cold.

'I can't go.' Emma pushed her paper bag at him. 'Ali's not well.'

She had sounded terrible, barely coherent, just kept saying over and over, 'Can you come, Em? Please, can you come?' and sobbing.

Adrian's patient sweetness slipped. 'I'll go on my own if you won't come with me,' he said huffily. It was just an excuse, he could tell. Emma was slipping away from him and he didn't know why.

'It's not that I won't; I can't. Ali needs me.'

They parted coolly, Adrian staying on the bus when they got to Earl's Court, and Emma walking along the familiar street with a sinking feeling in the pit of her stomach that grew as she rounded the corner and covered the last few yards to the front step. She had a flash of memory, of the last time she and Ricky had sat together on the stairs, crying in each other's arms. She missed him, painfully.

Alison's door was ajar but her curtains were still pulled, and she was in her dressing-gown. She had taken all her clothes out of the drawers and cupboards, then flung them around in a fit of impotent rage. The room smelled of unwashed bedding and stale cigarette smoke.

Emma pulled the curtains back and put the kettle on, then picked up all the clothes, folded them as best she could, and put them away. Alison lay with her face to the wall, scrunched up like a dead cat, and ignored her. Emma made coffee then rummaged under the sink for the bottle of expensive brandy Ali kept there for Harry and poured a generous slug into the cup. Then she took it across the room and rolled Alison over. She was stiff, her limbs curled as if in rigor mortis; Emma shook her.

'Here, drink this.'

Alison unwound herself and sat up obediently. She looked ugly, all her beauty washed away by hours of crying: swollen puffy eyes, cheeks blotched with tears, a dribble of saliva oozing from her mouth and down her chin. She wiped it away with the back of her hand and took the cup carefully in unsteady hands; the brandy made her gag. Emma sat next to her on the bed and waited.

She got almost to the bottom of the cup before she began to talk. 'He doesn't want the baby. He isn't going to marry me. He isn't even going to leave his wife. He says I can get rid of it, or I can keep it. He says he doesn't care which. He'll pay for an abortion, but if I keep it, he'll disown it. Do you know what else he said?' She laughed, high-pitched, hysterical. 'He said, "I'm a respectable married man and it'll be your word against mine."'

'But it wouldn't be. I'm a witness. And there must be dozens of others who know what's been going on.'

Alison's eyes filled with tears. They oozed between her red, swollen lids and ran down her face. Her nose dripped. 'There's no point.' She wiped it on her sleeve, leaving a silver snail-trail along the cuff. 'Don't you see, he doesn't want it. He doesn't want *me*. There's no reason for having it now. I only got pregnant because I thought … I thought …' She tailed off into silence, into more tears. 'You'll have to ring the clinic for me, Em. I can't face it, not on my own.'

Emma sat beside her on the bed and held her while she wept, leaving a large, damp patch on her shoulder, then found her a pile of hankies and rifled through the dressing-table for the address of the abortion clinic. She knew roughly where it was; Alison kept it in her top drawer, along with her contraceptive pills. Belt-and-braces she'd called it, laughing. Some joke.

It was cold, standing in the hall listening to the phone ring, and when Emma got through there was only a receptionist on duty.

'The consultant won't be here until Monday,' she said, disapproving. 'No, I don't know when he can fit you in. No, I don't know how much it'll cost. I don't deal with that sort of thing. I'm just a temp. You'll have to phone back Monday.'

Emma borrowed the spare blanket, added a couple of coats and slept in the armchair, afraid to leave Alison alone.

As she was slipping out for milk on Sunday morning she ran into Mabel coming in. 'Ali's ill,' she lied. 'Flu I think.'

Mabel sniffed. 'Flu my eye. I heard them on Friday night, bellowing at each other. The girl's a fool.' She tucked her chin in, puffed out her ample chest and harrumphed on her way upstairs. 'Let me know if there's anything I can do.' She'd tried interfering once and it had been a disaster. From now on if anyone wanted help they'd have to ask for it. Alison's problems were Alison's problems. She left Emma staring open-mouthed at her stout legs moving stolidly up the stairs, wondering whether she knew her aunt at all.

Emma didn't see Adrian watching her from the basement window when she came back with the milk and two packets of cigarettes. She stayed with Alison all day, tending her with endless cups of tea and just listening.

'What do you think, Em, maybe I should talk to him again? After all, it must have been a terrible shock for him.'

A cigarette, another cup of tea.

'Do you think I should go and see his wife? I'm sure she's putting pressure on him. I know he'd have been okay about it if it wasn't for her.'

Another cigarette, more tears, another cup of tea.

'Do you think I should ring and apologise? Maybe I was taking too much for granted? Maybe if I tell him I'm sorry?'

Sorry for what, for getting involved with the creep in the first place?

On the second night Emma waited until Alison finally fell into an exhausted sleep, then went downstairs to see Adrian and ease her nagging conscience.

Bill came to the door doing up his fly, half dressed, embarrassed, and she caught a glimpse of a naked man, a stranger, diving for cover behind him.

'Hello, darling, what a surprise.'

'I can see that. Sorry, Bill.' Emma was embarrassed too, as if she'd actually caught him in the act. 'It was Adrian I wanted. Is he in?' Stupid question, you'd hardly be prancing around nude in the hall if he was.

'They're all out, all except, um, me.' Bill began to button his shirt, pull himself together. 'Have a good holiday?'

'Yes thanks, you?'

'Mmm. Everything all right with you and Adrian?'

'Yes, fine. Why?'

'No reason, just like to know my favourite girl's okay. Any message?'

Emma shook her head, backed away towards the area steps, hesitated. 'Just tell him I was here, will you? See you, Bill.'

Emma was late for college on Monday. She had to wait until nine o'clock to phone the clinic and make an appointment in Alison's name. Ali seemed calmer once it was done, relieved that a decision had been made.

'I'll phone you at lunchtime, okay? *Ali!* Is that okay?'

'Yeah. Yeah, fine. Thanks, Em.'

She was on her way out when the phone rang, and Alison leaped up, galvanised into life. 'It'll be for me. It'll be Harry.' She barged past Emma to get to the phone and her face lit up. 'It's him,' she mouthed and Emma felt better about leaving her. Thank God, it was going to be all right, after all.

Once the day had started Emma lost herself, as she almost always did when she was working. There was no reply when she phoned Ali at lunchtime. Good, she thought, out with Harry, and relaxed a little.

She spent the afternoon in the cutting-room, working on a *toile* that had to be finished by the end of the week, then around four she remembered the work she had left untackled at home, panicked, and took Bill to one side. They had exchanged only a brief greeting so far, both uncomfortable that she had caught him out the day before.

'Do me a favour, Bill? Check on Ali for me when you get in? She's not very well. I'd do it myself, but I've got to get home, I'm all behind with a commission. Tell her I'll ring around seven to make sure she's all right.'

She started work as soon as she got home, keeping herself going with a packet of chocolate biscuits and six slices of Hovis spread thickly with butter and Shippam's sardine and tomato paste. It was nearer eight than seven when she finally made it to the phone, and there was no reply. Ali must be with Harry. Or maybe Bill had taken her out for a drink to cheer her up, or for a meal. She'd be hungry by now. She plodded back upstairs to work for another hour before she tried again.

She didn't recognise the voice. 'Who is this?'

'Penny.'

'Penny who? Which room are you in?'

'Room two,' said the voice and Emma said, 'Oh,' rather blankly. That was her old room. 'Well, could you knock on Ali's door, number one, for me, please?'

There was a pause, then Penny again, hesitant, slightly higher-pitched than before. 'Ah. Can't, I'm afraid. She's ill.' A pause. 'Actually they've carted her off to hospital.'

'What?' Emma felt suddenly chilly. A goose walked over her grave and her skin tingled.

'They've taken her to hospital,' the girl repeated. Her voice was flat, monotonous.

'Which hospital?'

'Dunno . . . Um . . .'

Emma's patience frayed at her stupidity. 'Get Auntie Mabel then.'

'Who?'

'Auntie Mabel!' Emma shouted. 'Miss Bentley! Your landlady!' Stupid cow.

'Oh. Oh no, I can't. She's not here either. She went with the ambulance.'

'George then, or Bill.' Emma hesitated. 'Or Adrian. Any of the boys in the basement.'

'Who?'

Emma counted to ten. 'The basement. Go and get someone from the basement.'

'Oh, right, hang on.'

She heard the phone clatter as the silly bitch put it down, then her footsteps receding. She leaned against the wall, listening to the blood thumping in her ears and closed her eyes. Don't panic. It'll be something silly, too much booze or flu or something.

Penny returned. 'There is someone there, but he says he's only just got in and could you ring back later?'

'Who was it?'

'Who was who?'

Emma gritted her teeth. 'Who was it you just spoke to?' You stupid, cretinous, half-witted apology for a human being.

'Oh. Don't know his name. Er, thin, mousy hair, about five foot ten?' Emma slammed the phone down. If he'd just got in, Adrian wouldn't know anything anyway.

She sat on the stairs and went through the phone book. Western Hospital, that was the nearest. 'No, no one of that name has been admitted.' Hammersmith Hospital. The receptionist there didn't know. 'There's been an accident on the flyover this afternoon and we've had a lot of casualties. What's she in for?'

'I don't know,' said Emma helplessly. She couldn't think who else to try so she sat on the stairs in the dark until after ten. Then she tried again; surely there must be someone there by now.

The phone was picked up almost immediately.

'Where've you been?' Emma shouted into the handset. 'What's going on? I've been frantic.' The silence lasted so long she thought she'd been cut off and began to bellow '*Hello? Hello?*' into the mouthpiece.

'Hello, Emma dear. Look, um, look, it's Alison ...' Mabel's voice, sounding as if she was five hundred years old, talking in slow motion, as if Emma was deaf or retarded.

'I know it's Alison. That girl, the one in my room, she said – what's happened? Is she all right? Where is she?'

Another pause, then Mabel, wearily, 'Sit down, dear.'

'What?'

'Sit down, Emma.'

'All right, now tell me.'

'She's dead, dear.'

'Dead? Who's dead?'

'Alison, dear.'

Emma understood then why Mabel had told her to sit down. She suddenly discovered that her legs wouldn't hold her up, and she slid down the wall to land with a thump on the stair. The goose galloped over her grave again, with hobnailed boots on; she felt suddenly freezing cold.

'Emma! Emma, are you there?'

She nodded, then thought, don't be silly, she can't see you nodding and said, 'Yes.' Her voice sounded peculiar and her teeth chattered. 'Auntie Mabel?'

'Yes, dear?'

'She can't be dead. I only left her this morning. She was fine. Well, not fine exactly, but she was all right ...' Oh God, she was talking to Harry Passmore.

'I'm sorry, dear,' said Mabel. 'Bill found her. About six. She'd taken some pills, they think, and some brandy. Emma, how much brandy did she have left when you were here?'

'Lots.' There was lots, the bottle was three-quarters full when I left.

'Only, the police will want to know.'

'Police?' The conversation drifted into the surreal. 'What police?'

'In cases of suicide, dear, you know—'

'Suicide?' Emma didn't believe it. 'Don't be silly, Auntie Mabel. Ali wouldn't commit suicide. You know what she's like. You know Ali. She couldn't.' She screwed up her eyes, fighting the nausea that was threatening to swamp her, swallowing the lump in her throat that was constricting her breathing.

'She has, dear. Emma, call a taxi and come over here, then you won't be on your own. You can sleep in my—'

'*No!*' That sounded too vehement, she mustn't hurt Auntie Mabel's feelings. 'No, it's all right, I'll go to bed. I can't, um, I can't face ... I'm tired, Auntie Mabel. I'll ring you tomorrow. okay?'

'All right.' Mabel sounded resigned, too exhausted to argue. 'Shall I get Adrian to—'

'No!'

'All right, dear.'

Emma stayed where she was. She was freezing cold but it seemed easier to sit than to move. She could hear her own voice every now and then, silly, whimpering noises, and she was vaguely aware that she was rocking rhythmically backwards and forwards on the stair, her hands clenched into fists and pushed into her mouth to stop her teeth clattering. Somebody clambered over her at some stage and asked if she was all right. 'Yes,' she said, 'I'm fine,' and nodded vigorously to prove it.

It was an hour before she moved. By the time she had climbed the single flight of stairs to her room she felt as if she had climbed Mount Everest without oxygen. It was hot – she'd left the gas fire on when she went out – but she was still cold. She huddled over the heat in a state of shock.

It couldn't possibly be true; it had to be a mistake. 'She was all right,' she said aloud, her voice echoing unpleasantly in her ears. 'She was all right when I left.'

But you should have stayed to make sure; you knew she was miserable.

Miserable doesn't mean suicidal; she wasn't suicidal.

She's dead though, isn't she? Not just dead miserable, she's dead. And I'm so *cold*.

She thought she'd go to bed, but she couldn't bear the thought of undressing, so she stayed where she was.

She came to with a start at around three, lying on her side with her mouth open in front of the dead fire, and for a moment she had no idea where she was. She was freezing.

It took her minutes on end to find her big bag and tip the contents out all over the carpet to find some shillings so she could feed the meter. She lit the fire with hands that trembled uncontrollably and crouched over it trying to keep warm while she shovelled her bits and pieces back into her bag. She avoided looking at Ricky's brooch, deliberately pushed it deep down so she couldn't see it. It was too close, reminded her of Alison and what had so suddenly, so brutally, gone from her life.

Right at the bottom of the untidy pile was a folded piece of paper. She couldn't think what it was.

'*Come live with me and be my love.*'

She stared at it stupidly, then crumpled it into a ball and threw it across the room at the waste-paper basket. It missed.

She glared at it for twenty minutes before she retrieved it. It took her another half an hour to get as far as the landing, to dial his number, and she was just about to put the phone down when he answered.

'Jay Hammond.' He sounded sleepy and annoyed.

Emma stared helplessly at the mouthpiece.

'Who is this?'

'. . . Jay?'

There was a long silence, then he said sharply, 'Em? Is that you, Em? Say something! Emma?'

'I . . . It's . . . me.'

'Where are you?'

'Here.'

She heard him sigh. 'Where's here? Are you at home? Emma!'

She nodded stupidly.

'Emma, are you at home? Just say yes or no.' His voice took on the timbre people use to talk to small children and idiots.

'Yes.'

'I'm on my way,' he said, and put the phone down.

She was still sitting on the stairs when he arrived but she didn't hear him coming. He paused on the landing below, and stood looking up at her white, hunched figure, his face distorted with loneliness and covetous longing. Then he climbed the stairs and bent over her, touching her shoulder lightly so as not to startle her. When she raised her eyes his face was calm, shuttered.

It was nearly four. He picked her up and carried her up the stairs to her stifling room, laid her carefully on the bed and turned off the fire. She sat up, drawing her knees into her chin.

'I'm sorry,' she said. 'I didn't mean you to come all this way. I just ...' She rubbed her nose with the back of her hand, scratched the side of her face where she'd been leaning against the wall. 'I just needed to talk to somebody.' No, not somebody, you. For some obscure reason I wanted to hear your voice. Nobody else's, just yours. 'She's dead,' she added loudly, meaning to shock. 'Alison's dead.'

She caught the disbelief on his face, in his voice when he said soothingly, 'You've been dreaming.' She wiped her tired, stinging eyes with her fingers. He stared hard, then came and sat on the bed beside her, his weight distorting the cheap mattress, tumbling her towards him. He pulled her in close against his thick woollen sweater, wrapping one arm round her waist, the other round her shoulder, and she leaned gratefully into his warmth. He didn't ask any questions.

She went to sleep almost immediately, and he sat perfectly still, watching her as the room cooled down. When she stirred he stroked her forehead or her hair to comfort her, and when it grew so cold he thought it would wake her, he dragged the blankets from the bed and wrapped them round her as best he could. He listened to her breathing and watched the night sky lighten outside.

The police came at eight.

Emma woke with a start when the banging began. Jay unfolded himself stiffly from the bed and went to open the door. On the landing, looking harassed, stood a sergeant and a woman constable. They seemed disconcerted to see him.

'Miss Versey?'

'Do I look like Miss Versey?'

The sergeant was middle-aged, plump and out of condition. He was sweating from the stairs and he didn't need any smart-alec remarks. Jay stood back and ushered them in, then waved an elegant hand at the white-faced crumpled mound of blankets on the bed.

'Miss Versey,' he said sarcastically, as if, thought the sergeant, he couldn't have worked that one out for himself. Smarmy bugger.

'Morning, Miss.' He hated these jobs. This one looked terrible, but at least they didn't have to break the news... Someone else had clearly done that. 'Apologies for calling so early, Miss, but we've got to get a report in as soon as possible. If we might just ask you a few questions?' His sonorous voice rolled around the room and Emma stared at him, confused. What a noisy man.

Poor little thing, the female constable thought, only looks about fifteen. She'd come to the conclusion it didn't pay to be clever really. More suicides to the square inch with all those brainboxes at London University than pigeons in Trafalgar Square. First one they'd had from the Art School though.

She hovered uncertainly, waiting for the Sarge to tell her what to do, then when no one said anything crossed the room to sit down. The girl sitting on the other end of the bed bobbed gently in unison with her as she lowered her weight, then closed her eyes. The freckles stood out brown on her white skin, as if someone had spattered her with paint. The constable noted with interest that they weren't just sprinkled across her nose, they were all over, arms as well, what she could see of them. She'd always fancied a few freckles, but not that many. Went with that red hair, she supposed, sticking up all wispy round the kid's head and escaping from its thick plait. Pretty girl, if she wasn't quite so corpse-like. The constable shifted her weight, trying not to bounce, and settled herself more comfortably. Not as corpse-like as that other one though. Genuine article that one had been.

She suppressed an unsuitable smile at her little joke, thinking how hard she was getting, then noticed the dark man watching her as if he knew what she was thinking and made a big thing of finding her pencil, embarrassed by his unblinking gaze. Cool customer that one.

'And who are we, Sir?'

'We are a friend.'

Jay lowered his head to rest on his hand, raised a sardonic eyebrow, implied that the sergeant wasn't doing too well so far. The sergeant bristled, couldn't stand these stuck-up, intellectual types. He treated Jay to his interrogation stare and Jay stared back, impassive. The sergeant looked away. Bloody Clever-Dick, he thought, surprisingly intimidated.

He wanted to know everything. 'How long had you known the deceased? What time did you last see her? What sort of state was she in when you left?'

'All right,' said Emma, 'she was all right when I left. She was better. She was smiling.'

'And why was that, Miss?'

'Because he phoned, just as I was leaving, so I thought ... I thought it was going to be all right.' She peered around the room, looking for some familiar landmark to focus on, finding only a strange place that she wasn't used to, didn't know. She latched on to Jay's feet, still in a pair of soft, indoor moccasins stained dark on the soles with wet. She wondered if he was wearing pyjamas beneath his jumper and jeans, remembered that he didn't wear anything in bed, and felt an unexpected, unsuitable stab of lust. Here was Alison lying stone-cold dead somewhere and she was thinking about sex. She felt the colour flooding her cheeks and lowered her head hurriedly.

'And what was it that was going to be all right, Miss?' The sergeant's equilibrium was restored now he was on familiar territory. He moved slightly, deliberately blocking Jay's view of Emma.

'Well, you see ...' Emma stopped, frowned at him. 'I don't know that this is any of your ...' It's none of your business, standing there with your fat red face, asking questions about Alison's private life.

He shifted tack. 'Did she have any reason to be depressed, Miss?' They often clammed up, realised they were talking to complete strangers and suddenly wondered why they were doing it. It was a case of roundabouts, you got your information in the end, but sometimes by a roundabout route. The sergeant was a patient man.

'Who was it phoned, her boyfriend?' Put some ideas in her head, give her a prod.

'Yes, her boyfriend.'

'So they'd had a tiff, had they? She and the boyfriend?' Have to spell it out, otherwise they lost the track sometimes.

'Well, sort of. Yes, I suppose so. She was pregnant.' Oh, thought Emma, I didn't mean to say that. Ali wouldn't want everyone to know that.

'Ah,' said the sergeant heavily, and glanced meaningfully at the constable, who was dutifully scribbling copious notes in her little book. 'Tell us about the boyfriend, Miss.'

A spasm of rage swept Emma and she told them. 'He's a tutor, at our, at my college. He's married, with three children. He promised her, she told me, promised! And then he went back on it, said it was her word against his and—'

'Whoa, Miss, one thing at a time, if you please. Now, let's start again at the beginning, shall we? Let's have the gentleman's name.'

It went on for hours, question, answer, question, answer, until Emma forgot what she had told them, repeated herself, began to muddle dates, names, and Jay rose and said peremptorily, 'That's enough.'

He placed himself between Emma and the sergeant, shoved his hands in the pockets of his jeans and stared the man down, daring him to ask another question. Then he leaned across and took the constable's notebook from her protesting hand, flipped it over until he found a clean page, wrote swiftly and held it out to the sergeant.

'Miss Versey is suffering from shock; I'm taking her back to my place for a few days. If you have any more questions you can contact her there. Perhaps you would let her aunt, Miss Bentley, know where she is. My telephone number's on there as well. All right?'

'Your name, Sir, I must have your name.' The sergeant was sweating again. Arrogant, jumped-up young pup ... Who does he think he is?

'It's on there.' Jay waved his hand at the notebook, sent the sergeant's blood pressure up another point.

'Ah.' The sergeant peered suspiciously at Jay's sprawling signature. 'Right. In that case, we'll not trouble you any further, Miss.' He had to peer round the man to address the girl, and his spleen rose again. 'For the moment, that is.' Just let me catch you speeding, Smarty Pants. I'll throw the bloody book at you. The constable stood up.

Jay closed the door behind them, listened for a moment to the sound of their footsteps retreating down the stairs, then said, more to himself than to Emma, 'Clean clothes,' and wandered off towards the cupboard. She heard him ferreting around, watched as he moved about the room, her half-full rucksack in his hand. He found jeans, a jumper, underwear, even her nightgown, retrieved her washbag from the bathroom, toothbrush, flannel, shoved it all into the rucksack, then dumped it by the door and came back for her.

'Right,' he said briskly. 'Let's go.'

She did as she was told, followed him meekly down the stairs and sat in his car while he stowed her stuff in the back. Then she closed her eyes and went instantly to sleep, waking with a start only when he killed the engine in the car-park outside his flat.

She couldn't manage the stairs but when Jay hauled her up and led her to the lift she jibbed at it, shook her head and said in a dried-up, throaty whisper, 'I can't.' So he carried her, long legs dangling, dead weight, resting on the landings, all the way up to the third floor, then propped her carefully against the wall while he found his keys and caught his breath, pushing his hair out of his eyes, sweating. Then he carried her again, to his bedroom.

He undressed her as if she was a small child, unplaited her hair and put her to bed. It felt nice: clean sheets, warm blankets. She felt the movement beneath her as he sat on its edge, then his fingers, cool on her forehead, stroking. She ought to say thank you. She would in a minute, when she could summon up the energy, she'd just lie still for a moment.

When she woke, he was sitting in exactly the same place, as if he hadn't moved.

'What's the time?' she asked, turning her head towards the window and blinking at the bright light.

'Nine. I have to go out. I'll be back at lunchtime.'

'Nine?' Lunchtime? Nine in the morning? How could it be nine in the morning? 'What day is it?'

'Wednesday.'

Emma lay still, frowning heavily, while she worked it out. That meant she had slept almost twenty-four hours. She couldn't have. 'It can't be.'

Jay laughed at her. 'Need anything, sleepyhead?'

She shook her head, remembered him unplaiting her hair yesterday, the brief surge of libidinous pleasure his fingers had caused.

'I'm sorry,' she said.

'What for?'

'For involving you in all this.'

He shrugged. 'Coffee?'

He brought her coffee in a brown earthenware mug and she sat up to drink it, clutching the sheets tight around her naked breasts. He laughed at her.

'Don't worry, your virtue is intact this time. You ought to take your pill though. They're in the bathroom.'

She was shocked, that he could think about her pills when Alison was dead. It was almost as bad as wanting sex because your hair was being unplaited.

'I've left you a key,' he went on. 'It's on the hall table, but unless you have to go out I should stay here; the police will be back, either today or tomorrow. I must go.'

He leaned across and kissed her cheek. Emma was tempted to turn her face so he would kiss her mouth, but she didn't. Alison was dead.

'See you later.' He rose and moved towards the door.

'Jay?'

He paused, waiting.

'Thank you.'

'For what?'

'For being there when I needed you.' Why was it you I needed? Why wasn't it nice, kind, dependable Adrian, or Auntie Mabel. Why didn't I yell for my mother, or . . .? She pushed the thought away.

He laughed at her again. 'Pure self-interest,' he said calmly, then blew her a kiss with his fingers and disappeared.

She lay and listened, heard the front door, strained her ears, tried and failed to hear his car starting, then turned over and went back to sleep.

Later, she had a bath, washed her hair and felt better, dressed in jeans and a sweater. The flat was warm, silent, only the faint hum of the traffic below disturbing the quiet. She wandered from room to room with her damp hair hanging down her back, prying into his things, his books and music, pushing Alison to the periphery of her mind to be dealt with later.

He'd slept on the sofa; his bedding was stacked neatly against the sitting-room wall – blankets, two pillows. She caught her breath again as a trickle of remembered pleasure ran down her spine. He could have shared her bed. Now that *would* have been comforting. The thought reminded her that she hadn't taken her pill and she padded back to the bathroom, silent in her bare feet.

How, she wondered, could she have failed to register when she'd bathed that he'd laid her things out as if she lived there: her toothbrush cosying up to his in the glass; flannels overlapping, cuddling over the rail by the basin; pills laid neatly on the shelf below the mirror next to his razor? Cut and thrust, she thought in swift, involuntary word association, and crossed her legs, enjoying the sensation despite herself.

Her mood swung. Arrogant bastard, taking me for granted, making assumptions. I'll show you; I'll go home. She found her washbag, tucked neatly in the cupboard next to his, flung things angrily into it, then jumped when the phone rang and dropped it upside down on the floor.

'Damn . . . Hello?'

'You all right?' She could hear people, voices, glasses clinking in the background.

'Yes, fine.' Where are you, you arrogant bastard? What do you do with your life when you're not rescuing maidens in distress out of pure self-interest?

'I'll be home in an hour.' He rang off.

As she put the phone down it rang again; she thought it was Jay and said, 'What?' in aggrieved tones, but the voice was impersonal, unfamiliar.

'Miss Versey?'

'Yes.'

'Sergeant—'

Her heart jolted in her chest. She didn't hear his surname, she was busy panicking.

'Just a few more questions, Miss, then that'll be all until the inquest.'

Emma gulped. 'Inquest, what inquest?'

'There'll have to be a post-mortem, Miss, and then an inquest. It's the law when a death isn't . . .' the sergeant coughed tactfully, cleared his throat '. . . straightforward, so to speak. They'll need you to give evidence to the Coroner, Miss, being one of the last to see her alive, if you get my drift.'

'Oh!' said Emma blankly and it all came flooding back.

When Jay walked through the door she was sitting on the floor in the hall by the telephone, her head buried in her arms, knees drawn up tight.

'Something wrong with my sofa?'

'No. No, I was just on the telephone.' Just on the telephone an hour ago and I haven't moved since because the policeman on the other end was talking about cutting Alison up and I had a sudden vision of that beautiful girl lying on a slab, like the sides of beef one sees at the butcher's, while somebody fished around inside her to see what they could find, held up bits of her for inspection.

'Who was it?'

'Who?'

Jay sighed, slid down the wall to sit beside her. 'Who was it on the phone?'

'The police.'

'Ah. Are you going to tell me about it?'

She related it in fits and starts because her voice kept letting her down. Then the word for cutting people up and depositing bits of them in specimen jars deserted her.

'Autopsy?'

'Post-mortem,' she remembered. 'And when they've finished with her there'll be an inquest. I'm supposed to be the star witness. Fame at last.'

Her own levity made her sick, she felt as if she was personally responsible for the whole thing. It occurred to her suddenly that she *was* responsible. It was all her fault. If she'd been there she could have stopped it happening.

'Standard procedure,' said Jay, watching her face. He rose, pulled her to her feet, stood for a moment quite still, holding her hands, very close. She smelled his skin, needed him to take her in his arms and wrap her up in his warmth. 'Lunch,' he said briskly and walked away.

Emma was embarrassingly, disgustingly hungry, ate everything he put in front of her, then asked for cheese, ate it in chunks without bread or biscuits. 'If I'd known I was feeding the five thousand,' said Jay, amused, 'I'd have laid on extra loaves and fishes.' When Emma smiled she found her cheeks were stiff, the muscles unused for two, three days.

The police arrived shortly afterwards and wiped the levity from her face very effectively.

The questions were the same as yesterday, with the added dimension that they had found an empty bottle of sleeping tablets in Alison's room.

'Have you ever seen this bottle before, Miss?'

'No, Ali's never taken sleeping pills. She never needed them.'

'Do you know anything about the appointment Miss Brown made with a clinic in Stanmore?'

'Yes.' Emma shifted uncomfortably. God, it *was* all her fault. 'I made it for her.'

'And did you know that Miss Brown cancelled it on the Monday morning?'

'What?'

'The day she killed herself,' the sergeant added helpfully, as if Emma could possibly miss the significance.

'No, I didn't.'

'And can you explain the empty bottle of brandy in her room?'

'Empty? God!'

It all went into the notebooks. How many boyfriends had she had? Did Emma know of any other problems she might have had: money worries, family tensions?

'It's all relevant,' said the sergeant, 'all contributes to the picture, Miss.'

It was after three when they left and Emma was shattered. Jay made her coffee and sat with her on the sofa, waiting.

'It's my fault, you know.'

'Oh? You got her pregnant, did you, and then chucked her? Shame on you, Em. How could you do such a thing?'

'Shut up. I should have gone back at lunchtime on Monday. I nearly did, but then I got busy, no, that's not true, I was enjoying myself. I was on my own and I didn't want to spoil it. I thought she'd be all right so I left it. If I'd gone back I might have found her in time, and I should have taken the bottle of brandy away. I should have told Auntie Mabel. She would have sat with her. She would have been all right if I'd gone back, if I'd stayed a bit longer, if I'd waited.' She paused for breath. 'Oh, God.'

Jay ridiculed her. 'And supposing you had, supposing you'd done all those things. Supposing you'd saved her? Then what would you have done, stayed with her for the next three weeks, three months? Don't be naïve. If you want someone to blame, blame Passmore. He was old enough to know better. Or blame Alison. She knew what she was doing when she got herself into it.'

'I'm going home,' said Emma angrily, hating him for his hardheaded logic. 'I don't want to talk about it any more,' and she struggled up from the sofa, making for the bathroom and her things. Jay made no attempt to stop her, but when she got there he had picked everything up from the floor and put it all back, the toothbrush, her flannel, her pills, all laid out neatly as if she had never touched them. Her temper rose anew, she flung everything topsy-turvy into her rucksack, then flounced out into the hall to get her coat. Jay was leaning against the wall by the sitting-room door with his arms folded.

'Thank you,' she said, adding silently, you supercilious bastard.

'You're welcome.'

As she passed him, it occurred to her that she was being churlish and ungrateful, and she hesitated. 'Really,' she repeated, 'thank you. I'm very grateful, honestly,' and she reached up to kiss his cheek.

'Honestly?' He smiled and turned his face at the last minute, doing what she had almost done that morning, so that she kissed him inadvertently full on the mouth.

It was hopeless. Once she'd started she couldn't stop; her arms went round his neck and she pressed herself hard against him, hungry for physical comfort, for sex. She wanted what she had discovered with him before, what only he could provide. *Catching*, he had said, likening sexual desire to the common cold.

He wasn't expecting her. She caught him off-balance, knocked him backwards against the wall, then slid down helplessly to land with a thump on top of him. He grunted, and his breath, forcibly expelled from his lungs, whistled past her ear.

'Ah! Ow, you're – get your knee out of my balls, for God's sake! Em, what are you do— Emma!'

She was triumphant. She had him now, stretched out breathless beneath her, and when he found his voice and gasped, 'Ow! God ... Ouch! Emma, don't ... !' She found herself doing things she had never done before.

'No, oh ... no, don't stop ...' He relaxed, let her, encouraged her. 'There, oh, yes, do that some more...' Finally, heaving beneath her hand, he groaned, dropped his head against her shoulder and murmured, 'Ahhh ...'

'Oh!' she exclaimed, caught by surprise.

They lay still for a few minutes, Emma wildly keyed up, waiting for something but she wasn't sure what, Jay relaxed again, limp, and then she felt his fingers at the waistband of her jeans. 'Your turn,' he murmured in her ear, and chuckled.

This, she thought later, as she lay with arms and legs akimbo on the hall floor, this delight, this skin-tingling, bone-melting pleasure, is as contagious, as compulsive as drugs, as alcohol, as gambling, all the vices rolled into one. Only better. And I seem to have lost the use of my legs.

When she turned her head to look at Jay she burst out laughing. His top half was respectable, if crumpled – shirt, tie, sweater – his bottom half naked to the shins, where his trousers were concertinaed around his ankles. He was still wearing his socks and shoes.

'It's no good laughing at me.' He was unfazed by her derision. 'Take a look at yourself.'

She lowered her chin to her chest, said, 'Oh!' and began to giggle. Her T-shirt, rucked up under her arms, exposed half a white bra, one pink-tipped breast standing proud, then below that naked skin, hollow belly, protruding hip-bones, a red triangle of pubic hair, long legs splayed out in an attitude of complete abandonment and the whole finished off with a pair of black and white striped socks. She brought her legs together with a thud, then blushed scarlet in sudden, excruciating embarrassment as Jay leaned across to kiss her exposed nipple and pop her bosom neatly back into its lacy cup, tidying her up. Just moving her legs exhausted her.

Then, unexpectedly, his face twisted as if he hurt inside and he bent his head to whisper, 'Stay with me, Emma . . . please?'

He ran a bath, poured liberal amounts of Radox, then picked her up, carried her to the bathroom, staggering under her weight with post-coital lassitude, and finished undressing her.

'God,' he murmured as he dumped her unceremoniously in the bath, 'I think my arms are about to fall off.' Then he shed the last of his clothes and climbed in after her. When they were no longer sticky, he took her to bed, wrapped her in his arms and held her until she slept – about thirty seconds.

When she woke in the early hours Emma was warm, hungry, disoriented. She lay listening to her stomach rumble, staring at the lights from the street below making shifting traceries on the ceiling. It was raining and the drops ran sideways above her head, magnified in reflection, flickering and rippling.

She turned to look at her sleeping companion, watching the patterns playing on his face in the half-light. He was lying on his side, dark lashes shadowing his cheeks, resting his head on his hands like a child and he looked different, younger, vulnerable. When she reached out a tentative hand to touch, he opened startled eyes, then smiled sleepily, a slow, affectionate twist of his mouth, none of the usual sarcasm.

'Hello,' he said. 'I thought you were going home.'

She smiled in return. 'So did I. You appear to be irresistible.'

'Good.' He grunted, mumbled, rolled over and presented his back to her. 'Em?'

'Mmm?'

'I love you.' Then he slept again and Emma lay, head pressed to the pillow, heart pounding, staring in terror at his dark head.

Oh Lord, what have I got myself into? 'Don't say that,' she begged his dormant figure. 'Please don't say that,' but he was deaf to her entreaties, comatose. So what to do, run away? She sighed, the terror subsiding. Much easier to burrow down beside him and go to sleep. Tomorrow, she thought, I'll run away tomorrow.

He was a generous lover. He led her into raptures she had never felt before, and she responded voraciously, took what he offered like a greedy child in a sweet factory, always craving more.

But you can't make me love you, she taunted him silently; this is sex, sex with a capital S, but still just sex.

Just sex? It was voluptuous delight. It was hopelessly, deliriously addictive. She should have listened to the doctor at the Brook Advisory Centre who had lectured her all those months ago about the dangers of promiscuity.

It was three days before she remembered Mabel.

'Where on earth are you? I've been worried sick.'

'Didn't the police tell you?'

'Yes, the police told me, gave me some address in Putney and the name of a man I'd never heard of. That doesn't tell me where you are, or . . .' pause, then, sounding distraught, 'what you're up to.'

'I'm staying . . .' Emma hesitated, glanced across to the kitchen where Jay was standing, leaning against the doorjamb. Why did he never stand up straight? He was always propping himself up against something. 'I'm staying with a friend.' A grin from Jay, an inappropriate, suggestive one. 'I didn't want to be on my own and I – I couldn't bear to come back to – to . . .' Her eyes filled suddenly, irritatingly, with tears, and Jay wiped the smile from his face, uncoiled himself from the doorway, poised to hold, to comfort her. Emma felt threatened by the movement; he was breaking down her walls, chipping away at the cement, demolishing her barriers brick by brick. She must go home before it was too late.

'What friend?' Mabel wasn't finished with her.

'Um, you don't know him, Auntie Mabel.' Change the subject. 'Is Bill okay?' It must be so much worse for Bill, he'd found her.

'He hasn't gone back to college yet, if that's what you mean. Says he can't face it.'

Oh, thought Emma, is that my fault too? And college, I'd forgotten college. How could I have forgotten college?

'That frightful Brown person's been here again.' Wild ridiculous hope flared. Oh, Ricky! 'Been kicking up a stink, wanted to know where you were ...'

So, how do you propose to handle that, Emma Versey, Rick returned and you still warm and damp from another man's bed? Oh, oh, this is awful, wonderful.

'Alison's father is without doubt the most unpleasant man I have ever come across.'

'What? What are you talking about?'

'Alison's father. Haven't you been listening? He came round, wanted to know where you were.'

'Oh,' said Emma blankly as hope died, swallowing the tears that threatened again and staring malevolently at Jay. If you weren't here, she thought, if I weren't here, I could sit down and weep for that misunderstanding. She placed her hand over the receiver, said nastily, 'Bugger off, Hammond, this is a private conversation.' He didn't move.

'I didn't tell him where you were, of course. The man is outrageous! If he'd been a better father the poor child might not have – well, that's all water under the bridge, so to speak. Oh, and Adrian came to see me. He's been round to your flat.'

'Adrian?'

'He was worried about you, wanted to know where you'd got to.'

'Oh.' Emma glanced at Jay again, blue eyes fixed on her face. 'Did you give him this address ... ?'

'No. Should I?'

'No!'

'I see. That sounds fairly definite. What should I tell him then?'

'Um, tell him I'll – no, just tell him I'll get in touch.'

'He'll want to know when.'

Emma was acutely aware of Jay, no longer relaxed, putting two and two together. 'Just tell him I'm sorry, but no. Okay?'

'Can't you do your own dirty work?' Mabel was tired, annoyed. 'I'm too old to start composing Dear John letters on your behalf. You ought to tell him yourself.'

'Please, Auntie Mabel . . .'

'All right.' She sounded querulous, ancient. 'On one condition. You phone your mother, the minute you put the phone down.'

'Yes, Auntie Mabel.' I'll do anything as long as I don't have to face dear, kind Adrian and tell him I don't want to see him again. 'Thanks.'

'All right, dear. Take care.'

'And you. I'll call you soon.'

As she said goodbye Jay advanced into the hall, took the phone from her hand and dropped it carelessly back on its rest. Then he turned abruptly, backed her up against the wall and placed his hands deliberately either side of her shoulders, trapping her between his arms.

'Look at me.'

Emma squirmed.

'Was the last part of that conversation anything to do with me?'

'No,' she said vehemently. 'Nothing at all.'

It was only because she was looking straight at him that she caught it, a brief, startling glimpse of what it was like to be Jay Hammond beneath the impassive veneer. She dropped her eyes hurriedly, feeling like an intruder on his pain. 'Yes,' she said, to stop him hurting. 'Yes, it was.'

He bent his head and kissed her, touching nothing but her mouth. When she leaned towards him to reciprocate, he took his lips from hers, muttered, 'Good,' then turned and walked away.

She stood where she was, incapable of moving, for almost five minutes. Then she made for the bathroom, going home.

It was only when she had collected all her belongings together that she remembered she had promised to phone her mother. There was no reply. Relieved, she phoned Earl's Court again, to tell Mabel that she'd tried, but it was Bill who answered the phone.

'You all right?' he asked.

'Yes. You?'

'Fine . . . No, now you come to mention it, not. Not fine at all. I can't believe it, Em. I can't believe she's gone. She has – she had, so much energy. Where's all that gone? Where's she gone, Em?'

'Oh, Bill, don't.'

They were both in tears. 'She's not the type,' Bill kept saying. 'She's just not the type.' Emma blew her nose hard, tried to speak, failed, hiccupped with misery.

'Fucking bastard Passmore!' shouted Bill.

'Enough,' said Jay from behind her and took the phone away. Then he held her while she cried, heavy, hopeless sobs that wrenched her guts and made her jaw ache.

He was big and warm and comforting; she found herself mumbling into his shirt, 'Can I stay, please?'

'For ever,' he said, loosening another chink in her armour, and she wished she had kept quiet.

He took her back to Baron's Court to change and pick up clean clothes.

She was shocked at how small and shabby the flat looked. Worse, it didn't feel like home, it didn't feel safe and she was glad to get away from it. She wondered if she would ever feel safe on her own again.

On the way back to Putney they stopped at a café and Jay fed his baby cuckoo. While Emma ate they talked about work, about Mabel, Josie, Bill, even about Alison, but they avoided discussing how long Emma was staying. Emma felt as if Jay was waiting for her to admit she wanted to be with him, to make a commitment so he could say, 'It was your decision. You made up your own mind.' He watched her all the time too, and the constant scrutiny made her feel uncomfortable, like a rabbit being mesmerised by a hawk ... or was it stoats that mesmerised rabbits, stoats and weasels? She longed for Ricky to come and rescue her, wondered where he was, whether he knew about his sister. Did he ever think about her, or had he forgotten her very existence?

Woats and Steasels, she found herself chanting silently, madly, as they crossed Putney Bridge. Woats and Steasels.

CHAPTER NINETEEN
• • •

Jay cleared a space in his wardrobe for her, found hangers, gave her a drawer for her underwear. He shoved her nightgown negligently into the bottom of a cupboard. 'I want to feel your skin,' he said, grinning.

'Only for a few more days,' Emma kept saying. 'It's only for a few more days.'

'Okay. Whatever you like.'

She had already missed a week at college.

The only time he let his guard down was in bed. During the day he was cool, sarcastic, in complete control. Emma was in such a turmoil that she didn't even try to analyse where she wanted to go from here. She just needed him. Especially at night.

She went back to college the following week. Jay dropped her off on his way to deliver some work to a client. It was a disaster: everyone knew; everyone stared. People she was barely acquainted with came up to her, shuffled their feet, mumbled with embarrassment. 'Sorry ... Awful ... Anything I can ... ? Why ... ? Why did she ... ? Did you know ... ? Sorry ... Dreadfully sorry ...' Even Ian, who hadn't spoken a civil word to her for months. Others avoided her, as if she carried the plague. I'm a bubonic rat, she thought as yet another familiar face turned away, pretending not to have seen her.

Bill was still not back, and everywhere she went reminded her of Alison. She spent half the morning hiding in the loo in floods of tears, then got on the bus and went back to Putney.

Jay was out, and she was devastated by his absence, went completely to pieces. She wandered aimlessly from room to room, tears streaming down her face, then collapsed on the bed and slept, exhausted.

He returned just after five, not expecting her to be there. He switched on the light as he came into the bedroom and she woke with a start, blinking her sore eyes. He took one look at her swollen, puffy cheeks, her red nose, and sat heavily on the edge of the bed to take her in his arms.

'Poor babe,' he said. 'You weren't ready, were you?'

'I don't think . . .' She accepted his handkerchief, blew her nose loudly and snuffled into his shirt. 'I don't think I can do it.'

'Do what?'

'Go back. Go back there. She's everywhere. Do you know someone told me Harry Passmore's still teaching as if nothing had happened? How can he do that? How can he bear to? How can he look at himself in the mirror every morning? Bastard!' she shouted, red in the face with impotent rage, 'Bloody, bloody bastard!', desperate to put the clock back, so that none of it might have happened.

'Shh.' He held her close, stroked her hair, until she went limp against him. 'Just give it time. It's too soon, that's all.'

The inquest date came through a few days later. Emma spoke to Mabel on the phone, but she couldn't bear to go back to Earl's Court. She phoned Josie briefly, but when she heard the sympathy in her voice, the tears her mother was shedding for someone she had hardly known, she was incensed, and put the phone down.

She missed another week at college, then another.

The inquest was set for the 16th of February, a Thursday; Bill got Emma's number from Mabel and rang a few days earlier. 'Are you all right?' he asked. 'Is Jay looking after you?'

'Yes,' she said. 'He's been wonderful.'

'Must be standing behind you,' said Bill with a flash of his old humour. 'Got you in an armlock, has he?'

She laughed, to please him. 'He's not here. He's at work.'

Wherever that is, she thought, her mind drifting. I know no more about you, Jay Hammond, than I did when I moved in, which wasn't much. You come and go erratically, no pattern, no routine, and the paintings on the walls change almost daily. About your meetings, your business transactions, you speak hardly at all and I don't ask. You work frequently at home, shut in your studio with your music playing and when you are here and the sound of Beethoven or Brahms begins to drift out into the hall, I make myself scarce. I deliberately show no curiosity, no desire for any more closeness than we have now, which is almost all to do with bed, because I don't wish to get close to you, and you know it. I don't love you and you know this too. The arrangement is temporary, a convenient stop-gap until I can sort myself out, decide what I wish to do with my life.

She dragged her mind back to Bill. 'Are you at college?'

'Yeah. I, it's—'

'Difficult?'

'Difficult. Joe's helped, he – well, we pop out. For coffee, you know. When it gets too . . .'

'Much?'

'Much. I seem to be getting very incoherent in my old age. God, Em, if you knew how old I feel. I must have got through enough coffee to refloat the *Titanic*.'

'You're a sensitive little flower.' What had happened to the other man, the one she had seen in the basement that night?

'Em, are you coming back? Everyone's asking. I mean you've got to sooner or later, haven't you? I know it's—'

'Difficult?'

'Difficult.' The conversation had come full circle. And it wasn't difficult, at the moment it was impossible.

She had tried, gone up on the bus towards the end of January, still unable to face the Tube, walked along the Charing Cross Road with her heart thumping and sweat trickling down her back, then lost her nerve and diverted into Foyles. She'd wasted half an hour in there, pretending she was going on in a minute, bought a couple of books for Jay, then come out, turned left, away from college, and caught a bus straight back to Putney.

'Soon,' she said, prevaricating. 'I'll be back very—'

'Soon?'

She worked hard over the week leading up to the inquest, using the desk in Jay's study to keep up with college work, fabric designs, commissions, and during the hours spent poring over her easel she got it into her head that she was sliding into a comfortable routine. Her nightmare had ceased to haunt her; the black cloud of depression had lifted; she could stand on her own two feet now. It was time she went back to Baron's Court.

'I'm going home,' she announced, then cleared out all her things, leaving what she couldn't carry to be collected later.

Jay made no attempt to stop her, just shrugged and said calmly, 'Make sure you've got everything.' He didn't offer to take her back to Baron's Court.

She spent the first night without sleep, afraid of the dream returning, then worked frantically through the next day, muttering, 'I'm fine, I'm fine, I'm perfectly all right,' as her panic and loneliness grew. She bought and ate two packets of ginger nuts, a box of Lyons Cup Cakes, lemon and orange, then made herself a leathery three-egg omelette, stretching her culinary expertise to the limit. At two in the morning on the second night she called a taxi and went back to Putney.

She let herself in silently, dropped her bags and her clothes in the hall, then tiptoed the length of the corridor to the bedroom and slid through the half-open door like a wraith. As she reached the bed Jay rolled over and sat up, wide awake. 'What kept you?' he asked.

She crawled in beside him and they made love until she was satiated. 'I missed you,' he said, but Emma didn't hear him. She was already asleep.

CHAPTER TWENTY

• • •

It rained on the first day of the inquest. Mabel was there when they arrived, with Bill, who was grey with nerves and wearing an ill-fitting suit he'd borrowed for the occasion. Jay came to hold Emma's hand. She would have begged him if necessary, but she didn't have to; he seemed to take it for granted she needed him. The fact that he was right rankled all the way there.

Alison's doctor was called first, and questioned about the sleeping tablets. She'd had a perfectly plausible story: student, exams approaching, difficulty sleeping. 'It happens all the time,' he said phlegmatically. He knew nothing about her pregnancy, or her boyfriend. As far as he was concerned, she was just another student, cracking under the strain.

The Coroner was deaf. 'Speak up,' he kept saying. 'The court can't hear you.'

Bill had to give the details of how he'd found her, lying on her bed drowned in her own vomit. Emma hadn't known about that. Poor Bill. Nearing the end of his evidence, he leaned towards the jury and said vehemently, 'She was still warm, you know, when I found her. If I hadn't stayed at college to finish my *toile* . . .' The jury exchanged uncomfortable glances. *Toile*? What on earth was a *toile*? 'And then when I got home I had a cup of coffee.' His voice rose. 'Twenty minutes. It was twenty minutes before I went upstairs. And she was still warm.' He stopped, confused, ran his hand over his eyes. Why did I say that? he wondered. Is it my fault she's dead?

Jay took them all down the road in the rain for beer and

sandwiches. 'Will that be it?' Mabel asked Bill, staring curiously not at him but at Emma's mystery friend.

Bill shook his head. 'They've hardly begun. They haven't started on her, her state of—' He scowled ferociously, trying to get his brain to focus.

'State of mind,' prompted Jay. 'They won't finish today.'

Mabel watched him. An oddball that one, she thought, hidden depths. I hope Emma knows what she's doing. But there's no doubting his partiality for her; he hardly takes his eyes off her, anticipates her every move. That's nice, nice to watch, and just as well; poor Emma's very jumpy. It's going over this awful business. It brings it back, sitting in that stuffy courtroom listening to all the sordid details.

She stared vaguely at the rain dripping from the eaves outside the window. I should have done something about it, she castigated herself; I should have taken young Alison in hand. We could have worked something out, made her see sense. And now look what I've done with my 'nothing to do with me'. Look at these whey-faced children, facing death when they've only just started out on life. Except for that one. She glanced again at Jay, leaning back in his chair watching Emma. He's faced it before, that one.

The proceedings were adjourned at three o'clock, until the next day.

They were already there, waiting in the corridor, when Jay and Emma arrived, Alison's father and a man so like Ricky that for a moment Emma thought it was him and stopped breathing, almost fell down.

But this Brown was bigger, heavier set, exuded Alison's confidence, her charisma. He was Ricky six, eight years older, without the hang-ups.

Jay, watching Emma's pale, set face, followed her eyes, saw the likeness to Alison and guessed. 'Is that him?'

'No.' She dragged her gaze away. 'It's his brother Pete and his father, Ali's father.'

'Well, well!' Brown's voice boomed down the corridor. The place was crowded. Heads turned, craning to see who was making the noise, conversations died. 'If it isn't the little tart!' He moved sideways, keeping Emma in his sights and she shrank back against Jay, searched for and found his hand, hung grimly on to it as on to a lifeline.

'Come away, Dad,' said Alison's brother, his voice loud in the sudden hush. 'Let it be.'

'Let it be?' Brown roared, shaking off his son's restraining hand. '*Let it be?*' His voice rose hysterically. 'My girl's gone, and you say let it be? Bloody hell, boy. I—'

'It's nothing to do with her, Dad.' Pete Brown began to tug at his father's arm. 'It's not her fault.'

'Nothing to do with her? Not her fault? Whose frigging fault is it then? Mine? My Ricky's gone. My Ricky. God knows where. And my beautiful . . . my beautiful—' He began to cry, big, ugly hiccupping sobs that echoed round the wide space, ricocheted off the walls, thumped inside Emma's head, and his son led him away, holding tight to his elbow, past Emma standing frozen beside Jay, still clutching his hand to stop herself from drowning in shame.

Jay moved, ready to protect her, but it wasn't necessary. All the fight had gone out of Brown, he looked like an old man, shrunken, defeated, ashen with misery.

'I'm sorry,' said the son, talking with Alison's mouth, staring at them with Alison's black eyes as they drew level. 'I'm terribly sorry. Really. He doesn't mean – you know what it's like . . . no, I don't suppose you – I'm sorry. He doesn't mean it, really. He just can't, well, you understand . . .'

He guided his father away down the corridor to the big double doors at the end and Emma felt suddenly, violently sick.

Jay pushed her across to one of the benches that lined the walls. 'Down.' He dropped his hand to her shoulder, shoving hard until her head was between her knees, and she found herself contemplating the shiny brown floor beneath her feet, tasted bile in the back of her throat, and gasped for breath.

She heard the clerk summon the crowd into the courtroom, then her own name and Jay's voice saying, 'She's not well.' After that feet, shuffling, clicking, thudding past to take their places, then blessed, blessed silence.

After a couple of minutes Jay let her sit up and she leaned gratefully against the wall, able to control the waves of nausea that had threatened to overwhelm her.

Bill came back out, looking anxious. 'You okay, dear girl? They're doing Mabel. Then it's Passmore, then you. Will you be—?'

'I'll be all right.' She smiled to prove it, swallowed hard.

'God,' said Bill. 'I wish it was all over.' He was sweating with nerves.

He took one arm and Jay took the other, as they had years ago, when she'd got tipsy for the first time, before things got so complicated. She felt a rush of longing, to go back, to start again and do everything differently, then glanced surreptitiously at Jay's impassive face, and wondered whether he'd wanted her even then.

The venue was different, the questions the same. There was a jury, seven men, five women, their faces registering alternately boredom, repugnance, disapproval, fatigue. Emma's sergeant sat at the front and perspired freely, mopping his brow with a large grubby handkerchief. She couldn't see the constable, but she supposed she must be there somewhere.

Passmore was there, the first time Emma had seen him since before Christmas. As she sat down between Bill and Jay he rose from the floor and made his way to the stand to give his evidence. She stared at his handsome face and wondered, why did I never notice how shifty you are? Why did I never register that you do not, cannot, quite look anyone in the face? Why did I not see how phony your smile is, how it lifts the corners of your mouth, but doesn't ever quite reach your eyes? Why did I fail to register the whine inherent in that charming voice of yours? And why didn't I see all these things in time to warn Alison that if she tried to snare you, you would slide out from her trap like a woat or a steasel?

She choked with sudden, inappropriate hilarity, clapped her hand over her mouth and shrank into her seat, small involuntary explosions of mirth escaping from her mouth. Oh God! Oh, somebody get me out of here!

'... A brief liaison,' Passmore was calling it. The Coroner's batteries were running low. 'A what?' he demanded irritably. 'A deep elation? Hardly appropriate, surely?'

'Liaison, Sir. Brief.'

'Stop mumbling, man. I can't hear you.'

'A brief liai— affair! Short! A short affair!' Passmore bellowed, pinkened, and Emma choked again.

A brief liaison? A short affair? She glanced back at the woman who had been seated next to Passmore, and realised with a shock who it was. That plump, mousy woman was his wife, the mother of his three children. She was staring at her husband, her face pale and strained, but loyal, giving him the benefit of the doubt.

Emma could see her hands from where she sat, twisting nervously in her lap. How had he explained those nights? Not just the nights when he had rolled home at two o'clock, but the nights when he hadn't gone home at all. Had she guessed? Had she turned a blind eye because she was frightened of losing him? It wasn't as if Alison had been the first, or would be the last.

'And did you know of the young lady's pregnancy?'

'No, Sir, I did not.'

Emma caught her breath. Liar, barefaced liar! Woat! Steasel! Hysteria assailed her again and she lowered her head, biting her knuckles to stop the snorts of dreadful merriment from escaping.

'She had, of course, already had one abortion. A fellow student, I believe.'

'A what? A yellow student? Do you mean an Oriental? For God's sake say what you mean, man.'

'Student! Fellow!' Passmore bawled.

The Coroner was puzzled. 'D'you mean a student or a fellow, man? Make up your mind.' Didn't know they had fellows at these arty establishments. Thought fellows were just university. It was time he invested in a new hearing aid.

'I am prepared to admit,' said Passmore nervously, choosing his words with extra care, 'that I was weak and easily led.' He enunciated each syllable gingerly, terrified by now of every sound that left his mouth. 'She was a very attractive young woman. But completely without scruples.'

What did the man say? Roubles, rupees? The Coroner opened his mouth, thought better of it, shut it again.

'Makes you want to throw up, doesn't it?' said Bill to no one in particular. Emma wished he hadn't reminded her and felt sick again. They called her shortly afterwards.

There was a discrepancy between her evidence and Passmore's, even the Coroner grasped that. 'And you say the affair had been going on for almost two years?'

'Yes.'

'Speak up young woman. Let the jury hear.'

'*Yes!*' she bellowed.

Never mind the jury, you deaf old fool. What gives you the right to sit there and pontificate upon Alison's life and death, to decide what happened?

'Yes, Mr Passmore did know about the pregnancy. Ali— Miss Brown thought he would be pleased.' She glanced across at Passmore, shaking his head for the jury's benefit as if to say, you liar. 'She thought he was going to marry her. He'd promised to leave his wife.'

The jury all stared at Passmore, and Emma felt a brief stab of righteous triumph. That'll show you. That'll teach you to malign poor Alison when she can no longer defend herself.

She realised when she looked at his wife what she had done. The woman seemed to wither. She had sat stoically all through, showing the world she was behind her husband. She had persuaded herself that what she wanted to believe was true. And in the space of a couple of seconds Emma had shattered all her illusions for good. She suddenly wished she could rescind the words, tell her she hadn't really meant it, but it was too late. The damage was done now.

When the jury retired Jay took her outside into the cold street, and the others trooped out behind them to stand on the courthouse steps.

'Did she fall or was she pushed, Your Honour? What would Sherlock Holmes do now?' said Emma in a ghastly attempt at levity and they all looked at her as if she was mad.

The voice came from behind them, sounded as hysterical as Emma felt. 'You do realise you'll lose your job, don't you? And we've got three children to feed and clothe? Although I'm surprised you can still remember their names, the amount of time you spend with them. Do you have any idea what it's been like, bringing up your kids all on my own, scrimping and saving, sitting at home night after night while you've been out with your teenage tramp?'

Emma stared in horror, felt Jay's hand under her elbow, and found herself propelled at speed across the pavement to his car. He opened the door and shoved her unceremoniously into her seat, slammed it hard behind her. She sat bolt upright and waited while he climbed in beside her, then collapsed with relief when he fired the engine and drove out into the traffic without looking, causing a man in a brand-new blue Mercedes to ruin his digestion as he swerved to avoid them.

Jay took her back to Putney, but he didn't stop when they got to the flats, just kept driving along the Embankment, then took a narrow slip road further on and bumped the car down almost to the water's edge. He parked beneath a tall tree, bleak in its winter nakedness, and took her for a walk, pushing her on for miles beside the grey, choppy water. It was freezing cold, but still he propelled her along the tow-path, into the wind, not talking, just holding her hand, wearing her out. Then he turned her round and walked her back again.

Emma would have braved the lift, she was so tired, but he made her take the stairs, and by the time they reached his front door she was ready to drop.

It was warm, silent. He removed her coat, poured her a large brandy, stood over her while she drank it, then put her to bed and stayed with her until she slept.

She'd missed another week at college.

They had their first row that weekend, because she tried to give him some money.

'I can't stay here for nothing,' she said. 'At least let me pay for my keep.'

'No. Not unless you move in. Give up your flat and move in properly.'

It was the first time he had made a specific demand, but Emma wasn't ready to give in and she insisted. When he flung the money back at her for the second time she tore the notes into little pieces and dropped them on the floor.

She had never seen him so angry; he frightened her, he was so icily insulted. He didn't once raise his voice, but he didn't need to, she got the message from his eyes, from the timbre of his voice. So she packed as much as she could get into her rucksack, shoved her current batch of work into her folio and went back to Baron's Court, leaving what she couldn't carry to be picked up later.

'Don't forget your toothbrush,' he flung at her back as she walked past him, and she slammed the door hard behind her.

The flat was freezing. She lit the fire, trying to ignore the shabby unfamiliarity of her surroundings, then huddled over it until the meter ran out of money and the gas hissed, popped and died.

She had no more shillings in her purse. She had to plod back down the stairs to get some food and some change. She was miserable; she wasn't cushioned from the world any more, but she made herself some soup, ate a couple of slices of bread and cheese and felt better with something inside her. Then she settled down with a cup of milky coffee and a sketch-pad to start on a new fabric design. After a while, when she still felt lonely, she turned on the radio, the Home Service so she could hear some voices, then worked steadily to the accompaniment of Harold Wilson discussing the current crisis in the Health Service. At ten o'clock she gave up and went to bed, pleased with what she had done.

She couldn't sleep. She missed Jay's double bed. She missed Jay's warmth, his breathing, the smell of his skin. She missed the sex.

On impulse, she got up, dressed again and went out on to the landing to phone her mother. Conscience assuaged, she thought virtuously as she sat shivering on the stairs.

Josie was almost incoherent to begin with, with mingled delight and distress. 'When are you coming home?' she asked plaintively when she finally found her voice.

'Don't know, Ma. I've been busy.'

'Where've you been anyway? I've rung and rung and some girl keeps answering the phone and she says she hasn't seen you for weeks, and when I asked Mabel she said you were staying in Putney or somewhere. What is going *on*, Emma?'

'I—'

'I know it's all been very upsetting and everything and I realise she was your best friend, but don't you think you could spare a thought for *me* occasionally?'

'I'm sorry, Ma—'

'I mean it's not as if I expect you to come home every weekend, I don't. I just think that once a term is too little time to spare, it makes me feel as if you don't *care*.'

'No, Ma, it's not—'

'And I don't complain about the fact that you never phone, although goodness knows I would be *perfectly* justified given the number of times I've spoken to you this year. It's just that I get the feeling you don't *think* about it any more, about me. You didn't even come home after all that trouble with your friend. And I found that *really* upsetting, Emma . . .'

'Look, Ma,' Emma shouted, furiously angry with herself, with

Josie, with everything. 'I've said I'm sorry. What more do you want? I'll come home as soon as I can. Okay?'

She put the phone down harder than she meant to, then imagined her mother sitting in her old green armchair, crying into her handkerchief until she went to bed.

Sleep still eluded her. Her thoughts switched from Jay to Ricky, to wishful thinking, to what might have been, and she felt worse than before. When she finally dropped off, just after one o'clock, she fell straight into the familiar nightmare, down the shaft into her black pit. She had thought herself free of that since she had been at Jay's. She got up at two and made herself a cup of tea, wondered whether Jay was still awake. 'Bet you're snoring your head off, you pig,' she accused him, unfairly, because he'd never snored while she'd been with him. She had a bowl of cornflakes, then worked until five, until her eyes stung and her back muscles tingled with exhaustion, then crawled into bed and tried to sleep for the second time.

It was not a good day to decide to go back to college. The first person Emma bumped into, literally, on the stairs as she rushed through the main entrance at ten past ten was Harry Passmore. She would have made some acid remark if she could have thought of one but the vitriol that surged up silenced her and she merely glared. Passmore, who had just attended an interview with the Principal and a couple of college governors, was too shaken to notice. He was trying to work out how to tell his wife that as of the end of the month he was an ex-college lecturer. And he was wishing he had never set eyes on Miss Alison Bloody Brown.

Emma struggled through the morning drawing class, sublimating all thought in work, then escaped to the annexe, to the printing department. She didn't see Bill who, to her secret relief, was working elsewhere, and went for lunch on her own. While she was in the canteen she picked up a paper someone had left behind and idly scanned the news.

It was on the fourth page, a paragraph at the bottom, between an article about a man who had named his infant son after the entire Manchester United football team and a short item about a new remedy for Athlete's Foot.

... recorded a verdict of 'suicide, while the balance of her mind was disturbed'. In his summing up, the Coroner delivered a stinging rebuke to the gentleman who had put Miss Brown in this invidious situation and then reneged on his responsibilities when his support was most required ...

Stoats and Weasels. Emma raised her head, stared at the students going cheerfully about their business and asked herself, what am I doing here? I don't belong with all these silly, frivolous people any more.

When she walked into the cutting-room the first thing she saw was the pale blue evening-dress Alison had finished at the end of last term. Someone had been clearing out a stock cupboard and not knowing who it belonged to, had left it draped over a dummy by the window to be claimed.

Emma stopped, stared, then turned away and found the *toile* she was working on. She regarded it blankly for a moment, without interest, then took it to the furthest corner of the room and sat down with it. As long as I don't look, she told herself, I will be all right. I will be fine.

'Ah! Just the girl, and about time too. Miss T. wants to see you, four o'clock on the dot.'

Emma jumped, stuck her needle in her finger, then sat back in her chair and sucked it, glaring at her tutor in startled bewilderment.

Good grief, thought Mrs Hills, you look dreadful, white as a sheet, black rings under your eyes, so thin. It's really shaken you up, all this. She opened her mouth, carefully expunged the sympathy from her voice. 'It's your attendance, Emma. She wants to discuss your attendance, just so you're forewarned. And don't be late, you know what she's like, stickler for punctuality. You're in enough trouble already.'

She turned to go, felt an unwonted rush of motherly concern

and patted Emma's shoulder. 'Poor dear,' she said, 'it must have been awful.'

She would rather have walked away, dealt with something less embarrassing, but watching the hazel eyes fill with tears she changed her mind.

'Do me a favour, would you, dear? Pop down to the photography department for me, and collect some pics. They've been siting there for weeks and I keep forgetting to retrieve them.'

Watching Emma disappear almost at a run through the swing doors, Mrs Hills congratulated herself. Good idea that, got the child out of the way for ten minutes.

Down in the basement, where the photography department was housed, Emma began to feel the walls closing in and panicked. When Eddie, the resident photographer, asked her to wait while he finished developing the prints he'd taken of her clothes, she shook her head vigorously, promised to come back later, then snatched Mrs Hills' pictures from his hand and bolted, almost suffocating with claustrophobia.

It wasn't Eddie's fault. He didn't give the pile of grainy black-and-white blow-ups a second thought when he handed them over. Three prints down, beneath a couple of shots of somebody's evening-dresses – Joe's by the look of all the frills and flounces – and one of a tank-top and a pair of hipster bell-bottoms, horizontally striped, was a photograph of Alison.

She was holding a cigarette between her fingers, and smiling seductively at the camera through a haze of tobacco smoke. She was wearing a pale, diaphanous organza dress, the one Emma had seen so recently in the cutting-room, backlit to highlight her long legs and slim waist through its folds; her head was tilted slightly, her lips parted provocatively as if she was about to kiss the cameraman.

She looked as Emma had seen her so often, giving the come-on to the camera as she had done to a hundred boys. Emma remembered her telling her about the session when they'd done it.

'Got completely kippered,' she'd said, laughing. 'If I ever decide to give up smoking, that's the way I'll do it.' She'd given up sooner than she'd expected.

'Oh!' said Emma out loud, and sat down with a thump on the cold stone step.

She left the pile of photographs scattered on the stairs and went back to the cutting-room. There, she picked up her bag, slung it over her shoulder and walked out.

She was halfway there before she realised she was on her way to Putney, but she stayed on the bus because Putney was where she needed to go. She ran from the bus-stop, her plait swinging heavily at her back, as if someone was pursuing her, saw his car in the car-park and leaped up the stairs two at a time, light-headed with relief. Then she froze on the landing, clutching her key but unable to make the last move, until Jay unexpectedly opened the door, on his way out.

He started, blinked, turned swiftly away from her back the way he had come, then faced her again with a face stripped so carefully bare of all emotion that he looked as if he had never laughed, never cried, never felt anything in his entire life. Oh God, he thought, don't do this to me.

Oh God, thought Emma, don't do this to me. I'm so crazily pleased to see you. Don't look at me like that, as if you don't want to see me at all.

'Come for the rest of your things?'

He managed somehow to expunge all feeling from his voice too. He might have been a robot, addressing another robot. Emma stood staring helplessly at him and waited, tongue-tied.

'You'd better come in then.'

He didn't move to let her pass, just propped himself up against the wall, arms folded over his chest, face completely shuttered against her. She sidled past him, inadvertently brushing his sleeve, and hesitated, longing for more of the warmth she had touched. He didn't move a muscle.

When she was past him, standing in the hall, he spoke from behind her. 'I'm just on my way out. All your stuff's in the spare room. Make sure you lock up when you leave.'

She heard the door shut, then his footsteps dying away on the stairs, and wanted to sit down and sob. 'You son-of-a-bitch!' she yelled at the silent flat instead. 'You pig!'

He'd laid all her things out neatly in a pile on the desk. 'You pig,' she snarled again. 'You beastly, arrogant, sarcastic pig, pig, *pig*.'

She moved everything into the hall, then rang for a taxi and settled down to wait. But after ten minutes she grew tired of contemplating the pathetic pile of her belongings. He'd even folded her unused nightgown neatly before adding it to the rest. How long, she calculated, how long had she been there, just over a month? It was time she stood on her own two feet again. 'Who needs you, Hammond?' she said, challenging him.

She thought she'd just check that he hadn't missed anything. After all, she didn't want to have to come back. She slung her bag over her shoulder so she would be ready the moment the taxi arrived, then began to wander from room to room, getting her bearings after two days away, wasting time.

The bed was still unmade, which wasn't like Jay. He'd been sleeping on her side too, there was a heavy indent in her pillow where his head had rested and his was neat and tidy, untouched. She stood in the doorway and stared at the rapidly blurring counterpane, blinking back the tears. She didn't need him, didn't love him, he wasn't worth shedding tears over. So why was she crying?

She didn't hear him. When he placed his hands on her shoulders she leaped like a startled rabbit and dropped her bag on the floor with a thud.

'Good while it lasted,' he murmured, his mouth tickling her ear, 'wasn't it, Em?'

'Pig!' She shook with rage.

'Anybody 'ome? 'Ullo, Taxi!'

Thank God. Just in time, the cavalry to the rescue. 'In here! . . . *Pig!*'

'Go away!' said Jay loudly, tightening his grip on her shoulders.

'I'll be right there!' Emma wriggled frantically. '*Bastard!*'

'Taxi?'

Jay released her abruptly and stormed off, making for the hall and the inoffensive middle-aged man standing halfway along it.

'*Bugger off!*' he yelled.

'Bloody Nora!' The taxi driver backed away towards the front door, then turned tail and fled. He tangled his feet in the pile of Emma's belongings as he passed, then hopped and slithered down the stairs with her nightgown wrapped around his left foot, trailing bits of lace and cotton as he went. Emma was suddenly suffused with helpless, inappropriate gales of laughter.

'Now,' growled Jay threateningly, his expression about as far from neutral as it could get. 'Where were we?'

CHAPTER TWENTY-ONE

• • •

He wouldn't touch her. He wanted to talk. Only when the conversation got nowhere did he succumb to Emma's increasingly desperate overtures and take her to bed. Then he made tea and they drank it with the sheets tucked up under their arms in case of drips. The preceding argument had left Emma angry and shaken, and she was still very far from regaining her equilibrium.

'You must make the first move,' Jay had insisted.

'Why must I?'

'Because I won't. And if neither of us does then it's finished.'

'Tell me,' she had said bitterly. 'Do you have any weaknesses at all?' He had stared at her until she had thought he would climb right inside her head, then said, 'Yes. Just one,' and Emma had known without a shadow of doubt that he meant her.

Now she gulped her tea, wincing as the scalding liquid went down her throat, leaned back on the pillows and complained resentfully, 'What do you want from me?'

'I want you to make a commitment. I want you to marry me.'

'No.'

'Why not?'

'I've told you. I don't love you, I love—'

He clapped his hand over her mouth, splashing her tea all over the sheets. 'Doesn't matter.' He dismissed the scalding liquid seeping through the cotton on to her bare skin. 'I can change them now.' Then added, continuing the previous conversation, 'All right, leave me then.'

216

'I ...' I can't, she thought, panicking, I've just tried and I couldn't do it.

'Well?'

'Well, what? I don't know. Why were you sleeping on my side of the bed?'

'Does it matter?'

'No – yes – I don't know.' She mopped herself, folding the sheet over to find a dry patch. 'Why were you sleeping—?'

He put his tea down, leaned across to take her mug away, then pushed her down savagely into the pillow. 'Because it smelled of you.' His voice, his face, were full of heat and fury. 'Now, are you staying or are you going?'

She mumbled, hedging her bets again; he persisted. 'Louder.'

'Ymmn.'

'Clearer. I can't hear you.'

'Oh, bloody hell! Yes!' she shouted.

'Yes what, staying or going?'

'Yes, staying.' Oh, Ricky, why aren't you here? You would save me from this, from Jay.

'Right.' He rose abruptly and stalked across the room to where she had dropped her bag, sweeping it from the floor on to the bed. His skin was still sheened with the sweat of energetic lovemaking and drops of tea. Emma wanted to stroke him dry with her fingers, write her name on his damp shoulder, or 'Kilroy wos 'ere' and one of those silly faces peeping over a wall. Hysteria, always close these days, rose at the thought.

'Where are your keys?' He rummaged around, then began throwing cheque-books, tissues, pens, pencils all over the counterpane. He found her keys right at the bottom, next to Ricky's brooch.

He took it out and stared at it. Emma hadn't looked at it for a week, a month; it sobered her up instantly, seeing it in the palm of Jay's hand. Watching his face as he registered the arrow piercing the tiny heart, the initials, R and E, she thought how easily she could get to hate that blank expression.

He put it back without a word, picked up her keys, tidied everything else away, gathered his clothes from the floor, then walked out of the room without even looking at her.

She heard him moving about, then the front door opening and closing and the silence of the empty flat. She reached across, fumbled, found the brooch and touched it, curling her fingers round it inside the bag. The she lay back and closed her eyes. 'I don't love him,' she said defensively, 'I don't love him at all, I love you. But you're not *here*.'

She slept heavily for nearly an hour, moving over to Jay's side where it wasn't so damp, breathing his scent as he had hers. It wasn't until she woke that she remembered Miss T., Head of the Fashion Department and a stickler for punctuality, who wanted to see her at four o'clock on the dot. It was dark outside.

She panicked, couldn't find her watch, lying on the floor beside the bed, rushed aimlessly around the flat, then pulled herself together and phoned the speaking clock.

'At the third stroke,' said the woman's voice, 'it will be five twenty-two and thirty seconds.'

She changed the damp sheets on the bed and went to soak in a long, hot bath.

Jay was away for three hours. When he returned he was laden down with her possessions, and he smelled strongly of whisky. Emma had never known him touch whisky before.

He had all her clothes in a big suitcase, one of his, and he'd filled her smaller one with towels, washbag, books, sketch-pads. He'd loaded her folio up with as much of her work as he could find, brought her easel, coloured inks, and all her pens.

'It's all right, little Em,' he said as he passed her startled face for the third time. 'I've left enough so you can escape if you want to.'

For the first time that day she smiled at him, felt a rush of . . . what was it, affection? Not lust certainly, she was too tired.

Perhaps it was relief, that she'd made a decision, at least for the time being. Whatever it was, it wasn't love. She knew the difference, even if Jay didn't.

He took her out for dinner and sat back to watch her attack a large curry. 'Why did you come back to me?' he asked.

'I went to college.' She put her fork down, lowered her head. 'I lay awake all night thinking about—'

'Yes?'

'Thinking about—'

'What?'

'Us. Stop grinning, blast you, about you.' And about Rick, who isn't here.

'And?' He stopped smiling, his usual iron self-control weakened by alcohol, remembering the brooch.

'And then I went to college and there was Ali's dress sitting on the dummy and I was tired and Mrs Hills sent me down to, well, she was embarrassed because I— So she sent me down to get some— Water, I need some water, this curry is hot.' She gulped a glass of water, picked up her fork, took a mouthful, put it down again. 'I had to go down to the basement to collect some photos and Eddie was— I—Eddie asked me to wait but I— So I took them upstairs and one of them was— And I was supposed to see Miss T. at four o'clock and I came home instead and now I've missed it and she's going to be *furious*.' She raised her head, staring tensely at the tender amusement registering on Jay's face.

'You said home.'

'What?'

He repeated himself patiently. 'You said "I came home".'

'Oh.' Emma looked puzzled. 'Did I?'

'Why didn't you tell me?'

'Tell you what?'

'That you were going back to college.'

'You didn't give me the chance.'

'No.' He bowed his head in acknowledgement. 'I suppose I didn't. I'm sorry.'

'You? Sorry?' In all the time she had known Jay Hammond, Emma couldn't remember ever having heard him apologise to anyone. 'Could I have that in writing please?' she demanded, attempting a joke.

He laughed, fumbled in his pocket for a pen, then reached across for a spare table napkin, smoothed it out with long fingers. 'Would you like to dictate? No? Right, I'll have to make it up as I go along then.'

She watched suspiciously as he began to write, grew increasingly uncomfortable as he continued. When he was finished he pushed the napkin across the table at her. *Emma*, it said, *I apologise for my intransigence, my inability to compromise. I do not mean to be ruthless and overbearing. In my defence I can only plead that I love you. It muddles my thinking.* He had signed it with his big looping scrawling signature. *Jay.*

You know your faults quite well, she thought, staring dumbfounded at the billet-doux, and you know how to get round me, how to chip holes in my defences. Is that why I'm here?

'Well?'

'Well what?'

'Will that do?'

'I only wanted an apology, not a declaration of love.'

'The two are mutually inclusive. You are the only woman I have every apologised to.'

She raised her head, went to speak, thought better of it and shut her mouth with a snap. She had never been in any doubt about Ricky. She had known from the first moment that she loved him. With Jay the sex got in the way of everything else, muddied the waters. She couldn't get past it, but she didn't want to give it up, even if it meant giving in. It's very worrying, she thought as she helped herself to another chapatti, perhaps I have a cock fetish.

'Well, are you going to move in properly?'

'I don't think I can hack it.'

'What's to hack? You're already doing it, if you'd just stop hedging your bets all the time.'

'College.'

'What?'

'I'm talking about college. I don't think I can hack it.'

'Oh,' he said blankly, trying to pull himself together, to concentrate on the twists and turns of the conversation through the three large whiskies he had knocked back. 'Was it that bad? Maybe if you went in part-time for a while?'

'And what happens when you get bored with me?'

'When I—?'

'When the novelty wears off. What happens then? Do you throw me out into the street, leave me sitting on the pavement with my pathetic pile of possessions and take another in my place?'

'No, of course I don't. Why should I get bored with—?' He was slipping. He shouldn't have stopped at the pub, shouldn't have had those whiskies. It was finding the brooch that had done it. It seemed to be getting away from him.

'She was everywhere, you know, everywhere I went. It was awful. She always seemed so much more . . . *alive* than anyone else, she had so much energy. That's why I thought you'd fancy her. Do you know, when I went up for my interview she was the only person I noticed.' Emma picked up her fork and dug into her curry again. Jay ran distracted fingers through his hair. How long had she been carrying it around in her bag? How could he compete with that?

'So will you—'

'Did you fancy her? At the beginning, I mean?'

'No, I've told you, I only fancied—'

'But if I don't go back I shall have to find a job. I've got to pay the rent somehow. Do you think I could make enough with freelance illustration? I mean, I'm doing quite well at the moment, but I'm not earning enough to live on.'

'You don't have to earn enough to live on. If you come and live—'

'It's just that I don't feel as if I belong there any more, I don't seem to have anything in common with them somehow.'

'Well, maybe if you talk to Bill—'

'You haven't answered my question. What happens then? What happens when you get tired of me?'

'Emma . . .'

'Yes?'

Jay rubbed his hands across his eyes. 'Can we go home, please?'

'Oh,' said Emma. 'Yes, of course, if you like . . . Jay?'

'Mmm?'

'Are you all right? You're looking a bit peculiar.'

She rang the next morning, made an appointment to see Miss T. at eleven o'clock, then sat down while Jay moved to and fro across the kitchen, making breakfast. As he passed he tugged gently on her plait. Emma raised her head and smiled at him. You always do that, she thought, and I like it. It's a morning ritual, a shared habit. You tug, I smile, we share.

He leaned over her shoulder, put her coffee down beside her plate. You always put my coffee down on the wrong side too, handle facing left, because you drink yours with your left hand, although you're right-handed. It's a very endearing habit and I like it.

He sat down opposite her and ate his toast, reading a letter at the same time, frowning as if it irritated him, then tearing it across. She examined his face, the dark hair flopping heavily over his forehead, in need of a cut, wanted to push it back for him, so he could see better. He glanced up and smiled, the frown disappearing; she smiled back, wondered, are you becoming an endearing habit, Jay Hammond? Odd, if you are, because 'endearing' is not a word I would readily have associated with you.

The interview was short, pithy and to the point. 'Non-attendance, falling work standards, uncooperative attitude, erratic behaviour. Very disappointing. Would you like to explain?'

'Um . . .'

'Is that the best you can do?'

'I . . .'

Miss T. was short, round and solid, like one of those toys that pop up again, smiling, however hard you knock them down. She was formidably efficient, ran the Fashion department of one of the most prestigious Art Schools in the country, freelanced for a well-known suit manufacturer, lectured, toured the country acting as External Assessor for other colleges. Emma wondered how she'd found the time to get fat.

'I can't, Miss T. Explain, I mean.'

'Pity. Apart from a brief spell in your first year you seemed to have been doing all right until recently. Boyfriend trouble?'

'No.' No, and yes. 'It was Alison Brown, Miss T. It's . . . shaken me up a bit.' What a ludicrous understatement.

'Alison Brown? Ah. Friends, weren't you?'

'Yes.' How pathetic I must sound, Emma thought. After all, Ali is just a small blip in the statistics. Eighty per cent pass rate, fifteen per cent fail, four per cent drop-out, one per cent mortality.

'It was my fault you see.' Why am I telling you this? You don't care, why should you? 'I could have gone back at lunchtime but I didn't. And when poor Bill found her it was too late.' Poor Bill.

'Ah.' Miss T. shuffled papers, frowned, produced a pair of half-moon glasses and peered through them without putting them on. 'Appleyard. William Appleyard. Seems to be having problems too. Same address, I see . . . You two—?'

'No, Miss T. He's in the basement. Anyway, I've moved.' Bill and I? If only you knew. 'I haven't seen him since the inquest.' I've been avoiding him as he's been avoiding me. I dragged him into it, and he feels responsible now, as I do. Would people commit suicide if they could put themselves in others' shoes, know what it feels like to be left behind, to live with the constant subliminal 'if only'? But it was typical of Alison's selfishness. She never did give a tinker's cuss for anyone else's feelings. Emma closed her eyes momentarily. What a dreadful thing of which to accuse one's defunct best friend.

'I said, what are we going to do about you?'

'I don't know, Miss T.'

Miss T. shuffled papers again, put her half-moon glasses on, peered over them at Emma, pursed her lips. 'You have three weeks,' she said at last, 'until the end of term. If you can prove to me during that time that you can pull yourself together, I'll keep your place open. Otherwise I shall be forced to review the situation. We can't carry passengers here, you know.'

Emma went straight home. Jay was out. *Back late* said his note, and she missed him. Needing comfort she finished off the chilli she found in a saucepan on the stove, ate a ham and tomato sandwich, then laid out all her stuff in the spare room and got down to some work. I'll start back properly tomorrow, she told herself; one more day won't make any difference.

She was uneasily aware that it would probably make rather a lot.

It was after eleven when she heard Jay's key and she made eagerly for the front door, looking forward to seeing his face.

'Good day at the office, dear?' she asked facetiously.

'Not particularly.'

As he bent to kiss her the smell of expensive scent hit her. She jerked her head back and stared at him. Was he messing about with other women?

'What's the matter?'

'Nothing.' Except that you smell like the Perfume counter at Dickins and Jones and I am jumping to conclusions as to why.

'Didn't feel like nothing.'

'You reek of perfume.'

'Oh.' Jay dropped his coat over a chair, ran his fingers through his hair. 'I've been out with a . . . You look tired.'

'I'm on a final warning. Non-attendance and I'm falling behind with my assignments.'

'Sounds serious. How was it today?'

Emma raised a hand, picked at his jacket lapel, still breathing in that smell, French, expensive. 'I didn't stay. I came straight home after I'd seen Miss T. What sort of a—?'

'But if you're on a final—'

'D'you want a drink?' She turned away, the scent clinging to her nostrils and her fingers, a sinking feeling beginning in the pit of her stomach.

'Em, if you're on a final warning you can't afford to miss a single session. You'll get thrown out on your ear. Emma, are you listening?'

'Yes, of course I'm listening. Was it a client?' Good grief, thought Emma, you don't sound even vaguely casual, you sound like a jealous wife. 'You're not usually so late.'

'If it bothers you I'll explain.' Jay wandered into the sitting-room and flung himself down wearily on the sofa. Emma followed, the ache in the pit of her stomach increasing. 'I might as well tell you now as later, just in case.'

Just in case of what? Emma felt a surge of panic, then anger. It reminded her of how she had felt when things were going wrong between her and Ricky, only this was different, new. This was infidelity. She crossed the room to sit as far from Jay as possible on the other end of the sofa, and stared at him rancorously.

'I've been with another woman … Your face is a picture.' Emma flushed scarlet with rage at his casual amusement. 'I haven't even begun to explain yet and already you're jumping to conclusions. You're jealous.' It occurred to Emma suddenly that she was supposed to be, that he wanted her to be.

'No,' she said. 'No, of course I'm not. Why should I be? There's no commitment on either side.' She fumed silently, made a half-hearted attempt at levity. 'Anyway, I've got an insurance policy. I can always go back to Baron's Court if you do me wrong.'

'No, you can't. I won't let you. Anyway, I haven't done you wrong.' Jay regarded her dispassionately. 'I'm glad you're jealous though. Makes it all worthwhile.' He was taking his revenge for the brooch, enjoying the green-eyed harpie glaring at him from the other end of the sofa.

'I've told you, I am *not* jealous!'

'So you say. Why don't I believe you?'

'I can't imagine.' Emma began to feel sick.

'Do you want to know where I've been or not?'

'No, I do not want to know where you've been.' I want to cut your balls off. She mentally reviewed the kitchen knives, selected an implement suitable for slow castration.

'All right, I'll tell you then.'

He leaned back, lounging as he always did, draping himself negligently all over the furniture, only tonight it was unaccountably infuriating instead of endearing. Emma festered, crouching in her corner with her knees drawn up protectively, wondering why he couldn't sit up straight.

'Sit up straight,' said Jay, staring at her with overbright blue eyes. 'You're always huddled in a heap.' And you're jealous, which means you care. And I love you.

'All right!' She cut him off abruptly. 'Where have you bloody well been?'

He reached out to touch her bare foot and she snatched it away. 'I told you, I've been seeing another woman.'

'Oh.' Oh, god, you *have* been unfaithful.

He reached for her foot again. 'An ex-girlfriend.'

'Oh? And how "ex" is "ex"?'

'Since the first time I kissed you.'

'Oh?' She couldn't make herself any smaller and his arms were long. He began to run his fingers up and down her leg, from ankle to calf, inside her jeans. 'So why did you—?'

'Chuck her? Because of you.'

'No, not chuck her! Go and see her! Come back stinking of her perfume!' Her voice was squeaky with incipient hysteria. Jay wrapped his fingers round her foot, dragged it across the gap between them and placed it firmly on his lap. Emma wriggled, glowered.

'I'd been seeing her for six months, off and on. And when I dropped her she didn't like it. She's been making a nuisance of herself, started off phoning, then writing...' Emma rarely answered the phone, hadn't noticed any females calling him, had paid no attention to the piles of post that came every morning. 'I was getting bored with it. So I went round to tell her to leave me alone. What size are your feet?'

'Seven. Just like that?'

'Just like what? They're sexy, your feet.'

'You got bored, so you just dropped her?'

'Mmm. She tried to persuade me to change my mind. That's why I smell of her perfume. Your ankles are pretty sensational too.' He was stroking her foot, running his fingers across her toes; his touch was delicious, lust-inducing. She snatched her leg away and glared at him.

'Is that what happens to me? How long have I got, six months, a year? Or will you reach your boredom threshold sooner? And you want me to give up my flat?' She laughed manically. 'You must be mad. Did you kiss her?'

He looked surprised. 'No,' he said. 'Since the first time I kissed you I haven't touched another woman, haven't even looked. From then until the first time we went to bed together I was completely celibate.'

'How sweet.' Emma, still seething with possessive fury, took her revenge. 'I wasn't.'

She watched it come, that hard look creeping across his face like a shutter, blanking her out.

'I'm sorry,' she backtracked. 'I don't know why I said that.'

'And to think,' he sounded completely unemotional, looked completely impassive. 'I actually thought you were jealous. How stupid of me!'

'I was. Oh Christ. I didn't mean . . . It isn't as if you didn't know . . . I just wanted . . .' I just wanted to get my own back.

'You don't understand, do you?' Unexpectedly he turned his face towards her and dropped his guard, allowing her to see, for only the second time, the extent of his passion. It took her breath away. 'I've waited two and a half years for you. You're all I want.

I love you so much it hurts. I can't live without—'

'Stop it!' Emma leaned across and stifled the words with her fingers, then perversely found herself stroking his contorted face with the back of her hand, because she had no defence against his pain, couldn't bear his suffering. 'I'm sorry, I've said I'm sorry. Don't look at me like that. Please, Jay—'

'I can't bear the thought of that – that—' Jay closed his eyes, seeing the brooch, then began to laugh, covering his face with his hands and choking with mirth. But as swiftly as it convulsed him, the merriment died. 'Oh bloody hell,' he said bitterly. 'I've never got myself into this sort of a situation before.'

'What sort of a situation? I don't understand.'

'I've just dealt you all the aces in the pack.' He sighed resignedly, then leaned against the cushion behind his head, pushed his hair back from his forehead and closed his eyes again. He sounded flat, numb, as if he had emptied all his emotions out into a hole somewhere and buried them. He looked as if someone was torturing him.

Emma forgot that she didn't love him. She caught him by the shoulders and pulled hard, until he half fell against her, his mouth resting on her throat. Then she wrapped her arms around him and stroked his hair, murmuring over and over, 'I didn't mean it, Jay, truly I didn't mean it.'

She felt him give against her, his arms sliding round her waist, and he rolled towards her, pinning her with his weight. She tightened her hold.

'Emma?' His voice was muffled, breathless.

'Mmm?'

'You're suffocating me.'

She lay on her back, bruised and tender inside, feeling the warmth between her thighs where he had been, and contemplated the ceiling. 'What's her name?'

'Doesn't matter.'

'Did you sleep with her?'

Jay turned his head and smiled at her, replete, drowsy, recovered. 'I told you—'

'Not tonight. Before. Before me.'

'Oh ... Yes.'

A tidal wave of jealousy. 'And was she the one you were in love with?'

No, idiot, you were. 'No. Emma?'

'Mmm?'

'Where does ...' He stumbled, stopped, began again. 'Where does Alison's brother fit into all this?'

There was a long silence before Emma said sleepily, 'I don't know. I haven't managed to figure it out yet.'

She rose early the next morning and left Jay dozing while she settled down to some work. It was hard to concentrate to begin with – she made the mistake as she left the room of looking back at him. She liked to watch him sleep, he looked younger, softer, defenceless, made her feel ridiculously protective, almost maternal, towards him. She kept staring into space thinking about him instead of working.

By eight-thirty she had done an hour's work and wasted an hour. She made tea, taking the mugs into the bedroom to rouse him.

He was awake, propped up against the pillows waiting for her. He was still crumpled with sleep and he smiled spontaneously when she walked through the door, a rare, beautiful smile that transformed his hawkish face and made Emma go weak at the knees. His defences were still down.

She would have undressed and climbed back into bed with him, but he held her at arm's length. 'It's time I started earning my living,' he said. He caught her by the back of the neck, pulled her down to kiss her, then dived for the bathroom.

They drove in together, as if they were married, Emma thought, alarmed, and Jay dropped her at the top of Oxford Street. 'Will you be all right?' he asked, watching her pale, tense face.

'Fine. I'll be fine.' I think. But I wish you were coming too, to hold my hand. I wish I didn't rely on you as much as I do. She turned and smiled at him. I wish you were Ricky. I wish I wasn't so confused.

He leaned across and kissed her, then decanted her and her folio into the street. She stood on the pavement, early shoppers and late commuters swirling around her, and watched his car disappear into the traffic, then turned reluctantly to climb the stairs, trying to ignore her rising panic.

It was still there, Alison's dress, sitting on the dummy by the window. Emma stood and stared at it for a moment, then left, striding purposefully along, going nowhere in particular as long as it was away from that room. She fetched up on the third floor, staring blankly at the noticeboard. There was a Hop on Friday, in the Common Room.

'Life goes on.'

'Hello, George. You okay?'

'Yeah, great.' Unlike you. You look awful, so thin. 'Did I tell you Jilly and I are getting married in October? You're invited.' George paused, feeling he ought to say something, at least mention Alison's name. 'Won't be the same without Ali though.' He shuffled his feet, uncomfortable now that he had, unable to think what to say next.

'How're Bill and Adrian?' asked Emma, to help him out. George reddened.

'Bill's away again. Got a sick note and he's taking anti-something-or-others.' He laughed, a little too loud, a little too hearty. 'Must be pretty bad, he's gone home to his mum for the rest of term.' Oddly, Emma found it comforting that Bill was handling things even worse than she was. 'Adrian's ... er.'

'Adrian's ... er?'

'Got a girlfriend actually.' George picked at a spot on his chin. 'From the Central School, I think. Pretty girl.' He glanced at Emma to see how she was taking it, then away again. 'Still asks after you though,' trying to soften the blow.

'I don't mind, George. In fact, it's a relief. If he's got a girlfriend I can stop feeling guilty about him. It was all over in January, you know.'

'So what are you doing now?' George was grateful that he'd got through a potential minefield without blowing himself to bits. 'Got a boyfriend?'

'Mmm. I'm living with someone.' It was the first time she had accepted that the arrangement was anything other than temporary. The admission made her feel guilty, as if she was cheating on Rick.

'You? The Virgin Queen?' George was impressed. 'My, you have come a long way. Anyone I know?'

'Well . . . Yes. Didn't Bill tell you? It's Jay.'

'Jay? What, Jay Hammond?' George stared at her open-mouthed. '*No!* Good Lord – I mean, I say – that is, d'you know what you're doing, Em?'

'Probably not.' Emma examined George's ruddy face. He'd had a haircut lately, was beginning to look plump, grown up, respectable even. I've known you, she thought, for over two years now; we've shared the same address, the same jokes, the same friends, yet here you are hopping from one foot to the other, dying (what an ironic word) to get away from me. It's the bubonic rat syndrome again. I have the smell of death about me; I carry the plague. Or is it all in my imagination?

'Talking of boyfriends . . .' George, anxious not to be seen to be escaping, paused, wondered whether to mention it or not, then shrugged, thought what-the-hell and continued. 'I saw that other chap of yours recently.'

'What other chap?'

George blundered on. 'Ali's brother, Ricky, remember?'

Remember? Oh God, how could I forget? How could you ask? Emma toyed with the idea of falling down, rejected it in favour of white-faced silence.

'Mum ran into him at our local market up in Norfolk, didn't know who he was, just thought he looked vaguely familiar. She'd only met Ali once, that day we all moved in, but she'd stuck in her mind, she said. Well, she did, didn't she, stand out in a crowd? Anyway, he was on a stall selling jewellery, lovely stuff, Mum said, silver, very delicate. And he was taking orders for paintings. He does houses, you see. Mum had never seen anything quite like them, incredibly detailed, she said, just like Nicholas Hilliard, only buildings instead of people. Anyway, she commissioned him to do one of our place and he turned up just before Christmas, while I was home. Amazing, there's hardly any stutter at all now. D'you remember how he used to be, almost completely incomprehensible? It was absolutely stupendous, the difference; I mean he was perfectly coherent, and he loved the old place, said it was just the house he would buy when he'd made his fortune. But do you know, Em,' George puffed himself out indignantly, 'he called me a prat, just because I asked him if he remembered you.'

'Where is he?'

'Who?'

'Ricky.' Emma swallowed hard, tried to sound casual. 'Where is he?'

'Oh. Haven't a clue, sorry, he didn't mention, just disappeared when he'd finished—'

Emma gulped, resisted the temptation to punch George, hard, on the nose, opened her mouth to ask the thousand questions engulfing her, then discovered that her tongue had seized up, and abruptly turned her back, departing on legs that felt like unravelled knitting.

What the hell have I said now? wondered George, staring resentfully at her retreating plait. Why should she be upset merely because I was talking about Alison's brother? After all, it's not as if they were together very long. It occurred to him that Ricky Brown probably still didn't know his sister was dead. He hadn't been in touch with his family, he'd said. Why, George asked himself as he made his way down to his typography class, does everyone have to be so bloody sensitive?

Emma spent the rest of the morning hiding, leaning against the window in the empty Common Room, watching the traffic on the Charing Cross Road two floors below, right back where she'd started months ago, seething with impotent rage that Ricky was alive and well and not *there*. At twelve, she went out to eat because she couldn't face the canteen, but she jibbed at the Italian too, bought a sandwich that, rarely for her, she couldn't face eating, then made her way reluctantly back to college, only to hang around on the pavement fighting to staunch the flow of tears that threatened to overwhelm her.

She should perhaps have expected him, after all he had begun to make a habit of rescuing her, but Jay still made her jump when he appeared beside her. She flung herself into his comforting arms and clung to him until the rage and misery subsided, oblivious to the odd glances they were getting from the students pouring past them on their way back from lunch. When he led her to his car and tucked her into her seat she felt overwhelming gratitude: that he was there; that he loved her; that he hadn't run away like Ricky. She was bereaved all over again, not by Alison's death, but by Rick's apparently rude and unfeeling well-being. How *dare* he survive, even thrive, without her?

Jay, misunderstanding, took her home, fed her, then sat her down on the sofa and confronted her.

'Now what?'

'I don't know.' Emma stared at the rug beneath her feet, blues, blacks and ochres, rich ruby reds, and let him think it was Alison alone she grieved for. 'I can't seem to get my act together. It's okay in theory, but when I get to college I go to pieces. I saw George this morning. Do you know, I embarrassed him just by being there? I feel like a leper at a garden party. I make them all uncomfortable; they don't know what to say to me.' It was an accurate enough description of her isolation. But, oh, Ricky, she thought, where are you? How could you do this to me?

'So ring Bill. You could go in together. Mutual support . . .'

'Bill's off sick again. He's even worse than I am – according to George he's on pills and back home with his mum.' She forced a laugh. 'If I was having a nervous breakdown the last place I'd go is my mother.'

Jay regarded her impassively. 'Me too,' he said and Emma stared at him in surprise. It was the first indication he had ever let slip that he even had a mother, let alone that she was alive and kicking. Seeing her interest he swiftly moved the conversation on. 'You'd stay here, so I could put you back together again. Humpty Dumpty. Next decision: if you're not going back to college what are you going to do instead?'

'I don't know. I don't earn enough to live on just freelancing, not to keep my place and . . .' Oh Lord, what a stupid thing to say; you'd be only too pleased if I gave it up and moved in properly, made a commitment I'm not ready to make.

'I can afford both of us,' said Jay flatly, reading her mind. 'You can work as much or as little as you please, not at all if you like.' He grinned, trying to lighten the increasingly heavy atmosphere. 'You could even learn to cook in your spare time, or change your name to Hammond.'

She ignored the jibe; her cooking was a joke and the other suggestion a dangerous red herring. 'I'll have to get a job, but I don't know whether I can without qualifications.'

'Of course you can.' Jay accepted the equivocation without comment. 'We'll get a portfolio together and I'll take you round some of the agencies. You could sell some more fabric designs too. I've got contacts all over now – I can probably even find you a buyer without you having to do a print run.'

Oh, thought Emma as she trawled through the attic, rescuing a cut-glass vase from beneath a pair of broken fishing nets, and adding the nets to the growing pile of throwaways, how difficult it was to accept. Bit by bit everything Jay did bound me tighter to him, was carefully calculated to enmesh me into his life so I was less able to function without him. And how I resented it. He did all the hard work, chose the samples he thought would sell me most effectively, riding roughshod over my opinions in the process, found an old folder and cut the work to size, then mounted it professionally. 'Presentation,' he kept telling me. 'Presentation is the most important thing of all.' And he was right, infuriatingly right, though at the time I was not prepared to admit it.

She found a pile of old magazines, *Domus*, *Designers in Britain*, both long since out of print, remembered as she flicked through them how good her work had looked when it was properly laid out, then smiled, recalling the panic when she had realised that there were no photographs. They were all at college, in the basement with Eddie, waiting to be collected. Looking back on it now, at a distance of twenty-six years, she wondered whether Jay's enthusiasm for her decision to quit had been entirely without ulterior motive.

I used Alison's death as an excuse, she thought; told myself it was because of her entirely that I couldn't face college, when it was George and his big mouth, the knowledge that Rick was somewhere out there, surviving without me, that had finished me off that day.

Of all the places she did not want to go, the photographic studio in the basement was the top of Emma's list.

'I'll do it,' said Jay. He was lounging on the sofa while she sat on the floor leaning back between his knees, and he was drying her hair. 'Whilst you take your letter in to Miss T. I'll go and see Eddie.'

The relief was dizzyingly wonderful, like being unexpectedly paroled from a prison sentence, let out into the sunshine from the dark.

Conscience assaulted her. 'I'll have to go home. I'll have to explain to Ma face to face. She'll have forty-seven fits when I tell her.'

'Do you want me to come?'

'No!' she said vehemently. 'You'll only complicate things.' Ma will award you the status of putative son-in-law. You will go along with her, using your undoubted charm, and I will be left floundering helplessly in the middle trying to defend my freedom against both of you. 'I'll manage better by myself. I'll go this weekend . . . maybe.'

'Em . . .' Jay slid behind her to the floor, long gangling legs stretched out either side of her.

'Mmm?'

He dropped his head to her shoulder. 'Don't leave me for too long.'

He drove her in on the Friday morning, her letter of resignation (withdrawal, abdication, surrender?) clutched in her hand, and they parted on the steps, Emma to go up to what promised to be an unpleasant interview with Miss T., Jay to go down to Eddie in the basement to collect her photographs.

She had to wait; there was some other poor soul being read the riot act, and they were so long Jay caught her up, a fat brown package in his hand. He was looking pleased, triumphant even.

She turned the envelope over in her hands, reluctant to open it in case it turned out to contain incontrovertible evidence that she was not talented enough to survive in the real world, and asked tentatively, 'Well?'

'Well . . . Eddie says your stuff looks terrific.'

Emma regarded him sceptically. 'And?'

'And what? I have nothing to add to Eddie's diagnosis. Show them to her. Play for sympathy. She's got contacts in the rag trade I haven't.'

'You can go in now,' said the secretary, emerging from the office with a white-faced first-year boy.

'But I ought to warn you,' Jay stood with her, 'there're some of Ali in there.' He touched her cheek. 'Good luck.'

The interview began stickily. Miss T. read Emma's sycophantic letter in silence, then regarded her impassively over the top of her half-moon spectacles. 'Pity,' she said brusquely.

'Thought you might have pulled yourself together by now. So what do you intend to do?'

'Er, well, um . . .'

'Come on, dear, you can be a bit more articulate than that. We had high hopes of you for a while, you know. I'm told—' she shuffled papers, summoning up Emma's file '—you've already been picking up some freelance illustration work. Shall you be able to survive on that?'

Emma shook her head, shifted on the edge of her chair, and turned the brown envelope over and over in her lap. 'I was rather hoping . . .' what a cheek, to tell the woman she was throwing in the towel, then ask her for a favour in the next breath '. . . that you might give me some advice.' When she looked up Miss T. was observing her with condescending amusement.

How difficult it is, Miss T. was thinking, to take the child seriously, when she sits there picking at her skirt like a fourteen-year-old schoolgirl. Was I ever that thin? Pleasant child, but too sensitive for her own good. How will she manage the Rag Trade, if she can't manage college?

She accepted the brown envelope Emma pushed across the table at her and went through the photographs maddeningly slowly, in silence. Then she stacked them all up neatly and replaced them in the envelope.

'And what is your opinion of them?' she asked unexpectedly.

'I don't know.' Emma smiled, suddenly struck by the ludicrous situation she had got herself into. 'Actually, I haven't the faintest idea. I haven't seen them.'

'Well, you'd better have a look then, hadn't you?' Miss T. pushed the envelope back across the table, then reached into her desk drawer for paper. As Emma went through the fruits of her last eighteen months' work, she began to write, in a round, neat hand, at great speed, glancing up only briefly to ask, 'Well, what do you think?'

'On the whole,' said Emma at last, trying to avoid Alison's beautiful face as she leafed through them for the second time, 'I think they're rather good.' They were: neat, snappy little numbers – skirts, tops, trousers, all interchangeable, commercial, eminently wearable.

'On the whole,' Miss T. quoted back at her, her face studiedly bland, 'I am inclined to agree with you. They are, as you say, rather good.' Then she went back to her writing.

Emma sat in silence, watching the pen cover the page and waited patiently until Miss T. had finished, signed her name with a flourish, then folded the letter and put it in an envelope. She wrote a name and address on the front and held it out.

'Go and see him.' She waved a hand at the photos in Emma's lap. 'Take those and anything else you think might be relevant. He's a friend of mine, does your sort of thing, sportswear mostly, "mix 'n' match" as they say in this ghastly modern parlance. He'll be looking for someone in a couple of months' time. Show him the letter.'

She stood, indicating that the interview was at an end, held out her hand across the desk. 'Good luck, my dear. Let me know how you get on.'

Up in the attic, Emma smiled to herself as she moved a pile of old *Vogue* magazines, flipped idly through the pages and came across a full-page spread featuring a well-known designer. She had wondered at the time why Miss T. had allowed Bill so much time off, when she didn't her. It was only later that she found out. She reckoned Emma was good, talented, but she knew Bill was better. Bill was brilliant, up there with Ossie Clark and Bill Gibb, and she didn't want to lose him. He'd proved her right since, won all sorts of prizes: two British Fashion Awards, a Woolmark Exhibition, and last year the ultimate accolade, a retrospective at the V & A. Emma smiled at the glossy photographs. I had talent, she thought, Bill had, *has* genius. I can't wait to see him.

Where were her photographs? she wondered. Still in one of the packing cases? They had come in so useful, just at the right moment.

*

She went searching for Jay when she left Miss T., found him in the corridor, leaning against the wall with one leg bent in his usual fashion and a girl standing in front of him, a hand resting on his shirt front, her face raised so she could gaze into his eyes. When he saw her he left the girl abruptly and came to meet her.

'Who was that?'

'Another ex-girlfriend,' he said calmly. 'There are lots of them about, so you may as well get used to it. And while we're on the subject, I've just seen Ian. He asked me, rather inelegantly I thought, whether I had managed to screw you yet. I told him I hadn't, so I reckon we're about even, don't you? Now, if you've finished, can we go please?'

As he spoke he took her hand and made for the stairs. Neither of them said anything further until they were in his car, driving down Oxford Street.

'How did you get on with Miss T.?'

'But I didn't sleep with Ian. I bet you screwed that girl back there. And why did you tell him you hadn't screwed me?'

Jay sighed. It was going to be another of those conversations. 'Yes, I did screw her. And I told Ian I hadn't screwed you because I haven't. We don't screw, you and I, we make love.'

'Rubbish. What's the difference?' Emma shifted uneasily, wondering how she had managed to precipitate herself into a discussion about the nature of their sexual relationship and suspecting Jay of manipulation.

'I've been screwing since I was sixteen years old,' he said bluntly. 'Purely to satisfy my sexual appetite. What I do with you is quite different.'

'Rubbish.'

He glanced sideways at her, clearly amused by her discomfort.

'Okay.' He shrugged his shoulders. 'Suit yourself. You screw, I make love. We both enjoy it. Now, how did you get on with Miss T.?'

Emma opened her mouth to continue the argument, then

thought better of it. 'Fine. I got on fine. She's given me a letter of introduction. To . . .' She fumbled in her bag to hide her irritation. 'Solly Cohen. The company's called Mirico. I've heard of them, casual wear, well-finished stuff, nice. I've seen it in D.H. Evans and Peter Robinson's.' *You crafty swine. I've rumbled your game, trying to get me to admit that we share more than sexual satisfaction.* She turned her head resolutely away, staring out of the window at the passing traffic. Jay chuckled. *I will not give you the pleasure,* she taunted him silently, *of taking the bait you dangle.*

It was only as they crossed Putney Bridge that it hit her. She'd burned her boats at college now; she couldn't go back even if she wanted to.

The decision irrevocably made, Emma entered a strange state of semi-hibernation, eating, drinking, sleeping, making love, working sporadically in Jay's spare room at fabric designs and commissions, and taking each day as it came. She talked to Auntie Mabel, asked after Bill, still off sick and apparently as dazed and confused as she was, guiltily sent love by proxy to her mother, but she did nothing about Mirico. There was no rush, it wasn't urgent and it was too close to real life just then for her to cope with, so she put it off.

She was aware that Rick was slipping away from her, that she was in danger of losing him, but she couldn't seem to summon up the energy to fight the subtle protective web Jay began stealthily to weave around her. He seemed to know instinctively when to leave her alone and when she needed company, to understand her even better than she understood herself, but it made no difference, she persuaded herself – it could have been almost anybody feeding her, soothing her, wrapping her in a warm, comforting safety blanket and tiring her out with pleasure every night. Jay silently acknowledged the rules of the game, that no overt pressure must be used, breaking the unspoken ban only when her resistance was low, when they had just made love, asking her to marry him as she lay satiated in his arms. 'No,' she said each time, with brutal candour. 'I don't love you.'

Watching him with newly observant eyes, Emma confirmed what she had been vaguely aware of since the beginning. At the theatre, waiting for her in the foyer, or on the rare occasions he stood at the bar during concert intervals, Jay was always alone. He set up a barbed fence around himself beyond which no one was allowed to pass. He seemed to know a great many people, a great many women. They came up to him in bars, greeted him in restaurants. He occupied a space, propped up in a corner, one knee bent and foot flat against the wall, lounging in a chair or leaning on a bar. When acquaintances approached him, he was polite, contributed, but somehow he never allowed them to cross the invisible line he had drawn. He never initiated the contacts, never took up the invitations he received to dinner or to parties. When she asked him why he refused to socialise he looked surprised, then said disconcertingly, 'If I don't want to join in, what is the point of pretending that I do?'

Often, more often than not, when the curtain came down and the audience rushed for the bar or the exit, he would pull her down beside him and make her wait, sitting calmly in his seat until the bell rang to summon the faithful to the second act, or until they were the last ones left in the auditorium and the cleaners appeared to pick up the sweet papers, the programmes, the lolly sticks. Only then would he get up and leave. He lived in a space of his own upon which the outside world was allowed to impinge only so far. Except for Emma. He wanted Emma with him, inside his self-imposed exclusion zone looking out, observing but not participating. His peculiar detachment reminded her poignantly of Ricky.

Was it coincidence, she wondered, that the two men she had been heavily involved with should be so very much alike, so cut off from the mainstream? And it occurred to her that whilst she knew Ricky's reasons for isolating himself, Jay's were a mystery.

She glanced at her watch; the sun was climbing higher in the sky and the light outside the attic window was bright. Time for a rest. The Hermit would be back with the dogs by now, waiting for her downstairs, and she smiled at the pleasurable anticipation the thought aroused in her. She should have grown out of such childish enthusiasm, she supposed, after all these years. She shook herself, then began shovelling the throwaways into black sacks, tying their necks and dumping them by the door ready to go.

'Hoy!' His voice floated up the stairs. 'Come down, I've made fresh coffee.'

'On my way.' Did you read my mind? she wondered. And if so, how? Is it because we have been together for so long you can tell what I'm thinking, or because we're so sure of each other after all we have been through?

As she negotiated the narrow gap she had left by the door, a folder slid to the floor at her feet. It was something of George's, a workbook, and there was a photograph tucked into the sleeve at the back. She glanced at it, then looked again, at the fresh young faces, the outlandish clothes. It was her, them, the four of them, George, Bill, Alison and Emma, standing on the stairs at Auntie Mabel's, taken . . . when? She frowned at it, then remembered Jilly, the night she had poured a glass of wine over Ian's head. She examined her seventeen-year-old self, a skinny child in the first throes of love; Bill, a baby-faced innocent just learning corruption; and George, smirking for the camera, immensely satisfied with himself even then. She peered at Alison's lovely face, glowing from the faded photograph even in the dim light of the attic, so full of life, beauty, vitality, and sighed, then tucked it in the back pocket of her jeans and made her way gingerly down the steep stairs.

They were all waiting for her, Newton lying across the bottom step, panting, Flotman and his master together, the dog leaning against a damp, corduroy-covered leg, his tail waving gently against the carpet, the Hermit lounging patiently, one arm draped across the newel post and his face turned up expectantly, ready to greet her.

'Look what I've found,' she said, holding out the photo. He

took it from her and moved towards the next flight of stairs, examining it as he went, then flung her a quick glance over his shoulder.

'I see he's not in it.'

She caressed Flotman's ears as she passed. 'Of course he's not,' she said dismissively. 'Neither are you. Neither of you ever were.'

She followed him down towards the kitchen and coffee. 'Hermits,' she added. 'You were both hermits. And you still are. I wonder whether he still is too?' How many years is it now, since I saw his face for the last time? I wonder if his hair is white, if he is married, a father, if he is as happy as I am ... as he deserves to be?

'Poor you,' he said, waiting for her in the hall, 'having to choose between hermits.' He touched her cheek, smiled. 'I just thank God it was me you chose.'

It was two days before she returned to her task in the attic – there was a room to prepare for Bill and co., a trip to Cambridge with the Hermit to deliver a commission, and the weather was too good to be inside, the overgrown garden seductive in its early summer promise.

So she put it off, removed the black sacks, sighed at the amount of work still left to do, then shut the door firmly behind her and ran down to find the dogs and escape into the fresh air and the sunshine. It was Wednesday before she climbed the stairs again, the Hermit was in London overnight and it was time she stopped prevaricating.

What is it about attics, she wondered as she stood in the open doorway contemplating her task for the second time, that brings the memories flooding back so thick and fast?

CHAPTER TWENTY-TWO
• • •

By the time Emma felt ready to make an appointment with Mirico, and had plucked up the courage to tell Josie she was coming home to visit, summer had arrived.

Her interview was fixed for a Monday, and she went home on the Saturday. She would have gone on the Friday, but she'd spent the day completing her portfolio, and she was tired. That Jay had gone out, and wasn't due home until ten that night – the first time he had been late back since the French perfume incident – that she would have had to leave without seeing him (and making sure he didn't reek of someone else when he arrived) was irrelevant.

Since she was there it seemed churlish not to provide him with a meal. She grilled chicken breasts until they were dry and curling at the edges, then chopped salad – and her finger – to go with them. She managed the potatoes quite well, catching them just before they boiled completely dry, then cutting off the black bits and adding butter so he wouldn't notice. The smell of burned potato was rather overpowering, but otherwise she was quite pleased with her efforts.

He wasn't expecting her to be there. He smelled, unlike the flat, satisfyingly of Jay and nothing else, and he was starving hungry, but not for chicken salad. By ten past ten they were in bed, their clothes strewn all along the hall, and the salad, unlike Jay, was wilting in the kitchen.

Josie was upset. 'I cooked your favourite meal, made you a special pudding and everything, and you couldn't be bothered to come

home and eat it. What were you dong last night that was so
important?'

Fucking, Ma. I was fucking my lover.

'And why do you never answer your phone? They don't even
seem to think you live there any more.'

I don't, and now is the moment to tell you about it, about my
fucking lover. But I won't, because I'm a coward. I'll explain it
after the ubiquitous sherry, or maybe after two.

As the weekend progressed it became more difficult. There
seemed to be no opportunity to break the news that she hadn't
been to college for months, let alone that she was living with Jay.
To ease her conscience, hovering like a vulture on her shoulder,
Emma cooked Sunday lunch: frizzled lamb; underdone potatoes,
compensating for her previous attempt; mushy carrots. She plied
Josie with sufficient sherry that she might not notice, then offered
to wash up because the alcohol made her mother garrulous and
she didn't want to talk.

She stared out of the window at the suburban garden, everything just beginning to wilt in the summer heat, the roses in full
blowsy bloom, and felt like a stranger. She didn't belong here any
more. I'm homesick, she thought; I want to go home. Then she
poured more detergent into the already soapy water and involved
herself in a flurry of energetic mopping, to avoid the implications
of the word. When she'd finished, she took off Josie's apron and,
on the pretext of needing fresh air, walked down the road to the
phone box on the corner. It smelled of stale urine and damp
concrete and Jay answered almost immediately. She could hear
music in the background, his classical stuff, and his mouth was
full.

'What're you eating?'

'Chicken.' There was a pause, then his voice again, clearer. 'Is
there some problem?'

'No . . .' Make it easy, damn you. 'I just rang to . . . to . . .'

'To what?'

'To see if there was any . . . post.'

'For you? Dunno, hang on, I'll look.'

She heard the phone clatter.

'One,' he said. 'London postmark, typed. Is that the one you're waiting for?'

'Yes,' she lied.

'Do you want me to open it?'

'Yes – no, it's all right. It'll keep.'

There was a long pause, then Jay, sounding dry and amused, 'If it'll keep why did you need to ring about it ... ?' Another long pause, then just to make his point. 'Especially since it arrived before you left.'

Emma thought of various choice epithets in the silence that followed, then rejected them all in favour of simple abuse. 'You,' she said succinctly, 'are a mean, low-down son-of-a-bitch, and I don't know why I bothered to ring you at all.'

He laughed. 'Thank you, my darling. I shall take that as a compliment.' Then just as she was about to slam the phone down he added softly, 'I miss you too,' and hung up.

She left earlier on Sunday night than was strictly necessary, having told Josie nothing of her plans, because really, when she came to think about it, there was no point in alarming her unnecessarily; it would be much more sensible to get this job first, before she broke the news. The decision engendered enormous relief.

She willed the train to go faster, fumed across London on the Tube, gritting her teeth and tolerating the claustrophobia because she knew it would be quicker than the bus, then tore across Putney Bridge, watching the lights of Jay's block reflected in the river and wondering which flat was his. When she reached the embankment she stopped under a street lamp to check the time, just after ten, then peered up at the windows, trying to calculate which ones belonged to Jay. As she counted, working from the end, the lights she thought should be his, theirs, went out. Must have miscalculated, she thought, he'll be waiting up.

She broke into a run, even took the lift, fighting the panic as the doors clashed together, then stood in the corner with fists clenched and eyes shut, counting the seconds until it reached the third floor. She was getting better, she congratulated herself.

She let herself in as quietly as possible, hoping to surprise him, but the flat was in darkness. She was surprised how anticlimactic his lack of concern made her feel, but she told herself she didn't care. Who needed him anyway? It was just insecurity, that was all, what with missing Rick, and Ali ... She turned on some lights, rather more noisily than was strictly necessary, made herself a tomato sandwich, then went to the bathroom and left her clothes littered all over the floor in an untidy heap. Jay hated that.

She padded naked down the corridor to the bedroom, turning off the lights as she went, then stood in the doorway in the dark straining her eyes to see. She could make him out vaguely as she drew nearer – a hunched, indistinct shape beneath the bedclothes – and she could feel his warmth as she slid in beside him, but he didn't wake.

She turned her back on him and lay staring out of the window at the orange light from the street below, aching with disappointment, until without warning he rolled over, whispered, 'Hello, my love,' in her ear, and swarmed all over her.

'You,' she informed him bitterly just before she succumbed, 'are a complete and utter bastard ...'

'Why didn't you wait up for me?' she asked, struggling to keep her eyes open, and Jay laughed in her ear.

'I did. I watched you all the way across the bridge; I saw you looking for the lights; I listened to you as you came up in the lift – you must have been in a hurry. Then I waited for you to come to bed. You eat too much, Skinnyribs.' He wrapped his fingers round hers, then drew her in against his warm skin. 'Don't go away again,' he said softly. 'I don't like it.'

CHAPTER TWENTY-THREE
• • •

Solly Cohen was vast, as big as Alison's father, as big as a house. His office, in a modern block just off Oxford Street, was quite big too, but his presence in it made Emma feel as if she was stepping into a rather small cupboard with a large grizzly bear. His voice was as huge as his physical presence – deep, raucous, very loud; his cheeks were rosy; his hair an extrovert mass of brown curls, and his mouth a pink, incongruous rosebud. His handshake was crushing.

'What do I call you?' he boomed.

'Emma. Emma Versey.'

'Right, Emmie Ver-sea. Angelica says I should give you a go. (Angelica? Could Miss T. really be called *Angelica*?) Not too sure myself. No time for precious little petunias that wilt at the first sign of pressure.' Petunias? What on earth was the man talking about? 'Got to be tough to survive in this business.' He glowered at her menacingly with large bulbous brown eyes. 'You tough, Miss Emmie Ver-sea? Or a wilting petunia?'

She resisted the temptation to laugh. 'Don't know yet,' she said, catching his habit of starting his sentences in the middle.

'See you're leaving college early. Why's that?'

'Personal reasons.'

'What personal reasons? Pregnant, are you? Ha, Ha!' he roared.

'I'd rather not say.' Emma eyed him dubiously. You could get on my nerves, she thought, awfully easily.

He rummaged on his desk, an exuberant shambles of swatches,

248

costings, letters, sketches, found Miss T.'s letter, read it again.

'Well, at least you weren't thrown out. Something, I suppose.' He grinned, showing large, white tombstone teeth that jostled each other for space in that small, feminine mouth. 'Unless it's a forgery of course.'

His smile was infectious, enthusiastic and slightly goofy. Despite herself Emma smiled back. 'Rather easy to check, I'd have thought,' she said and he laughed, a dozen pneumatic drills all going off together.

'Right,' he bellowed. 'To business!'

There was clutter everywhere in his office: two leather arm-chairs draped with swatches; bolts of cloth leaning drunkenly against the walls; the enormous, abandonedly untidy leather-topped desk; filing cabinets hanging open, as if a burglar had been caught in mid-rifle; and a button-backed swivel chair into which he hurled himself, swinging wildly round in a circle before finally coming to rest facing her.

'Do a deal with you,' he roared. 'Not a great one for you Airy-Bloody-Fairy students as a rule. Come out of your swanky colleges with a piece of paper, inflated idea of your own importance, and no effing idea at all about the business. Can't sell half this crap.' He waved a huge, dismissive paw at her folder, lying open on his desk. 'Going to be any good, you'll have to start learning. Fast. Or I'll throw you out. Understand?'

'If you're going to throw me out, does that presuppose you're going to take me on?'

'Ruddy smart-arse,' he said, grinning cheerfully and Emma felt a rush of elation. 'Right, follow me.' He lumbered to his feet, towering over her, then roared out into reception. Emma followed him with extreme caution, as one might a charging rhino, to be frog-marched down a long corridor to the cutting-room.

'Girls!' He waved an enormous, expansive hand at half a dozen middle-aged women in nylon overalls, hunched over their machines zapping industriously along lengths of cloth.

'Clerical! Costings!' he bellowed as they passed glass-fronted cubicles on the left of the room, occupied by secretaries checking invoices, calculating prices, opening parcels full of braid, buttons, zips.

The space opened out at the end into an L-shape, where two men were working at huge tables, cutting out patterns. Beyond them rack upon rack of fabric, bolts, rolls, scraps were stacked ten feet high and to one side a row of irons was connected to the mains by heavy-duty cables dangling like school climbing ropes from the ceiling. There were ironing boards, a Hoffman steam presser, sleeve boards, trouser presses. The noise of the machines was awesome.

'All right, Cyril?'

'Aye-aye, Solly.'

'Head pattern-cutter,' bawled Cohen. 'Best in the business.'

Cyril, grey-haired, wiry, his face invested with a hundred creases, winked at Emma, then waited patiently for his master's bidding as Cohen began to raid the cloth racks, rooting amongst the fabrics, then dragging out one after another and throwing them to land with a thud on the end of the cutting-table.

When he had a dozen bales littering the table, he grabbed a pair of shears, cut swatches from each one, and flung the shears negligently on to the table, where they skidded and clattered noisily. 'Right!' he said, sweeping the pile of cuttings into his great fist. 'All right, Cyril?'

'Aye-aye, Solly,' and Cohen was off again, back the way they had come. It was like being escorted by a whirlwind.

Once in his office he flung himself into his chair, then threw the multicoloured pile at Emma. 'Right, what can you do with those?'

'What did you have in mind?'

'You're the designer. You tell me.'

Emma rifled through the pile. There was some decent cloth there, a fine wool, a linen mix, a sailcloth. There was a good quality barrathea, a lightweight worsted.

'Leftovers. Ordered last season, never used 'em. Going to waste.' He glanced up sharply. 'You know what sort of stuff we do?'

'Er, um, I . . .'

He didn't wait for her garbled answer, snorted like a steam train. 'Find out,' he bawled. 'Bloody unprofessional that.' He examined her, head on one side, swinging back and forth like a gigantic budgie in a cage. 'Range of suits,' he said at last. 'Nothing fancy, keep it simple. By the beginning of next week.' He beamed at her gleefully. 'Not going to pay you a penny either, not till I've seen 'em. If they're any good we'll make 'em up, if not forget it. Don't pay for failure. Flat fee if we use 'em, forty quid a garment. If . . .' He eyed her dubiously. '*If* they sell we'll talk about a retainer.'

He waited expectantly for a reply. When Emma said, 'Okay,' he nodded briskly and rose, filling all the available space between them.

'Right, Emmie Ver-sea,' he boomed. 'Take your stuff and bugger off. Busy man.' By the time she had packed up her folder and reached the door he was already on the phone. 'None of your ruddy excuses, Bernard, you promised me those buttons three weeks ago . . .' He didn't look up.

She went to Dickens and Jones and wandered round the dress department looking at the clothes. She examined Mirico's last collection, then the competition, Emcar, Reldan, Alexon, Berkertex, trying to work out what market she should be aiming for. It wasn't for kids, not Mary Quant or Biba, but it wasn't the Crimplene Granny end of the market either. After nearly an hour, when the assistant was clearly beginning to suspect her of shoplifting tendencies, she walked back to Oxford Street and, her head full of ideas and plans, caught a bus to Marble Arch.

She crossed the road to Hyde Park and strolled along beside the Serpentine, then sat on a bench in the hot summer sunshine to watch the world go by: mothers pushing prams, their shopping hanging from their arms, from the handles of their kids' bicycles or pushchairs, bigger kids trailing behind; businessmen in a hurry, looking to neither left nor right, avoiding distraction lest the urge to loosen their ties, take off their jackets and roll up their sleeves should overpower them.

She turned her face up, closing her eyes to feel the heat, then opening them again to watch the fluffy white clouds moving across the blue overhead. When Ricky forced his way into her head she pushed him resolutely away – no point in agonising over what couldn't be changed – but when Alison followed she let her stay, allowed herself to think about her for the first time in months almost without pain, without guilt.

Where had the Bastard buried his daughter when what was left of her was finally released by the butcher boys? There had been no word, no message except a bald announcement in the paper: *The funeral has taken place* ... You up there, she addressed her friend silently, give me a sign. Pay attention, I'm down here waiting for you to get in touch.

She held her breath for a moment, stupidly expectant, then sighed and rose to go home. It was only as she walked across the dusty grass towards the road that she remembered: Jay wouldn't be there, he had taken some pictures to sell today and wouldn't be back until mid-afternoon. Frustrated, wanting something to do in the absence of anyone to tell about her morning, but not ready to start work yet, she began to run. She would catch a bus to the Portobello Road; it was ages since she had been. She would browse amongst the stalls and fill in time until Jay was back to share in her exhilaration.

The market was teeming with people: American tourists in loud shirts and checked trousers accompanied by stout wives in pressed slacks and rhinestone sunglasses; groups of diminutive Japanese huddled in close formation, loaded down with cameras and snapping at everything; students hunting for the definitive bargain everyone else had missed, and lovers strolling in the sunshine holding hands. Emma wandered aimlessly past the stalls, reliving her successful interview as she negotiated the crowds, stopping on her way to rifle through the antique nightgowns and moth-eaten fur coats, the beaded flapper dresses and cloche hats.

She spent nearly ten minutes poring over a stand selling home-made sweets, fondant creams, crystalised fruit, truffles and white chocolate, then bought two ounces of sugared almonds and a piece of fudge, using almost all the spare change she had. The almonds, carelessly wrapped in a twist of tissue paper, reminded her unexpectedly of the brooch she carried in her bag, of the day Ricky had given it to her. She made for the nearest jewellery display, searching for something similar, knowing she would recognise his work instantly if – when – she saw it. Then, scolding herself for day-dreaming, she moved determinedly on, only to be stopped by a stall selling Edwardian miniatures, reminded of her conversation with George. Rick was out there somewhere, selling his paintings. The thought of him managing so effortlessly without her dragged her mood down, spoiled her enjoyment. What was the point of dwelling on him, when he was gone?

The road narrowed further along; the street vendors had packed their trestle tables in closely and Emma was brought to an involuntary halt by a solid phalanx of people, stuck in a traffic jam ahead of her. As she stood waiting for the congestion to clear she turned her thoughts back determinedly to her interview with Solly Cohen, then forward to going home, cheering herself, as design ideas began to form in her head, with the anticipation of Jay's certain pleasure in her success. Oddly, having managed since Ali's death to avoid thinking about him almost entirely, Rick now refused stubbornly to let her be, as if he was deliberately intent upon wrecking her buoyant mood.

The stall in front of her was selling old lace, doilies, collars, cuffs and antimacassars. As she picked uninterestedly through a pile of crocheted table runners, Emma listened to snippets of passing conversation and attempted, through Rick's insistent presence, to concentrate on planning her afternoon's work. When an altercation started behind the awning draped at the back of the next stall she was grateful for the distraction and eavesdropped shamelessly.

The woman's voice was shrill and accusatory. 'But I still don't see why you can't go on supplying me. You've made a packet out of me over the past few months, and I reckon you owe me, you dog.'

The man's voice was softer than the woman's, low-pitched, and he was clearly unmoved by the abuse. 'Come on, Annie,' he said, 'be reasonable. I've already told you why. This contract is going to take up too much time to make stuff for you as well. You've done very nicely out of our deal and as far as I'm concerned I don't owe you a thing. Look at the mark-up you've been charging; you can hardly complain about your profits these past few months, and I warned you at the beginning the arrangement would only last until I'd got myself established, didn't I? I don't know why you're getting so worked up about it—'

Annie's voice again, peeved, sulky. 'Because your gear sells like hot-cakes, that's why I'm getting so worked up about it, because none of my other suppliers can come even close to the sort of stuff you do. Come on, darling, give me break, I'm not asking for the moon, am I?'

Emma, peering through the gap between the stalls, caught a brief glimpse of luxuriant, brightly hennaed hair and leaned forward across the piles of lace, straining to see more. What was it about the man's voice? The timbre, the intonation reminded her of someone, but who . . . ? The answer hovered tantalisingly on the edge of her mind, just out of reach, and she moved nearer, pushing against the crowds in an effort to see round the corner.

'Oh, blast you,' came Annie's shrill voice again. 'Just sod off then, I'll manage without your bloody stuff.'

Emma imagined the shrug accompanying that elusively familiar voice. 'Okay, if that's the way you want to play it. I'll see you around, Annie.'

It was the sibilant that jolted her memory, the almost imperceptible hesitation between the 's' and the 'e'. It brought Emma's head up sharply, just as he appeared at the far end of the next stall and the crowd surged past her again, carrying him away from her.

His distinctive profile was unmistakable: rich golden hair, brown skin, the brilliant whites surrounding the black irises of his eyes. And when he turned his head, looking for the quickest way through the crowds, *oh*...

He was framed momentarily, between the awnings, like one of the miniatures she had been enjoying earlier. Emma caught her breath and stared, mesmerised by his proximity and immobilised by the intensity of emotion the sight of him triggered. He didn't see her.

For five, ten, fifteen vital seconds she remained rooted to the spot, convinced she had conjured him out of the air with wishful thinking and unable to believe she had actually heard him talking, articulately, coherently. He was even more beautiful than she remembered, still stoop-shouldered, but not so thin, not cowed any more. Maybe it was something about the way he moved, clad in a familiar leather jacket, or the way he held his head, with a confidence, almost an arrogance, that had been entirely missing when she first fell in love with him. By the time she had pulled herself together and persuaded her leaden feet to work he was moving away.

She pushed hard at the solid wall of humanity between them, not caring who she trampled so long as she could keep her quarry in view, and she alternately apologised to the obstacles she was shoving out of the way and shouted at his back. '*Ricky!* Excuse me, will you let me through, thank you ... *Ricky!* Oh, may I just get past you, would you mind? *Rick!* Sorry, would you please let me by ... *Ricky* ... *Rick!*'

Her progress was impeded by the bulky folder she still carried under her arm, and her voice rose with her desperation as his tall figure diminished ahead of her; by the time he made it to the edge of the crowd and began to move more freely, she was bellowing her head off, but it was no good. A couple of stalls further on there was a man selling lengths of Indian fabric, touting his sari-silk at the top of his voice, extolling the virtues of his wares, offering discounts, two yards for the price of one, a bolt for less than half-price, wonderful, marvellous stuff, buy some for your wife, daughter, granny, and every time Emma yelled he yelled with her, matching and outdoing her so her voice was drowned in the general babble and Ricky didn't hear.

It was like a bad dream she had had as a child, pushing through air as thick as treacle, her limbs refusing to work except in slow motion, pursued by shadowy night-time demons. Only now she was awake, the pursuer not the pursued, and the harder she strove to narrow the gap between them the further away Rick moved, until she was catching only occasional glimpses of his bright hair and she knew she was going to lose him again.

When she finally cleared the thick wedge of people that had been holding her back she staggered and almost fell, then stared frantically round the space into which he had vanished as if she could make him reappear just by wishing. 'Ricky!' she bawled. '*Ricky!*' Where the hell was he?

Please, please, she begged the empty street, don't be gone. She spun wildly, straight ahead, from right to left, back the way she had come, set off up one side street, then another, plunged into the crowd to fight her way back to where she thought she had started, panicking. The girl would know; the one he had been talking to. (Rick, *talking*? So it was true, what George had said. The *bastard*!) If she could find Annie she would be able to give her an address, a phone number, a clue. Please, please, Ricky, don't be gone.

She found her easily enough, recognised her hair instantly. She was standing by her stall complaining to a neighbouring vendor, waving her arms about and ranting. She was small and lightly built, pretty, but her chin was squarely determined, her brown eyes were sharp and the auburn curls that bounded on her shoulders were brassily flamboyant. She was dressed in crushed velvet, a demure high-necked blouse which flattered her pert face, but she wore a dirty canvas money belt around her waist and there was nothing ladylike about her demeanour. When Emma tugged at her sleeve she swung round and snapped irritably, 'What? Just hang on, will you, I'm talking! Choose what you want and I'll be with you in a tick!'

Emma turned away to stare at the stall beside her. She wanted to scream and stamp her foot, to demand attention, information, felt she would explode with impatience, and leaned forward to examine the goods laid out before her with no interest at all.

'Oh!' she said out loud.

It was Ricky's silver the girl was selling, delicate, filigree pieces with a distinctive style that could have been produced by only one pair of hands. She had *found* him. She was swept by delirious triumph. When at last the pretty face, with its bright cloud of hair appeared beside her and its owner snapped, 'Well?' she smiled widely, her impatience forgotten.

'You know Ricky Brown?' she begged. 'Don't you?'

The girl's sharp expression grew sharper. 'What if I do? I thought you wanted to buy something?'

'Oh. Oh, I do. But I need . . .' She grabbed at the nearest piece, a tie-pin. Its head was fashioned in the shape of a daisy, each petal subtly different from its fellows, the tiny pin-cushion seedhead at the centre perfect in every detail. It was exquisite.

'This one, how much is this one?'

'Five pounds, cash only.'

'*How* much?' She hadn't got five shillings. She'd spent all her money on sugared almonds. 'I've left my purse behind,' she lied. 'If you could put it to one side for me, I'll—'

'No chance. This stuff walks off the stall by itself. In fact, come to think of it, the price has just gone up. These are collectors' items now the boy's joined the ranks of the Filthy Capitalists.' Annie waved a heavily ringed hand at the dozen pieces she had arranged together on a scrap of dark green satin and Emma, recognising Rick's intricate workmanship on her finger, was hit by a wave of illogical fury. The bitch was wearing a ring he'd made. He hadn't made *her* a ring.

'Now, do you want to buy or don't you?'

'Yes, but I—'

'These are the last, I can't get any more.'

'Why not?'

'Because darling Ricky's gone and got himself a big contract, that's why not, some fancy jeweller on Bond Street or somewhere, offering him the sort of prices I can't even begin to compete with.' She leaned across and deftly removed the daisy pin from Emma's hand, adding tartly as she placed it back amongst its fellows, 'So if you can't afford to buy, don't mess with the goods, okay?'

'But I know Ricky. He's my . . . he used to be my . . . I mean, he's my boyfriend.' This was crazy. 'I've lost his phone number.'

The girl laughed, her bright hair bouncing on her shoulders. 'Oh, yeah?' she said witheringly. 'Pull the other one. I've been trying to get a phone number out of Ricky Brown for three months now. Ex-directory, he says, and when you say well give me your address then, he laughs, blows you a kiss, and disappears again to wherever it is he hangs out, leaving you as wise as you were when you started.'

He laughs? How *dare* he laugh. 'Norfolk. He hangs out in Norfolk,' said Emma.

'Oh?' Annie narrowed her eyes speculatively. 'You sure?'

'Positive. I know – I knew his sister—'

'So if you know where he lives, how come you don't know his phone number?'

'I told you, I've lost it.'

'Well, if you've got his address, do me a favour and give it to me, would you? It might be worth a trip to the sticks if I could get my hands on some more merchandise.' She grinned suddenly, her face softening. 'Wouldn't mind getting my hands on a certain Ricky Brown either, come to that.' She licked her lips with a pink, lascivious tongue. 'How about it? I'd make it worth your while . . .'

Emma stared at her blankly. This couldn't be happening to her, a stall full of Ricky's jewellery, a girl who'd been dealing with him for months, and no nearer finding him than she was when she started. 'Look,' she began, fumbling in her bag for a piece of paper, 'if I write down my number (Oh Lord, which number? Hers? Jay's?), you could pass it on to him. Surely he must've given you a contact, a post office box, *something* . . . ?'

It didn't matter which number, Annie wasn't going to play anyway. 'You're not getting the message, are you? He used to just turn up out of the blue with the goods. He's never even given me a written receipt for the money I've shelled out to buy all this stuff.' She was losing interest, realising Emma had no useful information, becoming annoyed again. 'In fact, when I asked him for one he got really shirty, acted as if I'd asked him to walk on water at the very least—'

'He can't write.'

'What? Don't be ridiculous. Course he can write. Rick's as sharp as they come: adds up pounds, shillings and pence like a bloody cash register; does it all in his head too.' She placed her hands on her hips and eyed Emma contemptuously. 'Now if you don't mind, I've got better things to do with my time than waste it jawing with a starstruck groupie. If you take my advice, you'll forget Ricky Brown. He's on the way up, that one, and nothing's going to stop him, so give up and find someone your own size to drool over. In the meantime, do me a favour and clear off, I'm busy.' She turned her back, terminating the conversation.

It took Emma forty minutes to find a bank. She made it through the door with seconds to spare before they shut for lunch, queued for five minutes to withdraw twenty pounds she couldn't afford, then raced all the way back, arriving breathless and triumphant at Annie's stall to find it packed up and its orange-haired owner nowhere to be seen.

'Annie?' shrugged the woman next door in response to her frantic plea. 'Buggered off. She was fed up, said she'd had enough for today. Who wants her?'

'I do. I mean, I want to buy . . .' Emma's eyes prickled with tears of frustration. 'When will she be back?'

'Monday.' The woman was fat, phlegmatic, and infuriatingly unconcerned. 'Maybe. She shares it, this pitch, with another girl, only comes one day a week and then only if she's got something to sell.'

'But—'

The woman turned her back. There was an American hovering over her stall and Yanks meant business. Emma walked slowly away, pushing angrily through the crowds towards the nearest bus-stop. So close. How could she be so close and still miss him? Why hadn't he sensed her presence, felt it instinctively? He should have known she was there, the blasted idiot. Her head ached and her stomach churned. It had seemed of such overwhelming importance to buy one of his pieces, to have some tangible proof that she had really seen him, and all she had achieved was the loss of the only contact who might have led her to him. She stood on the pavement waiting for the bus in a daze, and when the conductor asked her where to, she stared at him in bewilderment.

'Bond Street,' she said at last. 'I want to go to Bond Street.'

By four o'clock she was exhausted. She had trudged the length of Bond Street, peering into every jeweller's shop she could find, even showed her brooch. 'Do you know the boy who made this? Do you sell this sort of stuff? Brown, his name is Ricky Brown.' No one had heard of him. Reluctantly, facing defeat at last, she limped up to Oxford Street and caught a bus back to Putney. All the way there she kept thinking, I'm returning to prison, I'm going back to second-best, and it's not *fair*. After all these months of thinking she was almost cured, even allowing herself to get far too close to Jay, she was right back where she'd started when Rick first walked out on her. How could he do this to her a second time?

Jay was playing his music: Brahms, the Double Violin Concerto. She was learning his favourites, his moods, and when he appeared in the studio doorway he was smiling, that rare, spontaneous lift of his mouth which usually had such a weakening effect upon her resolve. This time it was as if he was laughing at a funeral, and she couldn't bear it. I can't stay here, she thought, panicking, I can't; I *won't* settle for what you have to offer, but she was too tired to do anything about it.

'Have a good day?' he asked.

She shook her head vehemently, remembered Mirico for the first time in hours, nodded, then moved slowly past him, offended by his very existence. 'Yes,' she said. 'I suppose I have.' *But it doesn't feel like it any more.*

She used Jay as a crutch, something to lean on to stop her going mad, but she wouldn't talk to him. During the day she worked solidly on her designs for Mirico, rebuffing all his attempts at conversation, waiting for him to leave her alone then perversely feeling only panic when he did because his presence, his concern, dulled the pain and eased the agony of losing for the second time the one thing she wanted above all else. At night she fell exhausted into bed and his comforting arms, allowing him to make love to her, no, wanting him to, justifying herself with the thought that if she couldn't have Rick she would have plenty of sex instead and to hell with him. But she was painfully conscious, as she lay listening to Jay's breathing in the dark, that merely by staying with him she was being unfaithful to Rick; she was only there, she told herself, because she couldn't bear the thought of being on her own.

She ate herself silly.

She made a second abortive trip to the Portobello Road the following Monday, but Annie's stall was loaded down with tacky enamelled earrings and Annie was nowhere to be seen. When she got back to Putney she had a brainwave and phoned Directory Enquiries.

'Which town please?' asked the operator.

'Um, Norfolk.'

'Could you be a bit more specific please, caller. Norfolk's a big county.'

'Er, I don't know ...' *Where was it George lived – Cromer? No, somewhere near Aylsham, wherever that was.* 'Aylsham, try Aylsham.'

'And what was the name again?'

'Brown, Ricky Brown.'

'Ricky. Is that short for Richard?'

'What? Oh. Yes . . . maybe, I don't know.'

'And what is the exact address, caller?'

Emma's eyes filled with tears, and she tightened her grip on the receiver. 'I don't know!' she said irritably. 'Can't you just look and see—?'

'Do you have any idea how many Browns there are in the Norwich telephone directory, dear? And then there's the King's Lynn area and the Yarmouth Area, and the—'

When, after nearly a week of frenetic activity, of eager, almost desperate lovemaking in the dark, and frosty silences during the day, Jay demanded to know what was wrong, she said briskly, 'I haven't a clue what you're talking about. I'm just working hard, that's all. I'm tired.' She was grateful for Mirico, she needed the distraction to stop her going mad.

Her appointment was for ten and by nine-thirty she was prowling Oxford Street staring sightlessly into the shop windows, her stomach full of butterflies, her mouth dry with nerves, but feeling better than she had all week because she had something to think about other than Rick and her rising guilt about the way she was treating Jay. By ten to ten she was sitting in reception, wiping her damp palms on her skirt and wishing it was over.

Solly Cohen kept her waiting for another forty minutes, then when she was finally ushered into his office, remarked witheringly, 'Looks like you've been burning the midnight oil! Harder than you thought, eh?'

He laughed raucously, then took her sketches and leafed through them with inordinate speed. Emma resigned herself to failure. He put them down, swung experimentally in his chair, picked them up and went through them a second time, more slowly, then a third time, more slowly still. He began to divide them, two piles, one much smaller than the other and Emma's hopes rose. Then he picked up the larger pile, shoved it unceremoniously back into the folder and flung it across the desk at her.

'Not those. Rubbish.'

Emma blushed scarlet, felt as she imagined a mother might feel on rejection of her favourite child. Cohen slapped the other pile with his enormous paw. 'Not sure about these.' He picked them up carelessly, spilling them across the table. 'Have to see Cyril.' Then he heaved himself from his chair, grabbed them again and took off, Emma following behind.

Cyril went through what was left of her sketches methodically, asking questions. 'Could we run that dart from the side seam instead of vertically? Where would you put the zip on that one? Is that a pocket or just stitching detail?'

There were a couple that seemed to be a problem. 'You'll never get that to sit right,' he said of one. 'That jersey's too soft to take it. But you could do it in the hopsack, that would work.'

'All right, Cyril. Get on with it.'

'Now, Solly?'

'Now, Cyril.'

'Right, Solly.'

'Put Paul on whatever you're working on. Want to see some *toiles* by . . . how long?'

Cyril considered. 'Could let you have a couple by . . . Thursday?'

'Good grief, Cyril,' bellowed Solly, and Emma caught Paul, the other pattern-cutter, out of the corner of her eye, flinching. 'At that rate I'll be collecting my old-age pension by the time you've finished. How many by next week?'

Cyril considered, head on one side, then leafed through the sketches, less than a dozen left of the nearly forty Emma had done, and stroked his chin with a gnarled hand. 'Five or six.' He shrugged non-committally. 'Maybe.'

'Right.' Solly thumped the table with his fist. 'Get on with it then. All right, Cyril?'

'Aye-aye, Solly.'

And off Solly charged again, back to his office with Emma trailing in his wake.

He fell heavily into his chair and waved a hand at her as he passed. 'Nine suits. Look bloody boring to me, but we'll see. Need you here nine o'clock, Thursday. What'd we say, thirty quid?'

'Forty.' What a cheek!

He chuckled, twenty hens clucking all at once. 'Just checking. Coffee?' He flicked the intercom. 'Two coffees, Lesley, and bring the cheque-book.'

Emma was too excited to drink the coffee when it came. Solly Cohen scribbled as he slurped, signed with a flourish and threw the cheque across the desk at her. 'Don't forget, nine sharp, Thursday.' Then he waved a vast hand in dismissal.

She was halfway across reception when she noticed. The cheque was for £270. It was the largest amount she had ever received in one go, and it took a few moments to sink in. He'd paid her £30 for each design. She stopped, turned, started again, hesitated. How stupid.

'Damn and blast,' she said out loud.

The receptionist sniggered. 'Short-changed you, has he?'

'Does he do it often?'

'All the time.' They grinned at each other, reluctantly admiring his gall together.

'And does he get away with it?'

'All the time.'

Emma giggled. 'Well, you can tell him he's just got away with it again.' Then she hitched her bag over her shoulder, hoisted her folder under her arm and left, walking on air.

She needed to get home to share her success but she couldn't see any buses. Reluctant to face the Tube, she began to walk towards Marble Arch, wandering aimlessly past the trinket sellers and the find-the-lady tricksters coming out like woodlice into the summer sunshine, weaving her way in and out of the crowds and wasting time until a Putney-bound bus came by. She bought an Orange

Maid, then stopped to watch a three-card-trick man packing up with frantic haste to avoid the uniformed constable bearing down upon him, and it was only as her bus appeared, just past Oxford Circus and moving slowly in the heavy traffic, that she realised she was standing on the corner of Bond Street, and remembered Ricky. How could she have forgotten, even for a minute?

She stepped back and watched the bus come, then allowed it to trundle past. She felt completely deflated, the euphoria induced by success spoiled for the second time by the reminder of last week's fruitless search. She didn't want to go back to Putney any more, she wanted to end this terrible limbo so she could get on with living her life, instead of being torn in two all the time. She took a deep breath, straightened her back and turned left to begin her search all over again.

She almost missed it. It was one of those expensive, understated emporia that rely on word-of-mouth recommendation rather than ostentatious self-advertisement, and it wasn't on Bond Street at all, it was halfway down the Burlington Arcade. Sitting in the window on a bed of lush, plum-coloured velvet and lit from above by its own spotlight, was a silver filigree necklace. Each link, tiny, intricately detailed facsimiles of ivy leaves, interlocked gracefully with the next, each delicately veined leaf and twining stem was slightly different from its neighbour. There was no price tag, no clue as to its creator, but she knew instantly whose it was.

'It's urgent,' she insisted. 'Family business, and I have to get in touch with him immediately.' Her heart was thudding loudly in her ears, her folder seemed to have increased in weight, dragging at her arms, and her mouth was dry, her throat inexplicably constricted.

The manager was sniffy, clearly not used to dealing with the *hoi polloi*. 'I must repeat, Miss, I am not in a position to divulge his whereabouts.'

'But it's a matter of life and death, it's—' Oh, can I really be doing this, have I really sunk this low? 'It's about his sister.' She stammered the words out before she could change her mind, went hot with self-disgust, then waited red-faced with shame while the man weighed her up, trying to gauge whether or not she was genuine.

'He will be here tomorrow,' he said at last, grudgingly, 'at around half-past ten. But I would be grateful if you would kindly conduct whatever business you have with him well away from these premises. This is a very exclusive—'

'Thank you.' Emma didn't hear the rest of his sentence, she was making for the door.

She bought a sandwich, because it was lunchtime, then caught a bus and sat on the top deck, staring sightlessly into space and not eating it. She felt elated, heady, sick with nervous excitement; it was only as she neared Putney Bridge on her way home to Jay that she began to think about the consequences of her discovery. What if he didn't turn up? What if he turned up and didn't want her any more? What if he laughed in her face? And what, oh Lord, what was she going to say to Jay?

CHAPTER TWENTY-FOUR

• • •

At ten o'clock she was standing on the corner of Cork Street, opposite the entrance to the arcade. She was wearing her Indian skirt and an old cotton blouse, not wanting Rick to get the idea that she was desperate. But she was painfully aware of the dark rings under her eyes, caused by a miserable, sleepless night, and she could still see Jay's face when, for the first time since they had been together, she had refused point-blank to make love, still hear the puzzled incomprehension in his voice when she had failed even to return his good-morning greeting. It made it hard to concentrate.

Rick probably wouldn't come anyway. Why should things go right now, when they had gone wrong so many times before? She would probably miss him. Worse, he would come, see her, cut her dead and walk away; he had done it before . . .

When he emerged from the Burlington Arcade at ten to eleven she was leaning heavily against the wall behind her with her eyes shut because she couldn't breathe and she was having trouble with her legs, which were threatening to collapse. She didn't see him striding across the road, and when he touched her she was so startled she leaped convulsively and squealed like a frightened piglet. It wasn't how she had planned it at all, and now that he was here, she didn't know what to do.

'I had to tell you . . .' she blurted out, unable to think of anything intelligent to say or even, after that first startled glare, to look at him. 'I had to – to . . . I'm not chasing you, I just thought – I thought you ought to know. . .' Oh God, oh, Ali, I'm sorry, what an awful, dreadful thing to do, but it can't hurt you now.

Rick stood quite still, staring at her. When Emma plucked up the courage to raise her head she was confused to find she had forgotten even since last week just how black his eyes were, how brown his skin. He was bigger than she remembered too, more solid, and the leather jacket he was wearing looked expensive, well cut and soft. He was wearing a shirt and tie, neatly pressed trousers, and he exuded confidence, charisma – his own, not a pale facsimile of his sister's.

'I thought – I mean, someone has to tell you about – about ...' She was sick, she must be. How cheap, how utterly pathetic, using Alison as an excuse.

'Oh, *Emma*,' said Rick softly. 'Shut up, darling,' and he reached out to touch her cheek.

She had planned it minutely the previous night, as she lay unsatisfied beside Jay in his double bed, had rehearsed their reunion, what Rick would say, what she would say, how they would rush into each other's arms, what his kiss would taste like after more than a year apart. But now he was here Emma was unexpectedly engulfed by a roaring tidal wave of anger. She pushed herself away from the wall that was propping her up, struck his hand away, and hit him, hard, across the face.

The blow jerked his head back, but he didn't take his eyes from her for a second, or move away. When she went to swing at him again he braced himself to take the impact, and said quietly, 'Go ahead, I deserve it.' She paused, her arm still poised in mid-air as if she was hailing a taxi, and then began to cry.

Rick moved closer, sliding his arms around her, enveloping her in the smell of leather, expensive this time and minus the bike oil, not like Earl's Court at all, and he bent his head to whisper in her ear, 'I'm sorry, Em, don't cry, please don't cry. I'm sorry.'

'*Sorry?* What have you got to be *sorry* about?' She fought viciously to free herself and flailed wildly at him, oblivious to the passers-by who were beginning to stare, almost trying to goad him into walking away. 'You only ran out on me without a word of explanation. You only left me to fend for myself while you swanned off to do as you bloody well pleased. You only didn't phone, didn't write—'

'Couldn't write,' he corrected.

'What?'

'How could I write to you? I've only just learned how to handle the alphabet—'

Emma felt the rage welling again, let it come, oblivious to everything except what he'd done to her. 'Don't give me that crap, you can talk, can't you?' She could hear her voice echoing in her ears, harsh with unreasoning temper, and began to hurl gratuitous insults, just to relieve her feelings. 'You're a dirty, filthy pig of a bastard! You're a pathetic, selfish excuse for a human being, an apology for a man, you're a – a stoat, a weasel—'

'Emma—'

'Shut up, you son-of-a-bitch, you – you pig!' She was running out of epithets, repeating herself, her mind filled with heat and noise, her fury threatening to suffocate her. 'Shut up! I haven't finished yet!'

'Yes you have . . .'

He held her while she sobbed, breathing the scent of her hair, noting how thin she was, feeling her tears soaking through his shirt, smiling, beaming from ear to ear over the top of her head, in danger of exploding with sheer, delirious happiness.

'Better now?' he asked, straightening his face with difficulty as Emma raised her wet cheeks at last and glared at him with red-rimmed hazel eyes. 'Or do you need a stiff drink?'

'Don't you *dare* make jokes at me!' she snarled. 'Where the *hell* have you been?'

'Not here.'

'I know *that*, you bastard.'

Rick began to smile again, because he couldn't help it, refusing to react to her insults. 'I mean we can't talk here. Please, Em.'

He walked her back up Bond Street, then down Oxford Street

all the way to Park Lane, aiming for the Grosvenor Hotel in the hope that its quietly opulent atmosphere might calm her down a little. He needed calming down too, he was shaking inside, his euphoria mingled with terror, that he'd messed everything up and he might not be able to put it right. He gazed hungrily at her sulky profile all the way there, drinking her in like a man who has reached an oasis after months in the desert. Oh, he thought, if you only knew how much I've missed you.

Emma leaned back in her chair and waited for her heartbeat to settle, relieved to be sitting down. 'How did you get so big?' she asked irrelevantly, because all the other questions swirling round her brain seemed to be too difficult.

'Shifting rubble.' Rick moved his chair nearer so their knees were almost touching and leaned forward, then rested his elbows on his thighs and clasped his hands tightly together between his knees to stop himself from touching her. She wasn't ready for that yet. He could feel her resentment; he must give her more time. 'I'm renting a place near Acle, east of Norwich, that's where this chap lives, the one I told you—'

'What chap?' Emma was deliberately frosty, enjoying making it difficult for him.

'The one who taught me. He was the one I was saving up for, remember, the s-silversmith—?' Emma's head came up sharply at the self-mocking hesitation and Rick unclasped his hands, clasped them again; she still wasn't ready. 'And when he moved up to Norfolk I followed him—'

'What rubble?'

'The place I'm renting, I'm renovating it. The owner let me have it cheap on condition I did it up.' He leaned back, away from temptation, giving her more space. 'I've filled five skips so far, with assorted rubbish.' He grinned, then flexed his biceps at her beneath his jacket, posing, trying to make her smile. 'Mr Universe, that's me. Show me the Bastard nowadays and I'd probably knock his head off altogether.'

The reference to his father was a mistake; it reminded them

both of Alison. Rick greeted the waitress with relief, grateful for the interruption and ordered coffee for two and scones with jam.

'Nowadays,' said Emma nastily, ignoring the girl's presence completely, 'even I could probably knock the Bastard's head off. You didn't see him at the inquest.' Oh, she thought, why did I say that? What if he doesn't know?

The smile faded from Ricky's face and he looked suddenly bleak. 'It's all right,' he said. 'I saw it in the paper.' He lowered his head, staring at the floor as he relived the shock, the sadness, the feeling of waste. 'I was eating fish and chips at the time. It put me off fish for ages, finding my supper wrapped in a coroner's report.' When he looked up his eyes were blurry with tears. 'Sorry, Em.' He turned away, embarrassed by his own weakness. 'You gave evidence, didn't you? You and what's-his-name.'

'Bill.'

'Bill.' Change the subject. 'I went round to see him last week.'

'Who?'

'I went round to Earl's Court last week, to see Bill, but he wasn't there.'

'He's been off sick since . . .'

'Since it happened. But he's back at college now. George told me—'

'George told you what?'

'That Bill'd taken a long time to recover,' said Ricky, accepting plates, cups, saucers, shuffling the milk jug and the sugar bowl, looking for something to do with his impatient hands. 'But he wouldn't tell me anything else. He said you'd left college, that you'd moved and you were sharing a flat with someone, but when I asked for your phone number he went all vague on me.' Shifty would've been a better word, the stupid twerp'd waffled and prevaricated, then pleaded an urgent appointment when Rick'd started getting annoyed and practically slammed the door in his face, the great fool. Rick had been steeling himself ever since to go back and beard Mabel in her den, but he didn't need to now. Another wave of delight swept over him, and he smiled again, ducking his head to hide it in case he antagonised Emma again.

'Why?'

'Why What?'

Emma waited impatiently while her coffee was poured, having difficulty with her breathing again, then reached for a hot scone and cut violently through it, scattering crumbs and currants across the table. 'Why did you want my phone number?'

When she looked up he was staring at her, an intense, intimate scrutiny, the way he had gazed at her in the early days, before things began to go wrong. That look had always made her feel as if she was unique, as if he couldn't get enough of her, as if he was crazy about her.

'Why do you *think* I wanted your phone number?' he asked gently. 'You idiot.'

'Oh . . .' She lowered her head to her plate and began to spread butter, spoon jam, then reminded herself that he had left her once already and flared up again. 'I can't imagine. And what makes you think I'd be interested anyway? After all, it wasn't me that walked away without a backward glance—'

'It wasn't *like* that.' He shook his head vehemently. 'It wasn't like that at all. Em, darling, if you'd just let me explain . . .'

'Go on then, Rick, *darling*, explain. And make it good, will you, I'm in need of a laugh.' Stop it, Emma berated herself, stop being such a bitch, give him a chance or you'll scare him away for ever. What's the matter with you? She stared past him at the revolving doors on the other side of the foyer, trying to get herself under control. Was it Rick, she wondered, making her so aggressive, or was it guilt? It wasn't as if Jay didn't know, she'd told him often enough, warned him that she didn't love him . . .

'Em!'

'Oh! I'm sorry.' She blinked, turned her gaze back to Rick's puzzled face, softened, told herself fiercely, it's worth all the pain, all the waiting, to see you again. 'I'm sorry,' she repeated, genuinely contrite this time. 'Rick, I don't mean to be—'

'I know. It's okay.' He reached across and took her hand at last;

now seemed like a good moment. It was warm, and her fingers were all buttery. 'I'm sorry too, that I've hurt you so much. I didn't intend to, I swear. I just—'

'Yes?' Emma prompted, tucking her legs under her chair and leaning towards him, demanding reassurance. 'Go on, tell me. I need to understand.' I need to know that I still mean something to you.

He could sense her doubts, feel her quaking beneath his fingers. He placed his other hand over hers and squeezed hard, then he began, haltingly at first, gaining in confidence as he talked, to explain, to justify himself. Emma sat quite still, temporarily as tongue-tied as Ricky had once been, while he deluged her in a torrent of words.

'I just had to get myself together, that's all. It wasn't going to work, you see, Em, not the way it was, not after everything that'd happened. All those words, all those awful things he'd said, and all I could do to retaliate, to defend you, me, us, was hit out with my fists. What good was that? And then, afterwards, when I came round to see you, to try and make you understand, your Auntie Mabel sent me packing, and when I hung around waiting for you outside college Ian said you'd gone home (she hadn't known about that; how typical of Ian, she thought, to cause trouble if he could), and I thought, what was the *point*? I couldn't say what I wanted to say anyway – oh, I could bellow it all out inside my head, but I couldn't string two bloody words together out loud, and all I wanted to do was tell you how much I loved you. So I thought the best thing would be to disappear from your life altogether until I'd sorted myself out.' He paused for breath, grimaced at her. 'I thought I'd ride back into your life on my white horse and carry you off triumphantly to live happily ever after—'

Emma found her tongue at last. 'Where did you learn to talk?'

'What?'

'I said, where did you learn to talk?'

He could see her anger rising again, triggered, ironically, by his fluency and bubbling rapidly to the surface, but he hadn't a clue

how to defuse it. 'I should've hit him years before I did,' he began.
'I should've thumped the living daylights out of him when I was
twelve years old. The cure started the moment I stopped being
terrified of him, and the further away from him I travelled, the
better I got.' He knew immediately he'd put it badly.

'And me?' Emma snatched her hand away, sat up straight.

'And you?'

'The further away from me you travelled the better you got, is
that what you're saying?'

'No! No, of course it isn't! Don't put words into my mouth. It
was nothing to do with you, except that I had to prove I could
make it by myself before we could make it together. That was why
I was trying to find you, because I've done it, I've just landed this
terrific contract, to supply—'

'I know!' she snapped, boiling over again. 'Annie told me. I saw
you, last week, in the Portobello Road, and I yelled and yelled at
you and you just walked away.'

He couldn't have looked more stunned if she'd thrown a bucket
of water over him, but she didn't care. She scowled murderously
at him, beset for the second time by an urge to hit him, harder this
time, in the balls, where it would really hurt, and had to clench her
fists tightly in her lap. 'So, it's terribly kind of you to consider me
after all this time, but what makes you think I want anything to do
with you, Ricky Brown? For all you know I've made alternative
arrangements over the past year, since you couldn't even be
bothered to pick up the phone and tell me you could talk.'

'I did.'

'You did what?'

'Pick up the phone to tell you I could talk.'

'No you bloody well—'

'Yes, I did. I got that girl, what's her name, the one who's taken
over your old room …?' He was triumphant, he could prove it.
'Penny, her name is. She didn't know where you'd gone, said you
hadn't left a forwarding address. That was months ago, way back
in January, before…' He couldn't quite bring himself to say

Alison's name, but she hovered between them for a moment, a tangible, almost solid presence. 'You didn't exactly hang about waiting for me, did you?'

They glared balefully at each other, until Rick reached out to bring her fingers up to his mouth, reminding her vividly of the first time they'd met. 'Don't fight with me,' he begged, soft-voiced, contrite, compelling. 'I love you, Em.'

'Oh . . .' whispered Emma, capitulating. 'Oh, I love you too.'

They walked across the road to Hyde Park and strolled in the sunshine holding hands – just like lovers, thought Emma, astonished, even alarmed by the speed with which she was being swept along – and Ricky grilled her.

'Why did you leave college?'

'Because of Ali. I . . . because of you. Because I couldn't bear it.'

'And why did you move?'

'Because of Auntie Mabel . . . Oh, because of *you*, you stupid idiot, because I couldn't face the thought of staying there if you weren't coming back.'

Oh shit, Ricky lashed himself, Dad was right, what a frigging moron I am. 'So what are you doing, how are you managing?'

'I've got a job, designing. Yesterday, that's how I found you, there weren't any buses so I walked and I – I had to know.' She came to an abrupt halt, just as a crowd of infant schoolgirls in identical panamas, blouses, gymslips, white socks and T-bar shoes came past, and she slid her arms around his waist beneath his leather jacket, needing reassurance again that he was really there. 'I searched every single jeweller's shop on Bond Street, because I had to know whether it was all in my head, whether I'd just imagined it—'

'Oh, Em . . .' he said, interrupting her. 'What a pathetic bloody fool I've been. I got it all wrong, didn't I?'

It wasn't like their last kiss; that had been a goodbye and this was a new beginning, but it wasn't like their first either, they had both come a long way since then. They stood locked together in the sunshine and tasted each other hungrily, oblivious to the giggling crocodile winding its way two by two round the unexpected obstruction in its path, and they parted just in time to hear the unruly party's harassed elderly teacher shoo the last of her fascinated charges on their way, muttering, 'Well, *really*! I don't know *what* the world is coming to! You should be ashamed of yourselves: it's positively *indecent*!'

She made them laugh, induced in them both a charge of optimistic enjoyment, and it occurred to Emma, watching Ricky's face, how rarely he had laughed the first time round. His face had filled out as well as his body, and the frown mark between his eyes was less pronounced. She smiled at him and he smiled back, a wide, dazzling grin which made her glow with delight and reminded her how much she had missed him, how long she had waited for him, then they walked on towards the Serpentine, still holding hands like the small girls they had just entertained so thoroughly, twining their fingers tightly together as if they were frightened of losing each other again. Rick, talking just for the sheer pleasure of it, began again.

'So are you all still friends? There were five of you at the beginning, weren't there: Bill, George, Ali, you and ... what was that other chap called, the one I never met? Ali fancied him, didn't she, only he fancied you, she said. Maybe if she'd persevered with him she might still be alive. What was his name?'

Emma went hot, cold, stared fixedly at the ground beneath her feet, unexpectedly gripped by an appalling attack of guilt. 'Jay,' she said huskily. His name stayed on her tongue and his face swam across her vision. She swallowed hard. 'Tell me how you got this contract.'

Rick didn't register the abrupt change of subject. 'Word of mouth. Everything that's come my way over the past year has been word of mouth, which is ironic really, when you think about it. So where are you living now? Who do you have to give notice to?'

'Give notice ... ?'

He brought her to a halt, sliding his arms around her waist and pulling her close again, wrapping her up in the smell of warm leather and clean skin. 'I've finished my business for today. We can go to your place and pick up your stuff right now. You can give notice and come back with me tonight; we'll take what we can carry and leave the rest to be picked up later. We can be together again, for good this time.'

His confidence was breathtaking. When he stopped to kiss her again, savouring her, she clung to him, needing some confidence of her own, but he hit her, before she'd even had time to get her breath back, with another startling suggestion. 'I'll find out about special licences, so we can get married straightaway. My landlord's an old-fashioned Norfolk farmer; he'll want us to be respectable.' He grinned, then tightened his grip and sobered up. 'Have you any idea how many nights I've lain awake, wishing you were beside me?'

'Yes,' said Emma, seeing Jay, imagining the shutters come down over his face as she broke the news that Ricky was back and she was going away with him because he was all she'd ever wanted. 'How can you ask?' But you don't know what a potent soporific sexual satisfaction can be, or that I've been using it as a substitute for love and failing miserably to fend off the man who, having rescued me from my black pit of despair when you weren't here, wants to be so much more than just a human sleeping draught . . .

Later, promised Rick, turning his face to breathe in the scent of her hair, I will tell you about Rosie, who is teaching me, slowly and painfully, to read and who occasionally fills the empty space in my bed. I will explain that she means less than nothing to me, and I to her, that I was just lonely, and she was willing . . .

He was paying Rosie for the lessons, had felt, to begin with as if he was paying her for the sex, until she reassured him. 'No commitment,' she said gaily when his conscience pricked. 'Free love, that's what it's all about, no strings attached. Now belt up and let's get down to it.'

'I'm sorry, Em,' he said, no longer terribly sure what he was apologising for. 'Believe me, you don't know how sorry I am.'

They sat down to rest on a bench because Emma was still having trouble with her legs, and he tried again, impatient to get things sorted out. 'So who are you sharing a flat with, is it far?'

There was no point in avoiding the question; he would have to know sooner or later. 'Jay.'

'Who? You mean . . . ?'

'I mean Jay Hammond, the one Ali fancied.' She stared across the wide greensward into the middle distance, and told him, very fast, as if the words might have less impact spoken at breakneck speed. 'I'm staying with Jay, because when I was falling to pieces after you left me he understood, and when Ali died he rescued me because it was all my fault and I couldn't stand it. He made the nightmares go away and he held my hand at the inquest and he took me home with him because I was terrified out of my wits at the prospect of being on my own without you, without Ali, without anything, and I've been staying with him ever since, because you weren't around and he was, and I was so *lonely* . . .'

'Oh.'

'And don't tell me you haven't – because I won't believe you.' She leaned back on the bench and closed her eyes, exhausted.

'All right, I won't.'

Emma raised her head, opened her eyes. 'You won't what?'

'Tell you I haven't.' Rick took a deep breath. 'There's this girl called Rosie, she teaches ...' he grimaced '... adult illiterates. I met her on Gentleman's Walk, in the middle of Norwich; there's a big market there and I sold her a scarf ring. She offered to teach me to read. But she doesn't mean anything; she isn't important.' He leaned across to nuzzle Emma's neck, pulling her towards him. 'None of it's important, from now on we're the only ones that matter, you and I.'

Neither of them asked the obvious question. It was easier not to.

They walked across Putney Bridge hand in hand, but as they approached the flats Emma became increasingly agitated and pulled away. What if Jay was around?

'You have to understand,' she blustered. 'He's been good to me, and I owe him.' She slowed down, making sure Rick was under no illusion, daring him to complain. 'I don't want to hurt him any more than I have to.'

'All right.' Rick swallowed his rising resentment. It was his fault, he reminded himself, he'd caused all this and if he got it wrong he could still spoil everything. 'Poor bastard,' he added, feeling sorry despite himself for the other man, so soon to lose his prize.

Jay, with immaculate timing, was in the car-park; he had just climbed out of his car, and he was unloading pictures, leaning each one carefully against the Jensen's wheel-arch, running his fingers through his hair to keep it out of his eyes, engrossed in his task. Emma stopped so abruptly that Ricky cannoned into her from behind, and stared at Jay as if she was seeing him for the first time. Had he always looked so vulnerable?

Rick was taken aback, felt his sympathy fade. He had imagined someone more ordinary, shorter, plumper, less – what, less like competition? Jay was older than he'd expected, too; he looked arrogant, affluent, cool, laid back. Stupid, he told himself, he should've reckoned, since Ali'd fancied the bloke, that he must have something. But why did the bastard have to be so tall?

'Em—' he began, forgetting his resolution.

'Shh.' She pushed him back round the corner, out of Jay's sight, then collapsed against the wall and closed her eyes. Once this was all over, she vowed, she was going to trade in her legs for a new pair. They kept letting her down at the wrong moment. 'I can't do it,' she blurted, not looking at Rick because it was too difficult. 'I can't do it like this. I can't walk out there and say, "Hi, Jay, by the way this is Rick and we've come to pick up my things." It's too brutal.'

'You mean you won't leave him?'

'*No!*' She opened her eyes wide, pleading with him to understand. 'I mean *yes*, I will leave him. Now, today, I swear. But I have to tell him my own way, and I need time to work out how I'm going to do it. I can't handle all this, it's too much. I hadn't thought further than finding you, and now suddenly we're getting a special licence and going to live in Norfolk with a boot-faced farmer and a teacher called Rosie ...' She stopped, breathless. Rick must have loose ends to sort out as well. The thought made her feel better, then reminded her disconcertingly that it wasn't only Jay she had to deal with, she had her whole life to rearrange – she had forgotten about Mirico.

'And I've just got a job. I have to think what to do about that. How will I earn my living if I'm buried in the depths of Norfolk?'

What the hell did it matter? This was *love*, not the local bloody labour exchange. Ricky clenched his fists by his sides. He wanted to drag her away by her hair, make her do as he wanted, force her into acknowledging that the bond between them was stronger than any stupid job, or some misplaced loyalty. But she was older than the girl he'd fallen in love with; she had lived through Ali's death, left college, found her feet without him. She wasn't so – what was the word – soft? pliant? any more. What if he pushed her in the wrong direction?

'How long do you need?' He watched the relief sweeping her face and wondered whether he'd done the right thing, letting her off the hook so easily.

'We have the rest of our lives,' said Emma softly, pleading with him to make it easy. 'Surely a few more days won't make any difference?'

'No. I suppose not. But, Em—'

'What?'

'Don't make me wait too long. We've wasted so much precious time already.' And I wouldn't trust that floppy-haired creep any further than I could throw him. He's too bloody *cool*.

'I promise.' She pushed herself away from the wall into his arms, and they clung to each other. 'I *love* you,' she said vehemently. 'That's the only thing that matters.'

'I can support you,' mumbled Ricky into her hair, gripped by a sudden fear of losing her again, 'if you have to give up this job. I'm making a lot of money; you don't need to work. You can do whatever you want.' The words sounded eerily familiar.

He gave her the number he had guarded so jealously from Annie, which made her glow with possessive satisfaction, and she gave him hers, not Jay's, her phone at Baron's Court. His face cleared when she explained about her flat. She was only staying with Jay, she reiterated, not living with him – the arrangement had never been anything other than temporary, at least (a silent caveat) not on her part. Then they shared a last lingering kiss, Rick said, 'I'll phone you tonight,' and Emma watched him walk away, torn between conscience and a stupidly romantic desire to leave everything and run after him, taking just the clothes she stood up in, in case she lost him again.

He turned when he reached the road and she smiled, reassuring him, then as he disappeared, making for Putney Bridge, she slid slowly down the wall to sit in a crumpled heap on the ground, no longer able to support herself.

She remained where she was for over twenty minutes, her arms wrapped round her ankles, chin resting on her knees, staring blindly out towards the embankment and the river, while she tried to work out how to tell Jay she was leaving him.

CHAPTER TWENTY-FIVE

• • •

It was easy.

Jay was sitting at the kitchen table, reading a letter when she let herself in. He jumped visibly when she appeared in the doorway and crushed it in his hand, then stared up at her as if she was a stranger.

'Are you all right?' she asked, alarmed by his unusual pallor.

He blinked, clearly trying to pull himself together. 'Fine,' he said. 'I'm fine. You've been a long time.' He ran his fingers through his hair, gazed as if hypnotised at the crumpled sheet of paper in front of him. 'Er, how did it go?'

'What, Mirico?' How could he have forgotten already? She pulled out a chair and sat down, because her legs were still shaky. 'I told you yesterday, Solly Cohen's taken nine designs. He says if they sell he'll put me on a retainer, and I start on Thursday morning.'

'Oh, yes, I forgot.' Jay rose abruptly and curled his fingers round his discarded correspondence, then threw it at the waste-paper basket and wandered across to the sink, where he stood staring out of the window. How could he have forgotten?

'Thank you for your interest.'

'Sorry.' He lowered his head, and when she looked at his hands they were clenched into hard fists on the edge of the sink.

'Jay,' she began. 'I have to talk to you—'

He didn't move, didn't react at all, and Emma's temper rose. She didn't need this, she'd spent twenty minutes steeling herself to tell him she was leaving, and now he was behaving as if she'd already gone, as if he'd forgotten her very existence.

'I've decided to go back to Baron's Court.' Jay's shoulders stiffened, at last a reaction. 'Er, just for a while.' Coward, chicken, useless pathetic *drip*, tell him straight, get it over and done with. 'I need time to sort myself out, decide where I go from here.' Let him down gently, don't hurt him merely for the sake of it. 'Look, I'm very fond of you, you know I am, and I'm very grateful for everything you've done—'

'Right. Whatever you like.' He didn't ask her to stay, didn't beg, didn't plead; he didn't even turn his head. It was almost as if he hadn't heard what she'd said.

She packed what she could manage, borrowing one of his suitcases, and called a taxi. She could see him as she moved to and fro past the kitchen, still standing at the window staring at nothing, and she was surprised how much his indifference mattered. After everything he'd said, his protestations of undying love, she would have expected him to put up at least a bit of a fight, but he didn't seem to care that she was leaving him at all.

By the time the doorbell rang her things were piled neatly in the hall and she was almost in tears. She strode back to the kitchen in a rage. 'The taxi's here,' she said briskly. 'So I'll say goodbye.' Last time they'd been in this situation, she'd called him a pig and he'd stormed out and told the taxi driver to bugger off. She stood and waited.

He turned very slowly, moving like an old man.

'Em . . .' he began. His face was as blank as she had ever seen it and her anger seeped away.

'Jay, I—'

'Don't,' he said. 'I can't—' He stopped, lowered his head and stared at the floor, started again. 'I can't handle it right now, Em. If you're going, just go, would you?'

'Oh! Right!' Still she hesitated. 'Bye then.'

'Bye.'

And that was it.

*

Work. She needed it; her mind was a turmoil. Baron's Court was dingy and unfamiliar, and the knowledge that her stay was only temporary did nothing to dispel her loneliness. Looking for reassurance she called Ricky the moment she got in, even before she climbed the last flight of stairs to her door, but there was no reply and she cursed herself for an idiot – he couldn't possibly have got back to Norfolk yet. What was the matter with her anyway? She should have gone with him, had the courage of her convictions. As she stood listening to the phone ringing in her ear and staring at the cracked, curling lino beneath her feet, she wondered again why Jay hadn't tried to stop her leaving.

It wasn't until she had unpacked her things, made a foray to the shops to buy provisions, and was settled on her tiny balcony high above the traffic fumes with the remains of a cheese sandwich, that she began to calm down. It was going to be all right, she told herself as she propped her easel against the fire escape and opened a packet of Cadbury's chocolate fingers. She had enough work to keep her occupied until she decided what to do about Mirico, and she'd got the breathing space she needed to sort herself out. It was going to be all right. She rifled through her bag for her pen, leaned back against the sun-warmed wall behind her and sighed. Between them, she and Rick would solve the problem of Mirico. All it needed was the will to sort it out, and if it meant so much to him, she could give up the job, it wasn't that important, was it? Maybe Solly Cohen would let her freelance, travel down to London a couple of days a week or something... Encouraged, she helped herself to a biscuit, took the top off her pen and settled down to work.

Her mind wandered. What was the matter with Jay? She had never seen him so odd, so vacant, and he had allowed her to walk away without putting up any fight at all. She had expected him to plead with her, beg her to stay, but he had barely acknowledged her departure. Her mood deteriorated again and she shivered although it was warm where she sat. Jay wasn't her problem any more, she reminded herself. Anyway, even assuming he eventually noticed she'd gone, what was it he'd said the last time? 'You have to make the first move, because I won't, and if neither of us does, then it's finished.' So that was it, wasn't it, and just as well; she was uncomfortably aware that she might not have been strong enough to resist him if he'd tried to stop her leaving. She shook her shoulders, settled down and began to work in earnest.

She moved indoors when the sun went down and continued, immersing herself, as she had done so many times before, in therapeutic creative activity. When she ran out of inspiration she took a break, phoned Josie, and Mabel, asked after Bill, better now and back at college, then returned to her easel to try again. She didn't mention Jay, or Ricky, or the possibility of a complete change of direction, and Mabel didn't ask. She was a big girl now, big enough to make up her own mind what she was going to do with her life.

She worked until ten, then thought she would take a five-minute break, fell into bed and slept like the dead. She didn't hear the telephone or the girl from downstairs knocking tentatively on her door, and when she surfaced abruptly at ten the next morning, wakened by a nightmare visit to her black pit of despair, there was a note on the floor. *Ricky phoned. Could you phone him back?*

She brewed tea, ate a bowl of cornflakes, then forgot about the tea and made coffee. Only when she had finished the chocolate fingers and run out of inspiration did she walk down the stairs, her heart thudding with nervous excitement, to ring him for the second time.

'Hello?' The voice was soft, faintly rural, and female.

'What number is this?'

'Great Yarmouth . . .' The number was right.

'Er, could I speak to – who is this?'

'Rosie Medler. Did you want to speak to Rick?'

Emma stared at the mouthpiece and went cold all over. What was going on?

'Yes, I—'

'He's not here I'm afraid, but if you'd like to leave a message I'll tell him you called … Hello?'

'Oh. Er … no, just tell him … just tell him – I'll try again later.' And she replaced the receiver in a hurry.

She worked frantically for the next two hours, sublimating all thought in work. Every time the phone rang downstairs her stomach churned with a mixture of hope and apprehension, and every time it was for somebody else.

As the afternoon drew on she gave up and went to sit on the balcony, staring across the jumble of roofs and listening to the muted roar of London's traffic. What was Ricky's teacher doing, answering his phone when he wasn't there? Why hadn't he phoned her back? What the hell was he playing at? The question she had deliberately not asked swirled around in Emma's mind, demanding an answer. Suppose she did give up Mirico before she'd even started, burned her boats by leaving herself without a steady source of income – was it a wise move, under the circumstances? At four o'clock, still unable to decide what to do, she picked up her bag, slung it over her shoulder, and made for the door.

'I thought I'd better come and see you. I, er, wanted to talk about …' she stammered.

'Good!' Solly Cohen slapped her heartily on the back. 'Shows initiative, like that.'

Emma staggered under the blow and struggled to catch her breath. That wasn't the impression she'd meant to convey at all.

He gave her no chance to explain. 'Cutting-room!' he boomed, waving imperiously at the receptionist as he passed. 'Want Francis! Find him!'

Francis was a dapper little man with wavy grey hair, small, chocolate brown eyes and the face of a benevolent pug dog. He was sporting a flamboyant waistcoat, pin-striped trousers, a bow-tie and a rose in his buttonhole, and he bustled on small, neat feet clutching a clipboard.

'Francis!' roared Solly by way of introduction. 'Bloody poofy name! Frankie Bunker – Emmie Ver-sea. Bunker!' the pneumatic drills erupted. 'Bunker indeed!'

'*Boncœur.*'

'What?' Emma jumped, her nerves showing.

'*Boncœur.*' The voice was plummy, well spoken, the antithesis of his master. 'Old French. That's where he gets Bunker from. He's been enjoying the joke for fifteen years now.' The little man dimpled at her. 'But you must call me Francis.'

'Emma,' said Emma and smiled back. What a nice face you have, she thought, how appropriate, *bon cœur*. It was wonderful, having something to do; she felt calmer already.

Rather a sweet child, decided Francis, but jumpy. I wonder what she makes of our dear Solly.

Cyril had made up a complete *toile*. Emma thought his industry amazing; Solly was unimpressed.

'That all, Cyril? What you been doing, sitting on your fat arse smoking those cheap cigars of yours?'

'Got it in one, Solly.'

'Don't know why the hell I pay anyone around here,' roared Solly cheerfully.

The *toile* looked nothing. Emma's heart sank when she saw it. Boring, far too simple, not enough detail, not enough ... something.

Solly examined it in silence, prowled round it, examined it again. 'Buttons!' he bellowed.

It was supposed to be a pale pink linen. 'Navy,' said Emma. 'Navy stitching, navy buttons.'

'What sort of buttons?'

Panic. Navy sort of buttons. How would I know what sort of buttons? Isn't that enough?

'Paul,' said Francis. 'Find that box for Miss Versey.'

A large cardboard box was produced and Emma searched gratefully through it. There were thousands of buttons, hundreds of navy ones.

'These,' she said at last, triumphantly producing a plain wooden design with two holes and a beading round the edge.

'Right!' Solly snatched it from her hand, then stabbed it through the dummy's breast with a large pin. 'There?'

'No.' She moved it an inch, added more. Any fool could see it looked better. It suddenly looked almost possible.

'Stitching!' bawled Solly and flung a ballpoint at her. She drew a careful dotted line on the calico. 'Pockets!'

They went through it step by step, inch by inch. The designs Solly Cohen had picked were almost all dress suits, plain shifts with short or cap sleeves, cropped boxy jackets. There was a problem with the dress that Emma didn't have the nerve to mention. Cyril had put in bust darts running from the side seams and it ruined the line. Her sketch showed a seam, incorporating the dart to give a clean unfussy silhouette. It was Francis who pointed out the anomaly. You dear little man, she thought, I could kiss you, Monsieur Boncœur.

'Well, blow me!' Cyril picked up the sketch and peered at it, scratched his head. 'Sorry, dear,' he said. 'Never noticed. I was so busy with the jacket I just assumed it was a straight shift. Soon mended.' He picked up the big, black-handled cutting shears and sliced across the calico. Then he fiddled, slashed again, pinned, pruned, until he was satisfied. 'Whadaya think?'

They stood back. It was too short now, but that didn't matter. Two minutes of snipping had turned a disaster into a success. They could all see it, including Emma, who had begun to think the *toile* would never remotely resemble the garment she had sketched. Even Solly could see it.

'Right, Miss Emmie Ver-sea,' he commanded by way of praise, 'you're on the payroll, three days a week to start with, we'll sort out the details later. Now bugger off. Cyril, want another ASAP and get that one made up in the linen. Frankie, you idle layabout, need the Roller.' He grinned toothily, nodded his head and strode briskly off. Francis paused, winked and followed obediently in his wake.

'But—' began Emma to the swirl of air they had left behind. It was only as she emerged into the daylight on Oxford Circus that she realised just how much she wanted the job.

There was another note on the floor. *Ring Ricky*, it said. *Urgent*.

'Where the hell have you been? I've been out of my mind.'

'Nowhere. I fell asleep.' Emma swallowed hard and picked her words carefully, making an effort not to overreact. 'And I rang you this morning. Your fancy woman answered the phone.'

'My what?'

'Your fancy woman. Your teacher friend. You didn't tell me she was living with you.'

'She's not.' Ricky sounded tense, impatient. 'She's volunteered to do my books for me, that's all. Now I've got this contract I have to produce invoices, receipts, all the paraphernalia. I can sign my name and string simple words together, but – Em, have you left him yet?'

Rick and Rosie. It sounded like something out of a children's schoolbook: Rick and Rosie learn to read; Rick and Rosie learn to write; Rick and Rosie go to bed together. 'Yes,' said Emma sharply, her temper rising with her insecurity. 'Yes, I have left him. Unlike your Rosie, who still seems to be in residence.'

'She is not *my* Rosie, I swear.'

Perfectly true as of last night. It had been a relief, clearing the air so quickly. 'Okay, darling,' Rosie'd said, when he broke the news. 'No sweat, there's plenty more where you came from. But we'll keep on with the other stuff, won't we? I need the money, to be honest, and it'd be a shame to stop the lessons now, just when you're getting somewhere. Pity though, it's been a great pleasure.' Then she'd grinned, smacked a kiss on his cheek and left, whistling. She'd taken her dressing-gown with her.

'Em, what are you doing about this job? When are we going to be together?' begged Rick, desperate to get on with it. 'I *miss* you.'

'Oh . . .' Emma softened despite herself, felt guilty again, about Solly this time. 'I didn't tell him. I couldn't, he's not the sort of man you can just walk up to and say sorry I've changed my mind. I went in today specially and he didn't even give me a chance to mention it.' She paused, wondering how to put it so Rick would understand, then gabbled it out before she could stop herself. 'And anyway, I'm not sure I want to give it up.' Silence. 'Would you give up your jewellery for me?'

Rick sighed. This was all because of Rosie; it had to be. 'All right,' he said, reassuring her. 'If you need more time that's okay. It must be possible to sort something out. I'm not far from Yarmouth and the trains aren't bad ... It's only going to be a problem if we let it. Em, can't we sort it out later? The important thing is to be together.'

'Yes, I know. It's just that I—' She stopped. He was right, the important thing was to be together.

'I love you,' she said.

'That's the whole point, isn't it?' replied Rick without hesitation. 'I love you, too.'

And she knew it was going to be all right.

CHAPTER TWENTY-SIX
• • •

It was late, well after ten, and she wasn't expecting him.

He was leaning against the wall at the top of the stairs with his fists tightly clenched by his sides, staring blankly at the floor, and he didn't move when she appeared in the doorway. He was unshaven, bedraggled; Emma opened her mouth to speak then shut it again, unable to think of anything to say. He looked awful. She'd never seen him look so dreadful.

'Are you all right?'

'No.' His voice was hoarse and he hunched his shoulders awkwardly, as if he was in pain.

'Are you ill?' She advanced towards him, suddenly anxious.

'No.'

She stopped, waiting.

'Are you coming home?'

'No.' Surely this couldn't be her fault? He'd hardly noticed when she left, had barely said goodbye.

'I need you.'

'No, you don't, you didn't even notice me leave.'

'I'd just had a letter. I couldn't—' Jay stopped short, pushed himself away from the wall and took a hesitant step towards her.

Emma watched him pityingly. Surely this couldn't be the result of her leaving, this disintegration? 'What letter?'

'*Please,*' he begged and she flinched, took an involuntary step backwards. '*No!*' he bellowed, thinking she was going to close the door, and covered the distance between them in two strides, catching hold of her and wrapping his arms so tight around her that she could hardly breathe. 'Don't!' he mumbled. 'Don't shut me out!'

She could feel him quaking, the beat of his heart loud in her ear, feel his elbows digging into her ribs. 'You don't own me,' she muttered resentfully, her voice stifled by his sweater. 'Don't pressure me like this.'

'Can't help it. Em, I—'

'Well try harder. It's too late to beg me now.' Emma squirmed ineffectually, short of oxygen and temper, remembering his brusque goodbye but wanting despite herself to comfort him for whatever was hurting so badly.

'I need you. I – something's happened and I can't deal with it by myself.'

'What do you mean, something's happened? What's happened?' She struggled to free herself, writhed against his restraining arms, alarmed by the desperation in his voice.

'I need you,' he said again. He loosened his hold, took her plait in one hand, wrapping it round and round his fingers in a thick rope, then tugged, pulling her face up to his. 'Please, Em!' He was shouting now. 'I can't do it by myself! Don't make me; it'll kill me!'

'Stop being so bloody melodramatic!' she shouted back. Then, unable to bear the look on his face, burrowed into his sweater again.

'I can't help it,' he complained to the top of her head. 'I thought I could handle it, but I can't. I need you. I *love* you.'

She could feel him waiting, holding his breath for a reciprocal declaration. No, she defied him silently, I won't, I won't tell you I love you. I don't love you; I love Ricky and I won't be blackmailed like this.

'Handle what?' she asked belligerently. 'You're a grown man. What's so awful you can't manage it by yourself?' She took a deep, shuddering breath, imbibed his familiar scent, and hesitated. 'Why do you need me?'

'There's something I have to do and I can't do it on my own.

Em . . .' He stumbled into silence and just stood, still holding her plait in his hand, his head bowed to her shoulder, his hair falling over his eyes. Then suddenly his face twisted as if he was in agony, and she couldn't bear it.

'All right,' she mumbled. 'What do you want me to do?' She felt him sag against her; that one small movement weakened her resistance irretrievably.

'Come back with me now. I have to go to Yorkshire.' He tightened his hold, frightened she might change her mind. 'Tomorrow afternoon. I have something to sort out and I can't do it without you.'

'All right,' she capitulated. 'For how long?'

'Just a couple of days.' He raised his head at last to look at her, brought his hands up to cup her face. 'Emma . . .' Oh, thought Emma, melting, how could she have forgotten the sex?

It was the first time they had kissed for days. It shattered what was left of her resolve completely, made her feel warm and soppy, and he took advantage.

'I love you, Em,' he murmured into her hair. 'I can't live without you.'

She gave in with hardly any fight at all, then cursed herself for a weakling and a fool. Jay packed manically, everything he could lay his hands on as if she was moving back permanently, until she told him sharply to stop, reminding him this was only a temporary reprieve, then lugged everything downstairs at breakneck speed in case she changed her mind. She stopped just before she shut the door.

'Wait for me in the car,' she said, appalled suddenly by what she was doing, aching for Rick, slipping inexorably through her fingers again. 'I have to phone—'

'All right, but hurry up.'

Rick answered almost immediately. 'Meet me,' said Emma. 'Tomorrow, in the restaurant at Bourne and Hollingsworth. Twelve o'clock.' High Noon, ha, ha.

'Does that mean—?' He sounded ecstatic.

'I'll explain tomorrow . . . Ricky?'

'Yes?'

'I love you, don't forget that, will you?'

Jay was waiting in the car, his head resting against the window and his eyes shut. The smile that spread across his face when she slid in beside him made her feel slightly better. It's only for a few days, she told herself.

'Thanks, Em,' he murmured, and he reached across to stroke her cheek.

''S okay,' she said. She owed him, after all.

The evening was weird. Having got her back Jay showed no inclination to talk; whatever grief he was suffering he was clearly not ready to share it and she wondered why he needed her at all. They ate supper in complete silence, and spent the evening listening to music, filling in the deafening lack of conversation. It was almost ten before Emma plucked up the courage to ask if he was feeling better.

'Yes,' he said, blinking at her as if he had forgotten she was there. 'Yes, I'm fine now you're back. D'you want a drink?' He rose and wandered across the room to pour himself a large brandy then, forgetting Emma, took it to the window and stood staring at the lights along the river, sipping at it distractedly.

'If I had killed a man,' he said suddenly, startlingly. 'Would you still stay with me?'

'Killed? Killed what man?'

'No one.' He turned to face her, frowned as if his head hurt. 'I just wondered, if I had . . .'

'But you haven't . . . You may be odd, but you're not a murderer . . . are you?'

'No. No, of course I'm not.' He turned away from her again, swallowed the last of his brandy, added cryptically, 'I just wondered, that's all,' then passed a hand over his eyes and wandered back across the room. 'I'm knackered,' he said. 'Think I'll go to bed.' He hesitated. 'Keep me company?'

There was a long pause before Emma said slowly, 'Yes, yes in a minute.' What now, she was asking herself; what do you do now, you silly bitch?

She sat on until the violins faded into silence, then rose, turned off the record-player, and moved across to the window to stare down at the traffic passing below. She thought back, to the misery she had felt when she had first moved to Baron's Court and confronted the prospect of losing Rick for good; to Alison and the weeks, months of patient, gentle support Jay had given her when she needed it. She owed him. And one more time wouldn't make any difference, would it?

She needn't have worried. Jay held her tightly in his arms, but he showed no inclination to make love to her, seemed to be in need of comfort rather than sex. When the moonlight on her face woke her in the dead hours of early morning, he was standing naked at the window, watching the Thames flow past on its long journey to the sea, and when he turned to come back to bed she caught the glimmer of tears on his cheeks.

She reached out instinctively to take him in her arms and stroked his hair until he slept. She would have felt less guilty if they had screwed all night.

Rick's face when she told him was punishment enough.

They sat in a dark corner holding hands across the table and Emma tried haltingly to explain that these new circumstances didn't threaten him; it was an uphill struggle.

'You don't know,' she began at last, desperate to make him see, 'what it was like when Ali died. I thought it was all my fault. I went over every conversation we'd had, wondering if I'd triggered her off with a word, or a phrase, relived everything I'd done, every move I'd made: should I have gone back earlier to check on her? Should I never have left her in the first place? Should I have taken the brandy away? Maybe if I'd tried hard enough I could have talked her out of starting the affair to begin with . . . I left her and went back to college when I should have been there, holding her hand. I didn't phone when I said I would. When I got no reply I

assumed everything was all right, when it was all wrong. I
offloaded my responsibility on to poor darling Bill, who found her,
choked on her own—'

'Stop it!' Rick turned his face away, unable to bear any more.
'And I wasn't there and he was. That's what this is all about, isn't
it – paying debts?' He tightened his hold on her hand, lying limp
beneath his on the tablecloth, and ran his fingers along the
freckled skin. 'You're paying back your debt to—' He couldn't
bring himself to say Jay's name, he thought he might choke on it.
'And I'm paying for not being here when you needed me ... All
right, Em.' A moron, he thought bitterly, a frigging moron. A
heroic half-wit, riding back on my white horse to rescue the
maiden in distress, when somebody else has already done the job,
hoisted his prize across his saddle and ridden off into the sunset
with her.

'It's only for a few days.' She watched his face, sharing his
misery. 'Just until he's sorted out whatever it is he has to sort out.
And then I'll see if I can come to an arrangement with Mirico.' She
leaned across the table, and squeezed his hand until his bones
cracked, reassuring herself more than Ricky. 'It'll be all right,' she
said vehemently. 'You'll see. It'll be all right, I promise.'

And then she went back to work, to tell Solly Cohen that she
had to leave immediately, that she couldn't even work the rest of
the afternoon.

Solly was out, to her inordinate relief, and Francis was
wonderful. 'I – er – it's a – it's a family problem,' she stammered.
'My, er, my aunt's been in an ... accident. I'm dreadfully sorry to
let you down when I've only just—'

'Right,' said Francis imperturbed. 'Leave it with me, sweetie.
I'll smooth the ruffled feathers. How long do you think you'll
need?'

'Oh, only a few days. He, we – I mean, I have to go to Yorkshire.
I could do an extra day next week to make up ... ?'

'Don't be ridiculous, dear girl. Solly'll be only too glad to get
out of paying you and Cyril's got plenty to keep him going till you

get back. Don't worry about a thing, just concentrate on looking after your dear old auntie.'

'What?'

Francis chuckled richly. 'Wish her better from me,' he said drily, and she realised he hadn't believed a single word she'd said.

CHAPTER TWENTY-SEVEN

• • •

Harrogate was a pretty town, genteel, stuffy, middle class. The hotel was old-fashioned, Gothic-Victorian, full of long draughty corridors and fancy cornices.

They had driven north in torrential rain and almost total silence, a state that over the past twenty-four hours Emma had come to regard as normal.

'Are you sure you want me to come?' she had asked as they loaded their bags into the back of the Jensen.

Jay nodded his head vehemently. 'Yes, yes, of course I do. I'm sorry, Em, it's just that I . . .' Then he'd tailed off into silence and stood staring at nothing, forgetting what he had started to say. 'We'll talk later, when I'm . . . Come on, we must get going or we'll be late.'

Late for what? Emma wondered again what was hurting him so much. *Would you stay with me if I had killed a man?* Was that what this trip was all about?

'Jay . . .' she began as she dumped her suitcase on the lumpy double bed, but he frowned and shook his head.

'Not now, please, Em, not now.'

He crossed the room from the window to hold her close, and Emma could feel the tension, like steel bands encircling her. She stirred uneasily within his embrace, and the resolution she had made during their silent journey, to stay detached, keep him at arm's length so she could walk away when this trip was over, melted like mist in the sun. 'But I might be able to help.'

'You are.' He kissed the top of her head and tightened his grip. 'You're here. I should have ... I would have told you months ago, but I couldn't face ... and there was Alison ...' He sighed, laid his cheek against hers. 'I love you.'

'I know.' So why won't you tell me what's going on? What is it that hurts so much you cannot even bring yourself to talk about it? And what does Alison have to do with all of this?

He released her, began slowly, reluctantly, to unpack his things. 'There's a concert tonight, the Hallé orchestra. I've booked tickets for it; Barbirolli's conducting.'

Emma stared at him in disbelief. 'Is that why we've come all this way, why I perjured myself signing the register, had to keep my left hand in my pocket in case they wanted to see my wedding ring? Just so we could go to a concert?'

He smiled at her, the first time for hours, days. 'Of course, Mrs Hammond. I brought you hundreds of miles just to see how being married would feel.' His smile widened. 'I rather like it. Why don't we—?'

'No! Don't cheat! If you knew what I've had to give up to come with you—' No, she thought, biting her tongue, of course you don't know, and I can't tell you, I can't do that to you, not now. 'That's typical of you,' she finished lamely. 'Always an eye to the main chance.'

'Why not?' The joke, not really a joke, missed, and Jay's smile faded into bitterness. 'It's the only way I can hope to sneak under your guard.' He turned away, stricken with hopeless longing, wishing he had left well alone, wishing he hadn't come, and the brief respite from gloom was over almost before it had begun.

The music soothed him. He timed their arrival deliberately so they took their seats only seconds before the house lights went down, and he held her hand tightly from the moment they sat down. During the interval, apart from a brief foray to the bar so Jay could knock back a large Scotch, they stayed in their seats in splendid isolation, and it was not until the white-haired Maestro took his final bow and the audience rose to leave that Jay leaned back and relaxed at last.

'That's better.' Emma touched his cheek with a comforting hand, encouraged by the improvement, then sighed resignedly and waited for the auditorium to empty, following the familiar pattern. She had filed Ricky for the moment, under 'pending'; she couldn't manage them both at the same time.

When they emerged into the foyer there was only one other couple left, waiting for a taxi. Emma paid them little heed, she was thinking prosaically about her stomach, and they were almost at the door when the man, middle-aged, plump, florid, left his companion and moved across their path.

He stared hard at Jay, examining him with watery blue eyes, then nodded triumphantly. 'It is, isn't it? James Hammond! Well, I'll be blowed! I thought it was you!'

Jay came to an abrupt halt, still holding tightly to Emma's hand and the man called encouragingly over his shoulder, 'It is him! I told you it was,' then held out his hand. 'Well, well. And how are you, old son? Funnily enough we were just talking about you the other day, what with Missy being so ... Well, I suppose that's why you're here, isn't it? Must have been a bit of a shock for you, eh?'

'Hello, Gerald,' said Jay. 'How's Muriel?' He took the man's hand reluctantly, loathing the touch of his damp palm, remembering his arse.

'Oh, much the same, you know. Muriel doesn't change. She's only just over there. Come and say hello.' He waved at his wife, still hovering near the exit. 'She'll be delighted.'

'I don't think ...' began Jay.

Muriel, grey like Gerald but still fadedly pretty, gave an almost imperceptible shake of the head and pursed her lips at her husband. Jay's fingers tightened round Emma's.

'How long are you up for?' continued Gerald, stubbornly obtuse. 'Have you seen Missy yet? You'll come over for a drink before you go of course... How many years has it been ... ?' He peered curiously at Emma. 'And aren't you going to introduce me, dear boy?'

'Another time, Gerald.' No, you malign old man, I am not going to allow you to sully my beautiful Emma by touching her. 'We're running late, we must go.' He manœuvred Emma sideways, away from the doggedly persistent questions, then towed her briskly towards the door, past Muriel standing by the ticket office regarding them with barely concealed hostility, towards the dark pavement outside, and escape.

'Give my regards to Missy.'

Emma caught a glimpse just before the door closed behind her, of Muriel wagging a furious finger at her loquacious spouse, hissing at him. For what, she wondered, for talking to Jay? And who was Missy? Looking at Jay's grim face, she didn't ask.

The fragrant night air improved his shattered mood. It was softly warm after the heavy rain, redolent of damp grass and wet pavements. They walked hand in hand from the theatre across the Stray, the wide greensward encircling the town, making their way slowly back to the hotel, where Jay had booked a table for late dinner. Emma's stomach rumbled with hunger as she walked, the only sound either of them made as they traversed the sodden ground.

They sat in a secluded corner and Emma watched Jay as he perused the menu.

'You're very patient.' He raised his eyes from the table d'hôte. 'Or not very curious.'

'Very curious,' she said, encouraged by the proffered opening. 'But frightened to ask in case you bite my head off.'

He put the leather-bound menu down, rearranged his cutlery, poured himself a glass of water, then lifted his head and looked straight at her. 'I've known Gerald since I was a small boy. I come from just the other side of Knaresborough, about ten miles up the road.'

'Oh,' said Emma, as the waiter arrived to take their order.

Unexpectedly, Jay smiled, soothed by their silent walk across the Stray. 'Is that it, "Oh"?'

'Um . . .'

'Um? Does that mean you can't think what to say, or that you don't know how to ask?'

'All right, what are we doing here? I'll have the steak, well done, and both sorts of potato, please. And could I have plenty of carrots too?'

Jay grinned, feeling better than he had for days, amused as always by her appetite. 'You are a greedy peasant. I'll have the steak too, rare. With new potatoes and a green salad. And bring me a large whisky.' He leaned back in his chair and regarded her inscrutably. 'Gerald is a friend of my mother.' He paused to run long fingers through his hair. 'No, that's inaccurate, he used to be one of her lovers. Still is for all I know. If you're curious I can ask her tomorrow.'

'I beg your pardon?'

'I said if you're—'

'I heard you. You said you could ask her tomorrow. Ask who?'

'My mother, who else?'

'You mean you're going to see your mother tomorrow?' Emma glared at him. 'You didn't even tell me you had a mother.' Yes you did, she corrected herself, remembering, you once let slip that you would not run to her if you were in trouble. The last place you would go, you said. Is that why we are here? Is this what that letter was about?

'Well, you know now. I have a mother and we are going to see her tomorrow. She is Missy, Melissa.'

'We?'

'We what?'

'*We* are going to see her?'

'*We* are going to see her. Anything else you want to know?'

Emma opened her mouth, shut it again. When the food came she attacked it with an enthusiasm born as much from discomfort as hunger and only when her stomach was nearly full did she feel strong enough to try again.

'And are we going to see your father too?'

Jay stabbed a slice of green pepper with his fork, expunged the amusement from his face. 'No. My father's dead. I killed him when I was sixteen.' He picked up the whisky the waiter had left by his place, drained it in one long greedy gulp, then sat staring at his glass, wondering what had driven him to make such a stupid remark.

Emma dropped her fork, gagging on the mouthful of food she was chewing.

'I'm sorry,' he apologised. 'That was unnecessarily melodramatic. He died. But I was responsible for his death.' His face was blank, as it almost always was when he was hurting, his voice expressionless. 'What would you like for pudding?'

Emma folded her knife and fork together and pushed her plate away. 'Nothing,' she said, no longer hungry. 'Explain.'

'Explain what?'

'For God's sake!' Her voice rose indignantly. 'You have just casually announced that you killed your father, and now you say "explain what?" as if we were discussing the weather. Explain what you are talking about. Explain why we are here – why *I* am here. What do you mean by it, sitting there calmly making such outrageous remarks without so much as a flicker of an eyelid?'

He put his knife and fork down in turn, waved away the waiter when he appeared to take the plates, then leaned across the table. 'We are here,' he said, '*you* are here, because I *can't* explain it to you. It's been locked inside my head since I was sixteen years old, and I can't get it out. I'm exorcising ghosts at your expense, because I can't do it on my own.' He leaned back, exhausted by too much whisky, by his earlier unexpected confrontation with the past, by Emma's puzzled attempts to understand that which he couldn't explain because he had yet to come to terms with it himself. 'You asked me once if I had any weaknesses, and I told you just one, remember? I lied.' He examined her shocked face, loving her freckles, unsullied by paint, her pale, generous mouth, her angry hazel eyes. 'You aren't my weakness, you're my only strength. You laugh at me when I tell you that I love you. But until you I couldn't . . . Because I loved my father and I killed him.' He took a deep breath. 'Tomorrow. I'll explain it all tomorrow. Tonight I want to go to bed, to feel your skin against mine. I'm cold, I need you to warm me.' He reached out to touch her cheek with a finger, smiled uncertainly, a child looking for balm. And for that brief moment, because he was hurting and despite all the defences she had erected against him, Emma loved him. Don't, she railed silently at him, seized by inexplicable apprehension, don't do this to me.

Sifting through the debris in her Norfolk attic, Emma came across a jewellery box, empty but for a broken string of beads and a brooch made of shells with the word 'mother' spelled out across it. It was the sort of trinket that children buy with loving enthusiasm, that parents exclaim over, grimacing indulgently at each other above their offsprings' heads, then push to the back of a drawer, guiltily never to wear. Holding it in her hand as she moved through the clutter she was reminded of her unwilling attendance during Jay's interview with his mother, and the memory brought her up short, tasting again the poison that had dripped between them, corroding the air like acid as they scored verbal points off each other.

Jay pointed it out from the other side of the valley, a butter-coloured stone mansion, standing alone in the midst of rolling parkland. Its size, its grandeur unsettled Emma, reminded her of her own semi-detached insignificance. The plain grey jersey dress she had packed for she-knew-not-what occasion seemed suddenly cheap and suburban, her feet too big, her hair too red. She wondered in passing why she should care what sort of impression she made on Jay's mother; it wasn't as if she intended to stay with him for any longer than was absolutely necessary.

Jay had taken no trouble with his appearance at all. He was wearing his oldest jeans, and a casual shirt with a sweater flung around his shoulders. He was driving badly too, careless of the twists and turns in the narrow country road, his hands gripping the steering wheel so hard his knuckles were white, and Emma grew increasingly nervous of the high hedgerows and blind corners, the lack of passing places and the speed at which they were travelling. She let go a sigh of relief when they left the highway to negotiate the gravelled drive, darkly enclosed between banks of tall, glossy rhododendrons, then had to curb the desire to run away when Jay finally brought the car to a halt before the magnificent stone portico and killed the engine.

'This is it,' he jibed, coolly sarcastic. 'Home Sweet Home.'

They were greeted by a manservant, invited to wait in a formal, intimidating library looking out across green lawns and a broad, still lake to the gently rising hills beyond. Jay prowled the room like a caged animal, looking at everything but the peaceful view from the window, until the servant returned to inform him that Melissa Hammond didn't want to see Emma.

'Not the young lady, Sir,' the man said firmly. 'Mrs Hammond has expressed a wish to speak with you alone.'

'She gets us both or no one,' Jay replied. 'Tell her she can take her pick.' The man inclined his head, then led them back across the imposing hall to a pair of panelled double doors, the mouldings picked out in gold leaf.

'If you would care to wait, Sir, I will relay your message to Mrs Hammond.'

'Let me go and sit in the car,' hissed Emma frantically while he was gone. 'You don't need me here.'

'Yes I do,' Jay hissed back. 'This is why you came, and I'm not staying unless you do.' Then he held tightly to her hand in case she should escape.

The man returned to announce, 'You may go in now,' and ushered them into an elegant drawing-room filled with flowers and sunlight. Then he retreated to the hall, closing the doors behind him. Emma hung back, letting go of Jay and screwing up her eyes, adjusting after the dim coolness of the hall.

'Been redecorating, Mother?' asked Jay of the apparently

empty room. 'Doesn't look like the place I left.'

Emma heard her before she saw her, a rustle of silk from the window as Melissa Hammond turned to face the room, a soft, breathless, feminine laugh, and the jingle of bracelets. 'Did you think I would have preserved it just for you? Silly boy.'

Her back was to the light. She could see their faces, but hers was indistinguishable, a tiny, dainty figure silhouetted against the bright lawn and the distant lake behind her. 'And who is this you have brought when I asked you to come alone?'

Jay fumbled for Emma's hand again, lacing his fingers through hers. 'This is Emma.' He tightened his hold. 'I brought her for protection.'

Melissa Hammond laughed again, said huskily, 'From me? How very amusing,' them moved away from the window, emerging into the light.

'You're looking thin, Mother. Been on a diet?'

'Since you are here, I must assume that you received my letter. I have cancer, as you are no doubt aware.'

'Good. Not long to live, I hope?'

Emma caught her breath, stared in horror at Jay's impassive face. His mother was unfazed. 'Three to six weeks, so I am told.'

'May every second be full of pain. How did you find me?'

Missy Hammond laughed again, then coughed; Emma heard the fluid bubbling in her lungs and felt sick.

'Easily, my sweet boy. You forget, you're famous. I saw your work in a magazine, put two and two together. A Jay Hammond who draws like an angel, a few discreet enquiries. You even executed a commission for me, just so I could be sure I had the right Hammond, a villa I was letting near Nice.' She laughed again, choked, caught her breath. 'Remember that brochure you did? You worked from photographs, made it look absolutely gorgeous.'

'*Le Canadel?* Yes, I remember. How much did I charge you?'

'A great deal of money, and worth every penny.'

'A pity. Had I known it was for you, I would have doubled my fee.'

Melissa Hammond smiled, gagged, coughed juicily, then advanced further into the room, allowing Emma for the first time a clear sight of her face.

Her make-up was faultless, an illusion of delicate beauty framed by a thick cloud of improbable blonde curls. But beneath the foundation and powder disease had ravaged her, shrivelling her skin, feeding on the flesh that stretched over her skull. Within the perfect porcelain mask only the eyes were still alive, blue, but not bright like Jay's. Melissa Hammond's eyes were pale and cold, glittering in their bony caves like freezing diamonds. Emma shifted uneasily and moved nearer Jay, looking for reassurance. He squeezed her hand, glanced down, smiled, then returned to the attack.

'Found a magic formula, Mother? I've never seen your hair looking so good.'

'It's a wig,' said Missy calmly. 'As I'm sure you have already noticed. The therapy makes one's hair fall out. The treatment has stopped now; they tell me there is nothing more they can do.' She advanced nearer to examine Emma dispassionately, then raised an exquisite eyebrow. 'She is very young, James. And I think our sparring upsets her.' Then, addressing Emma directly for the first time, 'Don't you think, my dear, you would find it preferable to wait elsewhere? My business with James will take very little time, and my man will give you a sherry, or whatever you young people like to drink nowadays.'

'Of course, I'll—'

'No.' Jay's voice grated after Missy's soft persuasion. 'Emma is staying. But I wish you would get to the point, Mother, so we can both leave.'

'You always were an impatient child. And your manners have not improved since last I saw you, James. Very well, but you will wait for coffee at least.' Missy pushed a bell on the wall beside the mantelpiece, waved imperiously at the damask-covered sofa by the fire, and took the velvet chair opposite, folding her hands in her lap, and crossing her thin legs neatly at the ankle. Then they sat in silence until the manservant appeared with a tray. Only when he had gone did she speak again.

'As I am sure you have deduced by now, I have asked you to come here because I am dying. Since all this—' she waved a skeletal hand at the room, setting her bracelets jangling again '—will shortly be yours, I thought it was time we mended fences, forgave the past.' She leaned against the cushions behind her, picked up her cup, tinkling it prettily in its saucer, and sipped at her coffee. 'You stand to inherit a great deal of money when I am gone. It seems only civilised that we should part on amiable terms—'

'Amiable terms?' To Emma's acute discomfort, Jay began to laugh, loud, hearty guffaws that reverberated round the room. Missy shrugged, persevered.

'When you were young and impressionable, you made judgements, misunderstood—'

'Misunderstood?' Jay leaned forward, abruptly serious. 'What did I misunderstand, Mother? Gerald's bare buttocks, humping you in your marital bed in front of my father? Did I miscount the number and variety of your lovers? Or was it your determined attempts to seduce the friend I naïvely brought into this house to keep me company over Christmas that I misunderstood? He was sixteen years old, Mother, did I misunderstand that too? You were lucky he never told, weren't you—?'

'Enough!' Missy began to cough, waved a dismissive hand. 'If you repeat such slanderous assertions outside this room, you will not get a penny piece from me—'

'Ah!' Jay nodded, seeing the light at last. 'So that's what this is all about, a little coercion to add to all your other sins. I ran into Gerald in Harrogate last night.' He put down his cup and stood up, towering over his mother. 'He never saw us, Mother, did he, never knew you had an audience that day? He sends his regards. Poor Muriel didn't look too pleased to see me though. She knew, didn't she? Still shagging his fat arse, are you?'

Missy pursed her lips in distaste. 'Such a vulgar expression. You

should have stayed on at school, James, instead of running away.'
Her mouth curved into a small smile. 'And, of course, if you hadn't
run away, your father might still be—'

'Be quiet!'

Missy laughed, choked, searched in her sleeve for a handkerchief and wiped the red spittle from her mouth. 'No, my dear, you
will hear me out. But I wish you would send this child away first.
I see no reason why she should be forced to listen to your foul-
mouthed fantasies.'

Grateful to be let off the hook, Emma rose obediently to leave.
But Jay blocked her way, turning his back on his mother to beg her
softly, 'Please, Em,' and she hesitated, then stood waiting, wishing
they would finish their hateful duelling so she could escape.

'It is a small thing I am asking,' continued Missy. 'Having
anticipated your unreasonable attitude ...' She rose in her turn,
dwarfed by her son, the two high spots of colour on her
cheekbones the only indication that she was under any strain, and
walked across the room to a pretty, inlaid bureau. She unlocked it,
collected a sheaf of papers and brought it back. 'This is an
undertaking not to discuss our family business after my death.
Once this is signed, my will comes into effect.'

'Is that all?' asked Jay. He sounded amused, casual, wanted to
take her out and drown her in the lake, where his father had begun
to die over twelve years ago. 'Just sign on the dotted line and I cop
the lot? How much are you worth, Mother, half a million, three
quarters?'

'More,' she said. 'Much, much more. Here, just sign at the
bottom, where the crosses are. If your friend is not to leave, she
can witness your signature.'

She held out the papers and Jay took them, lowered his head to
read, then smiled suddenly, chuckled, began to laugh. For the first
time Missy Hammond looked disconcerted, stepped backwards
away from his hilarity.

'*Now* what do you find so amusing?'

Jay struggled to bring himself under control. 'You're positive?'

he asked, making sure he had got it straight. 'This is all I have to do, and everything will be mine? The jewellery, the house, the stocks and shares? Do I get all those noisy gold bangles, Mother?'

'Of course. You could make a gift of them to your pretty friend. Everything will be yours. Just think what you could do with all this.' Missy waved her arm, setting the bracelets clashing musically and Jay stared at her, no longer amused.

'And if I refuse?'

'If you decide to be so crassly stupid, then I shall leave everything to the local parish council, for the good of the community. You will get nothing.'

'Except the incalculable pleasure of mounting the pulpit in Knaresborough church to read your funeral peroration. Thank you, Mother, but I just can't resist the prospect of giving you a last character reference.' He grinned, baring all his teeth, then deliberately tore the papers across and dropped them on the floor at her feet. 'I could invite the Press too, couldn't I? They love a nice, juicy scandal. Do you suppose the parish council will still want your money when I have finished? I could even tell them why my father died, couldn't I, Mother?'

The two scarlet spots on Missy's cheeks faded into pallor. 'I suggest you think about it rather carefully,' she said, her icy self-control slipping for the first time. 'Perhaps your young friend will be able to make you see sense. In the meantime, I have one other thing for you before you go.' She returned to the bureau, opened a small drawer, then came back to stand in front of him. 'Here,' she said, 'your father wanted you to have this and it's worthless to me. I'll have another set of papers drawn up. When you change your mind you know where to contact me.' She placed a small brown package in Jay's hand, and he closed his fingers over it.

'Is that all?'

'For now, yes.'

'No, Mother, not for now. This was your last chance.'

He paused at the door, waiting for Emma to pass him, then looked back at the tiny ramrod-straight figure standing in the middle of her beautiful room. 'May you die in excruciating agony,' he said, savouring the words. 'And may you rot in Hell thereafter.' Then he shut the door and ushered Emma across the hall, out into the sunshine.

He was all right until they got to his car. Then he collapsed into his seat, bowed his head down on the steering wheel and groaned. Emma leaned across, shielding him from the house, and said softly, 'Not here, Jay, not now. She's watching from the window.'

He raised his head, nodded, started the engine, and pulled away down the drive in a hail of gravel. He felt light-headed, faint and disoriented, tasted again the panic he had felt when he was sixteen years old, when he had run away. Emma had to stop him half a mile down the road, shouting at him to pull over, or he would have killed them both. The last time he had fled it had been a push-bike – a Jensen is a lot quicker, he thought, hanging on to his sanity by his fingernails.

He started the car again, pulled out more slowly, said wryly, 'You must learn to drive, Em,' then settled back in his seat and began to concentrate on the road. He drove west, not back towards the hotel but out past Ripley and on through Pateley towards Hebden Bridge. Then he turned off the main road and drove on steadily as high as he could go, until he ran out of road. When he could take the car no further, he parked and climbed out to stride away across the moors by himself. He stood on the horizon for almost half an hour, his hands in his pockets and his face turned to the wind, letting it whip his hair across his forehead and flap his shirt. When he came back his eyes were red and his cheeks were wet. He turned the car round and they drove slowly back to Harrogate in complete silence.

He behaved like a zombie that afternoon, incapable of anything but the simplest decisions. Emma knew what it felt like, that bone-crushing tiredness; she had suffered from the same thing when she lost Ricky, then again when Ali died. She knew what to do about it too, ordered him around as he had bossed her all those months

before, took him straight up to their room and, ignoring his
protests, put him to bed. When he clung to her in desperation she
undressed, blanking out everything but Jay's desperate need,
climbed under the covers with him and held him in her arms until
he sighed and laid his head on her breast, his tense muscles
relaxing for the first time in days.

He didn't want to play but she made him anyway: Nanny
forcing her charge to take his medicine because it would make him
better; after a while he would realise it was doing him good.

'Make love to me,' she murmured in his ear, choosing her
words with care, offering sweet inducements if her patient would
swallow his spoonful like a good boy, thinking about nothing but
the problem in hand. 'Please, Jay.'

He raised his head, tempted by the lure. 'You and I don't make
love.' He had taken the bait. 'We screw.'

'Stupid.' She guided him back to his medicine, ignoring Ricky's
silent cry of protest. 'Don't be stupid.'

He reminded her afterwards, demanding his reward. 'Christ,
that was a good screw,' and she duly obliged.

'You and I don't screw, we make love. Now, will you please get
off my leg before you do me a permanent injury.'

He rolled obediently away from her and lay on his back,
contemplating the ceiling. 'I love you,' he said, and held his
breath.

'Don't be greedy,' replied Nanny briskly. 'You've had enough
treats for one day.' But she turned her head and smiled at him,
taking the sting out of the rebuke with a touch of her hand. He
needed her so badly...

It wasn't until they stopped for lunch on their way back to London
the next day that Jay began to talk, but once he'd started he
couldn't stop.

They sat for two hours in the window bay of a pretty pub built
of pale yellow sandstone just off the A1 somewhere in Lincoln-
shire, and Emma, having prodded and prompted him to tell,

thinking it would do him good, listened as it all poured out in a great bitter flood of jumbled bits and pieces – twenty years of bile, misery and guilt – and wondered whether she should have left well alone.

'I caught her, you see, only I didn't tell. I never told about any of them until the end. I thought it would kill him.'

'Caught who? You thought what would kill who?'

'My mother. My father. He adored her. He thought ...' Jay laughed too heartily, then winced. 'He thought she was perfect. But I knew better. I used to spy on her when I was home for the holidays, because I wanted to know why she'd sent me away.'

'Sent you away? Sent you away where?'

'Aren't you hungry?' Jay pushed a menu across the table at her, wanting her to eat. Watching Emma eat would make him feel better; it would make him feel normal. 'They've got steak-and-kidney pie, do you want that?'

'Yes. Fine, whatever you like. So where did your mother send you?'

'Boarding school. When I was eight. She didn't want me around you see, I cramped her style. Do you want peas and carrots, or they've mashed swedes if you'd rather?'

'No thanks, I don't like swedes.'

Jay chuckled, felt the tension ease momentarily. 'It was worth coming all this way just to find out that you don't like swedes. What other dark secrets have you been keeping from me, little Em?'

Emma lowered her head, reminded suddenly of Ricky, waiting for her on their return, then pushed her dark secret away and said firmly, 'I don't like scotch broth. I don't like the thingummies they put in. Oh, and tinned peas. I hate tinned peas.'

'Thingummies ... ?'

'Mmm, you know, what-d'you-call-'ms ... um, pearl barley. Why didn't your mother want you around?'

'Because I played tricks on her. I used to wait until she was entertaining one of her gentleman friends and then I would wander in and ask loudly, 'Mummy, what are you doing in bed with Mr Braithwaite? And what is Mr Braithwaite doing that for?' He mimicked his childish voice, high-pitched and lisping, rearranged his cutlery for the third time, then straightened the table mat, sipped at his water and continued conversationally, 'Sex is pretty ludicrous when you stumble upon it from outside, especially if you're only seven or eight. It's all right when you're doing it yourself, but watching other people screwing is pretty ... pretty ...' he hesitated, raised his head and grimaced at her '... hideous. Only it went on and on, and there was a horrible sort of fascination about it that grew as I got older. We all used to talk about sex at school, but I had actually seen someone doing it.' He laughed again, but this time it sounded bitter, nasty. 'I achieved hero status for a while, being the only one who really knew what I was talking about. I didn't tell them it was my own mother I'd been watching.' He paused, staring at his hands resting on the white tablecloth. 'It became a sort of game after a while: she would try to sneak her lovers in without me knowing, and I would try and catch her out, because I knew if I caught her she would have to cancel her fun. She didn't drive, you see, so they had to come to her. And she liked the excitement, the added *frisson* that the fear of discovery brought with it, the thrill of getting what she wanted without getting caught. She was the most promiscuous woman I ever knew. And my father thought she was perfect.'

'But how did she get away with it? All those men, they must have had wives, or girlfriends. Why didn't they make a fuss? And your father, why didn't he guess?' As you will guess, sooner or later, about me and ...

'He was out all day, somewhere on the estate, or working at his office in Harrogate. He did a lot of business abroad too. And a couple of them did make a fuss. Muriel was one of them, Gerald's wife. She rang Dad and told him to tell Missy to stay away from her husband. He simply refused to believe her. He ridiculed her, told her it was her imagination. He wasn't unkind, said he quite understood that she might be jealous of Missy, but if she was having difficulties with her marriage it wasn't his problem. He suggested she take Gerald away on holiday, to see if they could patch things up. I heard him tell my mother about it over dinner that night, and she said, "What a silly woman," as if Muriel was an idiot. They laughed about it together, and I thought I would throw up.'

Emma thought of fourteen questions all at the same time, and asked none of them. 'So how did your father die?' she demanded just as the waiter appeared with their steak-and-kidney pie. It wasn't what she'd meant to say at all.

'He had a heart attack, brought on by the cold, but it wasn't the coronary that killed him. The pneumonia did that. I bumped into one of his friends in York and he told me there'd been an accident, so I went to see him in hospital, just before he died. He was wired up to all these machines, spitting up phlegm and he looked like a cadaver already, all yellow and waxy.' Jay raised his head and stared out blindly at the car-park below their window. 'Do you know, he spent most of the time I was there peering over my shoulder, looking for my mother, and when she walked in his face lit up with joy.' He frowned at his plateful of food, pushed a piece of pastry around with his fork. 'Eat your pie before it cools down.'

Emma glanced at her plate, then back at Jay. 'Brought on by what cold?' she asked, returning to his father. 'I don't understand.'

'No.' Jay stared at her bleakly for a moment, then helped himself methodically to vegetables from the steaming dish the waiter had set down between them. 'Of course you don't. I made up my mind because of Tristan . . .' He put down the serving spoons and ran a hand across his eyes.

'Who's Tristan?' Emma prompted in despair, sprinkling salt liberally all over her food, just for something to do with her hands. 'Start again, Jay, from the beginning.'

'He was my best friend, at school. She tried to seduce him while he was staying with me during the Christmas holidays. And when he demanded to be taken home . . .' he closed his eyes, tasting the panic again, that Triss would tell all his friends, that when he returned to school everyone would know, and nothing would ever be the same again '. . . I had to threaten him to make him swear not to say anything to anyone. And I decided then that even if it meant telling Dad, it had to stop. Why aren't you eating?'

Emma blinked. 'I'm not very hungry,' she said. Or to be rather more accurate, I'm feeling sick to my stomach listening to this charming tale of your innocent childhood, and I'm wishing I hadn't asked because now that you've started to unburden yourself you're not going to stop, and I've a feeling there's worse to come.

'I waited until the next time. She was entertaining Gerald that day, remember Gerald? Dad was in Harrogate but I called him, got him out of a meeting and told him there was an emergency, then when he got home I took him upstairs and we stood in the doorway of mother's bedroom side by side, watching Gerald's bare arse bobbing up and down. It wasn't a very edifying sight.'

'Oh, Jay, how awful, how absolutely bloody *revolting*.' Emma brought her hands up to her mouth, staring at him in horror.

Jay made a face at her in return. 'Oh,' he said, remembering the sick feeling in the pit of his stomach, the apprehension that grew and grew as he realised what he had done. 'That wasn't the worst bit. I thought he would confront her, stop her in her tracks. I was looking forward to it, finishing it all at last. But he didn't make a sound, he just stood there staring at Gerald's rump, then took me by the arm, dragged me all the way downstairs to the library, and began to shout at me. He called me a—' He stopped abruptly, reached for the water and gulped a whole glassful in one go, poured some more. 'Will you please eat?' he pleaded. 'Just eat a little, Em, for my sake . . . He called me a corrupt little pervert. He said that what I had just done was completely unforgiveable. And when I said, "But what about what *she* was doing?" he began to cry. Emma, please—'

'All right, all right, I'm eating.' Emma picked up her knife and fork and began reluctantly to pick at her unwanted pie.

'He told me I didn't understand. That when I was grown up I would realise. It was bearable, he said, as long as he could pretend it wasn't happening, as long as no one rubbed his nose in it, but I had made him face it, you see, and he couldn't stand it. Then he told me he couldn't bear to look at me any more, to get out of his sight, so I did. I walked upstairs to my room, packed a change of clothes and a toothbrush in my rucksack, and I left. I climbed on my bike and cycled all the way to York. I got a job in a hotel that same night. It was easy, coming up to Christmas, everybody needed staff and I was tall for my age, well built. I looked older than sixteen. Nobody asked any questions.' He placed his cutlery neatly together, resting on his uneaten food. 'I thought leaving would put things right.'

Emma followed his example, folding her cutlery and waving her plate away when the waiter appeared, then reaching across the table to wrap her fingers round Jay's. 'But it wasn't your fault. You can't blame yourself. It was your mother's fault. Surely you can see that now, can't you?'

Jay twisted his hand beneath hers, brought the other across to hold her tightly between the two as Rick had done the other day; the unexpected reminder made her wince. 'I haven't finished yet,' he said. 'He went out that night, after I'd gone, looking for me in the pitch black, without so much as a torch, in the freezing cold in his shirt-sleeves. He lost his footing in the dark and fell in the lake.' Emma was visited by a swift mental picture of the still lake she had seen the previous day, imagined the splash, the cold, the shock. 'He managed to drag himself half out of the water, then collapsed with a heart attack. It took them three hours to find him ...' Emma felt his fingers tighten round hers '... so you see, I did kill him; it was all my fault, because if I hadn't shown him ... if I hadn't run away, he would have been all right.'

'Would Sir or Madam like to see the sweet trolley?' The waiter made them jump.

'Yes,' said Emma firmly. 'I would, please.' She had another swift flash of *déjà vu*, remembered Jay ridiculing her when she had blamed herself for Alison's death, recalled the long, cold walk he had taken her after the inquest, trying to bully and exhaust her back into some semblance of normality. She owed him.

She ordered Black Forest Gâteau with double cream, then followed it with cheese and biscuits and coffee. She ate all the *petits fours* that came with the coffee, Jay's as well as her own, and it nearly finished her – she couldn't remember ever having felt less like eating – but it was worth it. Somehow the sight of her appetite restored Jay's equilibrium as nothing else had managed to do, and by the time they made their way out to the car he was beginning to recover.

'As soon as we get back,' he reiterated, just before he started the engine, 'you must learn to drive. I'm too tired for this.' He leaned back briefly in his seat and closed his eyes. 'Thanks, Em,' he said, and fumbled for her hand.

'My turn,' Emma shrugged dismissively. 'You're not as tough as I thought you were, Jay Hammond.'

'Never was.' He opened his eyes, smiled at her, fired the engine. 'I love you, Em.' He pulled slowly out on to the road. 'Have I mentioned it before?'

Emma felt suddenly, stupidly, protective towards him, had to fight the sentimental surge of affection that was threatening to swamp her. Examining his drained, exhausted face, it dawned on her: this wasn't the end of it; she wasn't free yet. How could she ever have thought it would be that simple?

It was during that journey back to London, Emma acknowledged, crossing the attic to place Morag's brooch on the saving pile just in case, that she had realised how unobservant she was, how awry her instincts had been, right from the beginning. She had misjudged Jay, misjudged Ricky too, read them both completely wrong until that harrowing trip to Yorkshire.

Returning to the space she had cleared, she tripped over a Bullworker. She picked it up and stretched it experimentally between her hands, then dropped it on the throwaway pile, chuckling. George's? He could do with it now. Over the past few years, George had indulged in too many power lunches, power dinners, nowadays even power breakfasts. Whilst Jilly had stayed sleek and elegant, 'worn well' as everyone said, George had ballooned into obesity, and that incipient pinkness to which he had always been prone now permanently suffused his face, roseated his nose. Against appearances though, he possessed the constitution of an ox, enormous physical stamina and the mental toughness to stay at the top of his profession. That, she mused as she worked swiftly through a pile of ancient paperbacks, was where she had gone wrong in her assessment of Jay and Ricky. In Rick she had mistaken physical handicap for emotional weakness, thought him infinitely vulnerable. And into Jay's ability to build protective walls around himself, she had read an assumption of impregnable strength. When all the time it was Ricky who was tough, Jay who was weak; Jay who struggled to survive, a non-swimmer in the deep end, paddling frantically and gasping for breath, while Rick lay on his back and floated effortlessly. It was Rick who had survived the trauma of his past, Rick who had grown stronger with adversity...

During those two days and nights in Harrogate she began to understand why Jay had been able to help her when she was falling to pieces. He knew about drowning, knew when to throw a lifeline, when to make her strike out for the shore under her own steam. But in the end she had not allowed the debt she owed him to make any difference. In the end, her choice had been down to pure, primitive instinct... and the decision had almost broken her in two.

She heaved a rickety bentwood chair out of the gloom and examined it, wondering if it was worth saving, then shrugged at the gaping holes in the rattan seat, the cracks and splits in the parched, twisted back, and dragged it across to the throwaway pile. Be ruthless, she reminded herself, George doesn't want all this junk.

She found a first aid kit in the space the chair had left: a square, white-painted tin with a red cross imprinted on its lid, just like the one Josie had had in Cheshunt when she was a child. She hooked her fingers under the rim of the lid and swore as it snagged her fingernail, then peered inside. There was nothing there but an ancient yellowing roll of bandage and a corn plaster. 'Physician,' she said out loud, 'heal thyself.' Then she sighed, closed it up again and dropped it on the pile, recalling Jay's solitary struggle to heal the wounds that final confrontation with his mother had inflicted upon his fragile protective shell.

CHAPTER TWENTY-EIGHT

• • •

Emma drank too much wine with her supper, giving herself Dutch courage, then escaped to find a phone box. 'I need a breath of air,' she told Jay when he asked where she was going. 'It's stuffy in here.' Then she took the stairs two at a time down to the street to find a phone box, wanting only to get it over and done with now she had made up her mind.

'I have to see you,' she gabbled at Ricky, pushing coins into the slot with a shaking hand, now, soon, tomorrow, before I weaken. 'We have to talk.'

Talking was what Jay was finding impossible. From the moment they had left the anonymous pub that had served as his confessional, he'd clammed up again. Upon their arrival home he had collapsed, exhausted, and slept for three hours, and now he was stretched out on the sofa with his head resting on a cushion and his eyes closed, waiting for her to accompany him to bed. She had known since lunchtime that she couldn't leave him.

She followed him along the hall at ten o'clock with the intention of seducing him again; it would help him, she justified herself silently to Rick's accusing question, it had before. But whilst he needed her physical presence – refusing to go to bed without her, as if he was frightened of sleeping by himself – when they climbed beneath the blankets he wanted only to hold her in his arms, to ease his pain with her warmth, not to take advantage of her willing appetite. And this time, all her gentle encouragement, all her hopeful overtures, were rebuffed.

*

Ricky was bewildered, hurt, and he'd already heard her explanation once.

'I got it wrong with Ali. I left her when she was down, when she was relying on me. Every day, every time I think about her, I think, if I'd been there, if I'd stayed with her when she needed me, been a little less selfish, she might still be alive. I daren't make the same mistake again.' Emma leaned urgently across the empty coffee cups, aware that she was repeating all the things she'd said before, that she was using Ali yet again to justify her own dubious motives. 'I can't explain it. I just have to be there, that's all. You can't imagine how awful, how *sickening* it all was. And now he's like a wounded animal who's crawled into a hole to lick his wounds, and if I leave him, he'll *die*.' Her eyes filled with tears. Rick, staring at her pale face, knowing that nothing he could say would make any difference to the decision she had already made, was completely, utterly helpless, because he understood only too well. He'd had ample opportunity over the past forty-eight hours to think about what she'd said, and he couldn't blame her; he'd left her when she needed him and now he was being asked to pay for the second time. It didn't make it any easier.

'This is still to punish me, isn't it? Don't you think I've been punished enough already these past few days, knowing you were with him?'

'*No!* I mean no, it *isn't*, it isn't to punish you at all. I didn't . . .' Emma tugged at his hand, felt his resistance. 'I didn't want this to happen, I wanted – oh, Rick, I wanted us to be together.' The tears spilled over, ran down her cheeks, and she began to plead again. 'I can't help it. You have to understand. I just need time, that's all, until Jay can manage by himself again. Why don't you—' She wiped her wet face with the back of her hand and sniffed loudly. 'Why don't we start making plans, so that when I – when he's well again, we can be together straightaway?'

Rick shook his head. 'Why don't you let me know,' he said harshly, 'when you're ready. In the meantime, I'll do my penance like a good boy; I'll wait for you.'

He rose abruptly from the table, clattering the cups in their saucers as he moved, and rocking the sugar cubes in their china bowl. Then he leaned across the table and rubbed her tears away with rough brown fingers. 'You know where I am,' he said, feigning a confidence he was very far from feeling. 'And sooner or later you'll come back to me. In the meantime, I'm not going to hang about waiting for some other man's leftovers. I want all of you, not what you can spare from tending your wounded animal.' He hesitated, his fingers still resting against her jaw, then bent over her to add fiercely, 'Just call me every now and then, will you? So I know you're all right.' Then he straightened up and left her.

It was only when she was accosted on her way out that Emma discovered he hadn't paid the bill. 'Oh, great!' she snarled at the startled cashier, fumbling in her bag for some money. 'That's all I damn well need!'

Jay's convalescence was slow and painful, almost, thought Emma in her darkest moments, as if he knew what would happen once he was well. For the first few days after their return he did no work at all, although there were half a dozen unfinished commissions awaiting his attention, and he ventured no further from the flat than the towpath along the river, going for long solitary walks, deliberately tiring himself out. Emma, watching him from the window, his hunched shoulders and bowed head, could see the weight of the burden he carried, ached with pity for his plight and felt, briefly, completely useless.

'You aren't going anywhere, are you?' he asked anxiously before he set off on the second day, and when she appeared in the sitting-room doorway on his return his face lit up with relief. She was, she realised, being useful just by being there.

She didn't phone Rick; she didn't think she would be able to bear hearing his voice, but by the following Tuesday Jay seemed to be improving a little and she began to hope.

'Go back to work,' he said as he prepared a supper he could work up no enthusiasm for eating. 'I'm fine now, and you can't afford to mess them about any more.' So she escaped, ostensibly to the off-licence for a bottle of wine, then took a deep breath and dived into a phone box.

'It's me.'

There was a long pause. 'Are you on your way?'

'No, I—'

'Are you all right?'

'I suppose so. Rick, you do understand, don't you?'

She heard him sigh. 'Yes, I understand, but it doesn't make it any easier. How long, Em?'

'Not long, he's getting better. He's told me to go back to work. Rick . . .'

'I know, he needs you. So do I, Em.'

'But you're stronger than he is.'

'Are you sure?' There was another endless pause.

'Not long, I promise,' she said lamely, to fill in the silence. 'Rick, I—'

'I know,' he said. 'Just don't say it. It only makes it worse.'

She could sense the tension when she left for work, carried Jay's face with her all day, phoned twice to make sure he was all right, and took the Tube home so she could get back to him more quickly. When she opened the front door and heard his music she thought he must be better, hoped again, but when he came down the hall to greet her, his face was grey with exhaustion, and that night was as lacking in passion as the ones that had preceded it. Ironically, his complete lack of interest in her physical attractions served only to strengthen her conviction; she was doing the right thing, the only thing she could have done.

'Boyfriend trouble?' asked Francis, when she cut him dead for the third time in as many minutes.

'What?' Emma dragged her eyes from the *toile* she was pretending to work on. 'Sorry, Francis, what did you say?'

'I said, boyfriend trouble?'

'Oh! Er, no, not really . . .'

Francis tipped his head on one side and regarded her shrewdly with his chocolate-button eyes, then adjusted his brocade waistcoat over his ample midriff and smoothed the material with a perfectly manicured hand. There had been something odd going on ever since the child had returned from her so-called family crisis, a certain vagueness, an inability to concentrate on the job in hand; in Francis Boncœur's experience that sort of thing usually meant love tangles. When asked, the child had mumbled something about a 'friend', then mentioned in passing the name of a well-known illustrator who was, he thought, at least ten years older than she and with whom, he had guessed from the few hints dropped, she was living. Perhaps it was not surprising she was having problems.

'You've hardly spoken two words since you arrived this morning,' he continued urbanely. 'And both of them were "um". So why don't you tell your uncle Francis all about it, sweetie? Get it off your chest and you'll feel better.' A trouble shared, Francis always said, was a trouble halved.

Emma sighed, then glanced at Cyril, busy at the other end of the cutting-table just then and paying them no attention, but well within earshot if he chose to be. 'I'm fine,' she said. 'Honestly, Francis, just a bit jaded, that's all.' She smiled, at herself as much as Francis, then added lamely, 'You know how tiring it is, getting used to a new job.' She turned back to her *toile*, her hand hovering indecisively over the button she was trying to place, her mind on Jay and his uncharacteristic lack of interest in sex, hurting because he was in pain and she couldn't help.

'Lunch,' said Francis firmly. 'That's what you need, dear heart. Lunch with an ageing Queen who knows how to be discreet.' Aha, he thought, as Emma turned her head and appraised him with sudden interest, that caught your attention, didn't it, my red-haired *ingénue*! He chuckled. 'Hadn't you noticed, poppet?' he teased. 'Why, what an innocent child you are.'

'Oh, no,' Emma protested, trying to be casually sophisticated about the little man's startling revelation and wondering, now that it had been pointed out to her, how she could possibly not have noticed before. 'No, I'm not at all. Actually, one of my best friends is a ... is a ...'

Francis chuckled again. 'The word you are searching for, dear girl, is "poof". Now, what about that lunch?'

He took her to a dimly lit bistro just off Berwick Street, watched with fascination as she tucked away enough food to keep an army marching for a week, and set out to cheer her up. He began, having just sent Solly Cohen on his way to a meeting in the Roller, by regaling her with tales of his master's flamboyant driving habits, amusing her with instances of Solly's unshakeable conviction that driving a Rolls-Royce entitled him to take precedence at all times regardless of what other vehicles might be on the road, then made her roar with laughter at stories of his boss's pathological hatred of woman drivers in general and elderly, respectable women drivers in particular. Relaxed by her companion's easy charm, Emma confided her trepidation about her recently commenced driving lessons, booked the day after their return by Jay, and now adding immeasurably to the worries already keeping her awake at night.

'And how does this man of yours feel about women drivers?' asked Francis, probing gently.

'Oh, he's not my ... I mean, he doesn't mind them at all. He's not a bit like Solly.'

'Ah, the archetypal English gentleman?'

Emma smiled. 'Hardly,' she said, amused by the thought. 'More like the archetypal mis – um, mis – oh, you know what I mean, Francis, I just can't think of the word. What do you call them?'

'What do you call what, sweetie?'

'You know, hermits, people who distrust people.'

'Misanthropes?'

'That's it: misanthropes. Jay's the archetypal misanthrope.'

Francis was becoming confused. 'But if he's a misanthrope,

dear girl, what's he doing romancing a delicate young blossom like you?'

Emma laughed. Francis had such a soothing effect upon her. 'Ah, he doesn't count me, you see. I'm not one of them, I'm one of, well, one of us, if you see what I mean.'

'Not really, but we'll let it pass. So was that the problem then? Was it his misanthropic tendencies that ruined your jolly hols?' He made no pretence of having swallowed her original sob story.

'Oh, no.' Emma helped herself to more cream from the jug in front of her, pouring it liberally over her half-eaten sorbet and watching it set hard as it froze, then confided without thinking, 'That was his horrible mother's fault.'

'Ah.' Francis was none the wiser for his probing. 'I see.'

'Trouble is,' Emma was talking to herself now, 'I don't know how to help him. It's all swirling around in his head but he won't talk about it. He looks terrible, can't sleep, won't eat, and I don't seem to be able to comfort him.'

'The power of love,' purred Francis urbanely, wondering what the devil the dear child was talking about, 'will cure all ills, given time. Just be patient, sweetie, make sure he knows you love him, and it'll all come right in the end. You'll see.'

Emma raised her head and stared at him, her spoon poised halfway between bowl and mouth. 'Oh,' she said, suddenly dismayed. 'Do you suppose that's the trouble, Francis? You see, I *don't* love him, and he knows I don't.'

Francis blinked, uncharacteristically nonplussed by the blunt confession, then re-adjusted his waistcoat and brushed an imaginary speck of fluff from his trousers. Should he, in the light of this unexpected admission, revise his opinion of the lovely Miss Versey? he wondered. Did there lurk behind those wide, seemingly innocent hazel eyes, a thick-skinned gold-digger?

'So why, if I may be so bold as to pry, are you, er . . . ?'

'Living with him . . . ?' Emma lowered her spoon and began to peel bits of frozen cream from her pudding. 'Well, because when Rick left me he was such a . . . and then when Alison died, I needed him so much . . .' She paused, thought about what she'd said, then added, anxious that Francis shouldn't get the wrong idea, 'Anyway, it's only temporary. I mean, it's not as if I don't care for him at all . . .'

'Well, that's a relief at least,' murmured Francis faintly.

'It's just that I don't, you know, because there's somebody . . .' Emma stopped in mid-sentence, remembering the meal she had shared with Jay in Harrogate after seeing Missy, recalling the moment when he had needed her so badly, and briefly feeling again what she had felt then. 'Well,' she amended, correcting herself, 'maybe sometimes I do.'

'I see,' said Francis. 'You do and you don't. Or rather, you don't but you do. It must be very confusing for you.' As it most certainly is for me, he thought, lowering his head to hide the smile that was creeping across his face despite his earnest endeavours to the contrary.

'Well, yes, it is rather,' Emma agreed. 'Because every time I try to get myself out of it, Jay goes and dishes me. He can be so . . . so . . .' She paused to take a mouthful of sorbet, then gazed into the middle distance as it melted against her tongue, momentarily forgetting her companion as an unwonted surge of guilt-tinged affection swamped her again.

'Mmm,' said Francis sympathetically. 'I can quite imagine that he must be.' There are none so blind, he thought, making a determined effort to straighten his face, as those who will not see.

She was awfully quiet for the rest of the meal.

'Thanks, Francis,' she said as they passed through reception on their way back to the cutting-room. 'You've given me something to think about.'

'All part of the service, dear girl.' Francis dimpled at her, gratified. 'Can't have you moping about the place like a wet weekend – Solly'll have my guts for garters.'

Emma smiled back, then bent and kissed his cheek. 'You don't fool me for one second,' she accused him. 'You did it purely to make me feel better, just because you're such a terribly nice man.'

'No good kissing Frankie,' roared Solly from behind them, making them both jump. 'He's a woolly woofter, y'know.'

'Solomon.' Francis straightened his waistcoat, and drew himself up to his full height, bringing his bright button eyes level with the knot of his employer's loudly tasteless tie. His face was pink with pleasure from his kiss. 'In the words of some famous poet, whose name at this moment unfortunately escapes me, "Do me a favour, dear boy, and button your lip."'

CHAPTER TWENTY-NINE
• • •

By the end of September Emma's suits were selling steadily and Solly had awarded her a small pay rise. She travelled in every Wednesday, Thursday and Friday on the Tube, almost completely cured of her claustrophobia, and had started work on a new spring collection. Her salary was more than enough now to pay her way and she was selling fabric designs too, to Heals in the Tottenham Court Road. Her professional life had never been more exciting.

Her private life had never been more confused. When Jay begged her one particularly difficult evening to move in properly, she took a taxi and picked up the remains of her belongings, just to reassure him. The incandescent smile with which he greeted her return was reward enough, so she didn't tell him she had kept the key. It made perfectly good sense though, she justified herself, she might need it if she wanted to go on working after . . .

She broke the news to Josie that she had left college, although she was too cowardly to do it face to face, or tell her she had made the decision months ago, before the Easter holidays. She sent her two cheques to pay back her grant contributions and felt briefly virtuous, then guilty that she had let her mother down. When Josie threatened to visit she told her at last that she had moved, but not, since it was only temporary, that she was living with Jay. Josie didn't need to know, she excused herself; it was none of her business.

She wasn't just a coward where her mother was concerned. As the weeks slipped by, so Ricky slipped again from her tenuous grasp. She knew it was happening but there was nothing she could do to stop it short of leaving Jay to go to Ricky, and that she couldn't do, not yet. Her lunch with Francis had added a new dimension to her dilemma, had made her realise just how difficult parting from Jay, whether wounded or recovered, was going to be. She was *used* to him, and with every passing day she grew more apprehensive at the thought of giving him up for the uncertain prospect of life with Rick in darkest Norfolk. She was frightened, she admitted in her more clear-sighted moments, terrified of the unknown, of trusting to her instincts.

Jay was working again, buying and selling his paintings, taking on new commissions, even asking her to marry him, but she wasn't convinced. On the surface he was almost back to his usual sardonic self, but his point-blank refusal to talk about their trip to Yorkshire, and more significantly, their still nonexistent sex life, proved to Emma that all was not well. Somehow those last two hurdles seemed to be too difficult for him to surmount and she didn't know how to help him over them. If she was honest his continuing need of support was a relief; it gave her an excuse to prevaricate for a little longer.

It was strange, since his hold on her had been based from the beginning almost entirely on physical pleasure, that Jay's complete loss of sexual appetite should serve to bring them closer in so many other ways. Of course it was mostly pity, Emma knew that, but as she watched him, frowning over a sketch or painting meticulously a tiny detail of a finished drawing, laughing at her tales of Solly Cohen's oddities or lounging on the sofa listening to his beloved music, the emotion she felt was so strong, so all-pervading, that it would have been easy, had she never been in love before, to mistake her attachment towards him for the real thing. She had only spoken to Ricky once since their last emotional parting. He had promised to wait, she reassured herself when the wistful longing, the fear of losing him, crept up on her, and until she had something positive to tell him, it wasn't fair to get his hopes up.

CHAPTER THIRTY

• • •

After her driving test Emma sat beside the instructor in his green Austin A40, clutching her certificate and absolutely bursting with impatience as he drove her back to Putney at funereal pace. She couldn't wait to tell Jay all about it, but he had an appointment in the West End for which, unless her infuriating chauffeur got a move on, he would probably already have left by the time she got home.

When she spotted the Jensen outside the flats, she was so pleased she leaped out of the car without so much as a goodbye and sprinted for the lobby, confirming her instructor's opinion that young people nowadays had absolutely no manners at all, then took the lift almost without a thought, tolerating the enclosed space with ease. On the landing she fumbled clumsily with her keys, impatient to get inside so she could see Jay's face and praying he hadn't taken the stairs.

He was standing in the hall waiting for her, leaning against the wall with his arms folded, smiling, and Beethoven's 'Emperor' Concerto was drifting through the open studio door. 'Well?' he demanded. 'Did you pass?'

'What are you doing here? You should have left twenty minutes ago.'

'I know.' He pushed himself away from the wall and advanced down the hall towards her. 'I'm just going. Did you pass?'

'Have you been waiting for me?'

'All my life.' He took her hand as he reached her, laid it on his chest over his heart, mocking himself, then covered it with both his own. 'Did you pass?'

'Yes, of course I did,' said Emma ignoring the provocation, then jumped up and down, unable to contain herself any longer and squeaked at him, 'I passed! I passed! *Liar!*'

'What?'

She caught her breath, triumphant at having found him out. 'I said *liar*. You told me there was someone else you wanted before me. You didn't manage to hook her, you said.'

'Oh.' He tightened his grip and the smile faded from his face. He looked disconcerted suddenly, vulnerable again. 'It was you,' he said, confessing his sins. 'I was talking about you all the time.'

'No, you weren't.' Emma felt strangely pleased, then indignant. Why did he have to do this to her? It wasn't fair, deliberately weakening her resistance, especially when he couldn't, wouldn't make love to her, when she couldn't leave him. 'We were alike, you said, because we were both loners, remember? And then you said—'

'I'm glad you passed.' It would have been better, thought Jay, watching the resentment creeping into Emma's face, not to tell her. He should have let her think she wasn't the only one he had ever loved, but it was too late now. Reluctantly, unexpectedly feeling stirrings of desire for the first time in weeks, he released her and turned away. 'I must go, I'm horribly late.' He retrieved his folio from the hall table, picked up his keys and bent to kiss her as he passed. 'I'll see you tonight.' He grinned, lightening the mood. 'Should we put an ad in the paper, do you think?'

'An ad? What for?'

'To warn the rest of London you're on the loose with a lethal weapon.'

'Pig.' Emma grinned back despite herself, forgetting her irritation. 'Get out of here before I hit you . . . Jay?'

'Yes, what? I'm late.'

'Kiss me goodbye . . . Mmm . . . Jay?'

'What?'

'Kiss me again.' God, she was hopeless. 'You haven't congratulated me properly yet.'

'Yes I have, I . . . Emma, I'm going to be late.'

'How late? Can't you ring them up and tell them you've broken down?'

'No, of course I— Emma . . . Oh, Emma, Emma . . .'

'Jay. You're going to be late . . .'

'Mmm. Very late . . .'

'I'm terribly sorry,' she said. 'But he's in bed . . . Yes, some sort of virus, I think.' She clapped her hand over her mouth, stifling the giggles, shifted her bare feet. 'Oh absolutely, I hope it's not catching, too . . . Yes, I'm sure he'll be in touch as soon as possible . . . Yes, I'll tell him. Bye.'

She paused in the bedroom doorway, still giggling. 'He said to send you his best wishes for a speedy recovery.' She wandered naked across the room and climbed back into the warm patch she had left beside him. 'He was awfully concerned that it might be catching.'

Jay chuckled. 'Who knows?' he said. 'Maybe it is. If so, I probably caught it off you, but there's only one way to find out.'

'Oh?'

'Well, I think I'm beginning to feel the symptoms coming on again, so we could try an experiment. If I just . . . and we both . . . then I could . . . and if you get the same sort of . . .'

'Oh! Ahhh . . .!'

'Well that proves it, doesn't it? Definitely catching.'

They spent the rest of the day in bed, and Emma, between snacks, plied him with the multitude of questions she had been saving up ever since their return from Harrogate, getting them off her chest.

'Why did your mother dislike you so much? She must have wanted you to start with.'

'No.' Jay sat propped up on his pillows, completely at ease for the first time in weeks, drinking tea. 'I was conceived before the war, in 1937, and she couldn't get an abortion. Otherwise she would have got rid of me. She told me.'

'You mean you'd never have been born?' Emma was shocked, confronting for the first time what the abstract term 'abortion' really meant. It occurred to her that Alison had been responsible for the obliteration of not one but two unborn human beings, taking the second with her into oblivion when she took her own life. She felt sudden overwhelming pity, for Alison's lost babies, for Jay, and changed tack slightly.

'And did you go home, when you realised your father was dying?'

'No, I told you, I went to see him in the hospital, but I never went back to the house.' Jay leaned into his pillows and closed his eyes. 'Mother arrived to visit him just as I was leaving ... No, that's not true, I left when she walked in, because he didn't need me there once he had her. She followed me out into the corridor so she could tell me how he'd managed to get himself into such a state; she wanted to make sure that I knew it was all my fault. She said she didn't want to see my disgusting face ever again. So I went back to my hotel job.' He raised his head, opening his eyes to grimace briefly at Emma's shocked expression. 'It was all right,' he reassured her. 'You'd have loved it: a warm bed and all the leftovers you could eat, twenty-four hours a day.'

Emma swallowed hard and reached for a bourbon biscuit. 'And then what?'

'I read about his death in the paper. He was far too young to die of a heart attack, only fifty-two, so there had to be a—'

'A post-mortem?'

'A post-mortem. Cause of death, pneumonia brought on by "pulmonary infarction", whatever that is. I went to the inquest, but nobody asked me what happened. Mother didn't even tell them I had been there, and I was frightened they'd blame me if I said anything. So they put it down as an accident. He often went for a late-night stroll, my mother said, it was just ghastly bad luck. When they came to his state of mind... Remember that, Em, remember "state of mind"?' Emma nodded silently, gulped too quickly at her tea, then put it down beside her to cool. 'She told them he was fine. They were planning a holiday together, she said, the following spring. There was no reason for anyone to doubt her word.' Emma was reminded of Alison's inquest, the lies Harry Passmore had told, and wondered whether, if she hadn't given evidence, he would have been believed too. 'I went out afterwards with some of the others from the hotel and got drunk for the first time in my life.'

'And did they know who you were, where you'd been that day, that you were his son?'

He shook his head. 'No, of course they didn't. I was just another unskilled bum trying to earn a crust.' He leaned across and tucked a wisp of red hair behind Emma's ear, smiled at her. 'I lost my virginity that night, with one of the waitresses. She was thirty-five, and she told me I was the most inept lover she had ever had.' He chuckled. 'I didn't remember a thing about it the next morning, so I had to do it again to see whether I liked it.'

'Ha Ha. Very funny.' Emma shifted her shoulders and reached for the bourbon biscuits again, annoyed. 'There's no need to go into all the gory details.'

'Thank you.' Jay wiped the crumbs away from her mouth, then bent his head and kissed her tenderly.

'What for?'

'For being jealous. I love you.'

'Oh . . . I'm not! I . . .'

'Go on . . .' Jay waited a moment, then sighed and lay back again, draining the last of his tea before placing the cup carefully on the bedside table. 'You may have just one more question,' he said. 'This is getting very tiring, Em.'

Emma discarded her half-eaten biscuit, finished her tea and put the cup down. 'How did you get into college,' she asked, taking pity on him, 'without any O levels?'

Jay chuckled. 'Now there's a question of earth-shattering significance.' She could hear the relief in his voice. 'I sweet-talked them. I told them I had nine O levels, which was true enough, but that I had no certificates to prove it.' He rolled over, dragging her down beneath the blankets. 'And because I am a genius, they waived the rules for me. They gave me a grant too, as a mature student.'

'But—'

'Em, even geniuses need to rest occasionally, especially when they've just used up a month's sexual energy. Now do me a favour – please, stop asking questions, shut up, and let me go to sleep.'

'Oh, I'm sorry, all right . . . Jay . . .'

'Mmm?'

'Nothing.' Just feeling soppy, that's all, as if I've cured you single-handed. 'Sweet dreams.'

She hadn't phoned Rick for weeks, hadn't thought about him at all that day, but there was nothing, she realised just before her eyes closed, to stop her ringing him now. She stretched out a tentative hand and touched Jay's shoulder; he shifted, mumbled, sighed and slept again. Or maybe she'd leave it, just for a few days, until she was sure Jay was strong enough to manage without her . . .

It was late afternoon when she found it, and the sun was slanting low outside the dusty attic window, stretching long black shadows beneath the trees, and rendering indistinct the pile of memories waiting by the door, destined for the dustmen or the bonfire.

'Oh!' she exclaimed, as it all came flooding back, and she sat down hurriedly on an empty tea chest. It was George's wedding album.

'Here.' Jay leaned across the breakfast table and dropped the letter on her plate. 'You can open this one, it's for both of us.'

The envelope was addressed to 'Jay and Emma Hammond', and Emma was annoyed by the distraction, by the inference. She was almost ready to leave for work, to phone Ricky and tell him the good news, that their long wait was nearly over. She frowned at Jay's expression, at the silent challenge she read in the grin spreading across his face.

It was from George. They were invited up to Norfolk, to his and Jilly's wedding. Jilly's folks, George explained in the accompanying note, came from Northumberland. *Much too far for all our friends to travel and Mum and Dad have just the place for the reception here at home.*

You must come, he wrote. *We're doing it the Scottish way, with a ceilidh in the evening. Bill's coming, and all the other old faces from the Earl's Court days, but it won't be complete unless you're both here too.* He was enclosing, he added, a list of local hotels in case they wanted to stay overnight, and a map of the area so they could find the house. It was set for a Friday, three weeks hence, and Emma was relieved. She wouldn't be here in three weeks, but now was not the moment to break the news to Jay; since Friday was a working day she could tell him with a clear conscience that she wouldn't be able to go, and avoid giving him hope of a future that was never going to happen.

By the time she had worked out what she was going to say, he was deep in his own correspondence and she had trouble getting his attention. 'When is it?' he asked impatiently when he finally dragged his eyes from the thick wad of papers in his hand, and when she told him the date he surprised her by shaking his head and saying brusquely, 'We can't go.'

She was so taken aback by his vehemence, she forgot the story she had decided upon and demanded indignantly, 'Why not? Surely there can't be anything so urgent—'

'We just can't. We'll be somewhere else.'

'Don't be silly, where would we be that we can't—?' The conversation wasn't going as she'd planned at all.

'We'll be away.' He plucked the top page from the pile in front of him and dropped it on her plate as he passed to rummage in one of the kitchen drawers. 'Read it,' he said shortly.

Emma, still holding George's invitation in her hand, followed his movements in bewildered silence. What was the matter with him? He was supposed to be cured, wasn't he?

He returned to the table with a large, used envelope, sat down heavily and carefully removed the staples holding the rest of the sheets together. Then he began systematically to tear the pages into tiny pieces, halving and quartering each one again and again until he had a growing pile of waste in front of him. Emma sat quite still watching him until he glanced up and waved his hand at the piece of paper still lying untouched in front of her. 'Read it,' he repeated. His voice sounded odd, harsh; his face was blank.

It was from a firm of Harrogate solicitors. It was pompous, rambling, and full of unnecessarily long words, but the gist of it was clear enough. Jay's mother was dead and he was invited to sign the enclosed documents, agreeing not to divulge any details of his family's private affairs, after which probate would be set in motion and his inheritance would be forthcoming. It was a straight-forward bribe, involving a quite staggering amount of money.

'Oh,' said Emma, trapped again.

Jay continued doggedly to demolish every single document he had in front of him; it was only when she got to the bottom line that Emma realised what he intended to do.

'No,' she said. 'I won't come with you.'

She startled him, he wasn't expecting such a categorical denial. 'You must,' he demanded. 'I can't do it on my own.'

'I know you can't. So you'll have to come to George's wedding instead, won't you?' Always one more hurdle to surmount, can't walk away yet.

Jay's attention was still hundreds of miles away, in Yorkshire. 'But I'm entitled,' he said stubbornly. 'Please, Em, you know I can't do it without you.' The mask slipped, exposing the pain beneath and he grimaced at her, begging.

Emma rose from the table and moved slowly to stand behind him, wrapping her arms around his neck. 'If you wish to go to Yorkshire,' she said, forgetting her own predicament and intent only upon calling his bluff, 'to stand up in the pulpit at her Memorial Service, then go ahead. I can't prevent you ...' she straightened up and moved so she could see his increasingly agitated face; he wasn't so good at shutting her out these days

'. . . but I won't come with you. I will not sit in church and watch you take your revenge on the dead. Do you understand?'

'Emma—'

'No,' she said, resigning herself to the inevitable. 'I'll write to George and tell him we're going, shall I?'

Jay lowered his head, ran his hands through the pile of waste-paper in front of him, letting the pieces trickle between his fingers, then gathered them all up and shovelled them into the envelope he had found, until there were no bits left on the table. Then he turned and caught hold of her, pulling her in close and burying his face in her shirt. How did you know, he puzzled, that I needed you to stop me?

'I love you, Em,' he mumbled, tightening his grip.

'I know.' Emma sighed and brought her hand up to stroke his hair. It was all slipping from her tenuous grasp again.

She phoned Ricky anyway, because she needed to remind herself that he was real.

'Not long now,' she said encouragingly. 'Just until after George's wedding.' She received in reply a snort of disbelief.

'I'm beginning to wonder whether you really intend to leave him at all,' said Ricky harshly.

'Of course I do. I've just told you—'

'What? *What* have you just told me, Em? That it won't be long? You told me that two months ago, nearly three. How long is long? If he's still so crippled he can't manage without you he should be in a home.'

'Don't,' she pleaded. 'Please don't. It's hard enough already, don't make it worse.'

'Why not? I want to make it impossible. I *love* you, Em.'

'I love you too.'

It was too dark in the attic to see properly. Enough, decided Emma, switching her attention back to the pile of rubbish she had sorted so far, I've done enough today. Tucking the album under her arm, she picked her way along the wide corridor she had cleared to the door and switched off the light. On her way out she scooped up a pile of yellowing newspapers, nationals and locals all mixed up together. They would be useful for lighting fires; the nights were still cold this time of year and with the Hermit away the smell of woodsmoke and the crackling heat would be comforting.

She fed the dogs, then made herself baked beans on toast, poured herself a glass of wine, and balanced plate and glass precariously on top of George's wedding album and the pile of newspapers. That didn't look like enough, so she added a box of Carr's Table Water Biscuits and a tube of Primula Cheese Spread with Chives, then carried her makeshift tray gingerly along the flagstoned passage to the small sitting-room overlooking the walled back garden.

She ate slightly less voraciously these days than she had when she was nineteen, yet she had put on some much needed weight over the years, 'plumped out nicely', as Auntie Mabel never tired of telling her. The thought reminded her – she must ring her tonight, see if she could get her up soon for a visit. The Hermit could collect her on his way back from London next time he went.

It was getting more difficult now Mabel's eyesight was too bad for her to drive. She still had her bedsits, nowadays a mix of students and professionals, and last year at the Hermit's insistence they had installed a stairlift to the second floor; she was finding two flights hard nowadays. But she had refused point-blank to move to Norfolk so they could keep an eye on her, despite all their pleading and encouragement. Her kids were sweet, she said, checked up on her every day, did her shopping, posted her letters, kept her company, 'whether I like it or not'. She would die in Earl's Court unless her mental agility deserted her. 'And, thank God, I can still run rings round most of them,' she insisted, snorting with laughter at her own high opinion of her intellectual faculties.

Emma put her tray down on the edge of the hearth, then set

about building her fire with some of the papers she had rescued from the attic, resisting the temptation to read them lest her supper get cold. Flotman appeared by her side, waving his feathery tail in greeting, then settled down, nose and front feet pointing towards the promised heat, and rumbled contentedly in the back of his throat. Newton followed to flop down beside him and rolled on to his side with a sigh. Flotman always bagged the best spot.

'You're both spoiled ...' Emma caressed them in turn, careful not to linger in case it looked like favouritism '... spoiled rotten.' They were as jealous as children. She smiled, recalling George's mother, Morag, holding forth about dogs on George's wedding day.

'No home,' she had said firmly in her soft Scottish accent, patting her elderly retriever as it waddled past, 'is complete without a dog. I simply cannot understand how anyone can exist without one.' Then she had patted Emma too, for all the world as if she also was a canine, and added kindly, 'Unless you live three floors up in a flat, of course. Then it wouldn't be fair to the dog.'

Shortly afterwards, George had opened his big mouth and put his great hoof in it, as usual.

'Do you want to stay the night, or would you rather drive straight back after the reception?'

Emma, curled up on the sofa with her toes tucked under a cushion, was trying to compose a reply to George's invitation. She was thinking, not about the wedding but about its aftermath, wondering, since the news of his mother's death seemed after all not to have disturbed Jay's fragile equilibrium too much, whether it would be a good idea to tell him as soon as they got back, get it over and done with.

'What time does the reception start?'

'Six.'

Jay raised his head from the drawing he was messing about with at the table and rose, making for the corner cupboard. 'Then we'll stay, Mrs Hammond.'

'What?'

'Do you want a brandy before we go to bed?'

'No, thanks. Why did you call me Mrs Hammond?' Emma glared at him. 'How many times do I have to tell you I won't—'

'I was merely pointing out that if we stay over, you'll have to perjure yourself again.' Jay changed direction and flopped down beside her on the sofa, fumbling beneath the cushion for her bare foot so he could run his fingers up and down her leg. 'You complained last time that you didn't like it.'

Emma subsided. Yorkshire was still too close to make light of it, and he was taking advantage. 'We could sleep in separate rooms,' she suggested defensively, trying to ease the guilt that had taken up permanent residence in her breast since the unexpected revival of Jay's sexual appetite.

He chuckled. 'We could indeed. How wonderfully virtuous that would make us feel. Or I could provide you with instant respectability.'

'Jay—'

'It's all right.' He leaned back and closed his eyes, sighing resignedly. 'I've no intention of straying into forbidden territory. I'm merely suggesting we could be better prepared than we were last time.' He turned his head, opened his eyes again. 'I want you to have it anyway.'

'Have what?'

'Nothing.'

'Right,' she said wearily. 'I'll ask Solly for the time off.'

Solly fired her.

It wasn't the first time. During the last two months she had been sacked three times, resigned twice. It was par for the course, Francis had assured her the first time Solly threw her out, a sign that he really liked her. Over the past fifteen years he had lost count of the number of times he had been told to remove his useless carcass from the premises; it was one of Solly's little games.

Never one to miss an opportunity, Solly tried first to inviegle her into working full-time in return for his largesse.

'No,' she said. 'I won't do five days a week. I have other commitments. It'd leave me no time to do anything else.' *Be* anywhere else.

'Blast you!' roared Solly. 'Cocky little Madam, I've said you can have your pesky day off. I've even given you a pay rise, so why not? You can start when you come back from ...' He waved a hand, dismissing Norfolk. 'And you don't need time for anything else. What could be more important than this?' He swung vigorously in his chair. 'Never bloody here when I want you!'

Emma focused as best she could on his wildly revolving figure. 'Yes, I am! And I've already said I'm prepared to change my days if you need me to.'

'I need you five days a week.' Solly scowled murderously. 'But if you don't want to work for a living, then I can always find someone who will.'

'Are you trying to blackmail me, Solly?'

'Course I bloody am!'

'Well, it won't work.'

'Bugger you, then!' pronounced Solly, and yelled for Francis.

Francis did not improve his mood. 'Gombrick's rang – the two bolts promised for tomorrow? They're going to be delayed. They've found a fault right the way through the production run and they've had to scrap the lot. Then they've got to set up the looms again and do a test run.'

He waited, gauging how much of Solly's limited patience was available, then continued. 'Either Cyril or Paul, neither of them are saying which, managed to cut all right-hand bodice fronts, then spent the afternoon wondering why the girls couldn't get them to fit together, so we're running behind with the special order.' He consulted his clipboard, winked surreptitiously at Emma, then added triumphantly, 'And that cloth you ordered, remember Solly, the very expensive Venetian? Well, the bolt arrived this morning.' He paused, impishly savouring the bad news, then pronounced with relish, 'Old Italian Socks. I warned you, Solly.'

'Old Italian Socks?' whispered Emma, and Francis dimpled at her.

'"Reconstituted fibres of dubious origin",' he quoted, 'and I told—'

Solly's wrath was awful to behold. He turned on Francis as if his misjudgement was entirely the little man's fault, and when he had finished with his chief executive he rounded on Emma, simply because she happened to be standing next to him.

'If you were here all the time things like this wouldn't happen. Trouble with you ruddy kids – think you can do just as you please. If you got off your bum and did a full week's work I might be able to run my business without a crisis at every turn!'

'But I was here all day today,' protested Emma indignantly. 'And anyway, I don't see what—'

Solly's colour, always high, increased to an alarming puce. 'Don't see?' he bellowed. 'Course you don't! Never here to see anything that goes on in this place! And when you do deign to turn up it's only to ask for time off! What the hell do you know about the Rag Trade anyway? You're fired, you hear? Fired!' and he strode away, apoplectic with rage.

'You can't fire me,' Emma yelled at his departing back, 'because I just quit!' She made a face at Francis. 'One of these days,' she said ruefully, 'he'll really mean it, and I won't believe him.'

Francis chuckled. 'My dear,' he told her, 'Solly has never fired anyone in his life, he's much too soft. He works on the principle that there is no point in keeping a dog and barking oneself, and leaves that sort of dirty work to me.' He helped her into her coat. 'Trouble is, I know I shouldn't, but I just can't resist winding him up every now and then. Can't forbear to say "I told you so" when one of his little enthusiasms goes wrong.' He patted her shoulder. 'Do me a favour, sweetie?'

'Anything.' Over the past couple of months Emma had grown increasingly fond of Francis. He was so patient, so understanding, and he reminded her of Bill.

'Give him one more day. That way he'll think he's won, you'll get another pay rise, and he'll get off my back ... Look at me, darling, browbeaten and bullied. I need a break ... Please?'

'Who do you think you're kidding, Francis?' Emma was amused. 'You have Solly wrapped round your little finger, as well as everyone else in this place. Without you to smooth his path, Solly would have disintegrated years ago. All right, you shall have your extra day. But I'm only doing it because it's you, and that's all I'll do. Four days is my absolute maximum. Is that okay?'

'Have a splendid time at your wedding.' Francis pecked her on the cheek, grinned, and watched her go on her way, her plait swinging heavily at her back. What a sweet child you are, he thought, and so wonderfully tractable. If I was into that sort of thing, I could get quite sentimental about you.

How had she managed to get herself talked into that one? Emma justified it to herself as she climbed the stairs to Jay's flat – it didn't matter. It wouldn't make any difference, she and Rick would work something out between them, and the extra money would come in useful. Maybe she could persuade him to move nearer London?

Jay was home, in his studio. She could hear de Falla, 'Nights in the Gardens of Spain', and she prowled around, frustrated, wanting to tell him she'd organised everything but knowing by experience not to disturb him when he was working.

She left it until there was a brief silence, then made him a cup of coffee. He was startled, hadn't noticed she was back, and dishevelled, as he always was when he was drawing; he had a habit of running his fingers through his hair to keep it out of his eyes, didn't even notice he was doing it, and his shirt was open at the neck, untidy. Looking at him, to her shame, she wanted him.

She talked nineteen to the dozen to distract herself, told him in minute tedious detail about every second of her day, saw the amusement in his eyes, wanted him again, then watched his attention wander to the drawing that was calling him and made a hasty exit. Then she hovered in the hall for ten minutes, mentally persuading Rick that it was unimportant, it was only sex, before making determinedly for the bathroom, to soak in hot water and calm herself down.

Jay's music started again, drifting across the hall, Albinoni, bitter-sweet organ music, almost unbearably sad, and she was hit by another pang of guilt. Why, she wondered, should such an apparently unsentimental man choose to play such heart-rending music? Was it the same contradiction that made him care so little for the human race *en masse*, yet apparently feel so passionately about her?

She lay back in the steaming water and thought about the future, about George's wedding and what lay beyond it. And her buoyant mood drained slowly away with the bath-water.

CHAPTER THIRTY-ONE
• • •

Jay produced a surprise just before they left: a ruby-red MG Magnette with four doors and a walnut dashboard – a present. It was big and solid and when he unlocked it to show her the inside it smelled nice, of warm, slightly musty old leather. It had semaphore indicators, small orange arms that flew out of the central door columns at the flick of a switch; the steering wheel was enormous, with chrome struts and a shiny dome in the middle; it had a push-button start and even an octagonal clock above the windscreen in the shape of the MG logo. It was a prize, Jay said, for passing her driving test.

'I can't,' insisted Emma, horrified by his generosity, racked by guilt. 'I can't possibly accept it.' Not least, she thought, as she leaned back against the worn beige hide of the driver's seat and ran her hands over the huge steering wheel, because it is quite the most fabulous present anyone has ever given me, apart of course from Ricky's brooch, and it would be dishonest to take it when I have no intention of giving you anything in return.

Jay didn't notice her vehemence, wasn't the slightest bit fazed by her determined rejection of his gift. 'Your name's in the logbook,' he said, offhand, 'so there's nothing you can do about it. And anyway, I've put the Jensen in for a service while we're away, so right now it's the only transport we've got.' Emma gave in, trapped again.

There was no syncromesh between first and second gear, it had to be double de-clutched and Jay had to stop twice on their way through London because it had a tendency to overheat, but once

348

out on the open road the big car settled down nicely. He made Emma drive from Thetford, all the way through Norwich and out along the Cromer Road towards the north Norfolk coast, teaching her as they went, and by the time they arrived at their destination she was white-faced, sweating with nerves, and in need of a drink.

The hotel was small, with only seven guest bedrooms tucked under the eaves, and they checked in just after one, in the middle of the lunchtime rush. Emma kept her gloves on when she signed the register, pleading the cold so she could share a room with Jay. Her conscience pricked her only slightly. After all, she had decided as she drove carefully through the tiny scattered villages of Norfolk, they had such a short time left together. Given what she was going to have to do to him sometime soon it seemed like a small enough gift to offer him, in return for all his tender loving care ...

Jay said nothing, but he managed to look inordinately pleased and she wished she'd stuck out for separate rooms. What if, she wondered guiltily as she followed him up the creaky stairs, she was only making it harder for him in the long run?

Lunch was soup, from a cast-iron stock-pot that simmered over an electric ring on the end of the nicotine-brown bar, full of chunks of beef and bits of carrot and so hot and meaty that Emma's pale cheeks flushed pink as she downed it. Jay laughed as usual at her voracious appetite.

'Shut up,' she complained. 'Can I have your bread if you don't want it?'

By the time they got to their next course, strong home-made paté, served with hot toast dripping with butter, the room was filling up with locals: county types with loud, braying voices and hearty laughs, who all seemed to know each other and who leaned against the bar in preference to using the mismatched tables and chairs. Jay and Emma sat in a dark corner next to the smoky log fire, screened from the bar and their landlord.

'Here,' said Jay casually once the noise and bustle were loud enough to drown any objections Emma might have, and dropped a small hinged wooden box in her lap.

He had had less than half a pint of bitter, but Emma was already on her second pint, calming herself down the easy way. She had managed to push all thoughts of the future to the back of her mind, and she was feeling warm, well fed, and inclined to be sleepy. She picked up the box and stared at it without much interest. 'What is it?'

'Open it and see.'

Inside was a small pile of silver resting on a bed of cotton wool. It took her a moment to work out that she was looking at a trio of rings and Jay caught her by surprise for the second time that day, temporarily vulnerable. She laid the linked circles on her palm and peered at them, trying to make out the detail, but she wasn't alarmed – it wasn't as if he had presented her with a diamond engagement ring – just mildly curious. The one she picked out was plain, except for a tiny hand, palm down, outstretched along the slender circle as if about to shake another.

'Look.' Jay reached out, impatient to show her, and plucked a second ring from her palm. Like the first it was plain except for a hand, facing upwards this time. It was only when he gathered up the third ring that she noticed the tiny silver heart at its rim and bit her lip, reminded of Ricky's brooch tucked away in the bottom of her bag and suddenly suspicious. Jay didn't notice, he was concentrating on his task, sliding the two rings he held together so the hand clasped the heart.

'Give me the other one,' he said, still not looking at her. Obediently, she held it out so he could slide it close against the other two and she saw. Two hands, cradling a heart between them.

'Oh,' she said blankly. 'How . . . clever.' What was he playing at?

'My father bought it.' His voice was flat, devoid of emotion, but when she looked at his face his mouth was twisted ironically, and he raised his head to smile crookedly at her. 'He gave it to my mother, years ago, when I was quite small. He found it in an antique shop, and it appealed to him; he thought it was romantic.' He took her hand and turned it palm up, then placed the three bands, now locked tightly together, in the hollow at its centre. 'It's called a Gimmal ring. This one's very old, sixteenth-century, I think.' He ran a long finger round it, tickling her skin. 'Mother didn't want it. She called him a cheapskate, told him if he wanted to impress her with his generosity he would have to do better than this, so he took it back and said he would keep it for me when I was grown up. He wasn't angry, just teased her, said, "You have no soul," and they both laughed.'

'Jay—'

Abruptly, he took hold of her fingers and folded them over, pressing so hard that Emma could feel the tiny hands digging into the inside of her knuckle. 'It was what she gave me when we went to see her,' he said. 'Do you suppose she's burning in Hell yet?'

Emma, who had been about to hand him back his treasure, to tell him he was wasting his time, froze, remembering what was happening in Yorkshire today. She had been so busy thinking about her own problems she hadn't taken Jay's into account at all.

'Originally they were given as a token of love and faith between partners.' He held her fingers closed and as he felt her stir he tightened his hold, but when Emma looked up his face was carefully impassive. 'I'm not asking you to accept anything,' he said, 'except my love. What you do with it is in your hands.' Then he released her and sat back, sipping his beer and watching the solid wall of humanity milling around the bar in front of them as if nothing had happened at all. After a while, as Emma sat staring at him helplessly with the Gimmal ring burning a hole in her hand, he put his beer down, peeled back her fingers one by one and removed it. Then he slid it carefully, almost stealthily, on to the third finger of her left hand, touched it lightly, smiled, said in a voice that wobbled only very slightly, 'Now you won't have to keep your hand in your pocket.' He picked up his beer again without looking at her; Emma let him get away with it, didn't even try to work out why, sat with a ton weight hanging from her finger and said nothing, did nothing, because she simply couldn't bring herself to fling it back at him. It was ten minutes before he dared to meet her eyes.

'I suppose you think you're very clever,' she said. She wanted to hit him, to get up and walk out, away, anywhere, as long as it was far from Jay and the trap he had laid for her. 'Damn and blast you,' she said instead. 'I need another drink.'

When he came back with a pint of bitter and a brandy she was sitting staring at her left hand. It was clenched tightly into a fist, and the ring was standing proud of the skin just below her white knuckle. So, she was mocking herself, what are you going to do now, Miss Clever Clogs?

'I've ordered you some pudding,' said Jay. 'Lemon meringue pie.'

'Did you ask for extra cream?'

'Of course.'

She took her beer without another word, and gulped down almost half the contents before her pudding arrived. Then she lowered her head and began doggedly to demolish her pie while Jay sipped at his brandy, deliberately not looking at her. When she had finished, she drained her mug, pushed her plate away and rose from the table. 'Time we changed,' she said calmly. If she pretended it hadn't happened, perhaps the problem would go away.

The wedding was at three, in George's local parish church two miles up the road, and they were back in their room by two o'clock. Emma, fuddled by the beer and shaken to the core by what she had allowed Jay to do, quickly became belligerent.

'You're in my way!' she complained as he stepped across her path to reach his bag. 'No, don't put it there! Why do you have to spread yourself around so?'

He hesitated, his bag swinging in his hand. 'Go on then, say it,' he challenged. 'Get it off your chest.'

'Say what? Get what off my chest?' She pulled her woollen jumper over her head, emerging flushed and dishevelled in her underwear to find him watching her as he unbuttoned his shirt. 'And what are you staring at?'

'Nothing. Nothing at all, honest.' Jay raised his hands, mock-pleading not guilty, and she softened, helplessly, irritatingly, disarmed by beer and a familiar, irresistible stirring of warmth. What was the *matter* with her? Why was she so weak-willed, so pathetic? Jay returned to his buttons, fumbling slightly as he went and trying not to let his jubilation show.

'Here,' said Emma, involving herself in practicalities. 'Let me do it. We'll be all day if you don't get a move on.' She closed the narrow gap between them and took hold of his shirt, discovered once she'd started that she was even clumsier than Jay, then forgot about his buttons as his fingers found that spot at the back of her neck and slid down to unfasten the band around her plait. He said nothing at all, just began to unravel the braid, standing very still and close with his arms encircling her shoulders. Emma sighed and dropped her head to his bare chest.

'We'll be late.' It's just the beer talking, nothing more.

'Mmm . . .'

'Jay, we'll be—' Too much booze, it weakens my resistance.

'Mmm . . .'

'Jay . . . Oh, I . . .' And anyway I want to.

'Emma . . .'

'What?' It's not important, after all, the sex.

'Would you please undo my . . . ? Mmm . . .'

They missed the wedding. While George and Jilly were promising to love, honour and in Jilly's case, obey, Emma was sleeping the sleep of the confused, her cheek tucked into Jay's right shoulder and her mouth slightly open. Jay was trying to ignore the pins and needles running up and down his arm, flexing his fingers surreptitiously in an effort to keep the blood circulating. In his left hand he was holding Emma's, their arms folded up against the cushion of her breasts as if about to begin an arm-wrestling contest. He could feel the Gimmal ring against the soft pad of skin at the top of his palm, and despite his discomfort he was grinning broadly.

By the time the congregation gathered outside the church in the pale autumn sunshine for the official photographs, they were both fast asleep, still holding hands.

'Tea.' He put the tray he was carrying down on the dressing-table by the window. 'And fairy cakes.' Then he snapped the bedside light on and leaned over her, taking her wrists in his hands and raising her arms over her head to kiss her lightly on the mouth. 'It's a quarter to seven and we're late.' He was supremely unconcerned, freshly shaven and fully dressed, in his best dark grey suit, a white shirt and a knitted silk tie in deep blue. Emma hauled herself up sleepily in bed and watched him pour the tea. She ought to panic, but just now she couldn't be bothered. She would panic after she'd had her tea and fairy cakes ... panic about what, being late, or being here at all?

She left the saucer behind, holding the cup in both hands and it was only as the silver absorbed the heat to warm her finger that she remembered the Gimmal ring. She ignored it, merely shifting her left hand so it wouldn't burn. She would have to deal with its implications sooner or later, but not now. She could put it off until tomorrow.

Jay moved around the room, sipping tea with one hand, laying out her party clothes on the end of the bed with the other. She felt a surge of sentimental affection, smiled, then, irritated by his calm self-satisfaction and her own weak inability to resist him, demanded crossly, 'Where's my fairy cake, then?'

Jay drove slowly, putting off their arrival. The sky was clear, an almost full moon rising to light the unfamiliar patchwork of fields and woods. It was bitterly cold for late October and the road was beginning to freeze, making it slippery under the Magnette's big tyres. He aimed back the way they had come, over a humpbacked bridge towards the small market town through which they had passed earlier in the day, then branched off down a narrow country lane overhung with thinning autumn trees, starkly silhouetted against the night sky. A mile further on the wall began, crumbling red brick, eight feet high, braced at intervals with heavy wedge-shaped buttresses, then tall wrought-iron gates, wide open against the grass verges with a gravelled drive running through them, curling round to the left of a low clipped box hedge. Beyond the hedge and slightly to their right they could see the dim outline of a formal garden, borders and shrubs backed by taller trees, and as they neared the house the drive opened out into a wide turning circle, littered with cars parked at random before the floodlit façade. Jay brought the car to a halt and they stared.

It was very old: soft, mellow red-brick walls beneath steeply sloping pantiles. The house ends rose against the roof in elegantly curved Dutch gables and the chimneys twisted like sticks of barley sugar against the sky. Its face was criss-crossed with the thick grey branches of an ancient wisteria, which stretched across the brick as if its giant fingers held the fabric together. The sash windows were tall and multi-paned, only the left-hand ones on the ground floor showing light, and the whole had such an air of benign permanence about it that Emma smiled involuntarily at the sight of it. She was still sleepy, dreamy, and she wasn't thinking about Rick. Tomorrow, when this was all over, she had decided as they drove away from the hotel, then she would think about Rick, but not tonight. They followed the drive past the gable end, through more golden light spilling out from the same downstairs room, then on between a long wall on their right and a wide expanse of grass on their left, colourless in the moonlight and dotted with trees, their shadows stretching black across the ground.

'Oh ...' Emma was drowsily entranced. 'Why didn't George ever tell us how beautiful this place is?'

'Perhaps he's never noticed.' Jay moved on again, crawling in first gear round the corner and past the back of the house, just visible over the top of its walled garden, a confusion of crow's-foot gables, steep pitched gullies, and tiny dormer windows high up under the eaves. To their left the grass ran away into shadow beneath more trees before dipping down to a glimmer of water. As they followed the curve of the track the stream meandered nearer along a steep-sided channel, then swung away past the wide space ahead of them where more cars were parked in untidy rows outside a thatched, flint-faced barn. Even from inside the car they could hear the thump-thump-thump of loud music. Jay turned the car on to the verge and switched off the engine then sat gazing, not at the yellow light flooding out on to the gravel from the big double doors of the barn, but at the entrance to the walled garden, barred by an iron gate. This is it, he thought. This is where I want us to be. 'Em,' he began. 'What would you say to living somewhere like this?'

Emma just stared at him as if she hadn't heard, then climbed out of the car. Don't ask questions like that, she was thinking. Don't tempt me.

'Dress up,' Jilly had said, and Emma had taken her at her word. She was wearing a long-sleeved velvet dress, midnight blue with a scooped neckline and a wide hood lined in vivid fuschia silk draped across her shoulders. The pink clashed violently with her hair, twisted into a plaited red chignon high on her head, leaving a few tendrils deliberately to escape and curl about her face. The dress came down almost to her ankles, fitted from neck to hip then flaring out from the knee, but the vampish image was dispelled by the round toes and demurely buttoned straps of a pair of shocking pink Annello and Davide dance shoes.

The barn was stacked with straw, arranged in steps to form a bucolic amphitheatre, and floodlit from above, the pools of soft-coloured light picking out the Bacchanalian crowds lounging on the steep tiers, drinking, laughing, gesticulating and watching the revellers down on the floor dancing. Ali wouldn't have liked it; there was a big red sign on the door, saying, NO SMOKING.

'Where the hell did you get to?' George bellowed over the

music. 'We were expecting you at the church.'

'Sorry.' Jay dragged his eyes reluctantly away from the cold night outside. 'Car broke down.' He smoothed Emma's hood, rearranging it across her shoulders, then placed his hand on her neck and moved his fingers proprietorially against her cold skin. 'How was it?'

'Bloody freezing!' George grinned. 'Serves Jilly right. She was convinced it'd still be warm this time of year, and here we are in the middle of the second ice age. At least I managed to get a vest under my monkey suit.' He was wearing grey tails and striped trousers, even a cravat, looking plump, self-important and ineffably pleased with himself. Emma felt Jay's fingers move against her skin again and grimaced at him as they followed George across the floor.

'Stop it!' she complained desultorily. 'Behave!' He grinned, but he didn't take his hand from the back of her neck.

They were all there, twenty, thirty familiar faces to be greeted, people Emma hadn't seen since her last abortive forays to college after Alison's death, even Adrian with his latest girlfriend.

'Val,' he shouted over the noise, 'this is Em, the one I told you about.' He hesitated, frowned, clearly still not over her. 'And Jay.' Who stole her from me, the bastard.

Jay met Adrian's eyes, decided benevolently that he would let him live after all, then spotted Bill and moved on, genuinely pleased to see him. Emma, still sleepy, smiling and nodding over the noise, was taken aback when pretty, dark-haired Val stared at her coldly and mouthed, 'I've heard all about you.' She followed Jay, looking for reassurance.

'Em!' Bill held out his arms to embrace her. 'How's my favourite girl?'

'All the better for seeing you. Is Mabel here?'

Bill nodded, then linked his arm through hers and guided her further into the throng. 'Somewhere up there last time I saw her, holding forth.' He waved a hand at the platforms of straw rising towards the ancient roof trusses, then turned back to yell, 'Jay, I'm stealing your bird, okay?'

'Be my guest.' Jay's head was turned towards the door, away from the noise and heat. He looked mildly distracted, almost content.

'What on earth have you done to the man?' asked Bill. 'That's not the brooding Heathcliffe I know so well.'

'He's getting too smug and self-satisfied by half,' said Emma, waking up a little, and becoming annoyed at the inference implicit in Bill's words. Now that she thought about it, Jay seemed to have recovered awfully quickly from the giving of his gift, and it'd been downright sneaky, the way he had manipulated her into accepting it, the ease with which he had managed to seduce her afterwards. 'He's not the only man in the world, despite what he may think. I shall have to cut him down to size soon.'

Bill teased her. 'Oh, yes? And how do you propose to do that, given that you look almost as smug and self-satisfied as he does?' Emma was astonished, indignant, woke up a little more.

'No, I don't!'

'Oh, yes you do. Let's find Auntie Mabel.'

Jay watched them go, smiling indulgently, then turned and disappeared into the night.

It was a fabulous evening, at least until the end. Threading her way through the crowds with Bill, Emma began to relax for the first time in days, weeks. As she greeted old friends, exchanged news and gossip, she relegated both men, Rick and Jay, to the back of her mind and the relief was wonderful, rendered her light-headedly inebriated even before she started on the champagne.

She eyed Bill surreptitiously as they moved through the crowds, sizing him up. You look the same, she thought, taking in his rosy cheeks, the air of innocent boyishness he still retained, but you sound different, more camp, slightly effete. And you don't seem to have that 'oomph' you used to have. I wonder where it's gone, and why?

How thin you are, Bill was thinking, and you don't look smug at all, you look strained, as if you're under pressure. We must do something about that ... He tipped his head on one side, smiled at her, then squeezed her arm and nodded sagely. 'A drink,' he said. 'That's what you need, dear girl, a large glass of champagne.'

Emma finished her beans on toast and reached for the biscuits, then sipped her wine and munched as she turned the pages of the wedding album, smiling at the pictures. George and Jilly outside the church with their respective families; George and Jilly alone, Jilly, looking spectacularly beautiful, George looking pompous; George and Jilly with the rest of the guests, everyone but the bride and groom dated by their outfits, by the hats, the shoes, the suits, the trousers. Even Auntie Mabel had managed to get into a couple of shots, all in black like a dowager duchess in mourning, with Bill standing next to her beaming like a pony-tailed pixie in a shiny grey suit with a stand-up collar.

She sighed, remembering the peculiar suspension of reality she had allowed herself that night, the peaceful limbo in which she had briefly existed, blissfully free of doubt, confusion, guilt. She had even, for quite long periods of time, forgotten the problem of the ring she wore on her finger, persuaded herself that she could deal with it another day. Until the end of course, when George had put his great hoof in it and brought everything crashing down about her ears.

She rose to put another log on the fire, rubbing furry stomachs as she passed, and Flotman stretched his paws, sighing contentedly in the heat. What uncomplicated lives our dogs lead, she thought, giving them both one last caress. And how wonderfully uncomplicated it all seemed that night, until George opened his big mouth and brought me face to face with what I still had to do.

It was so lovely to see all her old friends. Alison's shadow no longer blighted the proceedings; time and distance had done their work, there was so much news to exchange, so many friendships to rekindle, that she faded into insignificance, almost into oblivion. Emma was transported back to the early days, before real life intruded, to pure, unadulterated *fun*, just as it had been at the beginning ...

They did their duty, admired Jilly and her dress, made appropriate noises about the presents, then went to sit with Auntie Mabel, magnificently got up for the evening in maroon lurex, ruched, swagged, twenty years out of date, and holding court before an admiring audience of current and ex-tenants, with the dregs of a large dry sherry in her hand. She despatched Bill to replenish her glass with a lofty gesture of dismissal.

'I've spent the last seven hours in your company, William, and I want to talk to Emma,' she said, folding her arms across her twinkling bosom and leaning back to observe her niece. 'So, where's your man, dear? Lost him already, have you?'

'No, he's here somewhere.' Emma peered into the well of the barn, running her eyes across the floodlit mass of people, but she couldn't see Jay. It was, she realised with an insight born of wine, a relief, now she came to think about it.

Mabel wrinkled her nose and adjusted the lurex over her bosom. 'Well,' she said comfortably, peering closely at her niece, 'you look quite perky, anyway. Must be looking after you, your oddball.'

'My what?' Emma straightened up to examine Mabel's flushed cheeks, the air of abandoned disorder she was exuding. Mabel chortled. 'Oddball. Your man, what's-his-name.' She waited, then when no reply was forthcoming, asked archly, 'What's the matter, dear? Cat got your tongue?'

'Auntie Mabel, you're tipsy!' accused Emma, shocked into attention.

Mabel beamed. 'Completely squiffy if you really want to know. Now, you were telling me about your man ...'

'Nothing to tell. He's here somewhere. I haven't seen him since we arrived. Where are you staying, Auntie Mabel? Surely you're not driving back tonight—'

'Don't be ridiculous, dear, of course not. I'm staying here.' Mabel leaned forward, squinting interestedly at her vacant niece.

'Such lovely people, Doug and Morag, said they wouldn't hear of me putting up in a hotel, not after I'd put up with George these past two years. True Scottish hospitality.' She sighed lustily, then added, shaking her head, 'Last time we'll all be together, you know. Poor Adrian's already gone, and Bill's moving out after Christmas.'

'What? He didn't tell me. Why didn't he tell me?' Emma was mildly hurt, even though this was the first time she had seen Bill since the inquest and she had spoken to him less than a dozen times on the phone over the past eight, nine months. He might have told her.

Mabel waited for her moment. 'Pretty ring, dear. Present, was it?' No reaction at all. 'Must be serious then.' Nothing. Emma was staring vaguely into space, switched off, no longer listening.

'So how's your love-life, Bill?'

'A mess if you really want to know.'

'Is that why you've lost your bounce?'

'Have I?' Bill leaned across and picked a straw out of Emma's hair, then sighed heavily. 'I can't get it right, Em. All the time I was at school I was confused. And then that first year at college, I kidded myself I'd got it sorted out. Except that when I stopped it was such a relief . . .'

'Stopped what?'

'Stopped bedding women.' Bill giggled, took another gulp at his wine. 'Remember when Griggsy told me to pull my socks up? I gave up women. And then I found, well, I got into this crowd and it just sort of . . . and . . .' He sighed, rolled over on to his stomach and began to pick at the bale beneath his fingers.

'It's all right, Bill.' Emma knew about queers now; it wasn't embarrassing any more 'You don't need to feel awkward about it—'

'Oh, I don't. It's not that; I came to terms with what I am ages ago. It's just that sometimes it makes me feel so . . . grubby. They're all so *promiscuous*. And it wasn't till a couple of months ago that I realised ...' He chuckled, hauled himself up to sit, his shiny suit dusted with straw and chaff. 'You'd love them, Em. I met Tel through college. He's a Display Manager for one of the big West End department stores. There're lots of fags in window-dressing; it seems to attract people like us. Anyway, he came to lecture about what he does, dressing windows, in-store displays and stuff, and we got talking. He took me home with him ...' Emma shifted uneasily. Being relaxed about queers was one thing, a blow by blow account of a male seduction was quite another. 'No, no, nothing like that. He took me home to meet his other half, Gordon.' Bill giggled. 'D'you know, it was the first time I'd come across a male couple who ... well, who really *belonged* together, if you see what I mean, like George and Jilly, or you and Jay.' Emma opened her mouth to protest at being bracketed with Jay, then shut it again. 'Tel's a drag queen in his spare time and he makes all his own frocks. We sat drinking port 'n' lemon, with Tel sewing sequins on one of his costumes and Gordon watching the telly with the sound turned up loud because he's a bit deaf, and they gossiped about their day, just like my mum and dad do every evening. They've been together for fifteen years, and oddly enough they're thinking of moving up to Norwich, apparently they're more tolerant of people like us up here. They were just like an ordinary married couple, only both men.' He sighed again, reaching across to tickle Emma's cheek with a wisp of hay. 'Trouble is, Em, I'm just a soppy old romantic. I want someone to come along and sweep me off my feet, you know, the complete works, hearts and flowers, violins playing in the background. All the slushy stuff. Only it seems to be rarer than snow in summer. D'you know what I mean?'

Emma, staring vaguely down at the groups mingling below them, was reminded suddenly, vividly, of Ricky, waiting for her somewhere out there in the dark, and that feeling, that moment of recognition, swept over her again, the instant revelation that he was the one person she had been waiting for all her life. 'Yes,' she said with feeling. 'Yes, I know what you mean.' She changed the subject hurriedly. 'Why are you moving?'

'I've found a flat by myself. I need more space than I've got, Em, and it's time I had a bit more privacy. Anyway,' another sigh, 'it's not the same without you and Ali upstairs, not like the old days. Did Mabel tell you, George and Jilly are having the whole of the basement from the beginning of next term? Adrian's gone—'

'Mabel said. Why did he go?'

'Because of you, I think. You rather broke his heart I'm afraid, dear girl.'

'Oh! But I thought—'

'Well, you thought wrong. He's far too polite to show it, but he was terribly cut up about you running off with Jay. Anyway, where was I?'

'George and Jilly.'

'Ah. Jilly's working now, at Coleman, Prentice and Varley, as a paste-up artist. She got a two:two this summer and she's earning quite good money, so between them they can afford the rent, and Mabel's knocked a bit off because they've offered to decorate. Mind you,' he giggled fruitily, 'Jilly's made it perfectly clear that she's only working until such time as George is in a position to keep her—'

'In the manner to which she intends to become accustomed.'

'And that the first minute he starts earning, she stops.'

Emma giggled, relaxed again. 'Presumably to allow herself more time to spend the stuff.'

'Got it in one, darling. Come on, more wine!'

It was over an hour before Jay was caught.

He had explored the whole of the first floor by then, standing silently in doorways, gazing down at the moonlit garden from bedroom windows, running his hands across the pale oak doors with their worn brass knobs, down the intricately carved newel posts at the top of the wide staircase, and he had prowled around most of the ground floor too. He had peered into the study, stood before the wide fireplace in the small sitting-room, spreading his hands against the bressumer and lowering his head to breathe in the distinctive smell of ash and tar. He had wandered the length of the dining-room, with its deep windows looking out over the floodlit gardens at the front of the house, and glanced into the cosy workroom. He had avoided only the room across the hall from the dining-room, judging from the line of light beneath the door and the murmur of voices that some of the immediate family were gathered there, escaping from the noise in the barn. Even in the house the base beat was audible, a faint regular thud, occasionally interrupted, that echoed through the brickwork and vibrated under the soles of his shoes.

He had entered via the walled garden, his feet crunching on the frozen grass; past the vegetable garden on his right, late cabbages and early Brussels sprouts surreal in the grey light; shrubs and trees on his left, ghostly white with hoar frost. He had found an unlocked door and a flagstoned passageway, and carried on from there, with no plan and no plausible excuse for if, when, he was caught. By the time he reached the heavily beamed kitchen, warmed by an old-fashioned Aga and lit, like the rest of the house, by nothing but the full moon outside, he was getting cocky. He could slip out the way he had come and no one would be any the wiser.

'And who might you be, young man?' Morag Campbell watched the tall boy by the window jump guiltily and suppressed a smile, then waited in the shadows by the door, arms folded, for a reply.

'Jay. Jay Hammond.' Jay hunched his shoulders, oddly tongue-tied, and continued to stare out at the grey grass and the frost-spangled trees on the lawn, catching the glimmer of water through the bare trunks of the small spinney beyond.

'And have you come to steal the family silver, Jay Hammond?'

He could hear the amusement in her soft Scottish voice. Would she have been so sanguine if she had caught him in one of the bedrooms? he wondered.

'No!' He shook his head vigorously, and she advanced into the room, her low-heeled shoes making little noise on the stone floor.

'Greengages,' she said, appearing beside him, 'on the left nearest the end of the barn, then there's a yellow plum and a Russet. Those others are Coxes, and there's a Bramley behind . . .' she pointed '. . . away over there. They're all that's left of the old orchard.' She waited, recognising the signs, the dreamy look in the lad's eyes . . . No, not a lad, now she could see his face, a man. Older than the bairns in the barn, and wary, bristling with metaphorical barbed wire.

'I didn't touch anything. I didn't even turn any lights on. I haven't done any damage . . .'

'Morag. I'm George's mother.' She held out a cool, dry hand, and Jay took it, still completely at a loss. 'No, I'm sure you've not. Jay . . . You're the one with the talent, aren't you? And young Emma.' The man smiled at last, the girl's name triggering an automatic response. How much nicer your face is when you smile, thought Morag.

'Yes. I'm the one with the talent . . . and Emma. And I've been trespassing. But I couldn't stand the noise, and I—' He stopped, lowered his head, incapable of apologising but, rarely for him, embarrassed by his inability. 'I just wanted to see . . . to listen to the place breathe . . .'

'Ah.' Morag nodded and moved away, leaving him to recover as she bent to fumble in a darkened cupboard for dishes. 'It's got to you, has it?'

'Got to me?'

'This house. We've been here nearly twenty-five years, Doug and I, and all our children were born here, our Norfolk dumplings. It got to us, too, the first time we saw it.' She lifted a latch, disappeared briefly into what Jay guessed was a big pantry, still not using the lights, then emerged with a handful of rustling packets from which she dispensed peanuts and crisps, twiglets and tiny biscuits. 'As a punishment for your intrusion you can make yourself useful.' She held out a pair of dishes. 'A fee, for the unconducted tour.'

Jay took them dutifully, smiled again. 'Thank you,' he said.

'For what, my dear?'

'For not minding.'

'You're not the first.' Morag laughed. 'Now come away, you've not seen the best yet.'

'Would you ever sell?'

'Are you always this blunt, young man?'

'No – Yes. Sometimes. I want . . .'

'Ah. That bad, is it?' Morag paused in the kitchen doorway, her handsome face serene in the moonlight. 'I think I should warn you, Doug and I will be carried out of this house in our boxes, and not before. There are other houses . . .'

'Not like this.' Why do I fall so hard, he wondered, like wanting Emma so badly I can hardly bear it. And now a house. Am I mad? Am I obsessed?

'I have to tell you also, young man, that you are not the first in the queue.' Morag led him along the passageway and across the wide hall to the sitting-room door. 'There's another lad saving his pennies to make us an offer we can't refuse.' She stopped, waiting for him to draw level with her. 'He plans to bring his wife here, when he finds her.'

'When he finds her?'

'Mmm. He was here at the end of last year. He had temporarily misplaced her he told me, but I have no doubt he will find her, if he hasn't already. He seems a very determined young man.' She felt no temptation to laugh at Jay's palpable dismay. 'And when he does, he is going to bring her here, or so he informed me.'

And which would I choose, she wondered, if I had to entrust the old place to one of these intense young men? Would I give it to that serious fair-haired boy, with his black eyes and his plans, his complete determination that everything he wants will be his . . . or would I let this tortured soul, with his brooding face and his hunched shoulders, who doubts himself and everything around him, have it? And which of them will be prepared to wait for twenty, thirty years, until Doug and I are carried from this house on our last journey?

She didn't reveal the identity of Ricky Brown's wife-to-be, but then she didn't mention Ricky Brown by name either. Morag Campbell had heard all the gossip from George but she was rather more tactful than her eldest child.

She stood back to let Jay past, paused behind him while he was carefully vetted by Bess, the elderly family retriever, then waited for his reaction.

He stopped dead in front of her, leaning against the doorjamb so he could take it all in. When he turned his head he was smiling. 'Would you put me on the waiting list?' he said. 'Please?'

Emma leaned back in her armchair and closed her eyes, spreading her hands on the age-spotted album as the memories rushed back. With hindsight she should have paid more attention that first time, taken in more of the detail. But by the time she realised she was going to be living here, it was all settled, the decisions long since made, her life's path plotted, and in the end she'd had almost nothing to do with it. Rick and Jay had decided the whole thing for her, and George had forced her hand without even knowing he did it.

She shook herself, then rose and carried the album across to the heavy oak chest in the corner, so she would know where it was when they came on Sunday. Jilly would want it, even if George didn't. Then she tidied up the remains of her supper, called the dogs and preceded them down the passage to the kitchen for a last run before bed.

She snapped on the outside switch, flooding the orchard with light, then opened the door and followed their noisily erratic progress across the grass towards the spinney. The dew was already heavy underfoot, she could feel it soaking through her sneakers and creeping up the hem of her jeans. Where was he now? she wondered. Had he found someone else after she had been forced to choose between them, another place, another person to fall in love with? From the moment she had left him for the last time, she had heard nothing, not a word, not a sign. For all she knew, he might be dead.

She walked on, out of the light and through the gate into the darkness of the spinney, listening to the trees rustling above her head, the dogs snuffling and grunting in the undergrowth. Might have been, might have been. Would she change anything, if she had it to do again?

'Newton! Flotman! Come on, boys, time for bed.' Slowly, she retraced her steps, enjoying the night-time sounds: the owl hooting from the barn, the frogs croaking at each other down by the stream, as she followed the dark tracks she had made across the grass. The dogs raced on ahead towards the welcoming warmth of the kitchen, aiming for prime position in front of the Aga. She wondered why Newton made the effort – Flotman would win, he always did. To the victor the spoils, and Flotman was the stronger.

Would she, with the wisdom of twenty-five years' hindsight, have done differently? 'No,' she said out loud to the soft night air. 'I'd do the same again, do it with even more certainty, no doubts at all.'

As she did the last rounds, checking doors and windows before making her way slowly up the stairs to bed, she sighed. It would be comforting though, to know that he was all right.

It was getting late and the partygoers were thinning out: Mabel had retired to bed; Jilly had disappeared to change out of her dusty wedding dress, and George was at a loose end, waiting to carry her off to a carefully chosen hotel in Cromer for their first night of legal passion. 'Come and meet the folks,' he said, and Bill and Emma followed him obediently out of the barn into the cold and across the drive to the iron gate, the walled garden, and the house beyond.

Emma was entranced. The inside of George's family home was as beautiful as the outside, and she lagged behind, taking it all in. By the time she reached the open door of the big sitting-room Bill and George were already mingling. The space was full, both families, Jilly's and George's, aunts, uncles, cousins, both sets of parents. She stood for a moment just watching, taking in the long, heavily beamed room with its deep window bays, its slightly ramshackle air of comfort, faded chintz sofas, mellow oak furniture, soft lighting and the smell of applewood drifting from the smouldering logs that sat in the wide hearth, dribbling grey ash on to the bricks. Oh, she thought dreamily, I could be so happy in a place like this.

Jay was already there, propping up the wall, talking to George's mother. She couldn't remember ever seeing him look so peaceful. It was almost as if, the idea came unbidden to her mind, he had found his home at last.

As she made her way across the room towards him, he saw her and smiled. She said hello to Morag, who made easy conversation, petting the ancient retriever leaning cosily against Jay's leg, and talking dogs. And then George, dear, self-important, tactless George, sauntered across, kissed his mother on the cheek and remarked loudly, so that Jay heard every word, 'Oh, by the way, Em, I've been meaning to tell you all evening . . .'

Twenty-five years later, as she turned the light out and burrowed down beneath the covers to sleep, missing the Hermit to warm her chilly feet, Emma went cold all over again at George's capacity for inadvertent cruelty.

He talked about Ricky, about his recent visit to Earl's Court, explained how Rick had demanded Emma's new address, how diplomatic he had been on her behalf. 'Of course, I didn't tell him where you were, although he was pretty insistent. Didn't think Jay'd thank me if the blighter turned up on your doorstep looking for you.' He laughed, didn't notice Emma's rapidly paling complexion, or Jay's sudden attention, the way he stiffened, and pushed himself away from the wall as he registered her reaction. Morag noticed though.

'George, dear,' she said hurriedly. 'Time you found your new wife and got on your way, don't you think?' Sometimes she despaired of her much-loved son. 'If you don't get your skates on you'll find the doors barred against you, and you'll not want to spend the first night of your honeymoon in your car, now will you?'

George hovered, waiting for Emma to tell him he had done the right thing, for Jay to laugh at his little joke. 'Surprised he didn't buttonhole Mabel, though,' he added, oblivious. 'He was pretty annoyed by the time I'd finished with him, so you'd better be warned—'

'Go on, then.' Morag gave him a vigorous push, making sure he was on his way, then tucked her hand firmly under Jay's elbow and turned him to face the prettily framed painting on the wall behind them. Risky, she thought, glancing over her shoulder to make sure George was safely on his way, picking that particular piece of work, but needs must... 'You're the expert on these things, so George tells me.' She had caught his attention, good. 'Now tell me what you think of this.'

She talked easily about the style, the detail, avoided all reference to the artist, but she lost him quickly, saw his gaze wander back to Emma, pale and silent, behind them. 'It was so nice to meet you,' she said at last, admitting defeat. 'Perhaps you'll come again to see the old place.' She glanced from Jay's distracted face to Emma's, feeling the tension. 'You too, my dear,' she added, including Emma in her warm smile. But, she wondered as the child smiled politely back with everything but her panic-stricken hazel eyes, if you do come back, my pretty one, who will you be with? Poor things; there could only be one winner in the end.

They drove back to the hotel slowly, because the road was icy. As he took possession of their key at the reception desk Jay said quietly to the night-porter, 'We're not staying, after all, if you could make out the bill while we pack?' then made for the stairs and their bedroom without another word.

'Jay . . .' began Emma, following him at a run, but he shook his head at her and quickened his pace.

'Let's get home,' he said. 'Please, Em, I need to think before we talk.'

*

He asked only two questions during that long, slippery drive, the first as they passed through a village called Stratton Strawless, north of Norwich. 'Have you seen him?'

'Yes.'

The second question came the other side of Newmarket, as they drove along the straight stretch of road east of Babraham, and it was merely an extension of the first. 'Was that why you left me?'

'Yes.'

They spent the rest of the journey in silence, a hundred miles apart. Jay, who for so long had had other things on his mind, who had foolishly dared to think he might be winning his long struggle, was putting two and two together: going back over their trip to Yorkshire, to the week before, the frosty silences, Emma's sudden, inexplicable refusal to make love, the peremptory announcement that she was leaving, incidents which he had ignored at the time but which should have built up a picture, given him a clue. How could he possibly have been so unobservant?

The part of herself Emma had always kept from him had grown without his knowledge, been snatched from under his nose by a rival he had underestimated at every turn. And now he was going to have to pay for his stupidity.

CHAPTER THIRTY-TWO

• • •

It was after one when they turned into the car-park behind the flats. Jay leaped from the Magnette as if the devil was after him, collected the bags from the boot and set off for the lobby without looking back. Emma followed, her heart thudding in her chest with apprehension, telling herself over and over that she had done nothing to be ashamed of, that she had nothing to reproach herself for.

Maybe it was better like this. After all, she would have had to tell him sooner or later; he would have had to confront reality eventually, wouldn't he? She listened to his feet thudding on the stairs half a flight ahead of her, remembered his face as George chuntered on and realisation began to dawn. No, not like this, she thought, cursing George's big mouth, he shouldn't have had to confront it like this.

When she arrived, panting, on the landing, he was already inside, and the bags were lying where he had dropped them in the hall. He was in the sitting-room, his hands in his pockets and his shoulders hunched, standing at the window staring out into the dark.

'Tell me,' he said.

'Tell you what?'

A long pause. 'Tell me why you came back to me.'

'Because you needed me.'

'No other reason?'

Another long pause. 'Because I owed you.'

'I see. And how long did you intend to stay?'

'For as long as it took . . .'

'As long as it took for me to recover, or as long as it took to discharge your debt?'

'Neither.' Emma walked across the room to stand beside him. 'For as long as you needed me to stay.'

He lowered his head, stared down at her impassively. 'But I need you to stay for ever,' he said.

'No.' She met his gaze squarely. 'I told you from the beginning how it was. You knew what I would do if I was given the choice. You have a choice now. If you ask me to stay, if you still need me, then I'll stay.' She raised her chin, defying him. 'But I won't promise you anything. I never have. And when you're better, I'll go. I've never lied to you—' He turned his face away, accusing her, and she laid her hand on his sleeve and tugged, demanding his attention. 'I didn't tell you only because – how could I tell you? You turned up on my doorstep looking like something out of a horror film. I did the only thing I could do under the circumstances. You would have done the same for me.'

'All right.' He turned his head back, stared down at her with inscrutable blue eyes, and abruptly ended the conversation. 'It's time for bed. Last time, little Em.' How typical of Jay, that he should put up no fight at all.

He made love to her, for the last time. Emma resisted him; it seemed wrong somehow in a way it hadn't before, but he made her anyway. 'I'm entitled,' he said when she protested, and she gave in, let him, because if she was being honest, she wanted him to. Afterwards, as she lay in his arms, she thought he ought to know.

'I didn't . . .' she said. 'I swear. I mean I haven't . . .'

'I know you haven't.' Jay tightened his hold, so they were touching, skin to skin, all the way down. 'Don't you think I would have guessed?' Or would I? I missed all the other clues. I was so busy wading through my own private nightmare I didn't notice anything. Even when you left, I didn't wonder why, just stumbled after you to bring you home because I needed you. *If you knew what*

I've had to give up for you, you flung at me across a hotel bedroom when I dared to tease you about marrying me, and still I was too dumb to notice. 'Go to sleep,' he said. 'You have a lot to do in the morning.'

'What will you do?' she asked. 'After I've gone?'

'I'll make myself a cup of coffee and finish the job I'm working on, which is overdue. Then I shall go for a walk, and have lunch at the pub. I shan't bother to cook.'

'No, what will you do afterwards, about being . . . ?'

She felt him turn his head away, the warmth of his cheek removed from her hair. 'On my own? The same as I did before, I expect. There are plenty of girls I can call on to keep my bed warm.'

'Our—' Emma stopped short. *Our* bed, she was going to say, but she had no right any more. She shifted nearer, badly wanting reassurance that she wasn't losing him for ever. 'We will still be friends, won't we?' she asked, her voice dropping small into the silence she seemed to have made.

'No,' said Jay. He didn't sound angry, or sad, or resentful, he just said it. And when he added, 'We shan't see each other again,' it was said as if he was telling her the time, or discussing the weather. 'Now go to sleep,' he repeated. 'You have a lot to do in the morning.'

She was too tired to argue. She slept obediently in his arms, overcome by alcohol, lovemaking and terror of the unknown future into which she had been so unexpectedly precipitated. Jay lay wide awake, staring at the ceiling until his eyes stung, contemplating the future without her, and wondering how he could have been so dim. Why hadn't he seen it coming? He might have had a chance if he'd seen it coming.

Emma was up early, after a night punctuated by muddled, unsettling dreams. She thought she would take a taxi to Baron's Court and leave her things there temporarily, but Jay told her calmly not to be so silly. He didn't seem surprised that she still had the key to her flat.

'I bought the damn car for you,' he said. 'I don't want it, and I don't want the hassle of reselling it, so take it.'

Obediently, she loaded all her possessions into the Magnette, to the accompaniment of Beethoven's 'Pastoral' Symphony. Jay neither helped nor hindered her; he was just there. When she was ready to leave, books and suitcases obscuring the back window, the front seat piled high with polythene sacks full of clothes, the boot carefully stacked with folios, folders, inks in cardboard boxes, she walked slowly back up the stairs for the last time.

'You'd better ring,' said Jay, 'and tell him you're on your way.'

She picked up the phone in the hall but she dialled reluctantly, with a shaking hand, because he remained standing stubbornly behind her, refusing to go away.

'Hello?' Rick sounded sleepy. It was Saturday: he must be having a lie-in.

'. . . I—'

'Em?'

'Yes.'

'Are you on your way?'

'Yes.'

'Is he there?'

'Yes.' I can feel his eyes boring into my back, and my hand is sweating.

'Poor bastard,' said Rick. 'You'll need my address.' Hearing the exhilaration in his voice Emma began to feel better.

'Yes. Hang on.' She picked up a pencil from the table and prepared to write.

He gave her minute instructions so she couldn't possibly get lost, every twist and turn of the road, a detailed description of his location. 'How long?' he asked eagerly when he had finished. 'How long, Em?'

The pause was mountainous. How long? How long have I been with Jay? How long have I been without Rick? How long does it take to change my whole life? How long will it take to leave my security blanket behind and reach my heart's desire?

'I don't know.' She felt Jay behind her, glanced up at him over her shoulder. He was reading her shaky handwriting.

'About three hours,' he said, and she jumped.

'About three hours,' she repeated obediently. To reach my heart's desire.

'I heard,' said Rick, and raised his voice deliberately, for Jay's benefit. 'I love you, Em.'

'Yes,' said Emma, and put the phone down.

He was still standing behind her, and she knew he was hurting because his face was completely expressionless. She walked past him to the door, miles away from him already, then turned to face him for the last time. They stared at each other.

'Take care,' he said at last.

'I will. And you. I'll ring you, just to make sure you're alr—'

'No. No, it finishes here, Em. You can't indulge yourself. It's not fair to me and it's not fair to . . . him.'

In all the time they had been together he had never once used Rick's name. Why hadn't she noticed before? 'You'd better go. You don't want to keep him waiting.'

'Right.' She took a hesitant step towards him. He moved backwards, away from her. She stopped. 'I'll, er, I'll be going then.'

'Right.'

'Jay, you know I—'

'Yes,' he said. 'I know you do. But it's rather late in the day to say so.' He ran his fingers through his hair, made a stab at a smile. 'Muddled to the end, little Em.'

The music stopped and they stood. It seemed like an eternity to Emma before he said briskly, 'Bye then. Drive carefully,' and disappeared into his studio. She remained in the open doorway expecting his music to start again; it didn't. She waited, but nothing happened. As she turned to go she remembered the Gimmal ring. *I'm not asking you to accept anything, except my love. What you do with it is in your hands.* She placed it carefully on the hall table, next to his keys so he would find it. Then she turned, walked slowly back to the door and on across the landing, down the familiar stairs to the lobby and out into the sharp autumn air of the car-park.

She looked up as she pulled away, but he wasn't at the window. She looked back before she turned on to the bridge, but he wasn't at that window either. Then she set her shoulders and began to concentrate on her driving. So, that was that then, the end, easy really.

She didn't even try to wipe away the tears, they fell too fast, and welled too quickly to keep up with them, so it was easier to just let them come.

CHAPTER THIRTY-THREE
• • •

She cried all the way through London, and as she continued on up the A11 it began to rain, a heavy, dreary drizzle, the weather mirroring her mood. It wasn't until she passed through Attleborough, approaching Wymondham, that the sun broke out.

By the time she joined the queue for the traffic lights on St Stephen's in the middle of Norwich, she was feeling better. Nearly there now, only another ten, fifteen miles, and she and Rick would be together at last, for good this time. As the car in front of her began to move Emma smiled, depressed the clutch clumsily and jerked forward, then tried again, twice, double de-clutching into second as Jay had taught her. When was that, was it really only yesterday? She pulled away more smoothly into third, then top, and felt pleased with herself. Mabel would be the first to know, she would ring her tonight. 'And he's *wildly* successful now, Auntie Mabel, you were *so* wrong about him ...' She would enjoy her triumph, and Mabel would understand, she would be pleased for her. She could take him home to Ma too, now he could talk. Josie would think he was gorgeous; she would love him. She raised her face to the sky, and addressed Alison, as if she was sitting somewhere up above on a convenient cloud, waiting to hear the news. 'I've done the right thing, haven't I?' she asked, wanting reassurance, then made a face and shook her head at her own whimsy as Ali, cigarette in hand, said succinctly in her ear, 'Of course you haven't, bloody fool.' It was ironic really; any advice Ali had to give was unlikely, by definition, to be worth taking.

As she drove out of Norwich on the Yarmouth road, past

Postwick and Blofield, making for Acle and the last leg of her journey, reaction set in again, outstripping the delicious anticipation that had begun to grow as she left the rain behind. Her stomach started to tie itself in knots. 'It's going to be all right,' she told Ali out loud as she left Brundall behind. 'No, it's not going to be all right, it's going to be wonderful.' The words reverberated around the car, produced the desired effect, a surge of wild euphoria. '*Wonderful!*' she yelled, winding the window down to cool her face, convincing the whole world as well as herself. 'It's going to be brilliant, fabulous, marvellous, sensational, it's going to be *wonderful*!'

She left the A47 at Acle and followed the road through a tiny village, then turned off towards another scattering of houses huddled amongst trees on a south-facing slope. It had rained here too, and the roofs and windows glittered, drying out in the sun. What was Jay doing? she wondered. She glanced at her watch. He'd be out somewhere, having lunch by now. 'I shan't bother to cook,' he'd said. Which pub would he go to? Was he sitting somewhere on his own, missing her? She blinked at the sunshine, too bright; it was bringing tears to her eyes, then slowed to glance again at Rick's instructions and wiped her cheek with the back of her hand.

She came out into open country, on to the wide swathe of marshland running inland from the mouth of the river Yare at Great Yarmouth, reeds and lush green meadows criss-crossed by narrow waterways, marked by coarse grass and bullrushes that swayed and rustled in the drying wind. Everything glistened: the road, undulating gently with the contours of the wild open land over which it ran; the scanty hedgerows, festooned with sparkling cobwebs; the few stunted trees on the verges, showering drops of water as they dried out.

Turn right here, the instructions said, *a dip in the road, a milestone, 7 miles to Great Yarmouth, a farm track and a clump of trees. The house is hidden behind the trees, facing south*.

Emma slowed, swung the car on to the rough gravel track and

began to bump along it, but the mixture of terror and euphoria rising from the pit of her stomach made breathing difficult and she had to stop halfway along, her hands gripping the steering wheel as if it was the only solid object left in the universe, whilst she waited for her heart to slow down. Behind her the village she had just left was obscured by the trees, only the square flint tower of the church visible above the autumnal yellows and reds, ahead nothing, just a thick hedge of sloe and hawthorn, the last barrier between her and Rick, and a wide expanse of lonely marsh, the straight line where land met sky, broken only by a line of slow-moving cattle and a distant windmill, long since fallen into disrepair. Hermits, she thought, reminded of Jay again, he would like this, then shook her shoulders and moved slowly on. Now was not the moment to think about Jay. The sun disappeared behind a cloud and she felt suddenly cold.

As she rounded the corner on to a gravelled turning circle the house came into full view. It was red-brick, square, a child's painting of a house with a door in the middle, a window each side and three above, a chimney at each end and a neat picket fence surrounding the small vegetable patch to its left. There was a wooden lean-to attached to one end, with a window in the blanked off section at the back, looking out through the open doors to where she sat. She could see a big motorbike inside, with shiny chrome exhaust pipes and a blue faring at the front. Rick's? How had he passed his test to ride a bike that size? There was firewood too, stacked all along one wall, and she could smell it on the air, see the smoke drifting from one of the chimneys. A pair of ancient hawthorns stood sentry duty either side of the white-painted front door, sagging like old men towards the wet ground, weighed down by age and rainwater. As Emma sat clutching the steering wheel and staring, a sudden shaft of sunlight lit it all up: the freshly painted window-sills, the neat gutters suspended beneath the eaves, the steep pitched pantiled roof, catching a dozen panes of glass and turning the hawthorns' autumn coats a fiery gold. Her new home. She gripped the steering wheel tighter, panicking, and when Ricky appeared unexpectedly, straightening up from behind the bike and dropping the spanner he was holding with a loud clang, she jumped and began to shake with fright.

He strolled out into the sunshine wiping his hands on a piece of old rag. He opened the door for her, as if he was her chauffeur, stretching out an arm to help her from her seat and bowing.

'You're filthy,' she said, scowling fiercely at his oil-stained fingers.

Rick laughed, completely at ease. 'I've been mending the bike all morning. I needed something to do or I'd have gone mad.' He bent down, peered into the dim interior of the Magnette and grinned. 'I see you've not left anything behind.'

'No,' she said. Just Jay's ring. It's on the hall table, he'll find it when he goes out for lunch.

'Come on.' Rick was impatient to see her properly, hold her in his arms, so he could be sure it was really happening. He reached across her and took hold of her big bag, swinging it past her to tempt her out. Slowly, stiffly, Emma lowered her legs to the drive and stood up. Rick was swept by elation, smiled dazzlingly. 'Welcome home, darling,' he said.

For some reason she couldn't fathom, Emma found his unruffled composure unbearably aggravating. He was so effortlessly in charge of the situation. She was on his territory and the knowledge that she wasn't in control infuriated her beyond belief.

Rick stepped back and waved her over the threshold. Her resentment was palpable, and he resisted the temptation to repeat the endearment, overdo it. She was so beautiful, his darling ...

Emma brought her head up sharply as she passed him. Was he laughing at her? He smiled, oh ... *Alison*, and reached out to tug her plait, two odd sensations rolled into one, the reminder of his sister and Jay's affectionate habit; she flinched, disconcerted by both mental pictures. Why should you suddenly remind me of Ali now? she wondered. And don't think about Jay. This is too important, don't spoil it, don't complicate it.

'Where would you like to start?' Rick dropped her bag on a

chair by the door, then wiped his hands again, flung the rag outside, and offered her a conducted tour. Emma stared about her blankly.

'Did you do all this?'

'Every single bit.' He waved an airy hand at the room, heavily beamed and divided at the far end by open stud-work through which Emma could see a round dining-table and four balloon-backed chairs. The space in which they stood was dominated by a wide inglenook fireplace, the floor was laid with pamments, there was a brightly coloured rag rug in front of the hearth and another between sitting and dining areas. A steep staircase ran up one wall to the first floor. It was small, but comfortable, civilised, even stylish.

Rick pointed at the chimney breast. 'I excavated it with a club hammer and a chisel, inch by inch. Had to be careful.' He brushed the brickwork with affectionate fingers. 'These are hand-made Norfolk Reds, soft as butter, and they fall to pieces as soon as look at you. And all the beams'd been boarded in too. I had to sand them down by hand, couldn't afford a machine, and that oak's like iron. The outside was almost worse than the inside, piles of rubble and rubbish to be cleared.' He grinned. 'That's how I got so big.'

'You said. Mr Universe, right?' Rick was disconcerted by the tart rejoinder. Why was she still so angry? 'It's very nice,' added Emma grudgingly, and moved away from him, taking in the small touches, the pretty, chintzy curtains at the windows, the bowl of summer flowers dripping petals on to a table in a corner, the dried grasses arranged in a blue and white jug in the hearth ... Rosie's touch? She turned back to face him and glared belligerently. 'Is she still here?'

'What?' he asked, bewildered. 'Who?'

'Rosie. Your friend Rosie, the one who's—'

'No! And how many times do I have to tell you, she doesn't mean anything. She's just been teaching me—'

'I'll bet she has!'

'Emma, will you cut this out, please? I don't need it.'

Emma bit her lip. What was the matter with her? 'I'm sorry,' she mumbled. 'I'm just . . . Show me the rest.'

Rick let go the breath he had been holding. 'I keep telling you,' he said, trying to reassure her, 'she's unimportant, irrelevant. We're the only ones that're important, you and I. We're the only ones who matter. Everything, everyone else, is cancelled as of now.'

His confidence was astonishing. Emma went red in the face with suppressed fury, wanted to yell, '*Cancelled*, Jay? And Solly, and Francis and work; my friends, the rest of my life?' but she didn't. She sat down hard on the sofa, staring at Rick's decisive features, so much stronger than the first time around, so full of conviction that he was right, that he could wave a magic wand and everything would be perfect, and said nothing.

He sucked her into his vision of the future, lulled her doubts with his unshakeable belief in the indestructible bond that existed between them. He was right, she reminded herself; he was the first, the only one she had ever loved. And all the certainties that had been missing the first time were there now: she could see them in his face, feel them in the strength of purpose he exuded.

'Show me round,' she said at last. 'Show me everything. Show me where you screw your Rosie.' Oh Lord, that wasn't what she'd meant to say at all.

She rose to follow him stiffly round the ground floor with her mind in complete chaos. She pretended an interest in the kitchen, hand-built cupboards divided by brick piers, a flagstoned floor laid by Rick and a wide, wild view across the marshes towards the coast. She stared blindly at the home-made bookcase loaded with books belonging to the woman who didn't live there, the one who had taught Rick to read, blinked at the pile of invoices waiting to go out, written in an unmistakably female hand, and gawped at the jewel-like miniatures on the walls, like the one she had seen only last night, painted by Rick and displayed with an extrovert flamboyance that Jay had never possessed.

Rick took her through the scullery to show her the back half of the wooden lean-to, converted for use as a workshop: tools neatly hung on custom-made racks; piles of stones, semi-precious and base; a polishing machine; a magnifying glass on a stand for detailed work and a powerful spotlight on a bracket screwed to the workbench.

'I've a contract to supply two Norwich shops as well as the London one. And there's a new place opening soon in Bridewell Alley, near the city centre. They'll take as much as I can turn out. I don't paint at all now, haven't time. You don't know how wonderful it is, Em, doing something you love and getting paid for it.'

Oh, yes I do, thought Emma, reminded of Mirico, and her temper flared again.

'Have you still got that brooch I made for you?'

'Of course I've still got it, you stupid bastard!'

'All right, there's no need to bite my head off!'

They stood in the midst of his professional clutter glaring at each other, both furious now, until Rick, refusing to fight, relented with a sudden lightning-blast of a smile. He could light up a room now, thought Emma wildly, no wonder he had been able to find an accommodating female to furnish his home, share his bed, teach him to read and write. Why hadn't it been *her*? Resentment boiled. Why had it been someone else, someone 'unimportant'?

'*God*, I love you!' he said.

'Piss off!' she snarled, and pushed past him back through the scullery and the kitchen into the sitting-room.

Rick followed her, completely fazed by her belligerent refusal to play the romantic heroine, the grin fading from his face.

'What do you want to see next?'

'Upstairs.' Emma curled a scornful lip. 'I want to see where you sleep with your tart.'

'She is *not* a tart!' He caught her by the arm, spinning her round to face him, and shouted at her. 'And don't talk to me about sleeping around, not when I've sat here these past three months waiting for you night after night while you were fucking someone else!'

'I—I—'

'Yes?'

'Oh God,' she wailed, 'what is happening to me?' and she collapsed heavily on the stairs, lowering her head to her hands and rubbing at her face as if she could wipe away her bad temper. 'Why am I *being* like this?'

She felt him sit beside her, touching as he had at the beginning, all the way down. 'It's real life,' he said gently, reaching across to take her hands in his. 'We're not kids any more, playing at being in love. This is the real thing, Em. We've both grown up, become different people, and we have to start all over again. It's frightening, that's all. But we can do it, as long as we have the will.'

'I can't give up my job,' she blurted, raising her head to glare defiantly at him. 'I don't *want* to give up my job.'

'You don't have to. I've found a place.'

'What?'

'When you rang me and said "soon" I went out and started looking. I've found a place, in Essex, a tiny village near Nazeing. I thought about what you'd said—'

'What I said?'

'You asked me would I give up my jewellery for you, remember? And I had to think about the answer.'

'Are you saying you'll move, just for me?'

He smiled, lowered his head to meet her eyes and leaned against her arm. 'You have,' he said softly. 'You've left everything, packed up all your goods and chattels and jumped in the deep end for me ...'

Emma stared fixedly at her hands, entwined with Rick's, at her finger, no longer adorned with a silver ring. Did I jump though, she wondered, swamped by a wave of sadness, or was I pushed?

'It's near enough to London for you to commute, but quiet enough for me to work. I need the space to breathe, Em. I couldn't go back to living in London now, it would choke me.' She felt him shudder beside her, remembered Ali's warning, *Face it, Em, he's a hermit.* 'I've put a deposit down, and they're holding this place for me for another fortnight, so you can have a look before we commit ourselves. We can move in any time we like, next week if you want. I've the option to buy too, if we decide it's a good idea, and then we could really put some work into it. It's got enormous potential. I've worked it all out. We start at the bottom, somewhere small, do it up, move on to a bigger place, do that up—'

'What for?'

'To make a profit. Most people don't have the imagination.' Rick was excited, enthused, and he infected her with his ambition. 'They don't see the potential, the possibilities. Your room in Earl's Court, you made it different, stylish. We can do the same with houses, people will pay a premium for a place with style, and each time we move we'll be able to afford somewhere bigger, then we'll do that up, move on again, until—' No, don't tell her yet, don't frighten her with your plans for the next twenty years. Take it one step at a time. He rose and walked across the room, trying to damp down his excitement, waved his hand at their surroundings, illustrating his point. 'Take this place. You should have seen it when I started; it was a dump, and now look at it. But it's not mine; I don't own it. While I was still learning to make jewellery I painted houses to earn extra money—'

'I know. George told me.' I saw one of your paintings last night; it was the ultimate irony. Morag was trying to distract Jay with it, because her stupid son had just told him about us.

Rick hadn't finished. 'George's place,' he said. 'That was what started me thinking. You'd love it, Em, it's the most glorious—'

'I've seen it. I went to his wedding yesterday, remember?' No, I didn't. I missed the wedding. I was asleep in bed while he was tying the knot. I was with Jay. I wonder if he's all right . . .

'Then you know what I mean. But we'll never be able to afford somewhere like that unless we start now, at the bottom.' He grinned at her, moved back to sit beside her again. 'That was the last house I painted,' he said, 'and the most beautiful. I made up my mind that one day I'd live somewhere like that. But I need you with me to make it work.'

He rose again and walked across the room to the heavy oak chest beneath the window, while Emma watched from the stairs. He came back with a notepad and a pencil and stretched his legs beside her again.

'Watch,' he said.

He wrote slowly and laboriously with his left hand. When he'd said Rosie was teaching him to read and write, Emma had imagined a level of skill, but his writing was merely legible. He frowned as the pencil moved hesitantly across the page, and clamped his tongue between his teeth in painful concentration.

'There!' he said proudly as he handed it over.

I love you. The letters were crude and ill-formed, but they were correct. They were an unwelcome reminder of the two messages in her bag, written by somebody else: '*Come live with me and be my love*' and a confession written on a table napkin and signed with Jay's big looping scrawl, . . . *In my defence I can only plead that I love you. It muddles my thinking*. She pushed the thought away.

'How did you pass your driving test?'

'I learned the Highway Code by heart, so I could spout it parrot-fashion. I only passed a couple of months ago: it's taken me this long to get the alphabet sorted out so I could read the numberplates.' Not a miracle then: he couldn't handle the complete works of Shakespeare, he could just get by. Bitchily that made Emma feel better about the only-just-absent Rosie. She rose in turn, to collect her bag, then returned to his side and rummaged, ignoring the table napkin that found its way into her fingers, until she found it.

'Remember?'

He took the brooch from her and placed it in his palm, turning it over and over to examine his handiwork.

'The R's back to front,' he said. 'I'll make you another, a better one . . . Em . . .'

'What?'

He put his hand on her cheek, turned her face to his. 'I love you,' he said. 'Right from the start, I've never stopped loving you.'

'I know,' said Emma. She raised her hand to touch him in return, then closed the narrow gap between them and kissed him.

It was like the kiss in her dream, aeons ago, the one that had convinced her it was Rick she really wanted. Only this time there was no Adrian to drag her away from her heart's desire; no Jay, roaring like a lion; it was just the two of them, and they had the rest of their lives to finish what they'd started. When Rick took his mouth from hers and murmured her name she smiled at him, and when he said softly, 'Let's go to bed,' she smiled again.

'Mmm . . .' she said. 'Yes, please.'

CHAPTER THIRTY-FOUR

• • •

Emma placed the jug of flowers on the polished table, smoothed a crease from one of the bedspreads, then straightened up and took a last look around the room. She was longing to see them both. She bent down to retrieve a fallen rose petal and smiled.

Over the past twenty-five years it had become an unspoken joke between the three of them, a game played to tease. She would carefully separate the beds, setting them chastely three feet apart with an obstacle between them, a table, a chest of drawers or a chair, and they would move them back together, their second task when they arrived, preceded only by the ritual drinks. It made them feel naughty, added a little spice to their visits.

Bill was between collections at the moment, not quite so frantic as he sometimes was, and the Dear Old Thing (a new title, also calculated to tease) was going to have time on his hands now that he was retired. She couldn't imagine him pining; he was already threatening to take an interest in Bill's business, heaven help poor Bill.

'Are you nearly done?' He was standing in the doorway watching her, a long-stemmed glass of white wine in either hand, and as she raised her head he smiled, lighting up the room.

'Just this minute finished. I'm *dying* to see them.'

'Well I'm starting without them, and I'm taking the dogs out while it's still light. You coming?'

She took her wine and tasted it, then followed him downstairs, across the hall and out through the kitchen to stroll across the orchard towards the meadow at the back of the big barn, where the attic remnants were piled, well away from the thatch, waiting to be burned. The air was heavy with pollen, scented with apple blossom, and the dogs sneezed and snuffled as they investigated the smells. Flotman was in bullying mood, cuffing Newton with his shoulder, bouncing at him aggressively and growling in the back of his throat, pulling at his ears.

'Cut it out,' the Hermit admonished his favourite, laughing at his antics. 'That animal is a complete hooligan.'

'It's your fault. You're too soft with him.'

'No I'm not. I'm the original hard-man.'

Emma laughed at him. 'You might fool the rest of the world, but you can't kid me. You're the most sentimental man I know.'

'That doesn't make me soft. Even the Kray brothers loved their mum. And they probably cried over *The Sound of Music*.'

Emma sipped her wine as she walked. 'Okay, Hard-man. When shall we have our bonfire?'

He squinted at the white cotton-wool clouds moving across the sky above them, tinged with pink to the west as they caught the rays of the setting sun.

'Better wait for the wind to change; we don't want the barn to go up in smoke.' He wandered round the pile of broken chairs, tennis racquets, three-legged tables, the remains of fifty years all piled higgledy-piggledy in an untidy heap.

'Not the most scientific bonfire I've ever seen,' he remarked drily. 'And we'll need more kindling at the bottom otherwise it'll never catch. We'll leave it till Sunday night when they've all gone and then see what the wind's doing. Anyway, you know what Silly Jilly's like. If she sees this lot she'll probably want to keep it all, just in case it turns out to be worth a fortune.'

Emma slid her arm through his as they moved back towards the house. 'We'll tell them the deed's already done then, shall we? They won't venture this far from the house to look, you know what they're like. Too much fresh air isn't good for him, George always says, dilutes the vodka fumes, and Jilly's shoes'll preclude—'

'She'll have to take them off in the house,' he said, briefly allowing his antipathy towards George and his acquisitive wife to show. 'Otherwise she'll ruin the floorboards with the damn things.'

'Well you can tell her, I'm not going to—' The dogs drowned her words with a cacophony of barks and yelps, announcing intruders, then disappeared at a gallop round the end of the house, vying with each other to see who could make the most noise. Emma took another gulp at her wine and increased her pace, smiling with anticipatory pleasure.

'I think they're here.'

'Bill!' Emma flung her arms around his neck and hugged him enthusiastically. 'This was such a *brilliant* idea!'

Bill returned her embrace with interest. 'Wasn't it just! We should have given you time to get straight, but you know what the Dear Old Thing's like.' He puckered his lips at his companion of the past twenty-five years and mimicked him. '"No time like the present, William. Better make sure the children are settling in all right."'

'Well, you know what they say, dear heart ...' Francis blew Bill a kiss with stubby, beautifully manicured hands and beamed happily at Emma, his chocolate-button eyes disappearing in a myriad creases. 'Absence makes the heart grow fonder and all that.'

Bill had aged hardly at all over the years. His face was still round and unlined, shining with enthusiasm. George had been heard to say, loudly and frequently that he must have a portrait in the attic, a Dorian Gray. It was the only explanation he said, considering Bill's ramshackle lifestyle. Francis on the other hand looked more benevolently prune-like every year, and his beautifully coiffed hair was now snow-white.

The Hermit shook his proffered hand, chuckling with amused affection. 'Still a platitude for every occasion, Francis? How reliable you are.'

'Jay, and how are you, lovely boy?'

'Delighted to see you two.' Jay moved on to greet Bill, then led the way into the flagstoned hall, making for the big sitting-room and the welcoming fire he had lit earlier. 'Now come and have a drink. We've started without you, and Em tells me we've got to cheer Francis up this weekend.' He narrowed his eyes suspiciously at the little man. 'Although frankly, Boncœur, you don't look very suicidal from where I'm standing.'

'Ah.' Bill shuffled his feet sheepishly. 'That was a bit of an exaggeration. You see we thought—'

'If we merely invited ourselves to stay, you'd probably curse us, because of having just moved in and everything, so we—'

'Hatched a plot.' Bill giggled richly. 'Going for the sympathy vote, so you'd be extra kind to us—'

'After all, we're such a deserving cause, two lonely poofters . . .'

'Idiots,' said Emma.

'What a pair of shysters.' Jay poured wine and whisky. 'Here's Em up to her ears in bin bags, stripping walls with one hand and laying carpets with the other, and you two idle queens decide to descend upon us and make her life even more difficult. Look at her, worn to a frazzle, poor thing. Aren't you ashamed of yourselves?'

'Mortified.' Francis glanced across at Emma's beaming face and winked. 'I can see it was a great mistake to come, dear boy, and we will endeavour to rectify it without delay. Come along, William, let us go. Never let it be said that we stayed where we weren't wanted.' He rose to mince across the room towards the door and as he passed Jay held out a tumblerful of golden liquid.

'Try this, Francis,' he said, unperturbed by his guest's apparently imminent departure. 'It's an Islay malt, I got it in specially for you. Lagavulin.' Bill didn't move from the wing-chair by the fire where he had collapsed with a sigh of contentment.

'Ah . . .' He stretched his legs out to the applewood smouldering on the hearth. 'Just what the doctor ordered.'

'Now then, sweetie.' Francis took his drink and moved across the room to where Emma sat on the wide windowseat, perching daintily beside her with his short legs dangling. 'Solly sends fondest felicitations, and a message.' He tucked a thumb into his waistcoat pocket, puffed out his stomach and sat up straight in an effort to emulate their mutual ex-employer. '"Tell the silly bitch that now she's done the bucolic native bit she can stop pissing me about and come back to work."' He paused, enjoying Emma's laughter, and straightened his bow-tie. 'He's missing you dreadfully, dear girl, even after almost a year he's still not over your *defection*, as he persists in calling it. Now that Cyril and I've both gone he's threatening to pack it all in, leave it to his son to carry on.'

'How old is Solly now?'

'Coming up for seventy, and no one left to insult; it's heartbreaking to watch, sweetie, tragic. He's found a designer he can live with at last, brilliant child, just out of the Royal College, but the poor thing's a bit of a ... Oh, how did Solly put it?' Francis chuckled wickedly, then took a deep, appreciative pull at his whisky, rolling it round his tongue before he spoke again. 'A wilting petunia, I think it was—'

'Oh, Francis!' Emma clapped her hands with delight. 'That was *exactly* what he called me, the very first time I came to see him! "You tough," he bellowed at me, "or a wilting petunia?" swinging round in that ridiculous chair—'

'Gone. His orthopaedic surgeon said all that swivelling was exacerbating the back trouble. You can imagine dear Solomon's reaction.'

'Brave chap, that orthopaedic surgeon,' Jay contributed drily.

'One can only assume, dear boy, that the man has a secret death-wish ... Jay, this whisky is divine ... Mind you, he did also suggest that Solly give up driving and get himself a chauffeur so he could put his feet up in the Roller.'

'And how did that go down?'

Francis leaned back against the window and tittered, enjoying the joke all over again. 'Oddly enough, rather well. It gives him more opportunities, you see, to scream obscenities at the ladies; it's so much fun it almost makes up for the swivel chair. Charles, that's his new driver, was telling me about an incident the other day. Poor love didn't know where to put himself: there he was, just saying to Solly that he was awfully sorry, but he thought he'd got himself into the wrong lane, when an elderly lady in a Metro pulled up beside them, in the lane they should've been in. Must've been at least eighty, Charles said, if she was a day. Well, before you could say Jack Robinson, Solly had pressed the button on his window and was lambasting the dear old soul, accusing her of hogging the road as if it was all her fault. And being Solly, of course, once he'd started enjoying himself he couldn't stop . . .' The giggles increased and his infectious merriment set Emma off. 'Apparently the poor thing was so startled that when she went to pull away she stalled her engine. Then while they were waiting for her to get going again, Solly went into overdrive, called her a senile old tart, suggested in passing that her mother must have had an illicit liaison with a donkey to have produced her at all, and then capped that . . .' he paused to snort with laughter at the incongruity of Solly's insults '. . . by informing her that the only way she could possibly have acquired a driving licence was by sleeping with the examiner!'

He dissolved into helpless mirth, doubled up at this latest evidence of his erstwhile employer's mental instability and the others joined him, howling with laughter, not so much at the joke as at the little man's childlike enjoyment of it.

'Oh, Francis!' gasped Emma, when she could speak. 'And what on earth does his wilting petunia make of it all?'

Francis wiped his streaming eyes. 'He cries a lot . . .' he managed, before dissolving again into helpless hysterics.

They talked on as the shadows deepened in the corners of the room, swapping stories and gossip, exchanging news of mutual acquaintances Emma hadn't seen for almost a year now, with Bill contributing his bit when he could get a word in edgeways. Jay sat in his favourite armchair by the west-facing window at the far end of the room, half listening. Occasionally he rose to check on the supper or replenish the drinks, and every now and then, catching Emma's eye, he smiled, so she would know he was all right. He loved to watch her with Bill and Francis, laughing at their outrageously camp stories, enjoying their company. But sometimes he wondered whether his affection for their visitors was purely selfish. Was he fond of them because they didn't threaten to take Emma away from him?

Emma had resigned from Mirico, after more than twenty-five years, when she and Jay moved for the tenth time, to a draughty Victorian vicarage ten miles south of Norwich. The Putney flat was long-gone by then, and the commuting was becoming too time-consuming. Their new home, like every other place they had owned, needed more renovation than they had originally thought, and she was tired.

'Good,' said Jay firmly when she told him. 'Now you're not tied to that lunatic Solly you can come with me when I have to go away. We can be together all the time.'

She'd been surprised how much she missed Solly's eccentricities though, and had kept herself up to date with regular trips to London to meet Bill or Francis, sometimes both, for large helpings of lunch and gossip, until Jay heard the news that George's father was dying of cancer. Jay had kept in touch over the years, even visited occasionally. Somehow, from the moment he knew, it became desperately urgent that the vicarage, which had been progressing at a steady if somewhat leisurely pace, should be finished as soon as possible. He even began turning down commissions so he could work on it full-time. In the face of his almost frantic haste, Emma found it difficult to justify gallivanting off to London merely so she could see Bill and Francis.

Even before the place was finished, Jay put it on the market. 'Time we moved on,' he said when Emma queried the speed with which everything was happening, avoiding her eye.

He had never forgotten his conversation with Morag on

George's wedding day. Listening to her talk in her darkened kitchen that night, and later, seeing her with Doug, he had recognised a kindred spirit. He had a secret hunch that Morag would not long outlive her husband and he was right. Within three months, at the ridiculous, almost criminally early age of sixty-nine, she had begun to fade away, and five months to the day after Doug's demise, Morag Campbell was buried beside him in the double plot they had reserved nearly fifty years previously.

'It was as if,' said George sadly when he rang Emma to tell her about the funeral arrangements, 'once the Old Man went, she couldn't be bothered to hang around any more.'

Jay was surprised to find himself mourning her with genuine sorrow, but that didn't stop him making plans for the future. Morag would want the place to go to someone who loved it as she had, he told himself in justification, and two months after her death he made George an offer he couldn't refuse.

One of George's sisters was going through a messy divorce, the other expecting her fourth child and they wanted their share of the family inheritance as soon as possible. George closed the deal with almost indecent haste.

By the time their guests disappeared upstairs, giggling at Emma's predictable pangs of hunger, it was nearly eight o'clock, and the familiar sounds of furniture shifting were hurried and perfunctory. Jay grinned. 'They must be hungry too.'

'It's so lovely to see them both.' Emma was flushed with wine and glowing with pleasure. 'Aren't we lucky to have such wonderful friends?'

'Yes,' said Jay calmly, surprising her. 'I can't imagine anyone I'd rather spend time with.'

'Except, of course, for George ...' Emma skipped hurriedly past him, anticipating trouble '... and his lovely girls.'

Jay caught her plait as she passed, pulling her backwards into his arms. 'Lowest form of wit,' he growled in her ear, 'sarcasm.' Then he turned her round and kissed her.

'Get off!' she complained when he released her. 'If I don't eat soon I shall starve to death ...' But she lingered within his embrace, breathing his familiar scent, and there was a smile on her face as she spoke.

They ate by candlelight, mellowed into nostalgia by wine and whisky, and delved further back, sharing memories.

'What were we doing during those years?' Bill asked Emma towards the end of the meal, leaning back in his chair and patting his well-fed stomach. 'I remember Kennedy in '63, but that was before college. There must have been other things happening while we were growing up. There was Bobby Kennedy, Martin Luther King – the French students brought down a government in '68 for God's sake, and all I remember worrying about was whether I'd get my collection finished in time for my final show. I might as well have been on another planet. Why didn't we march to Aldermaston to ban the bomb, or join in the Grosvenor Square riots?'

'We were too busy.' Jay turned his eyes to his wife's freckled face. 'Falling in love, learning how to live.'

'Falling in love ...' repeated Emma. She searched for his hand beneath the table, found it, grasped it very tightly. 'Only some of us were too stupid to notice.' She squeezed his fingers and smiled. 'Some of us were very stupid indeed.'

'I've never seen the dear boy looking so contented,' said Francis, changing the subject. 'What have you been doing to him, sweetie?'

'Ah.' Emma raised her glass at Jay and her smile widened. 'That's nothing to do with me, Francis. It's because he's finally where he's wanted to be for the past twenty-five years. He's coveted this place ever since he first saw it at George's wedding.' She chuckled. 'We've done it in tiny, subtle steps, moving a little closer each time: Middlesex, Essex, Suffolk, creeping north into Norfolk, each house a step nearer than the one before ...' She rose and walked slowly round the table, watching Jay's face change as it dawned on him that she knew, had known for years, what he was doing. 'Each place carefully chosen, like his pictures, so we could buy cheap and sell dear, make a profit ...' she reached his side, enjoying his confusion, raised her glass again '... until we could afford it.'

She didn't mention the other equation that had had to be taken into account, the question Jay had avoided asking for twenty-five years. Even after all this time it had taken great courage on his part, to risk deliberately taking his prize so close to his rival's last known address.

'And now we're here until they carry us out in our boxes.'

Jay was reminded of Morag, of her other words all those years ago. *I have to tell you, young man, that you are not the first in the queue*, and he wondered, not for the first time, who the other man was, the one who had coveted this house? Why hadn't he come back to claim it? He had half expected him to turn up all the way through the negotiations, but when he'd asked George just before they exchanged contracts if there was anyone else showing an interest in the place, George had shaken his head, looked at him sideways, as if he was mad, and changed the subject.

Perhaps he *was* mad, to covet a pile of bricks and mortar for a quarter of a century, but then he'd coveted Emma too, and that had worked out all right ... no, not all right. That had been paradise on earth, so far. Would he have to pay for it later? he wondered, as he reached out to touch her hand.

CHAPTER THIRTY-FIVE

● ● ●

'Brought you a present,' said George, kissing Emma's cheek as he stepped into the hall. 'To say thanks for all the hard work you've done on the attic. They were Mum's, and Jilly didn't want them, so I thought you might like them instead. They're worth rather a lot of money actually.'

He handed her a small package wrapped in pretty paper, smirked as she peeled away the layers, puffed himself up importantly when she drew out a pile of gold bracelets. Emma blinked at them, embarrassed that George should give her so valuable a gift, wondering where she had seen something like them before, and puzzled as to why they should make her feel vaguely uncomfortable. After all, they were very beautiful.

'Oh, George!' she exclaimed. 'I couldn't possibly. They're far too valuable.' She pushed them back at him. 'You ought to keep them for the girls.'

'I *told* you!' hissed Jilly audibly at her husband. She hadn't wanted to come anyway, just to see Jay Hammond crowing over his bargain, but what did *her* wishes ever count for?

George ignored her. 'Go on, try them on, see how they look.'

It was only when the things were jangling on her wrist that Emma remembered where she had last heard that noise. She was back in Missy Hammond's sun-filled drawing-room, seeing again her disease-stricken face, hearing the fluid bubbling in her lungs and the bracelets clashing on her thin wrist. Oh Lord, she thought, glancing at Jay, and removed the things with indecent haste.

'No, George,' she said firmly. 'Jilly's right, I really can't. They should go to Antonia and Sophie. Anyway, you know me, I'd be sure to lose them the first time I wore them.' She patted him affectionately, trying to turn her churlish refusal into a joke. 'D'you know, I don't think I've managed to hang on to a single item of jewellery over the past thirty years. It's just as well Jay's not into buying me diamonds.'

Jilly sniffed. It was absolutely typical of those two – she'd spent half the morning making herself look nice, insisted on the girls wearing their decent dresses and neither Jay nor Emma had even bothered to climb out of their jeans to welcome their guests. 'Perhaps that's the problem,' she suggested tartly. 'Perhaps if Jay ever bought you any decent jewellery, you might look after it. About the only thing you've managed to keep is that funny little ring you wore to our wedding.' She pursed her lips, disapproving of Jay's miserly ways. 'And I'll swear he got the thing out of a Christmas cracker. Maybe if you'd mislaid that, he might have bought you a decent engagement ring.'

Emma glanced down at the Gimmal ring on her left hand, then up at Jay. 'Mmm,' she said, smiling at him. 'But on the other hand, where on earth would I wear a decent engagement ring? It's not as if we ever got officially engaged. All we did was get married, and then carry on as we had before.'

'True enough.' George was affronted by the rejection of his gift and disposed to sulk. 'The way you two sneaked off and did the dirty deed, we all reckoned Em must be pregnant. Talk about clandestine – you'd have thought you didn't have any friends worth inviting.' It had always bugged George that Bill and Francis had been witnesses, and Mabel and Josie the only other guests at the ceremony. After all, he was one of the original five, which was more than Francis could claim. Sometimes he wondered why he bothered with them at all ... although he supposed he shouldn't complain, Jay had been more than generous over the house, and all that clearing Em'd done – Jilly would've been *ghastly* about the whole thing, would've wanted to keep absolutely *everything* ...

'What ho, George!' Bill's voice came from behind them, stirring things up. 'You're just piqued, dear boy, because you weren't there. Anyway, you wouldn't have wanted to come if you had been invited; we weren't nearly flash enough for you.'

'Rubbish!' Emma defended her wedding indignantly. 'I must be the only female ever to go through a ten-minute ceremony in a registry office wearing a William Appleyard original. I was the best-dressed bride they'd ever seen.'

'Oh, Emma!' said Jilly. 'And nobody to appreciate it. Poor you, how awful, when you could have had a proper church wedding with all the trimmings. I don't know why you put up with it. It wasn't as if either of you had ever been married before. Jay, you should be ashamed of yourself. I don't think you have a romantic bone in your body.'

'No ...' agreed Jay, his gaze wandering from Jilly's smooth pretty face to his wife's, lovingly tracing the crows' feet around her eyes as she laughed with him, the wisps of fading red hair escaping from her thick plait. 'I don't think I can have. I don't know why you put up with me, Em. You must've led a dog's life all these years.'

Francis appeared behind Bill, his leprechaun face wreathed in smiles. 'Is it time for pre-luncheon drinks?' he asked of nobody in particular. 'And talking of canines, when my turn comes for reincarnation, I'm putting in a request to come back as one of Jay's dogs. That beastly Flotman's just purloined my chair again.'

They sat down to lunch at the long polished refectory table, Sophie and Antonia either side of Jilly and the others wherever they pleased, changing places to talk to each other as the meal progressed.

Jilly was jumpy and defensive. Jay was always so condescending, and Bill and Francis made her feel vaguely uncomfortable too. She had a sneaking suspicion, though there was never anything she could quite put her finger on, that Bill's wrinkled little gnome of a boyfriend was constantly laughing at her, and if there was one thing Jilly hated it was ridicule.

She wouldn't have come today if George hadn't insisted – just because Emma had cleared out the attic the great fool seemed to think they ought to be beholden. She glanced down the table to where Emma was sitting, elbows on the table, setting a bad example to the girls, chin resting on her hands, flashing those big hazel eyes at Bill. She'd never liked her much, too stand-offish by half, and nowadays she seemed more remote than ever. Of course, one had to feel sorry for her, no children, and although she said she didn't mind, it had to be a front – all women wanted children, it was a natural biological urge. Jay was watching her as usual, you'd think he'd be tired of gazing at all that red hair by now.

She flicked her table napkin irritably and draped it over her Chanel skirt. Of course, she thought, smoothing the linen across her knees, these pale-skinned women didn't wear terribly well, although she had to admit Emma had managed to keep her figure, actually improved it in fact, with that little bit of extra weight. Mind you, if you didn't have kids ... And what had she thrown away while she was rummaging in that attic – or kept more like!

'Do you remember?' Emma, reminiscing once again with Bill, was suddenly convulsed with laughter, recalling her wedding day. 'Josie was absolutely shocked to the core. She simply couldn't believe her eyes.'

Bill began to giggle with her. 'And dear old Auntie Mabel thought the whole thing was hysterically funny, sat on her gold chair with that ridiculous hat tipped drunkenly over one eye and snorted like a horse all the way through.'

'At what?' George was still sulking, feeling left out again. '*What* was so hysterically funny?'

'These two.' Jay rose grinning from the table and began to replenish the wine glasses, waving the bottle at Bill and Francis as he passed. 'They'd never met before and it was love at first sight, instant passion, just like in the movies, right down to the canned soppy music playing in the background. The moment Em introduced them—'

'Our eyes met—'

'Our hands touched, and—'

'Bingo!' said Bill triumphantly. 'The earth moved—'

'The violins played—'

'I play the violin,' piped up Sophie, wanting attention. 'Mummy said if I practised more often I could be another Nigel Kennedy.' There was a moment's silence while five members of the party tried valiantly to stifle the inappropriate hoots of laughter that threatened to overwhelm them, then Jay topped up Jilly's wine and moved on.

'Heaven help us all,' he murmured as he bent to refill Bill's glass.

He set Bill chortling again and Jilly bridled, disgusted by all this levity about such a risqué subject in the presence of her girls.

'That's enough, Jay!' she said. 'You shouldn't even be discussing such things in front of the children.'

'Oh, it's all right, Mummy.' Antonia leaned across to pat her mother's hand. 'Sophie and I know all about gays, they do that sort of stuff in Sex Education.' She smiled winningly at Francis. 'Although actually, I wish Uncle Francis would tell me how they actually *do* it, 'cause when I asked Sister Mary Gregora, she just went red and changed the subject.'

That was too much. The table erupted into howls of laughter, all except for Sophie, who hadn't the faintest idea what any of the grown-ups were talking about, and Jilly, who pursed her lips furiously and coloured with embarrassment and indignation. Even Antonia joined in the general hilarity, basking in the success of her inadvertent joke, although she hadn't thought herself that there was anything particularly funny about the remark. As for George, he practically choked on the mouthful of food he was masticating, and had to be patted on the back by Jay as he passed with the bottle.

'Oh, Jilly,' he berated his wife when he finally managed to catch his breath, 'for God's sake stop being such a *prude*.' Jilly sniffed angrily.

*

She took her revenge after lunch, as they sat drinking brandy and coffee, George putting off their departure just to annoy her. The dogs were stretched contently in an untidy pile on the rug; Sophie and Antonia were sniggering over photographs of their father aged seventeen, in a Mod's plastic mac and a pudding-basin haircut, and Francis was dozing in the wing chair by the empty hearth. Bill was working his way through George and Jilly's wedding album, chuckling at the ridiculous clothes all the protagonists were wearing.

She waited her moment until George and Emma came to a pause in their conversation, making sure they were paying attention, then produced the small square package she had carefully concealed in her bag before they set off that morning and raised her voice. 'Oh, I almost forgot . . .'

She rose and crossed the room, her stiletto heels clacking loudly on the pamment floor, to where Jay sat, set apart from the others as usual, looking west into the afternoon sun. 'This is for you, Jay. A present from us both.'

'What is it?' Jay was disconcerted. Jilly had no more time for him than he had for her and present-giving was a new innovation.

'Open it and see.'

George rose suspiciously from the sofa. Jilly hadn't said anything to him about bringing another gift. What was she playing at? Emma followed purely out of curiosity.

She didn't realise immediately what Jay was holding in his hands but George did, the minute he saw the prettily carved wooden frame emerge from its brown paper wrapping.

'Oh!' he exclaimed, rendered incoherent by surprise and irritation. Jilly knew how fond he was of the thing – it was one of his most prized possessions. Sometimes his wife could be an absolute *bitch*. 'I say – I mean – Jilly!'

'What?' Jay dragged his eyes away from the miniature in his lap, a delicate, exquisitely detailed likeness of the house in which they were congregated. 'What's the matter?'

'Absolutely nothing.' Jilly smirked triumphantly at her husband. 'George was just reminding me we must be on the road soon. It seems appropriate for you to have it, what with you being a connoisseur, and having the house it goes with—'

Emma stared at Jay's long fingers, curled round Ricky's painting. She remembered it vividly, remembered George plunging her headlong into decision making, Jay's distracted face. How strange, to see it again after all these years . . .

'But that's Granny's painting!' Sophie, arriving in the midst of them to see what was going on, was indignant. 'Daddy said it was an airloom—' Part of their Hermitage he'd called it when he brought it home after Granny's funeral and now Mummy had given it away. Daddy wasn't pleased, Sophie could tell, his face was going all red. Which meant a row on the way home, sure as eggs were eggs.

'Be quiet, Sophie, this is nothing to do with you.'

'Yes, it is, Daddy says—'

'Daddy is only too delighted for Jay and Emma to have it, aren't you, Georgie darling?'

George knew that tone of voice. It said no nookie for a month if you don't go along with what I want; it said cold meals, and icy disapproval; it said more money on the credit cards . . .

'Of course I am,' he capitulated. Spiteful cat. It was lucky poor old Jay didn't seem to have the faintest idea what was going on.

Jay couldn't fail to notice the drop in temperature. 'There's obviously been some misunderstanding.' He glanced dubiously from one face to the other. 'I don't want to take it if it's going to cause trouble.'

He re-examined the intricate miniature in his hand. Pity, it was a beautiful piece of work; he'd loved it from the moment he'd first set eyes on it, had even asked about its provenance on a later visit, when he was less distracted. Morag had been peculiarly unforthcoming. 'Oh, just some itinerant painter,' she'd said. 'I don't recall his name. Now come and look at this landscape I've found and tell me whether I've got a bargain . . .' He'd got the impression she

didn't want to talk about it, wondered in passing whether perhaps
it had been painted by his rival and she didn't like to say. Whatever
its history, clearly Jilly had only given it to him to get back at
George for some imagined slight.

He held it out, but Jilly wouldn't take it, and as he rose from
his chair, feeling hemmed in by all the attention, he caught
George and Emma exchanging meaningful glances. What the hell
was going on?

'Here.' He held it out again, annoyed now, but Jilly shook her
head.

'Really,' she persisted, daring George to disagree. 'We both
want you to have it, don't we, George?'

'Of course,' said George through gritted teeth, then winced as
Jilly added maliciously, enjoying herself, 'After all, Jay's never
been one to bear a grudge, have you, Jay?'

'A grudge? What are you talking about?'

Emma couldn't bear his bewildered face. 'Stop it, Jilly!' she said
sharply. 'It isn't funny.'

'Don't be ridiculous.' Jilly was pleased with herself, just for
once she had the upper hand. 'Jay won't care after all these years.
You wouldn't be so petty, would you, Jay?'

'I don't know what you're talking about.'

Emma could hear the edge creeping into Jay's voice. What was
Jilly thinking of, giving him Rick's painting? Was this her idea of
a joke?

'Stop it, Jilly!' she said again.

'Oh, come on, Emma. Don't be so overprotective.' Jilly began
to lose her cool. Why did they have to be so melodramatic about
everything? 'It was all over twenty-five years ago. Why should Jay
care?' She pursed her lips, wondering why they should go to such
lengths to shield him. Jay was the last person who should need
protection from anything, tough as old boots. 'And, after all, Jay
won in the end, didn't he?'

'What was all over? What did I win? Will somebody please tell
me what's going on?'

'Nothing!' said George loudly. 'Antonia, Sophie, it's time we made tracks for home!'

Francis woke with a snort, and Bill raised his head, startled by the sudden urgency in George's voice.

'Come along, Sophie! Em, it's been great, just like old ...' He faltered, then turned away, taking Jilly's arm as he went and deliberately tightening his grip until she squeaked in indignant protest. 'Bill, Francis, are you going to come and wave us off?'

'Em, what the hell is going on?' demanded Jay, staring in perplexity at George's back.

'*Bitch!*' George hissed in his wife's ear as he propelled her across the room and out into the hall. 'What the devil do you think you're playing at?'

'Oh, stop making such a fuss; he doesn't know who painted the stupid thing.' Jilly was sulking. Somehow her petty swipe at George had backfired, but she wasn't sure why. 'As far as Jay's concerned it's just a picture of his house.'

It was nearly an hour before the Volvo was loaded and the Campbells finally pulled away down the drive. Their departure was a relief to all parties, and having waved them off the four who remained grinned guiltily at each other.

'Doesn't time fly when you're having fun?' remarked Francis to no one in particular as he followed Jay back into the house.

Bill linked arms with Emma and held her back.

'What's going on, sweetheart? I sense a little atmosphere. Tell your uncle Bill all about it.'

Emma sighed. 'Nothing much to tell. Jay doesn't know, but Rick did that painting Jilly gave him. Morag commissioned it, years ago, and you know Jay ...'

'Ah.' Bill patted her arm reassuringly. 'In that case, for once I'm inclined to agree with the lovely Mrs Campbell; there's no harm done, is there? After all, just because the dear boy's been given a painting it doesn't follow that the perpetrator's about to leap out from behind the rhododendrons like a pantomime villain and claim you for his own after all these years, does it?'

Emma smiled at the thought. Bill was right as usual. 'I suppose not. Funny though, I've been thinking about Rick this past week, wondering what happened to him. It was clearing out the attic, you know how one wallows in nostalgia. It made me think it'd be nice to know that he's, well, all right, if you get what I mean.' She sighed again, and squeezed his arm affectionately. 'I've been so lucky, Bill. It'd be comforting to be sure that Rick's as happy as I am . . .'

It was as they were passing the signposts to St Faith's Crematorium on the edge of Norwich that George let Jilly in on the secret.

'Well how was I supposed to know?' she blustered defensively, shocked by what he told her. 'Anyway, if Emma was still upset she'd have reacted—'

'Emma doesn't know. I didn't tell her.'

For once in his life George had taken his mother's advice. 'No, don't,' Morag had said fiercely when he asked her what he should do. 'Don't breathe a word to a soul, because if you do it'll get back to her for sure. The poor child's just beginning her life. Telling her won't undo what's done, it'll merely hurt, so what's the point?'

'Well, if she doesn't know, there's no harm done, is there?' Jilly was fed up with the whole thing; she could feel one of her headaches coming on. 'But perhaps if you bothered to talk to me occasionally I might not put my foot in it quite so often—'

'Ha! You don't fool me for a second. You do it deliberately, just to annoy me. Anyway it was years ago for God's sake.' George subsided briefly, then attacked her again. 'I can't believe you've actually given the thing away, when you know what it means to me, and to Jay of all people. It's just pure spite, petty, pathetic vindictiveness. You're jealous because we've all been friends for so long—'

'Friends?' Jilly snorted derisively. 'Who d'you think you're kidding, George Campbell? The only reason Jay Hammond's stayed in touch with you all these years was so he could get his sticky mitts on your parents' bloody house, which should have been kept for our children—'

'Oh, shut up, you miserable bitch!'

'Daddy,' Antonia's penetrating voice rose from the back seat. 'You're going to have to stop somewhere. I'm absolutely bursting for a pee . . .'

Bill and Francis left earlier than they'd intended. For once, Jay couldn't wait to get rid of them and they sensed it, cut the proceedings short with invented tasks awaiting them at home, all to be done before Monday and impossible to delegate.

'Give us a ring soon, sweetie,' Francis murmured as he kissed Emma goodbye. 'Just so we know everything's all right.'

Emma laughed at him. 'Curiosity killed the cat,' she teased, then hugged him tight to reassure him. 'Bill'll tell you what it was all about. Nothing important, I swear.'

'Well?' Jay demanded as she flopped, exhausted, into the wing chair by the fire.

'Well what?'

'You know damn well what. All that stuff about bearing grudges and winning in the end.'

'Ah.'

'Ah.' He pushed distractedly at the dogs, pawing at his trousers, bidding for attention. 'Get off, Flotman, I'll take you in a minute.'

'We'll take them now, while it's still light.' Emma rose and walked across the room to where Jay had left the miniature on the window-sill. 'And I'll explain as we go.'

It was the first time, she realised as she scooped the pretty thing into her hand, she had touched anything of Rick's for twenty-five years.

CHAPTER THIRTY-SIX

• • •

It wasn't the sex. That was spectacularly, knee tremblingly successful. It wasn't Ricky's claustrophobic bedroom either, tucked under the eaves and reached by a door three inches shorter than Emma. It wasn't even the dream, the familiar slide into her black cavern of loneliness and despair, waking her in a cold sweat from her heavy slumber. It was Rick's words that did it, slithering into her mind as she recovered from her nightmare and finally making her realise she was in the wrong place.

'It's real life,' she heard him say, his voice reverberating inside her head. 'We're not kids any more, playing at being in love. This is the real thing, Em.' From there, it was only a short step to the certainty that it was time to go home.

She wrote him a note, scribbling hastily in the dimly lit room, a trite, trivial goodbye. She even told him, curbing her guilty impatience to get away only with great difficulty, that she hoped he would be happy without her, that he would have his Rosie to comfort him. Then as he slept on beside her in blissful ignorance, she fumbled for the filigree brooch, impaled the letter to the pillow with it, and fled, to drive blindly until she was too weary to go any further, and then to sit in a lay-by just outside a village called Six Mile Bottom, watching the sun go down through a blur of tears as she cried for the second time, for her lost illusions.

Jay was slumped on the floor when she walked into the sitting-room, leaning against the sofa with his long legs bent and his arms wrapped around his knees. He was haggard, dishevelled,

410

distraught, and there was no music playing.

She couldn't even begin to explain, and she was so tired it took most of her remaining energy simply to cross the room. She stopped in front of him, then slid her big bag from her shoulder and up-ended the contents into his lap. Then she went to bed, stopping on the way to pick up the Gimmal ring, still lying where she had left it that morning, and put it back on her finger where it belonged.

He picked up every last thing, pens, pencils, cheque-book, old receipts, sweet papers, used tissues, loose change, and then he crawled around on the floor like an animal, feeling with his hands in case he'd missed anything. Only when he was sure the brooch was really gone did he follow her.

Around midnight, when the need to stake his claim grew too much for him to bear, he made love to her as she lay sleepily in his arms. She made all the appropriate responses; only when he tried to withdraw did she open her eyes wide to command peremptorily, 'Don't!' and wrap her legs tightly round him to hold him inside her. Then she slept. She needed someone to fill the empty space, and only Jay would do. Once secure again, she sighed, smiled, and went back to sleep.

CHAPTER THIRTY-SEVEN

• • •

'So you see, it was just Jilly being bitchy.' Emma slowed her pace, raising her face and smiling to reassure him. 'If you want to put it on the bonfire then go ahead. I don't mind.'

'Are you sure?'

'Oh ye of little faith. How many centuries will it take to convince you?'

Jay grimaced, then slid his hand round the back of her neck, stroking with his fingers. 'At least another millennium. I don't think I can live with it, Em. It'd be a constant reminder that he's out there somewhere, that he wants you ... *and* this house. Why didn't I connect the two?' He took her hand and walked on as the dogs zig-zagged ahead of them, noses to the ground. 'We could give it back to George ... ?'

'No. For once in his life the poor boy was trying to be tactful just now. It'd be churlish to throw it in his face. And it would only be another bone of contention between him and Jilly.'

She reached the bonfire, hesitated, then stretched out her hand and placed the miniature firmly in the middle of the pile. No point in being sentimental.

'It's better this way.' She turned her head to watch the relief spread across his face, enjoying the familiar rush of love. 'It draws a line under it for good.'

'We need more kindling.' He examined her minutely, searching for signs of distress. 'I'll fetch some newspapers. Em, are you quite—?'

'Sure. Sometimes, Jay Hammond,' she reached up to touch him, running her knuckles down his cheek, 'you can be awfully thick.'

She watched him walk away, Flotman cavorting at his heel, looking for the touch of his master's hand. To the victor the spoils, but just this once the weak had been allowed to triumph over the strong. Somewhere out there Rick must be surviving without her. Jay wouldn't though, couldn't. The thought gave her a warm feeling inside.

He returned with the remains of the newspapers she had rescued from the attic and a bundle of dry kindling. He had a box of matches in his pocket. 'Wind's right,' he said, not quite meeting her eye, 'so we might as well get it over and done with, as long as you're sure.'

'Yes, I'm sure.' Damn Silly Jilly, why couldn't she have let well alone? Emma picked a paper from the pile, separated the sheets, rolled and twisted them, then reached for another. It was a local rag, the *Eastern Daily Press*.

'Oh!' she exclaimed, amused by the coincidence. 'Look, it's the day we got married!'

'What is?'

'This is.' She opened it up, then shook it at him, grateful for the distraction. 'I wonder what was happening in East Anglia while we were plighting our troth?'

She read bits out to him as he laid more kindling around the base of the fire: unimportant local happenings, a flower show, a revue of a local amateur production of *Oklahoma*, a golden wedding anniversary, a charity spelling bee at a junior school in East Dereham. It was only when her voice petered out into silence that he glanced up and registered her white face.

She felt the damp grass soaking through her jeans as she dropped to her knees. Oh, how could she have been so wrong? How could she have been so *stupid*?

Jay took the paper from her unresisting fingers. He had to read it twice, and he felt his guts cramp as it slowly dawned upon him that for so many years he'd been preparing to fight a rival who was never going to show.

In the early hours of yesterday morning that notorious stretch of the A47 between Acle and Great Yarmouth, known as the Acle Straight, claimed yet another victim when a young motorcyclist left the road a mile east of the Stracey Arms. The body of an unidentified man was later removed from a water-filled drainage dyke by local rescue services.

The cause of this latest accident is as yet a mystery. Weather conditions were good, and police say the motorcycle, which they estimate to have been travelling in excess of eighty miles per hour, was almost new and mechanically sound, although the number-plates were missing. The rider, who died instantly, seems to have made no effort to brake as the machine left the road, and he was not wearing a crash helmet. No other vehicles appear to have been involved.

The police are appealing for witnesses to come forward with information about the accident. They are particularly anxious to trace relatives or friends of the dead man, who was carrying no identification, and have issued the following description in the hope that someone may recognise him.

The deceased was in his early twenties, around six feet tall and heavily built, with fair hair and dark brown eyes. He was wearing a black leather jacket, blue jeans, and a plain white T-shirt. Also recovered from the scene of the accident was a silver brooch incorporating a heart pierced by an arrow, at either end of which are the initials R and E. The R is back to front.

Anyone recognising this description is asked to contact Great Yarmouth police on the following number . . .

'It was him or me,' said Jay at last. 'Who would you have chosen, if you'd had to use a gun, pull the trigger? Would you have shot me or him? You chose to stay with me. Was that a sham? Have you been lying to me all these years?' He dropped the paper to catch hold of her arms and shake her, hard. 'Who would you have shot, Em? If you'd had to choose which one to kill?'

'You know who.' She stared at him, swamped by guilt, sorrow, horror. 'I chose you. But I didn't want him to die. I didn't mean to kill him.'

He raised his hands to cup her face. 'It was him or me. If you hadn't killed him you would have killed me. Don't you understand that?'

She nodded, then began to cry, the tears trickling down her cheeks and dripping off her chin. 'I love you, you know I do, just you, nobody else.' Just Jay. Nobody else. But what if . . . ? 'But what if I hadn't—'

'What, slept with him? Silly fool, you had to sleep with him.'

Emma stared at him in astonishment. 'But I never told you, you never said, never asked . . . How did you know?'

'Because I love you. Of course I knew. He left his fingerprints all over you.' And I didn't mind, much; I even felt sorry for the poor bastard. It was the only time I didn't want to kill him. How ironic that he should have done the job himself.'

'But how could you possibly have—? I stopped. I stopped at a hotel in Harlow, barged into the middle of a Wallace Arnold tour party and slipped up the stairs while they were milling about in reception. I found a bathroom and I had a bath. I scrubbed him out of my system.'

'Why, so I wouldn't know?'

'No, I would've told you if you'd asked. Because I didn't feel clean, because he wasn't you.'

'Poor bastard.'

'Poor bastard.' Her mind skidded on the words. 'That was what he said. About you. He'd learned to read, did you know?' She fumbled in her pocket for a tissue, blew her nose.

Jay hesitated, then leaned across to pick the miniature from its place on what had suddenly become a funeral pyre, and laid it carefully on the ground, well away from any possibility of damage. How could he take it away from her now?

He picked up one of the scattered pages of newspaper, rolled it diagonally, tied a knot in it and tucked it deliberately into a gap at the base of the pile. He followed it with another, and another, placed kindling carefully, and struck a match. Then they kneeled side by side and watched the flames begin to nibble at the edges, curling and crackling as they took hold.

'You had to choose,' he said again. 'It was his life or mine.' Then he reached behind her and began to unravel her plait.

'Jay...?' She dragged her eyes away from the tiny yellow tongues licking at the twisted paper. 'What are you ... ? No ... No, not here, not now. Oh, please, Jay – ohhh ... *no* ...'

She fought him, writhing beneath his hands, sobbing and pleading, but he took no notice. He knew what she needed. He needed it too.

As the fire caught and began to burn, reddening their bare skin with the fierce energy of its heat, he made love to her, holding her down until she gave in, kissing her wet cheeks, reminding her, and afterwards she clung to him as if she was drowning, listening to the fire snapping and crackling somewhere behind her as it soared high into the darkening evening sky. When at last he rolled reluctantly away from her to kneel on the trampled ground, she reached across to where the miniature lay unscathed beside her. It was her turn now.

She made sure he was paying attention before she threw it. It landed deep in the glowing heart of the pyre, sending up a shower of exploding sparks and they sat back on their haunches watching the flames creeping upwards, licking round the frame, feeding on the dry wood, then creeping inwards, melting the canvas.

It burned fiercely once it took. Emma could feel the heat warm on her face, but it was not as warm as the glow in her belly where Jay had left a part of himself. She turned her head to look at him kneeling beside her, his skin flushed gold in the firelight.

A contradiction in terms, murmured a soft, insidious voice in her ear, happy, and ever after.

'I must make a start on the dining-room tomorrow,' she said wearily, 'if we're to be straight by Christmas.'

The Windfall

Prue Carmichael

Although they had not seen each other for twenty years, a
curt telephone call was enough to tell Minou that little had
changed between herself and her half-sister, Bitty. For poor,
plump, manipulative Bitty has always resented the uncalled-for
presence of her beautiful French creole sibling. Even more so
since she suspected that their late film director father had
always loved Minou best.

Nevertheless, Minou is baffled by the summons to Southern
Spain - a wind-battered enclave on the coast, peopled by such
idiosyncratic characters that only the English can produce.
Her journey, while partly to satisfy her curiosity, is also to
see her gorgeous but confused twenty-year-old nephew, Titus,
a product of Bitty's love affair with Spain.

There Minou discovers her sister fraught and distracted in her
large but dishevelled home, her legacy from their father. Titus,
too, appears more wayward than ever and as Minou, gentle and
elegant in her approach, delves deeper, she discovers a host of
half-truths and deceits that will affect not only her family and
new-found friends, but also - most surprisingly - herself.

Wickedly funny and poignantly sad, *The Windfall* is a bitingly
perceptive novel heralding the debut of a talented new writer.

Fiction
0 7515 1641 4

<u>Downtown</u>

Anne Rivers Siddons

Set at the dawning of America's great social movement, in
the year before the peace and love yielded to militancy and
hate, *Downtown* is the story of Smoky O'Donnell; the story
of her career and her heart in a time and a place the like of
which would never be seen again.

Arriving in Atlanta in the autumn of 1966, Smoky is at once
thrilled and chastened by this dazzling and hectic young city.
Offered a plum job on *Downtown* magazine, the award-winning
journal epitomizing Atlanta's new vibrancy, Smoky soon realizes
her life is about to undergo momentous changes and throws herself
whole-heartedly into the dizzying aura of a city on the move.

The choices Smoky must face, and her ultimate decisions, create
an utterly compelling and completely captivating story of the end
of innocence, in a joyous novel that will enchant and delight
Anne Rivers Siddons' growing number of fans.

Fiction
0 7515 0890 X

A Dangerous Happiness

Hazel Hucker

Abbotsbridge is an ancient Hampshire village containing
a thoroughly modern mixture of inhabitants: rich and
poor, old and new.

Louise and her partner Simon led a contented and, she believed,
thoroughly fulfilled life in London. But when Simon's career
move takes him to rural Hampshire and he begins to talk of the
delights of country living - and of starting a family - she is
not sure she can become the woman he wants her to be ...

After the death of Maggie's two-year-old daughter, she
is desperate for another child. But her solicitor husband
Jack feels strongly that three sons are more than enough, given
the cost of private education ...

Middle-aged Brozie, mainstay of the village horticultural
society and the church flower-arranging rota, is trapped in a
loveless marriage to the horrible Hubert. She longs to escape,
but in his illness he relies upon her and perhaps she is too
old to shake off her chains ...

Then, into the Old Barn moves Charley St George,
erratic, energetic and brimming with ideas to solve their
problems - ideas that will change all their lives.

Fiction
0 7515 1625 2

Regret Not A Moment

Nicole McGehee

The year is 1930. Beautiful, spirited and independent,
Devon Richmond is the daughter of a prominent Virginia family.
Though many men have asked for her hand, none has captured
her heart - until John Alexander, a dynamic business tycoon,
walks into her life and Devon knows that the love will never
stop flowing between them.

Their electrifying passion is celebrated in marriage and a fairy-
tale future seems preordained. But Devon can foresee neither
the terrible tragedy that will blight their union, nor the
conflicts that will drive deep divisions between them.

From the dizzying sophistication of New York to the thrilling
bazaars of Cairo, *Regret Not a Moment* spans the unforgettable
life of a breathtaking woman: Devon Richmond.

Fiction
0 7515 0752 0

☐ The Windfall	Prue Carmichael	£5.99
☐ Hill Towns	Anne Rivers Siddons	£5.99
☐ Downtown	Anne Rivers Siddons	£5.99
☐ Colony	Anne Rivers Siddons	£5.99
☐ The Aftermath of Oliver	Hazel Hucker	£5.99
☐ A Dangerous Happiness	Hazel Hucker	£5.99
☐ Regret Not A Moment	Nicole McGehee	£5.99

Warner Books now offers an exciting range of quality titles by both established and new authors which can be ordered from the following address:

Little, Brown & Company (UK),
P.O. Box 11,
Falmouth,
Cornwall TR10 9EN.

Alternatively you may fax your order to the above address.
Fax No. 01326 317444.

Payments can be made as follows: cheque, postal order (payable to Little, Brown and Company) or by credit cards, Visa/Access. Do not send cash or currency. UK customers and B.F.P.O. please allow £1.00 for postage and packing for the first book, plus 50p for the second book, plus 30p for each additional book up to a maximum charge of £3.00 (7 books plus). Overseas customers including Ireland, please allow £2.00 for the first book plus £1.00 for the second book, plus 50p for each additional book.

NAME (Block Letters) _____

ADDRESS _____

_____

_____

☐ I enclose my remittance for £ _____
☐ I wish to pay by Access/Visa Card

Number ☐☐☐☐☐☐☐☐☐☐☐☐☐☐☐☐

Card Expiry Date _____